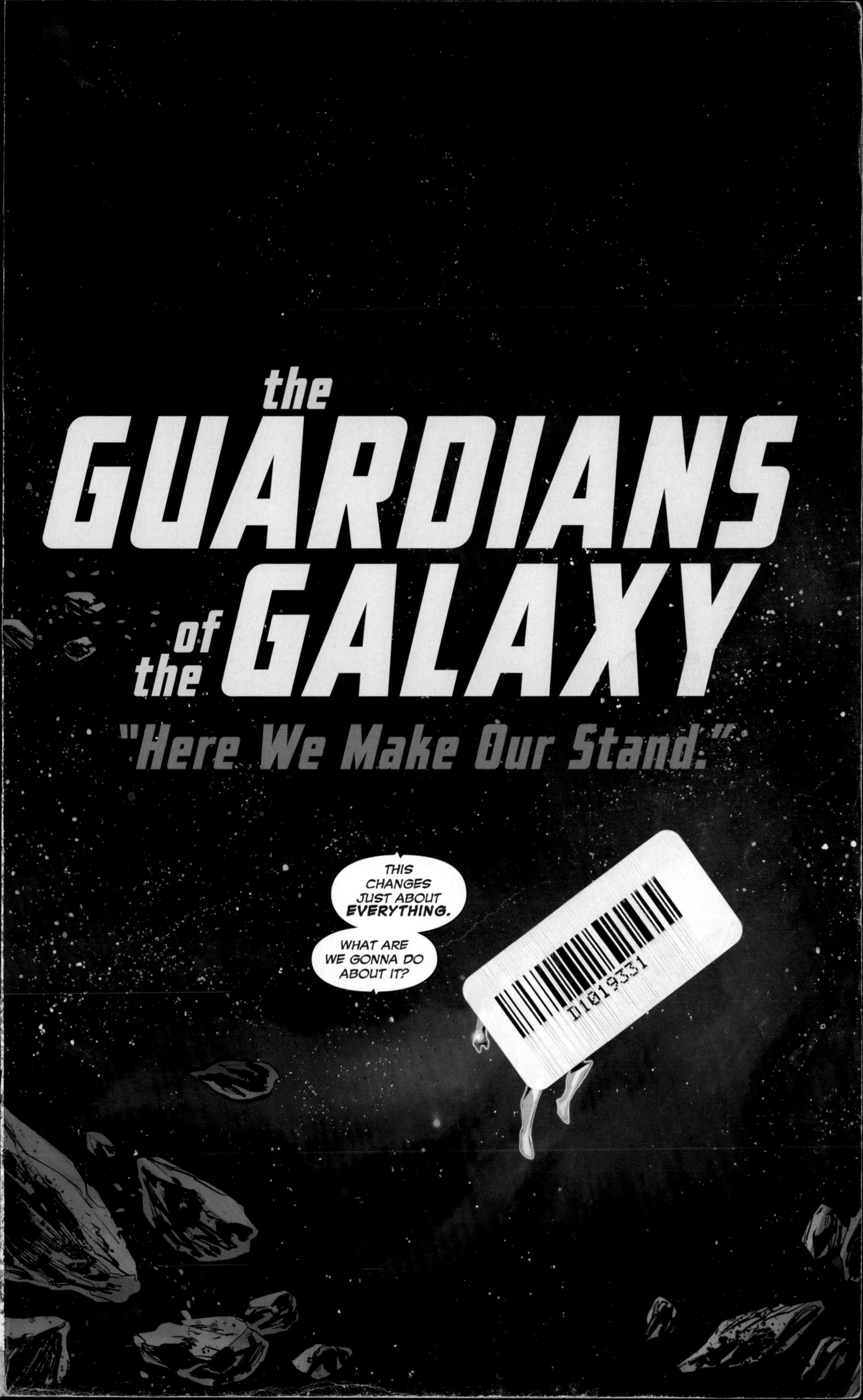
the GUARDIANS of the GALAXY
"Here We Make Our Stand."
THIS CHANGES JUST ABOUT EVERYTHING.
WHAT ARE WE GONNA DO ABOUT IT?

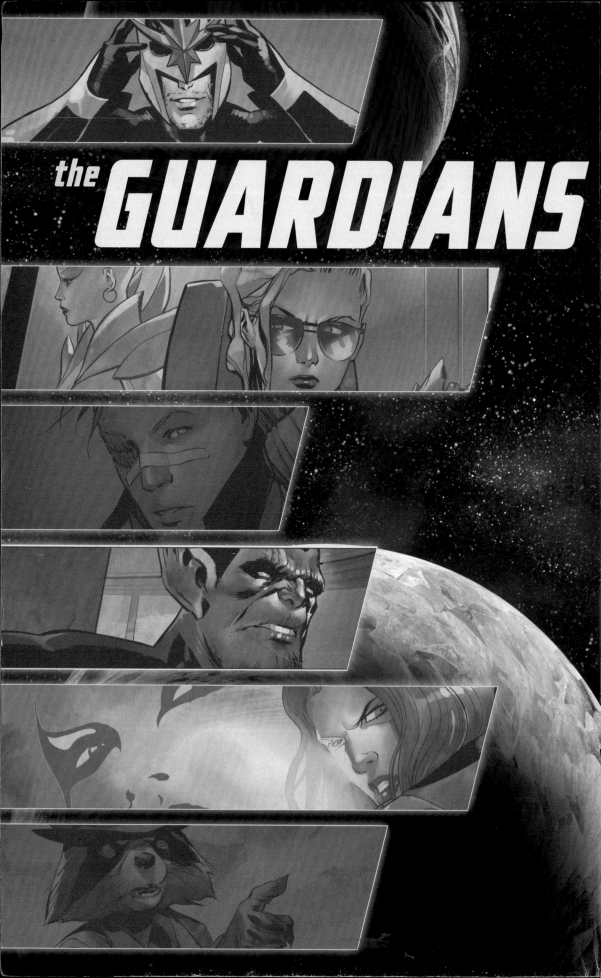

the GUARDIANS

of the GALAXY

"Here We Make Our Stand."

WRITER: **AL EWING**

ARTISTS: **MARCIO TAKARA** [#6-8] &
JUANN CABAL [#9-12]

COLOR ARTIST: **FEDERICO BLEE**

LETTERER: **VC's CORY PETIT**

COVER ART: **RAFAEL ALBUQUERQUE**
WITH **MARCELO MAIOLO** [#10-12]

ASSISTANT EDITORS: **LAUREN AMARO** & **KAT GREGOROWICZ**

EDITORS: **DARREN SHAN** & **MARK BASSO**

COLLECTION EDITOR: **JENNIFER GRÜNWALD**   ASSISTANT EDITOR: **DANIEL KIRCHHOFFER**

ASSISTANT MANAGING EDITOR: **MAIA LOY**   ASSISTANT MANAGING EDITOR: **LISA MONTALBANO**

VP PRODUCTION & SPECIAL PROJECTS: **JEFF YOUNGQUIST**   BOOK DESIGNER: **JAY BOWEN**

SVP PRINT, SALES & MARKETING: **DAVID GABRIEL**   EDITOR IN CHIEF: **C.B. CEBULSKI**

GUARDIANS OF THE GALAXY BY AL EWING VOL. 2: HERE WE MAKE OUR STAND. Contains material originally published in magazine form as GUARDIANS OF THE GALAXY (2020) #6-12. First printing 2021. ISBN 978-1-302-92076-0. Published by MARVEL WORLDWIDE, INC., a subsidiary of MARVEL ENTERTAINMENT, LLC. OFFICE OF PUBLICATION: 1290 Avenue of the Americas, New York, NY 10104. © 2021 MARVEL No similarity between any of the names, characters, persons, and/or institutions in this magazine with those of any living or dead person or institution is intended, and any such similarity which may exist is purely coincidental. **Printed in Canada.** KEVIN FEIGE, Chief Creative Officer; DAN BUCKLEY, President, Marvel Entertainment; JOE QUESADA, EVP & Creative Director; DAVID BOGART, Associate Publisher & SVP of Talent Affairs; TOM BREVOORT, VP, Executive Editor; NICK LOWE, Executive Editor, VP of Content, Digital Publishing; DAVID GABRIEL, VP of Print & Digital Publishing; JEFF YOUNGQUIST, VP of Production & Special Projects; ALEX MORALES, Director of Publishing Operations; DAN EDINGTON, Managing Editor; RICKEY PURDIN, Director of Talent Relations; JENNIFER GRUNWALD, Senior Editor, Special Projects; SUSAN CRESPI, Production Manager; STAN LEE, Chairman Emeritus. For information regarding advertising in Marvel Comics or on Marvel.com, please contact Vit DeBellis, Custom Solutions & Integrated Advertising Manager, at vdebellis@marvel.com. For Marvel subscription inquiries, please call 888-511-5480. **Manufactured between 4/9/2021 and 5/11/2021 by SOLISCO PRINTERS, SCOTT, QC, CANADA.**

10 9 8 7 6 5 4 3 2 1

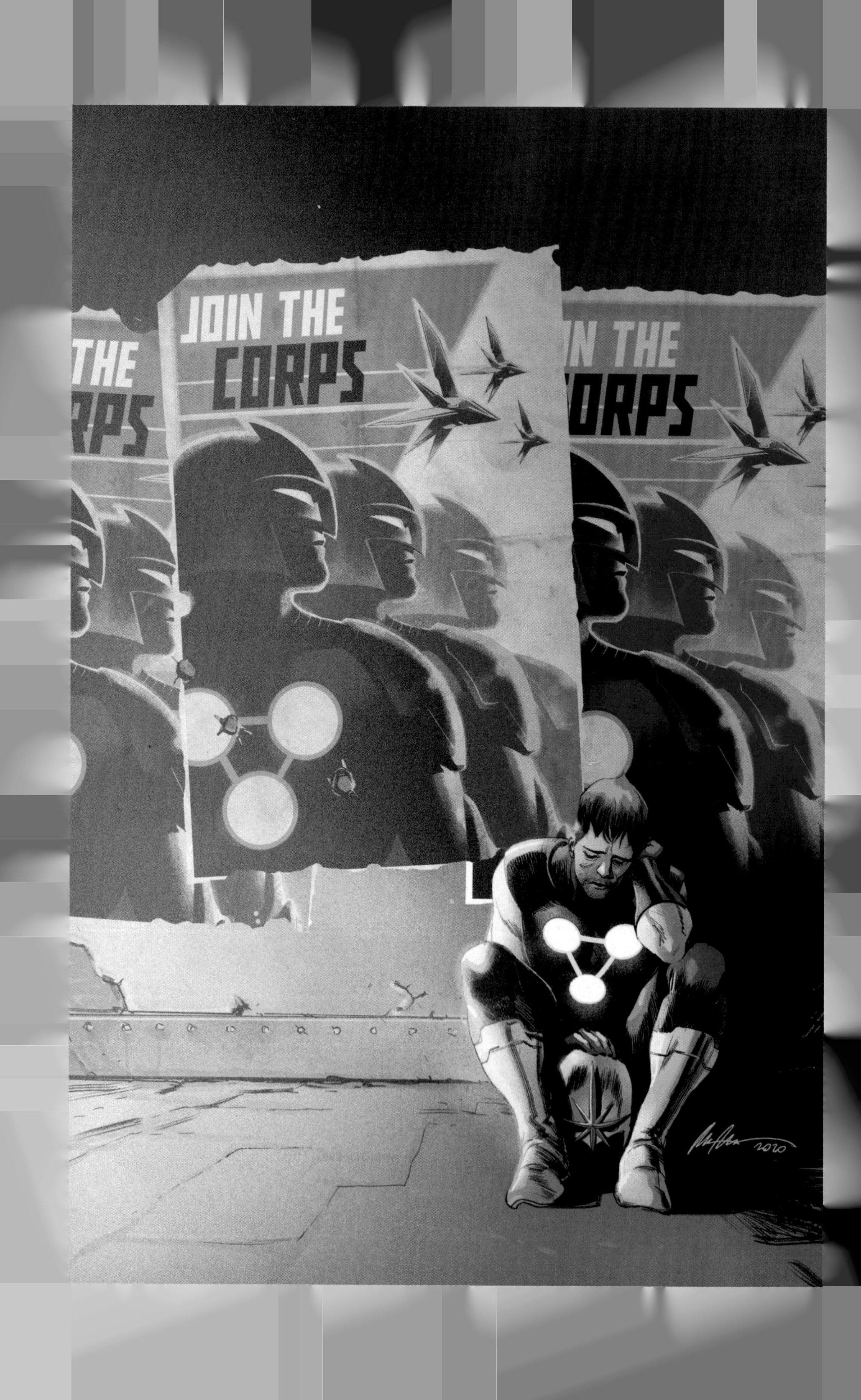
JOIN THE
CORPS

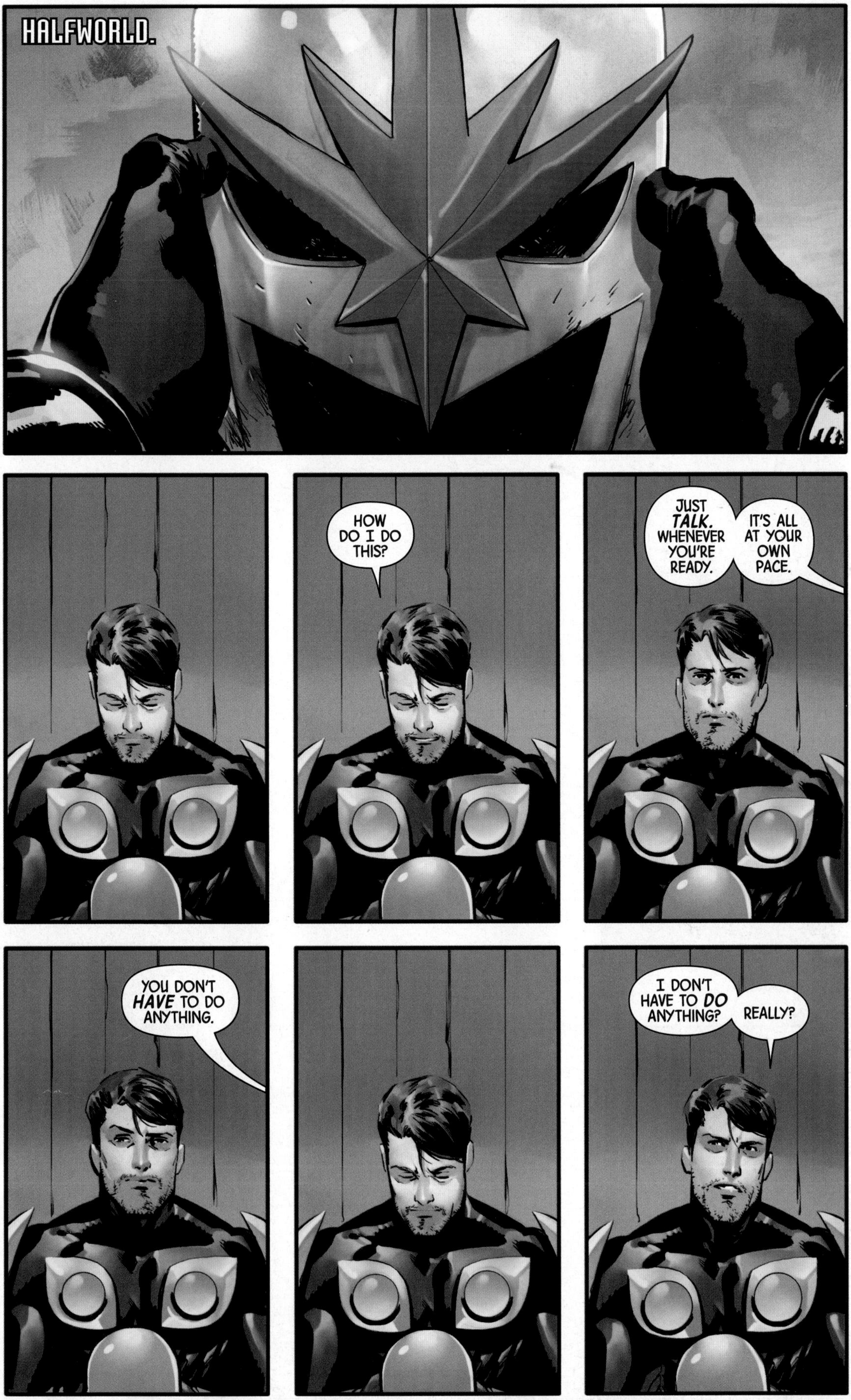
HALFWORLD.
HOW DO I DO THIS?
JUST TALK. WHENEVER YOU'RE READY.
IT'S ALL AT YOUR OWN PACE.
YOU DON'T HAVE TO DO ANYTHING.
I DON'T HAVE TO DO ANYTHING?
REALLY?

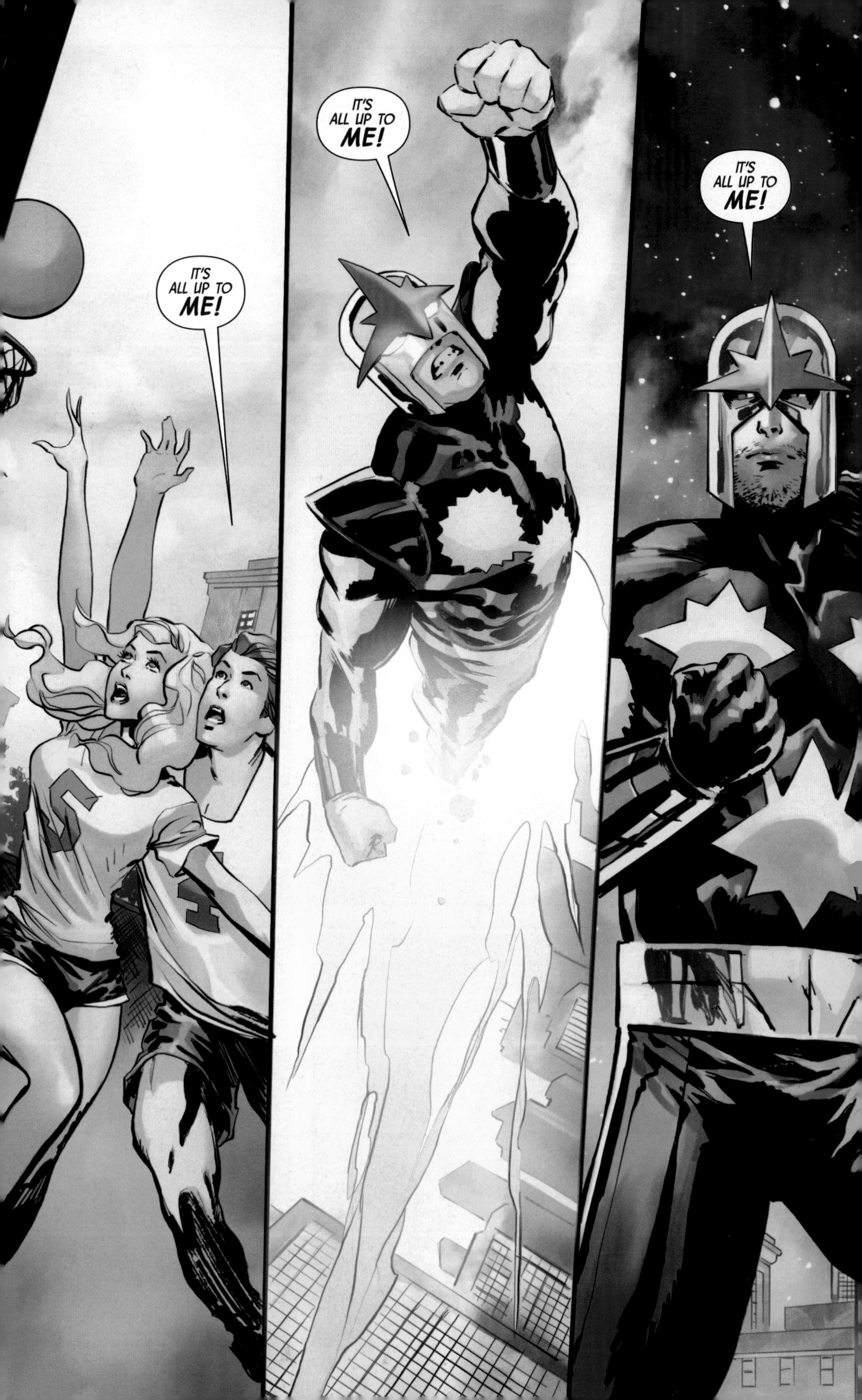
IT'S ALL UP TO ME!
IT'S ALL UP TO ME!
IT'S ALL UP TO ME!

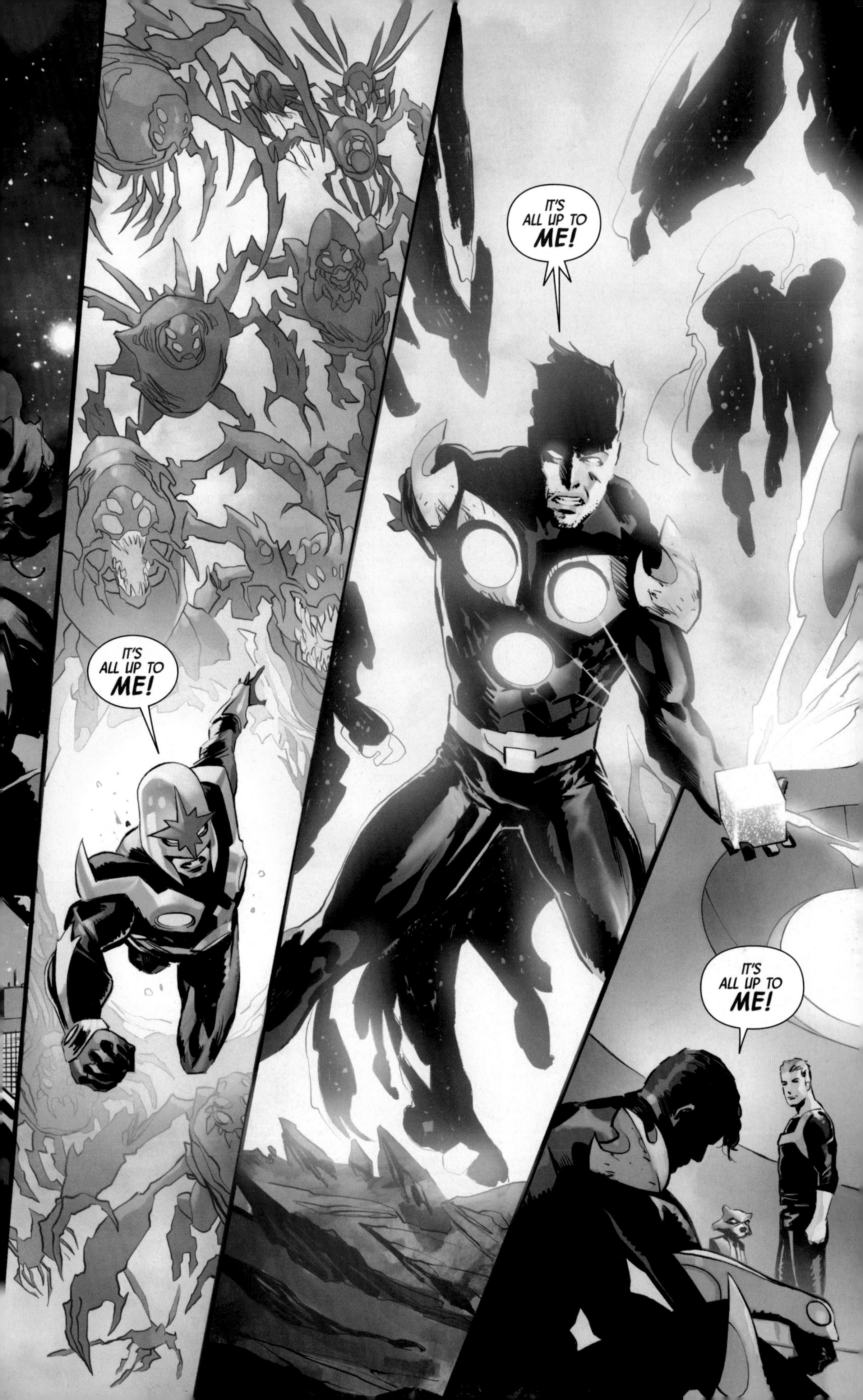
IT'S ALL UP TO ME!
IT'S ALL UP TO ME!
IT'S ALL UP TO ME!

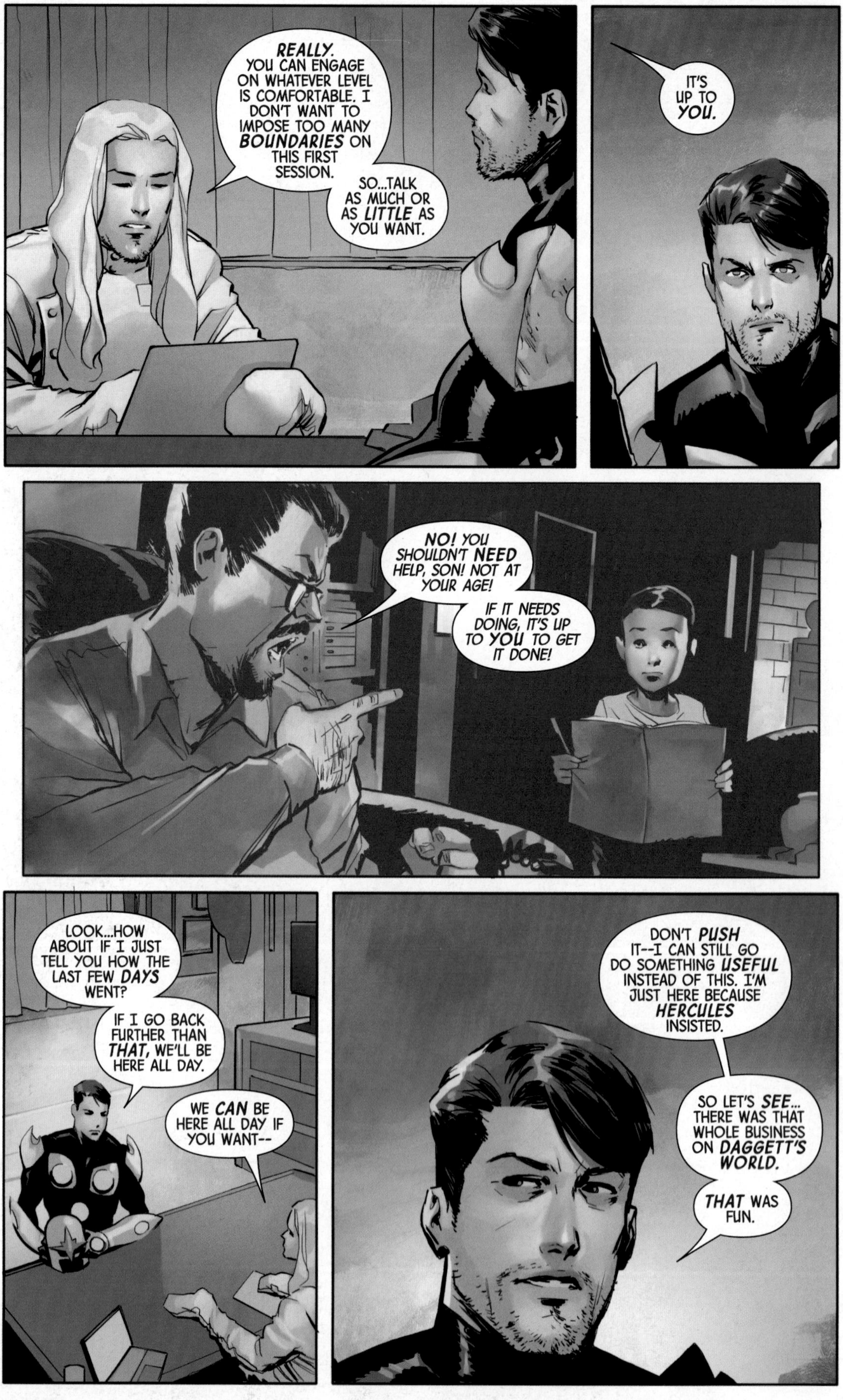
REALLY. YOU CAN ENGAGE ON WHATEVER LEVEL IS COMFORTABLE. I DON'T WANT TO IMPOSE TOO MANY BOUNDARIES ON THIS FIRST SESSION.
SO...TALK AS MUCH OR AS LITTLE AS YOU WANT.
IT'S UP TO YOU.
NO! YOU SHOULDN'T NEED HELP, SON! NOT AT YOUR AGE!
IF IT NEEDS DOING, IT'S UP TO YOU TO GET IT DONE!
LOOK...HOW ABOUT IF I JUST TELL YOU HOW THE LAST FEW DAYS WENT?
IF I GO BACK FURTHER THAN THAT, WE'LL BE HERE ALL DAY.
WE CAN BE HERE ALL DAY IF YOU WANT--
DON'T PUSH IT--I CAN STILL GO DO SOMETHING USEFUL INSTEAD OF THIS. I'M JUST HERE BECAUSE HERCULES INSISTED.
SO LET'S SEE... THERE WAS THAT WHOLE BUSINESS ON DAGGETT'S WORLD.
THAT WAS FUN.

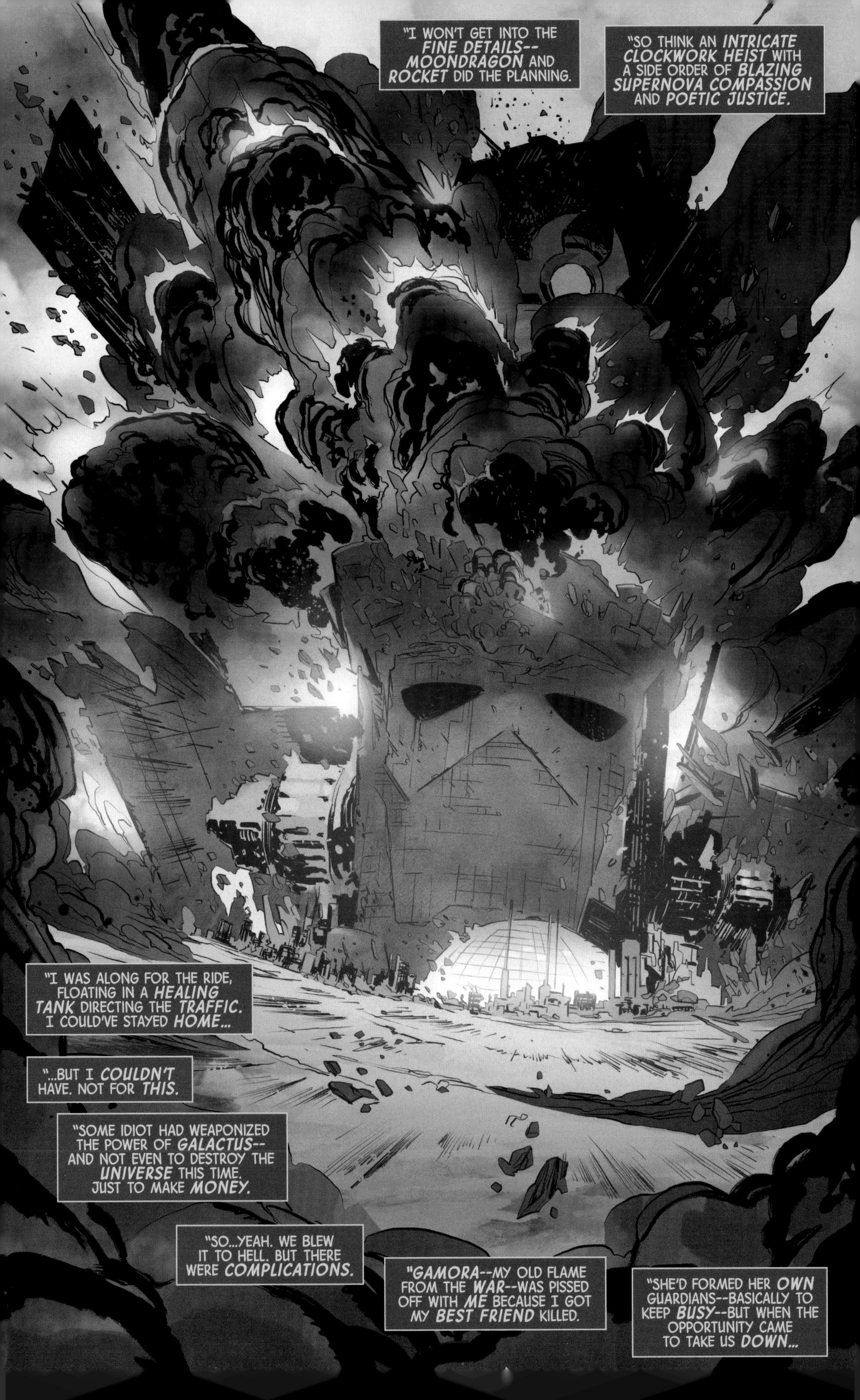
"I WON'T GET INTO THE FINE DETAILS--MOONDRAGON AND ROCKET DID THE PLANNING.
"SO THINK AN INTRICATE CLOCKWORK HEIST WITH A SIDE ORDER OF BLAZING SUPERNOVA COMPASSION AND POETIC JUSTICE.
"I WAS ALONG FOR THE RIDE, FLOATING IN A HEALING TANK DIRECTING THE TRAFFIC. I COULD'VE STAYED HOME...
"...BUT I COULDN'T HAVE. NOT FOR THIS.
"SOME IDIOT HAD WEAPONIZED THE POWER OF GALACTUS--AND NOT EVEN TO DESTROY THE UNIVERSE THIS TIME. JUST TO MAKE MONEY.
"SO...YEAH. WE BLEW IT TO HELL. BUT THERE WERE COMPLICATIONS.
"GAMORA--MY OLD FLAME FROM THE WAR--WAS PISSED OFF WITH ME BECAUSE I GOT MY BEST FRIEND KILLED.
"SHE'D FORMED HER OWN GUARDIANS--BASICALLY TO KEEP BUSY--BUT WHEN THE OPPORTUNITY CAME TO TAKE US DOWN...

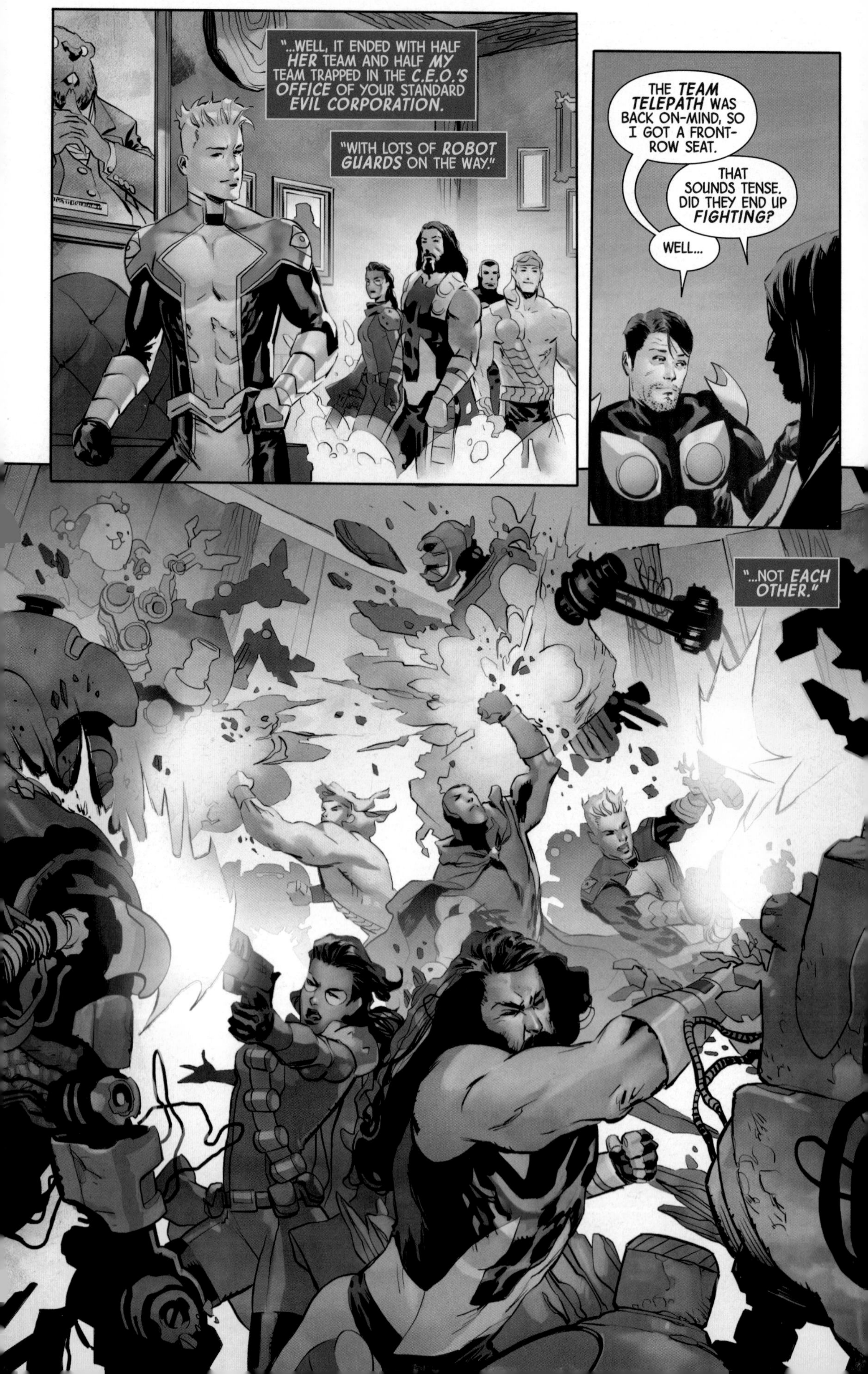
"...WELL, IT ENDED WITH HALF HER TEAM AND HALF MY TEAM TRAPPED IN THE C.E.O.'S OFFICE OF YOUR STANDARD EVIL CORPORATION.
"WITH LOTS OF ROBOT GUARDS ON THE WAY."
THE TEAM TELEPATH WAS BACK ON-MIND, SO I GOT A FRONT-ROW SEAT.
THAT SOUNDS TENSE. DID THEY END UP FIGHTING?
WELL...
"...NOT EACH OTHER."

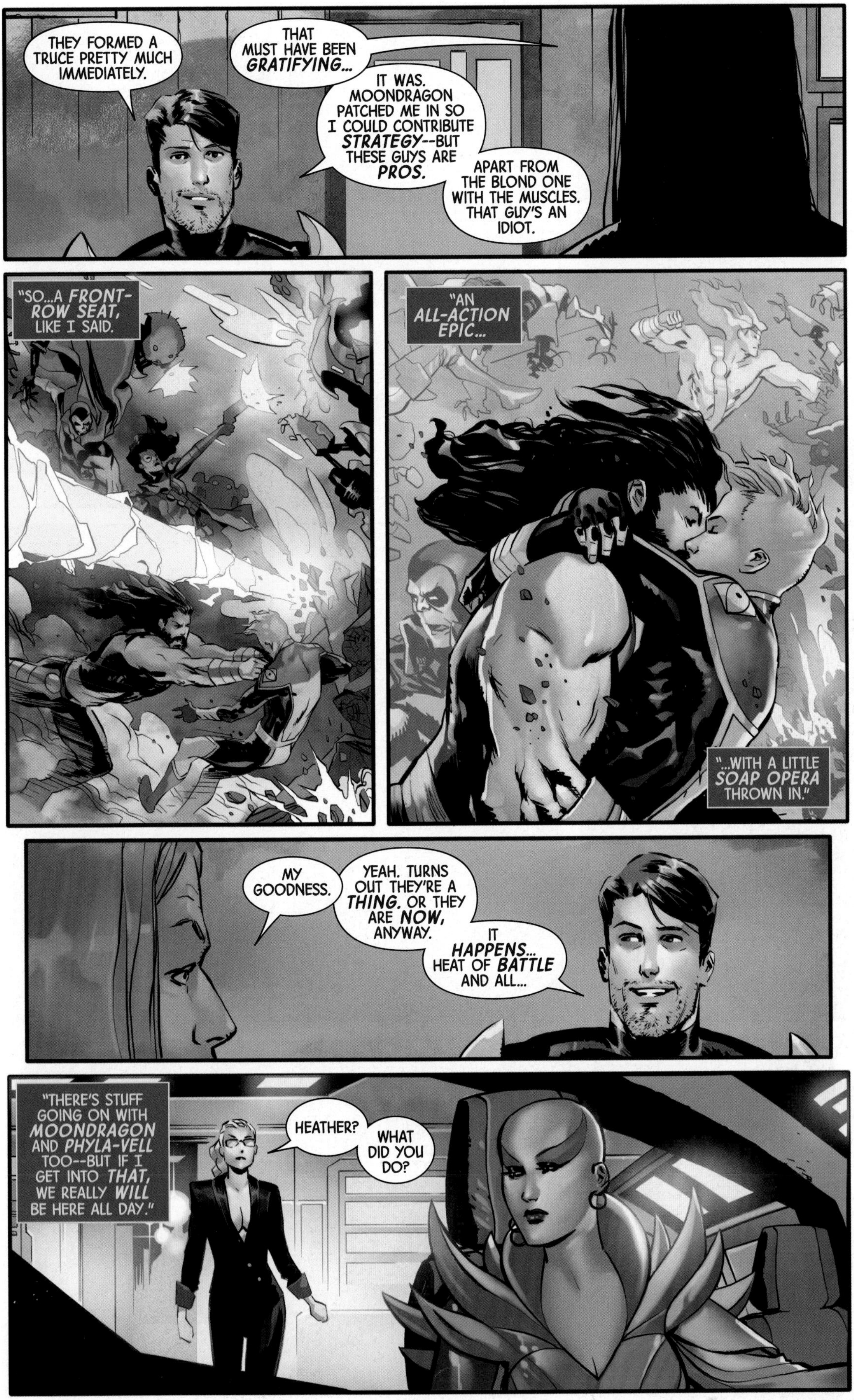
THEY FORMED A TRUCE PRETTY MUCH IMMEDIATELY.
THAT MUST HAVE BEEN GRATIFYING...
IT WAS. MOONDRAGON PATCHED ME IN SO I COULD CONTRIBUTE STRATEGY--BUT THESE GUYS ARE PROS.
APART FROM THE BLOND ONE WITH THE MUSCLES. THAT GUY'S AN IDIOT.
"SO...A FRONT-ROW SEAT, LIKE I SAID.
"AN ALL-ACTION EPIC...
"...WITH A LITTLE SOAP OPERA THROWN IN."
MY GOODNESS.
YEAH. TURNS OUT THEY'RE A THING. OR THEY ARE NOW, ANYWAY.
IT HAPPENS... HEAT OF BATTLE AND ALL...
"THERE'S STUFF GOING ON WITH MOONDRAGON AND PHYLA-VELL TOO--BUT IF I GET INTO THAT, WE REALLY WILL BE HERE ALL DAY."
HEATHER?
WHAT DID YOU DO?

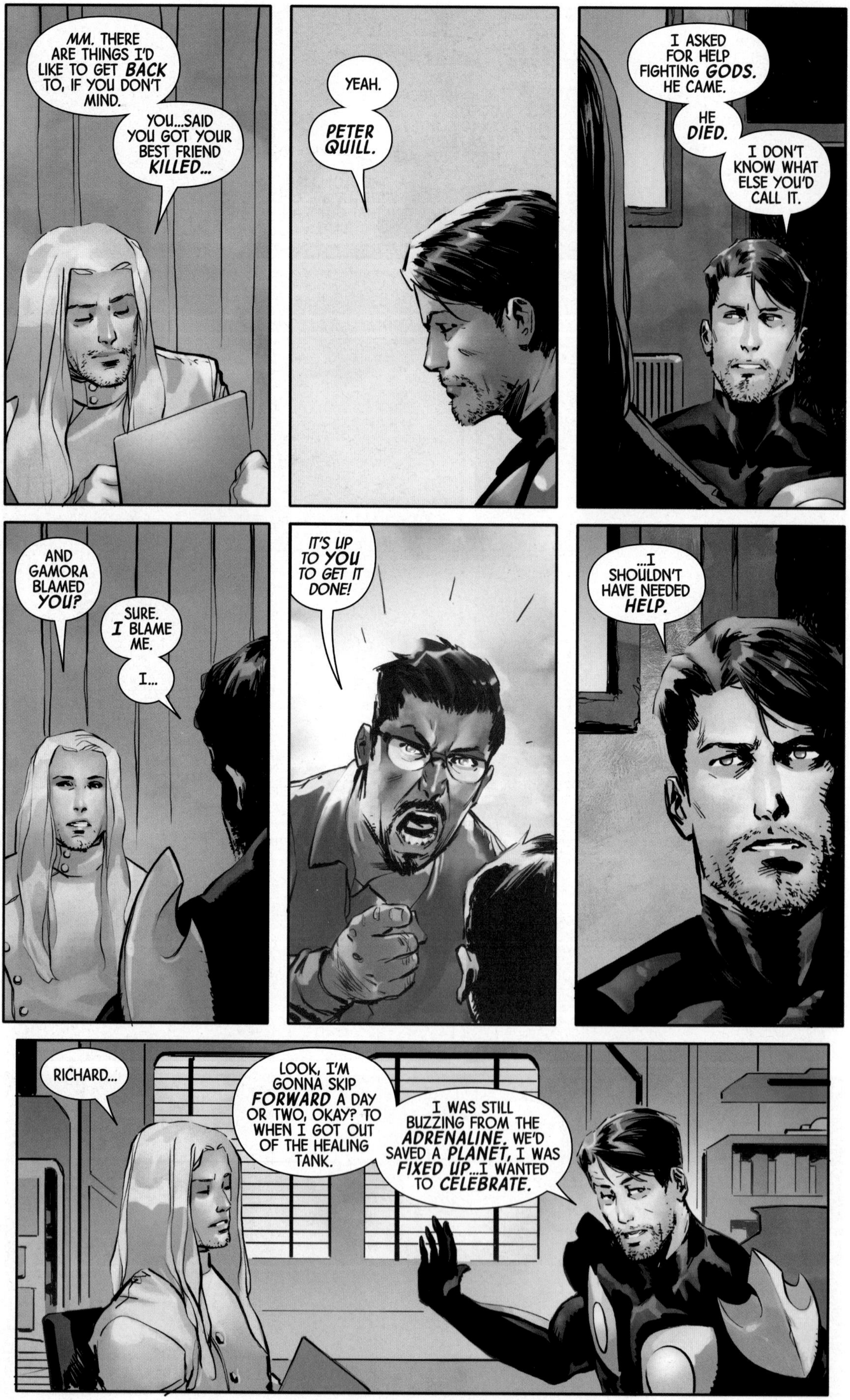
MM. THERE ARE THINGS I'D LIKE TO GET BACK TO, IF YOU DON'T MIND.
YOU...SAID YOU GOT YOUR BEST FRIEND KILLED...
YEAH.
PETER QUILL.
I ASKED FOR HELP FIGHTING GODS. HE CAME.
HE DIED.
I DON'T KNOW WHAT ELSE YOU'D CALL IT.
AND GAMORA BLAMED YOU?
SURE. I BLAME ME.
I...
IT'S UP TO YOU TO GET IT DONE!
...I SHOULDN'T HAVE NEEDED HELP.
RICHARD...
LOOK, I'M GONNA SKIP FORWARD A DAY OR TWO, OKAY? TO WHEN I GOT OUT OF THE HEALING TANK.
I WAS STILL BUZZING FROM THE ADRENALINE. WE'D SAVED A PLANET, I WAS FIXED UP...I WANTED TO CELEBRATE.

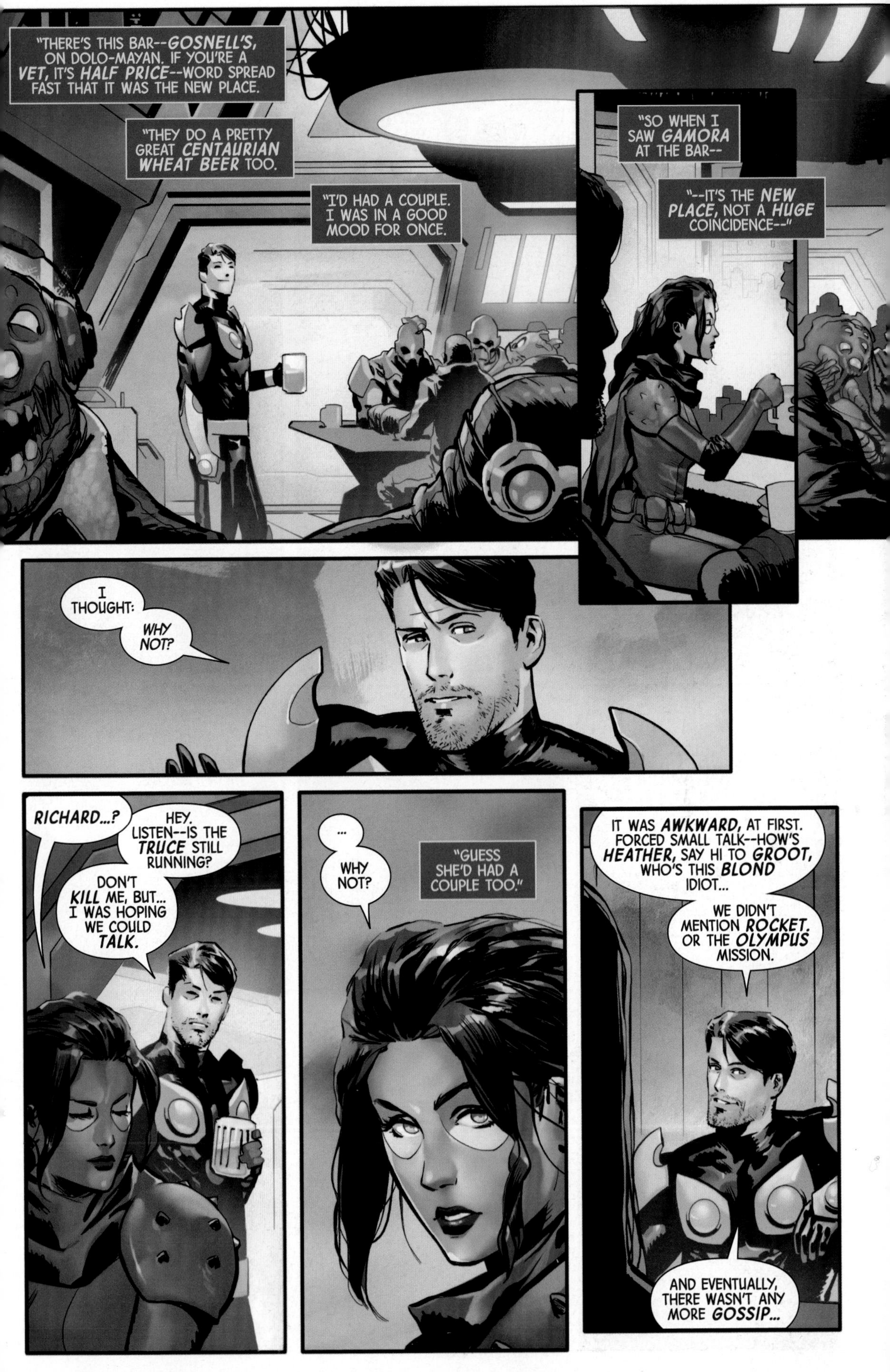
"THERE'S THIS BAR--GOSNELL'S, ON DOLO-MAYAN. IF YOU'RE A VET, IT'S HALF PRICE--WORD SPREAD FAST THAT IT WAS THE NEW PLACE.
"THEY DO A PRETTY GREAT CENTAURIAN WHEAT BEER TOO.
"I'D HAD A COUPLE. I WAS IN A GOOD MOOD FOR ONCE.
"SO WHEN I SAW GAMORA AT THE BAR--
"--IT'S THE NEW PLACE, NOT A HUGE COINCIDENCE--"
I THOUGHT: WHY NOT?
RICHARD...?
HEY. LISTEN--IS THE TRUCE STILL RUNNING?
DON'T KILL ME, BUT... I WAS HOPING WE COULD TALK.
...
WHY NOT?
"GUESS SHE'D HAD A COUPLE TOO."
IT WAS AWKWARD, AT FIRST. FORCED SMALL TALK--HOW'S HEATHER, SAY HI TO GROOT, WHO'S THIS BLOND IDIOT...
WE DIDN'T MENTION ROCKET. OR THE OLYMPUS MISSION.
AND EVENTUALLY, THERE WASN'T ANY MORE GOSSIP...

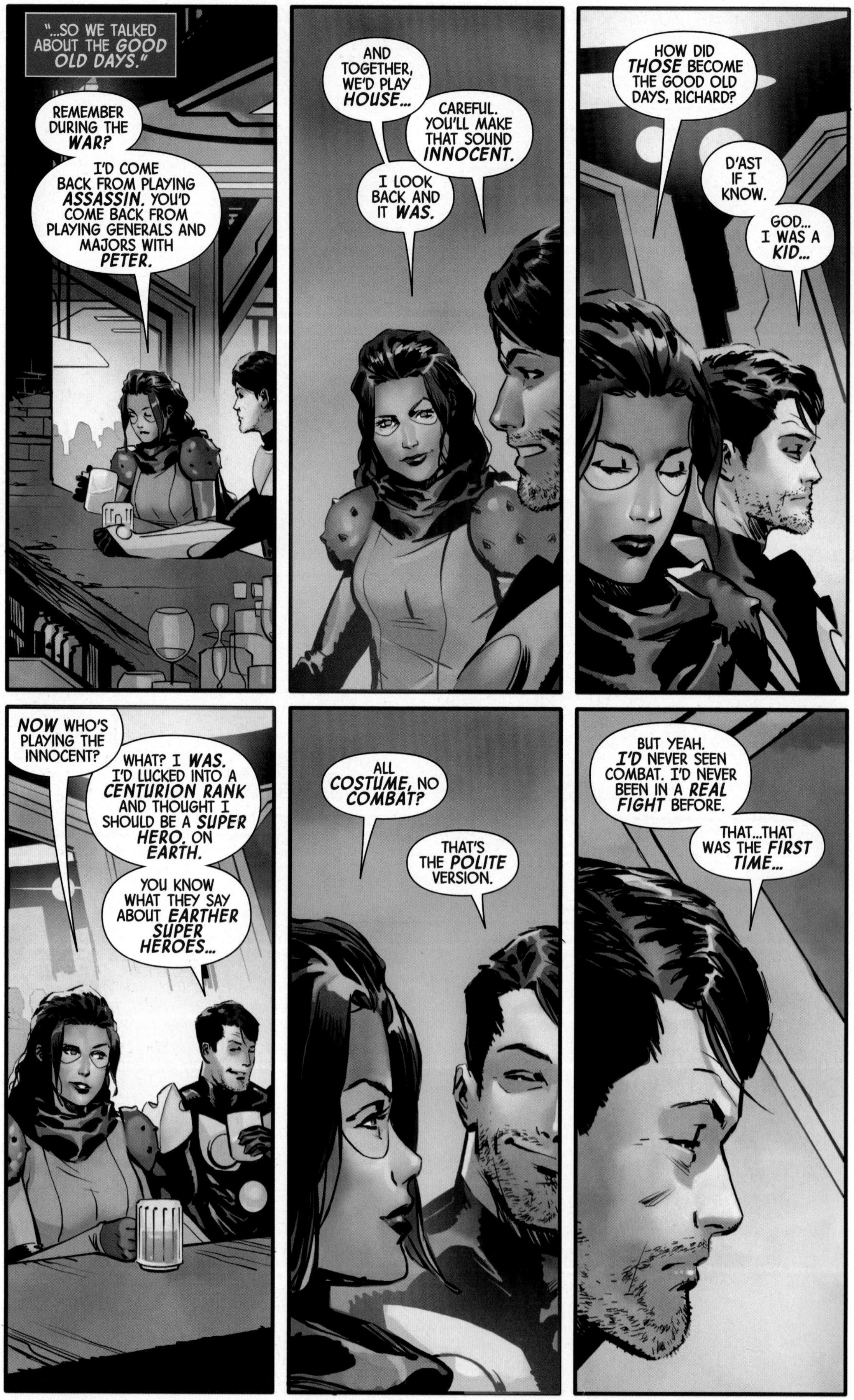
"...SO WE TALKED ABOUT THE GOOD OLD DAYS."
REMEMBER DURING THE WAR?
I'D COME BACK FROM PLAYING ASSASSIN. YOU'D COME BACK FROM PLAYING GENERALS AND MAJORS WITH PETER.
AND TOGETHER, WE'D PLAY HOUSE...
CAREFUL. YOU'LL MAKE THAT SOUND INNOCENT.
I LOOK BACK AND IT WAS.
HOW DID THOSE BECOME THE GOOD OLD DAYS, RICHARD?
D'AST IF I KNOW.
GOD... I WAS A KID...
NOW WHO'S PLAYING THE INNOCENT?
WHAT? I WAS. I'D LUCKED INTO A CENTURION RANK AND THOUGHT I SHOULD BE A SUPER HERO. ON EARTH.
YOU KNOW WHAT THEY SAY ABOUT EARTHER SUPER HEROES...
ALL COSTUME, NO COMBAT?
THAT'S THE POLITE VERSION.
BUT YEAH. I'D NEVER SEEN COMBAT. I'D NEVER BEEN IN A REAL FIGHT BEFORE.
THAT...THAT WAS THE FIRST TIME...

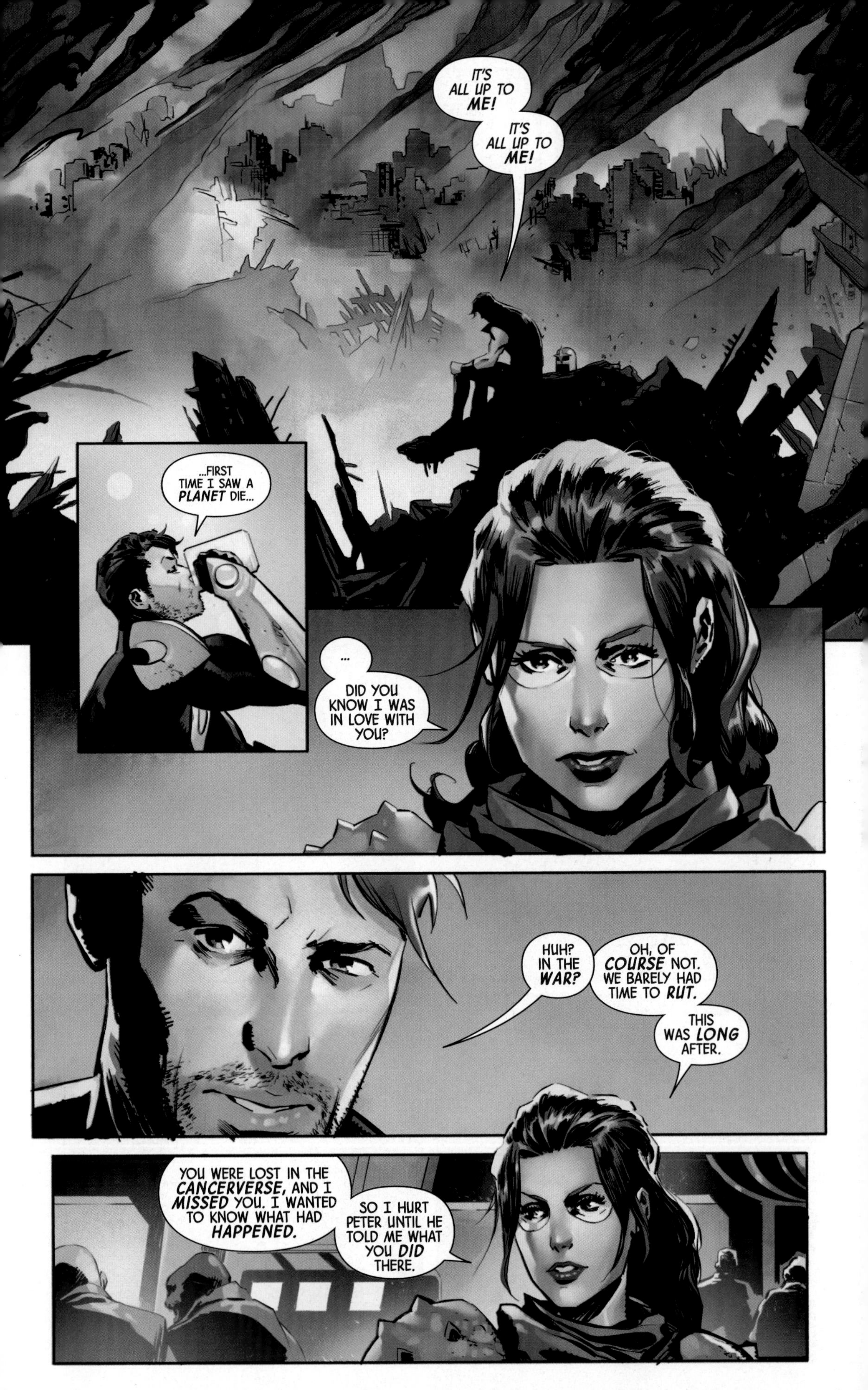
IT'S ALL UP TO ME!
IT'S ALL UP TO ME!
...FIRST TIME I SAW A PLANET DIE...
...
DID YOU KNOW I WAS IN LOVE WITH YOU?
HUH? IN THE WAR?
OH, OF COURSE NOT. WE BARELY HAD TIME TO RUT.
THIS WAS LONG AFTER.
YOU WERE LOST IN THE CANCERVERSE, AND I MISSED YOU. I WANTED TO KNOW WHAT HAD HAPPENED.
SO I HURT PETER UNTIL HE TOLD ME WHAT YOU DID THERE.

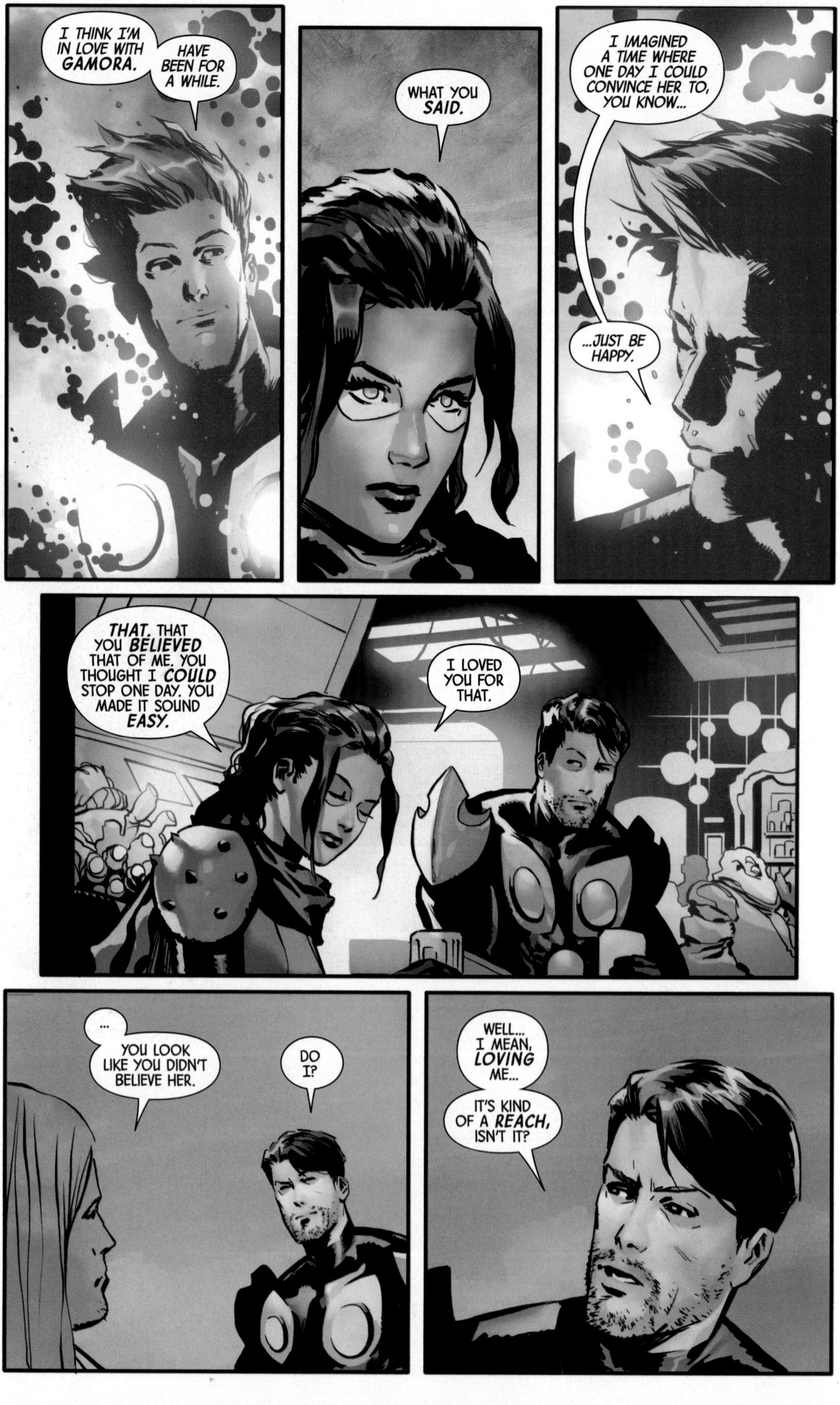
I THINK I'M IN LOVE WITH GAMORA.
HAVE BEEN FOR A WHILE.
WHAT YOU SAID.
I IMAGINED A TIME WHERE ONE DAY I COULD CONVINCE HER TO, YOU KNOW...
...JUST BE HAPPY.
THAT. THAT YOU BELIEVED THAT OF ME. YOU THOUGHT I COULD STOP ONE DAY. YOU MADE IT SOUND EASY.
I LOVED YOU FOR THAT.
...
YOU LOOK LIKE YOU DIDN'T BELIEVE HER.
DO I?
WELL... I MEAN, LOVING ME...
IT'S KIND OF A REACH, ISN'T IT?

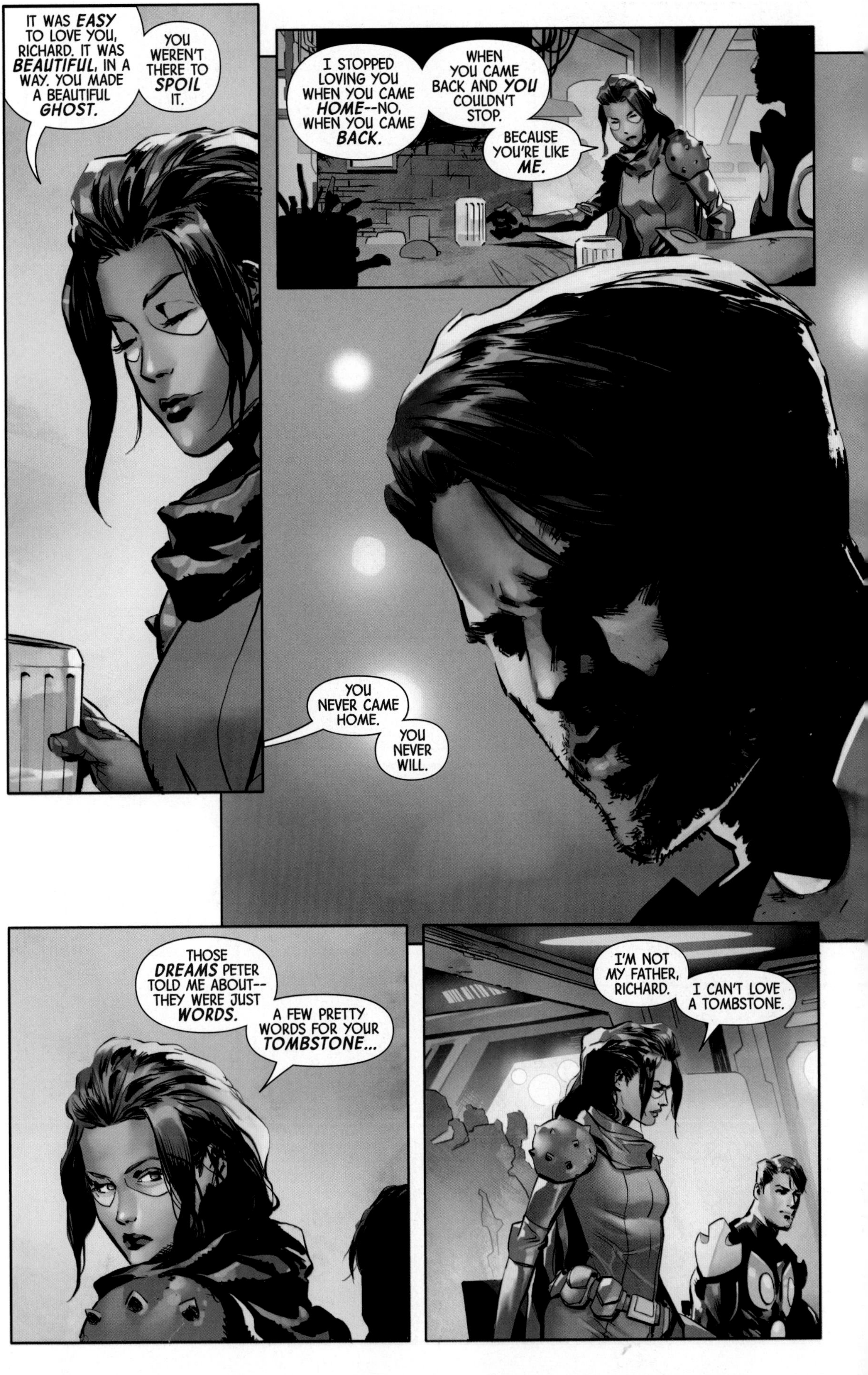

IT WAS EASY TO LOVE YOU, RICHARD. IT WAS BEAUTIFUL, IN A WAY. YOU MADE A BEAUTIFUL GHOST.
YOU WEREN'T THERE TO SPOIL IT.
I STOPPED LOVING YOU WHEN YOU CAME HOME--NO, WHEN YOU CAME BACK.
WHEN YOU CAME BACK AND YOU COULDN'T STOP.
BECAUSE YOU'RE LIKE ME.
YOU NEVER CAME HOME.
YOU NEVER WILL.
THOSE DREAMS PETER TOLD ME ABOUT-- THEY WERE JUST WORDS.
A FEW PRETTY WORDS FOR YOUR TOMBSTONE...
I'M NOT MY FATHER, RICHARD.
I CAN'T LOVE A TOMBSTONE.

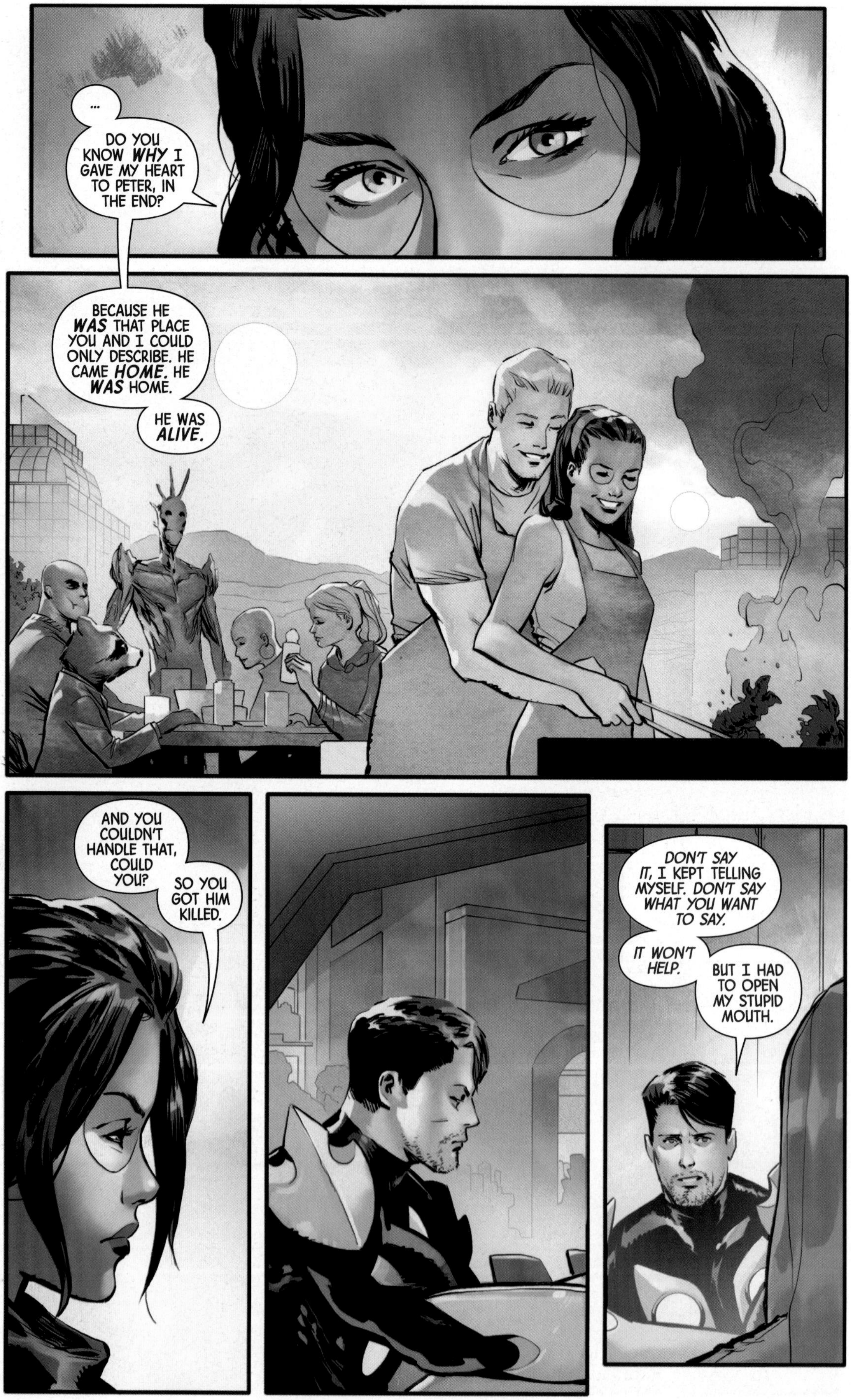
...
DO YOU KNOW WHY I GAVE MY HEART TO PETER, IN THE END?
BECAUSE HE WAS THAT PLACE YOU AND I COULD ONLY DESCRIBE. HE CAME HOME. HE WAS HOME.
HE WAS ALIVE.
AND YOU COULDN'T HANDLE THAT, COULD YOU?
SO YOU GOT HIM KILLED.
DON'T SAY IT, I KEPT TELLING MYSELF. DON'T SAY WHAT YOU WANT TO SAY.
IT WON'T HELP.
BUT I HAD TO OPEN MY STUPID MOUTH.

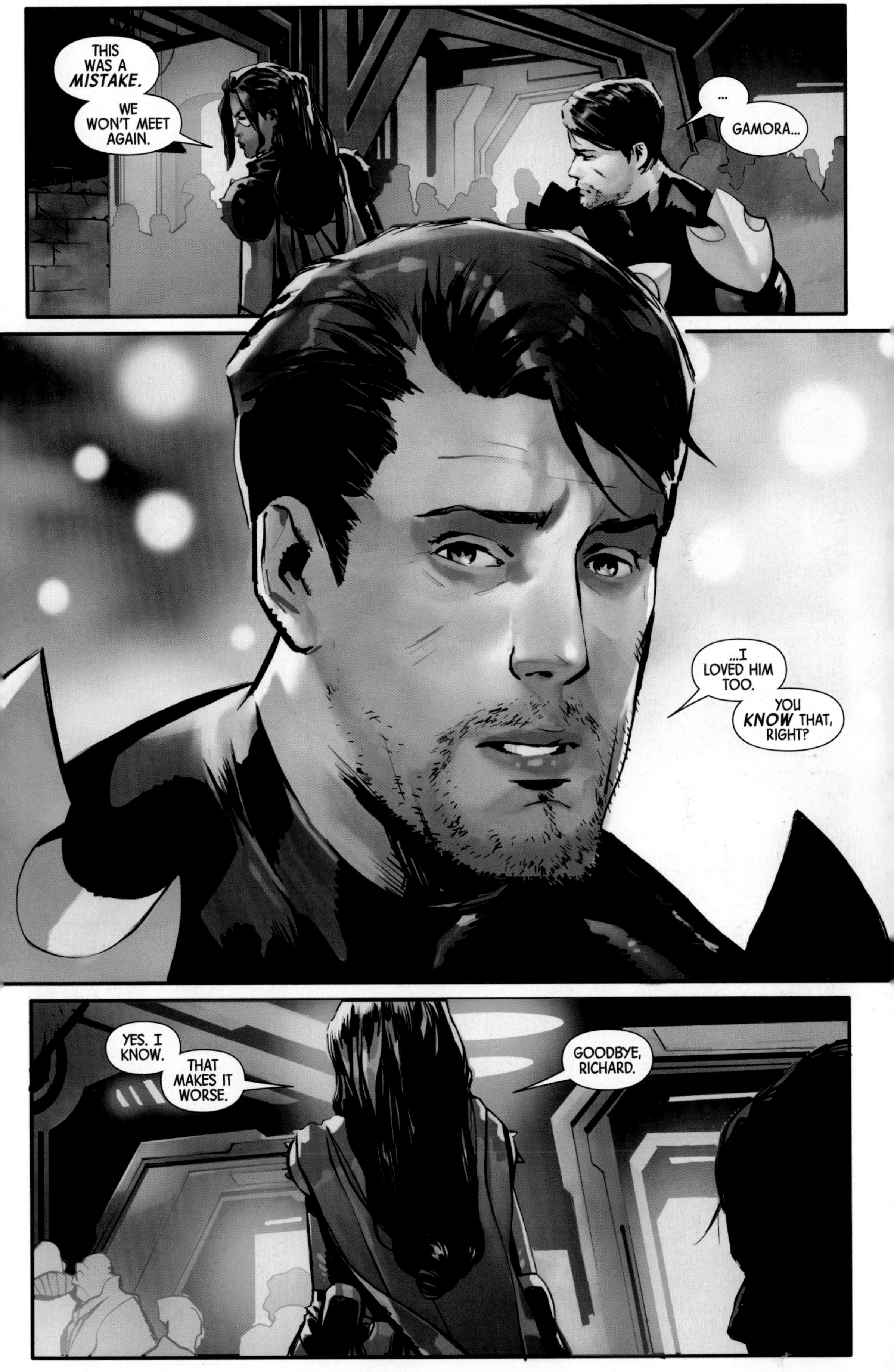
THIS WAS A MISTAKE.
WE WON'T MEET AGAIN.
...
GAMORA...
...I LOVED HIM TOO.
YOU KNOW THAT, RIGHT?
YES. I KNOW.
THAT MAKES IT WORSE.
GOODBYE, RICHARD.

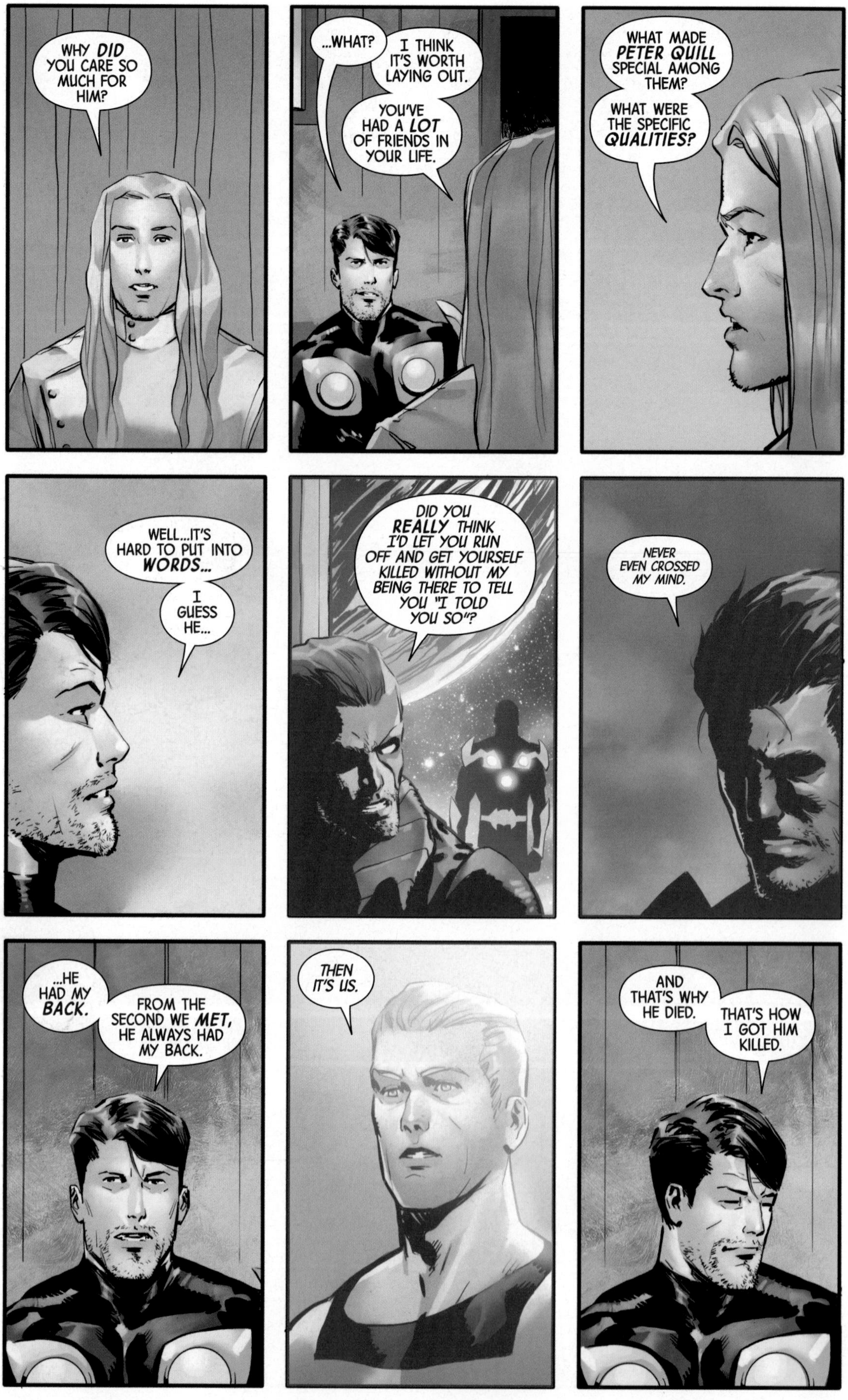
WHY DID YOU CARE SO MUCH FOR HIM?
...WHAT?
I THINK IT'S WORTH LAYING OUT.
YOU'VE HAD A LOT OF FRIENDS IN YOUR LIFE.
WHAT MADE PETER QUILL SPECIAL AMONG THEM?
WHAT WERE THE SPECIFIC QUALITIES?
WELL...IT'S HARD TO PUT INTO WORDS...
I GUESS HE...
DID YOU REALLY THINK I'D LET YOU RUN OFF AND GET YOURSELF KILLED WITHOUT MY BEING THERE TO TELL YOU "I TOLD YOU SO"?
NEVER EVEN CROSSED MY MIND.
...HE HAD MY BACK.
FROM THE SECOND WE MET, HE ALWAYS HAD MY BACK.
THEN IT'S US.
AND THAT'S WHY HE DIED.
THAT'S HOW I GOT HIM KILLED.

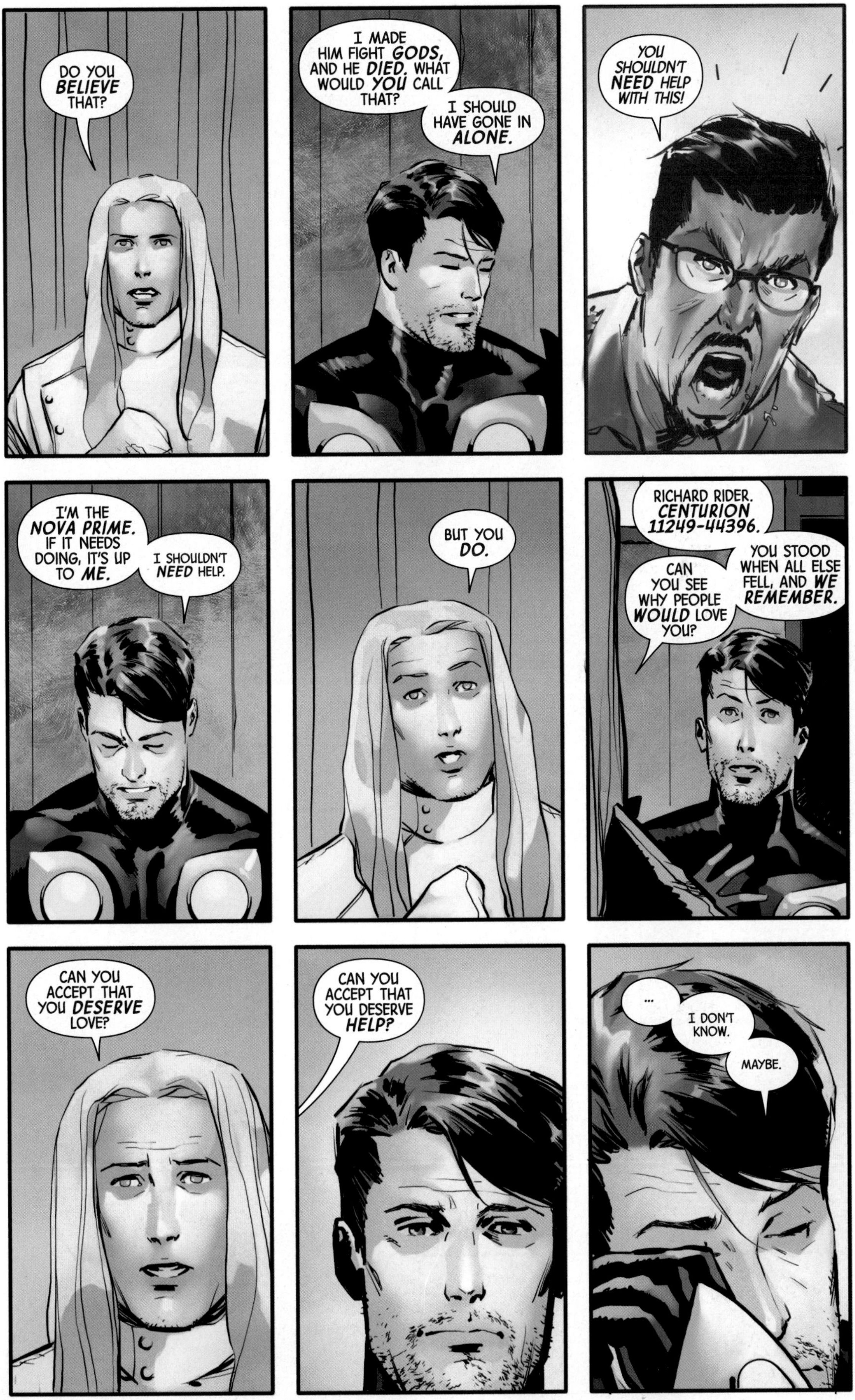
DO YOU BELIEVE THAT?
I MADE HIM FIGHT GODS, AND HE DIED. WHAT WOULD YOU CALL THAT?
I SHOULD HAVE GONE IN ALONE.
YOU SHOULDN'T NEED HELP WITH THIS!
I'M THE NOVA PRIME. IF IT NEEDS DOING, IT'S UP TO ME.
I SHOULDN'T NEED HELP.
BUT YOU DO.
RICHARD RIDER. CENTURION 11249-44396.
YOU STOOD WHEN ALL ELSE FELL, AND WE REMEMBER.
CAN YOU SEE WHY PEOPLE WOULD LOVE YOU?
CAN YOU ACCEPT THAT YOU DESERVE LOVE?
CAN YOU ACCEPT THAT YOU DESERVE HELP?
...
I DON'T KNOW.
MAYBE.

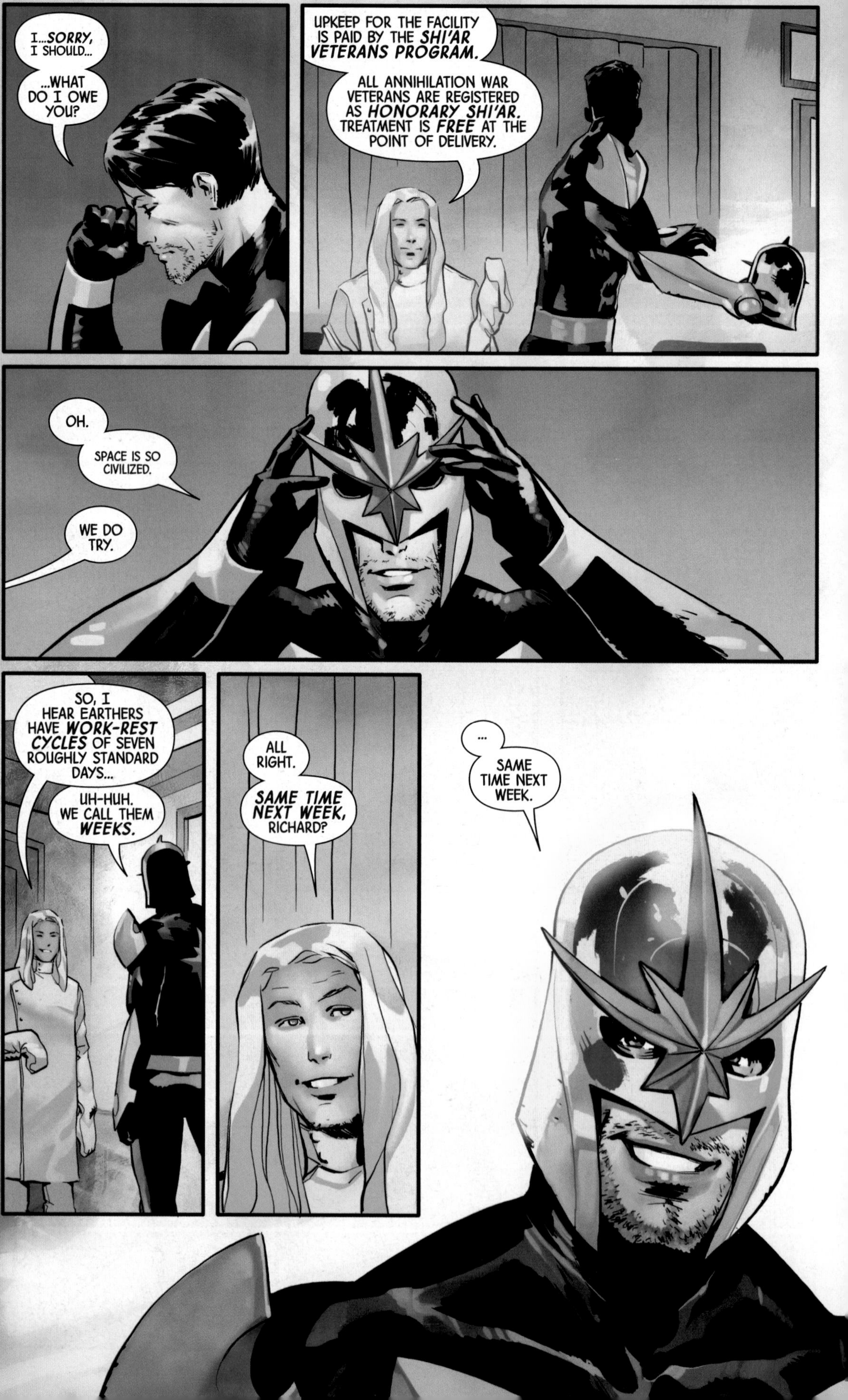
I...SORRY, I SHOULD...
...WHAT DO I OWE YOU?
UPKEEP FOR THE FACILITY IS PAID BY THE SHI'AR VETERANS PROGRAM.
ALL ANNIHILATION WAR VETERANS ARE REGISTERED AS HONORARY SHI'AR. TREATMENT IS FREE AT THE POINT OF DELIVERY.
OH.
SPACE IS SO CIVILIZED.
WE DO TRY.
SO, I HEAR EARTHERS HAVE WORK-REST CYCLES OF SEVEN ROUGHLY STANDARD DAYS...
UH-HUH. WE CALL THEM WEEKS.
ALL RIGHT.
SAME TIME NEXT WEEK, RICHARD?
...
SAME TIME NEXT WEEK.

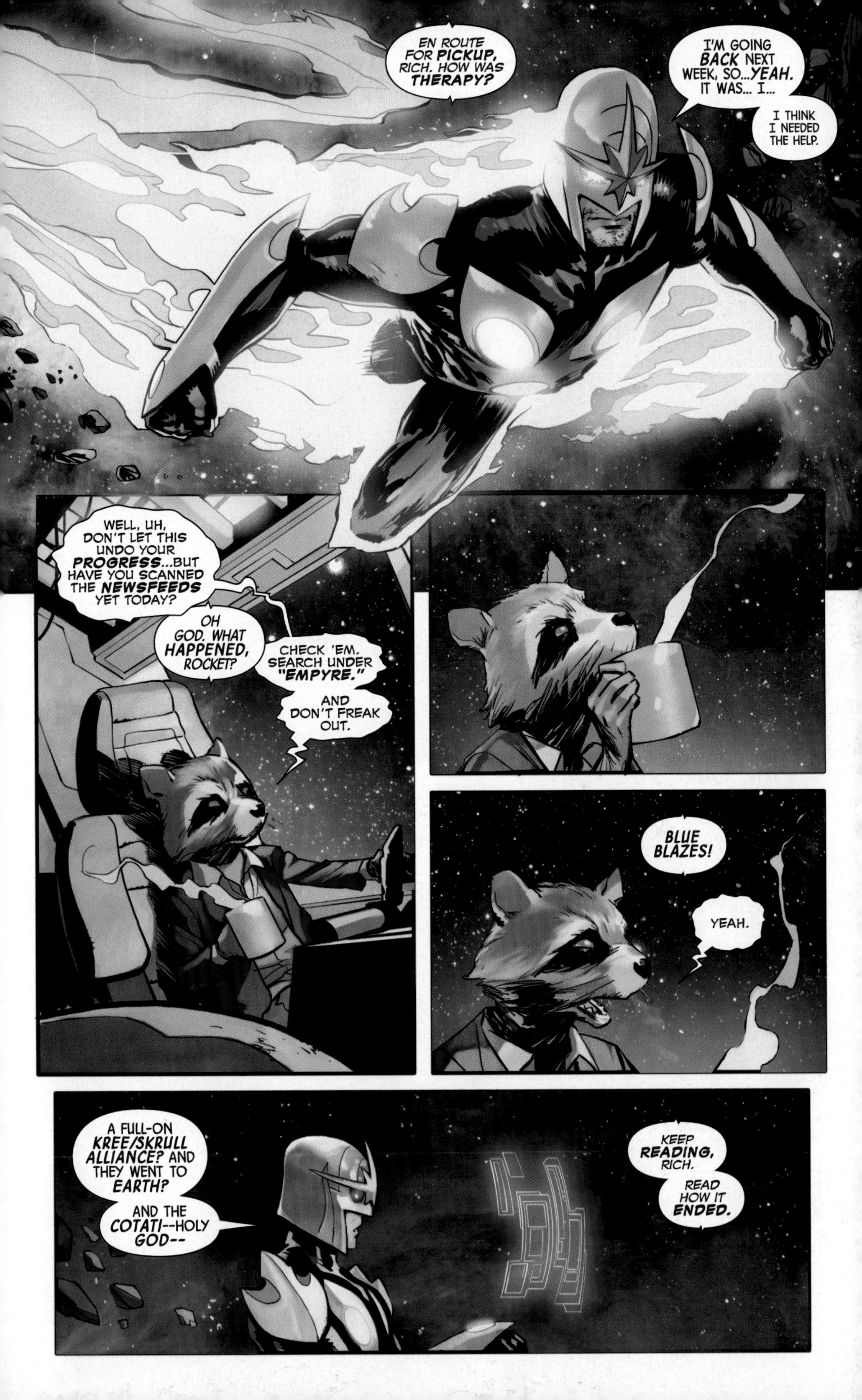

EN ROUTE FOR PICKUP, RICH. HOW WAS THERAPY?
I'M GOING BACK NEXT WEEK, SO...YEAH. IT WAS... I...
I THINK I NEEDED THE HELP.
WELL, UH, DON'T LET THIS UNDO YOUR PROGRESS...BUT HAVE YOU SCANNED THE NEWSFEEDS YET TODAY?
OH GOD. WHAT HAPPENED, ROCKET?
CHECK 'EM. SEARCH UNDER "EMPYRE."
AND DON'T FREAK OUT.
BLUE BLAZES!
YEAH.
A FULL-ON KREE/SKRULL ALLIANCE? AND THEY WENT TO EARTH?
AND THE COTATI--HOLY GOD--
KEEP READING, RICH.
READ HOW IT ENDED.

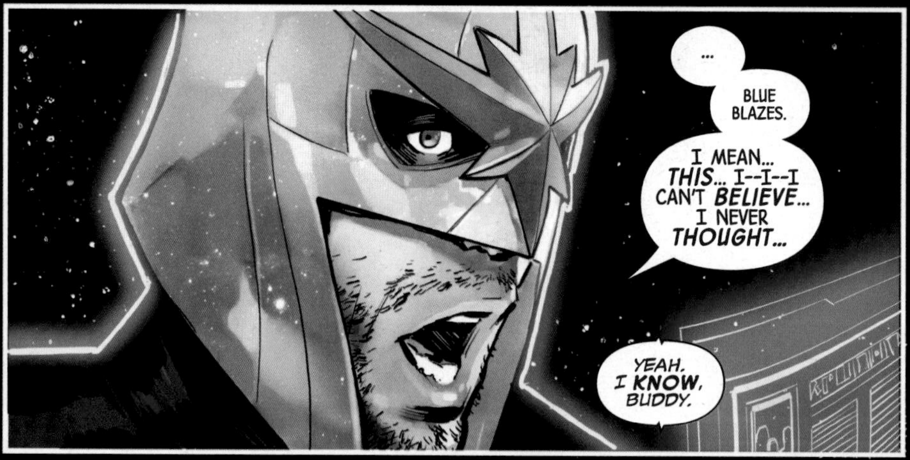
...
BLUE BLAZES.
I MEAN... THIS... I--I--I CAN'T BELIEVE... I NEVER THOUGHT...
YEAH. I KNOW, BUDDY.

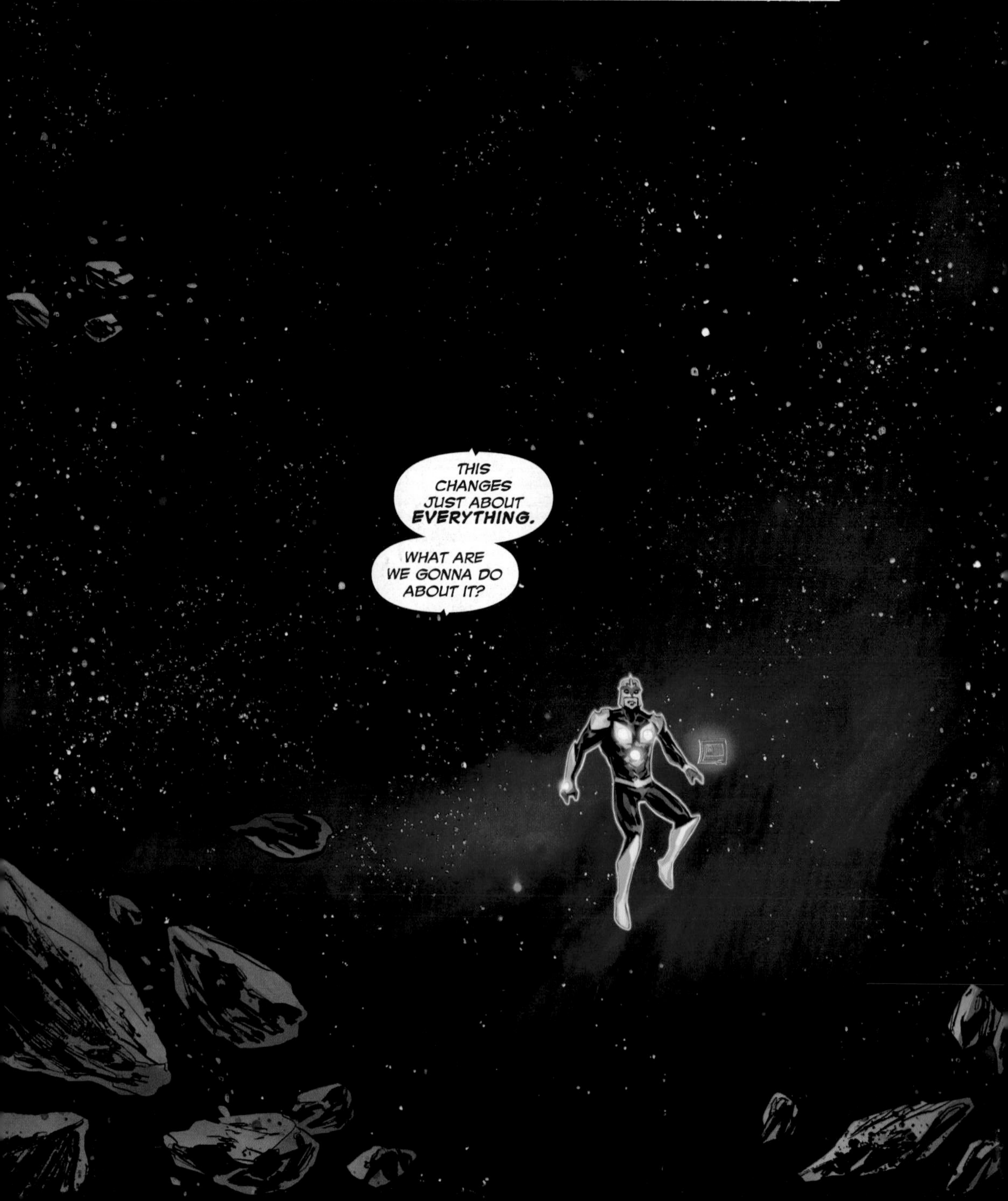
THIS CHANGES JUST ABOUT EVERYTHING.
WHAT ARE WE GONNA DO ABOUT IT?

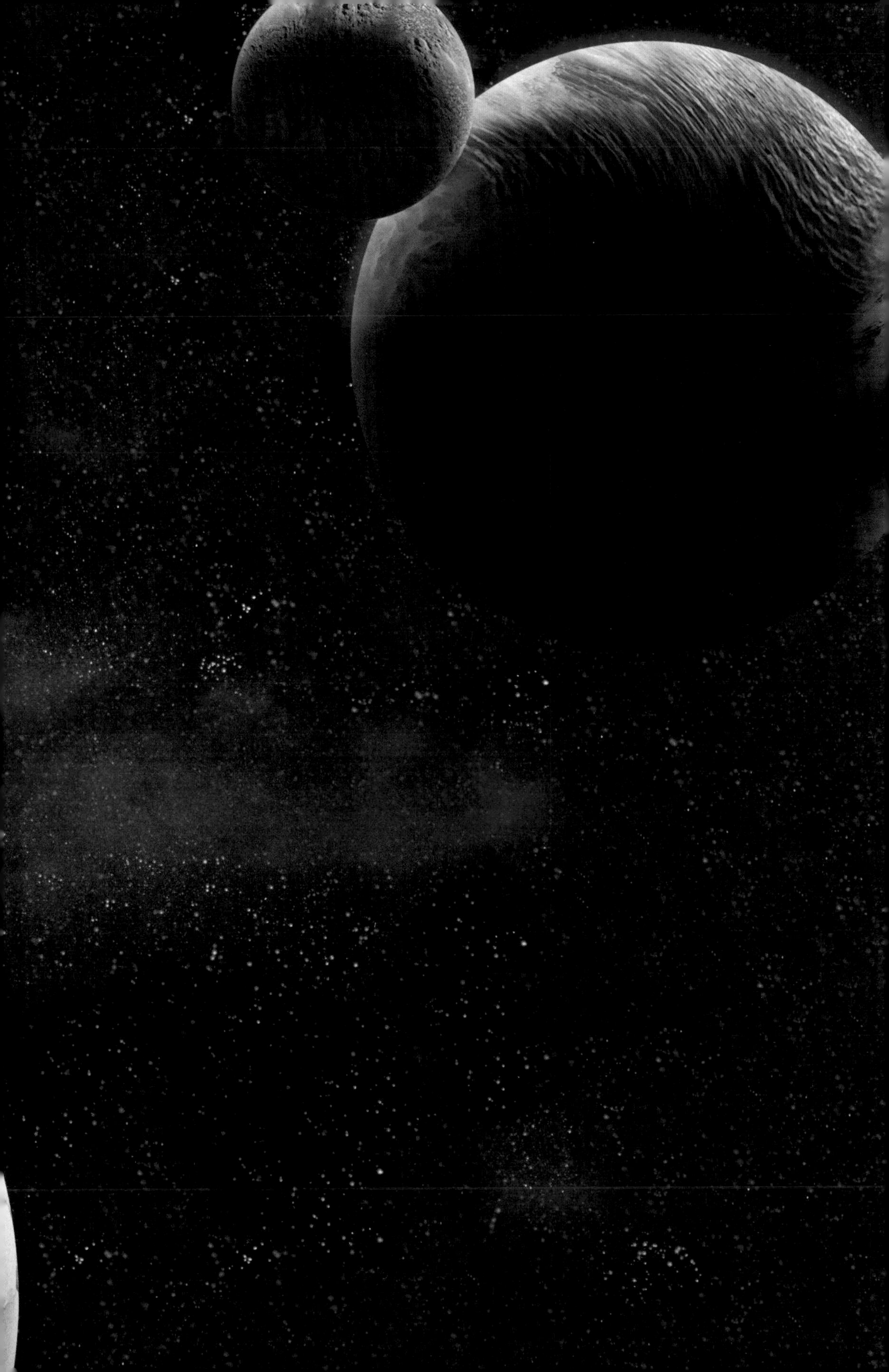

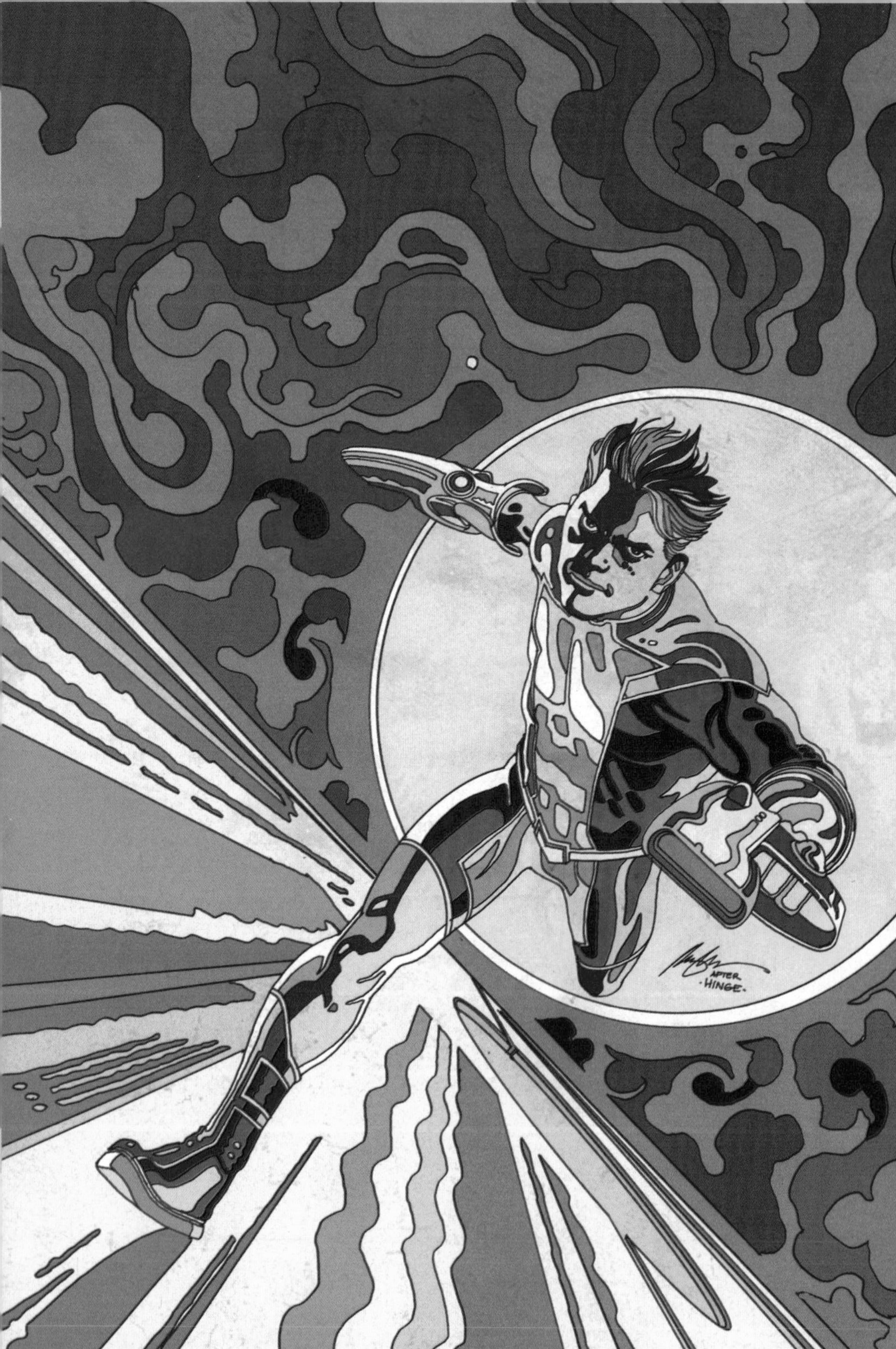
AFTER
-HINGE-

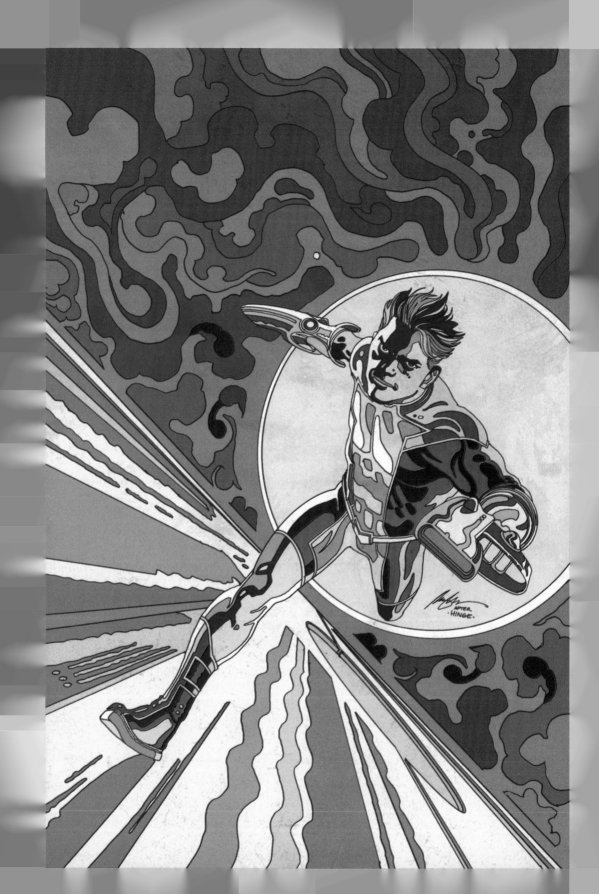

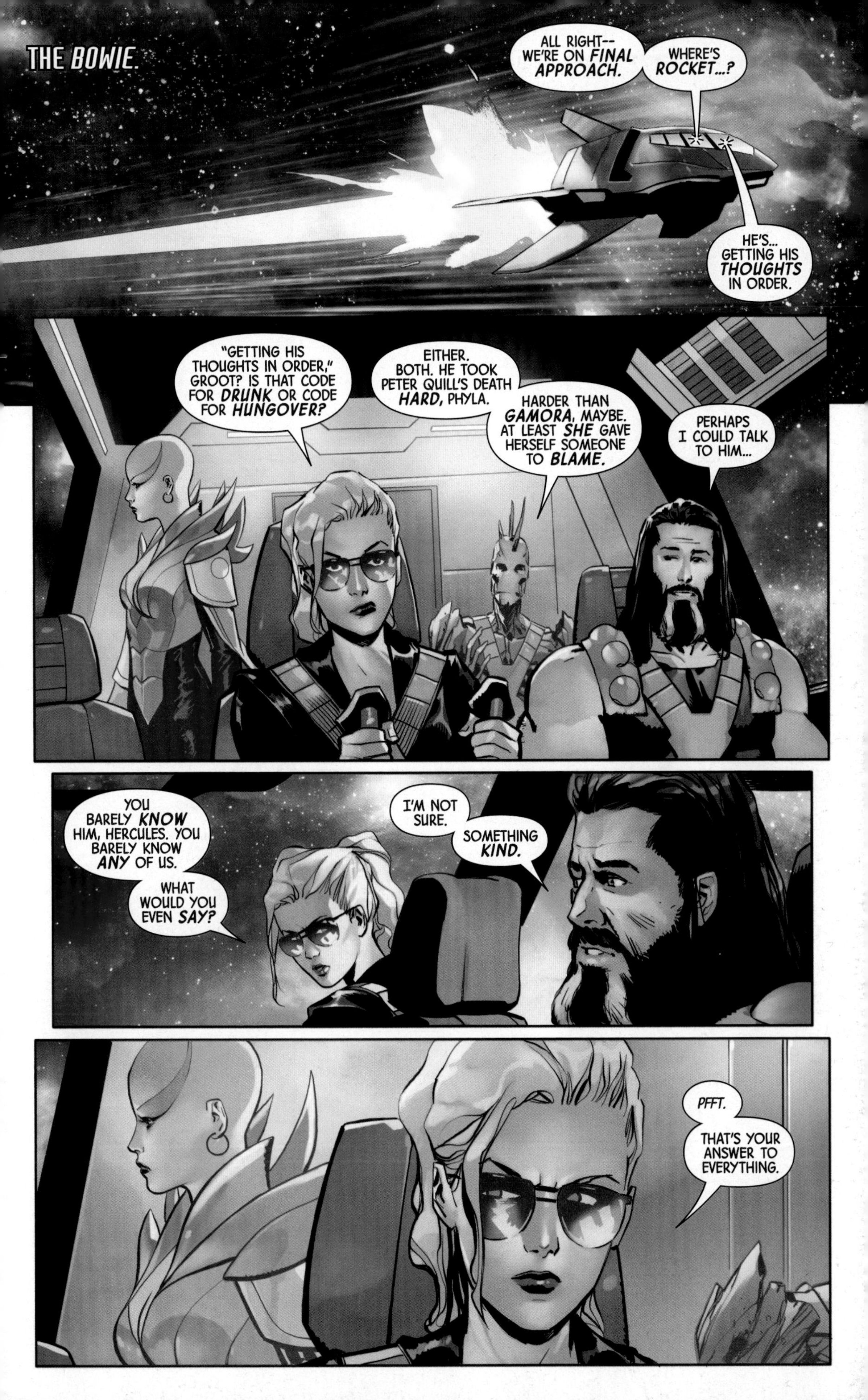
THE BOWIE.
ALL RIGHT-- WE'RE ON FINAL APPROACH.
WHERE'S ROCKET...?
HE'S... GETTING HIS THOUGHTS IN ORDER.
"GETTING HIS THOUGHTS IN ORDER," GROOT? IS THAT CODE FOR DRUNK OR CODE FOR HUNGOVER?
EITHER. BOTH. HE TOOK PETER QUILL'S DEATH HARD, PHYLA.
HARDER THAN GAMORA, MAYBE. AT LEAST SHE GAVE HERSELF SOMEONE TO BLAME.
PERHAPS I COULD TALK TO HIM...
YOU BARELY KNOW HIM, HERCULES. YOU BARELY KNOW ANY OF US.
WHAT WOULD YOU EVEN SAY?
I'M NOT SURE.
SOMETHING KIND.
PFFT.
THAT'S YOUR ANSWER TO EVERYTHING.

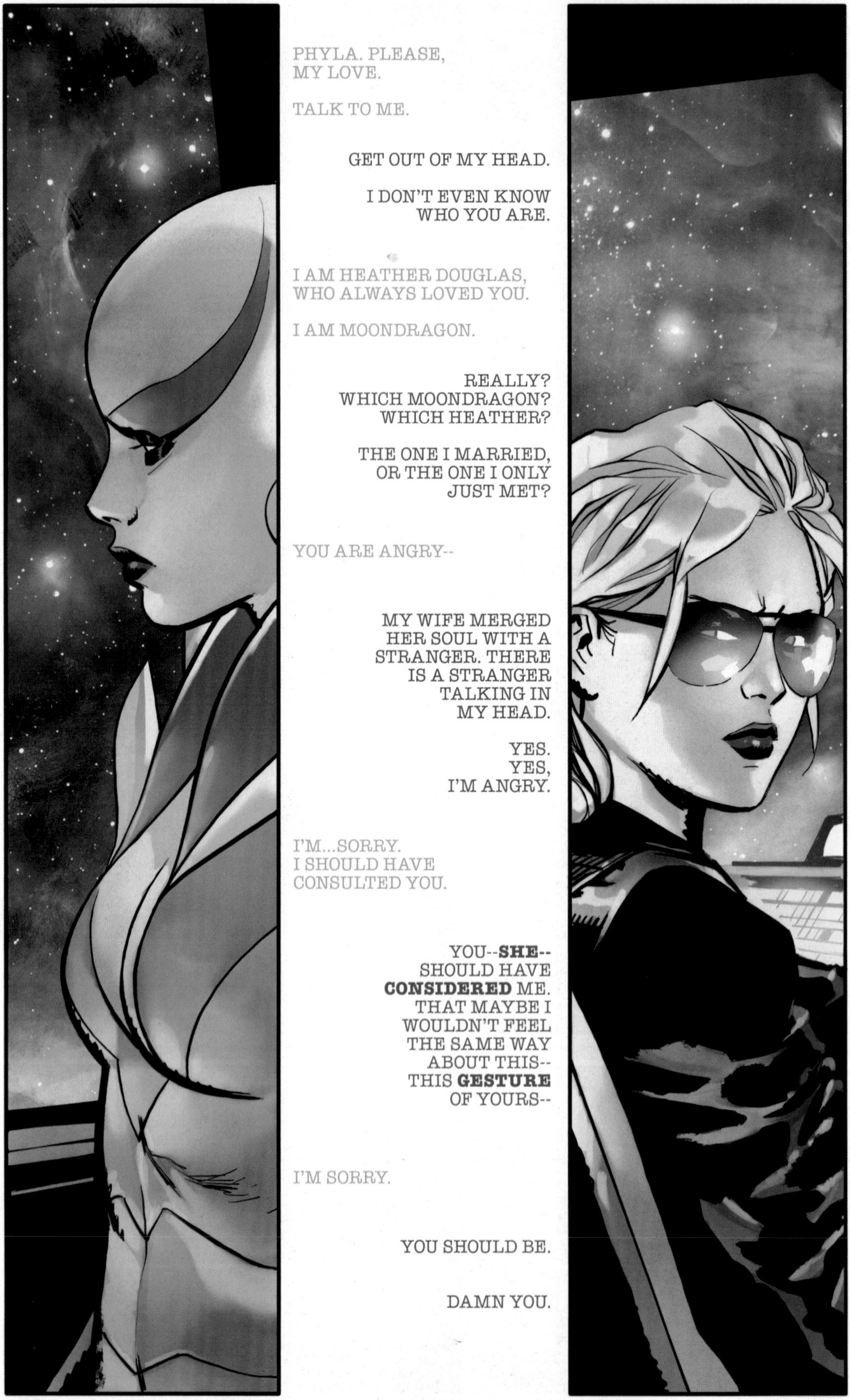
PHYLA. PLEASE, MY LOVE.
TALK TO ME.
GET OUT OF MY HEAD.
I DON'T EVEN KNOW WHO YOU ARE.
I AM HEATHER DOUGLAS, WHO ALWAYS LOVED YOU.
I AM MOONDRAGON.
REALLY? WHICH MOONDRAGON? WHICH HEATHER?
THE ONE I MARRIED, OR THE ONE I ONLY JUST MET?
YOU ARE ANGRY--
MY WIFE MERGED HER SOUL WITH A STRANGER. THERE IS A STRANGER TALKING IN MY HEAD.
YES. YES, I'M ANGRY.
I'M...SORRY. I SHOULD HAVE CONSULTED YOU.
YOU--**SHE**--SHOULD HAVE **CONSIDERED** ME. THAT MAYBE I WOULDN'T FEEL THE SAME WAY ABOUT THIS--THIS **GESTURE** OF YOURS--
I'M SORRY.
YOU SHOULD BE.
DAMN YOU.

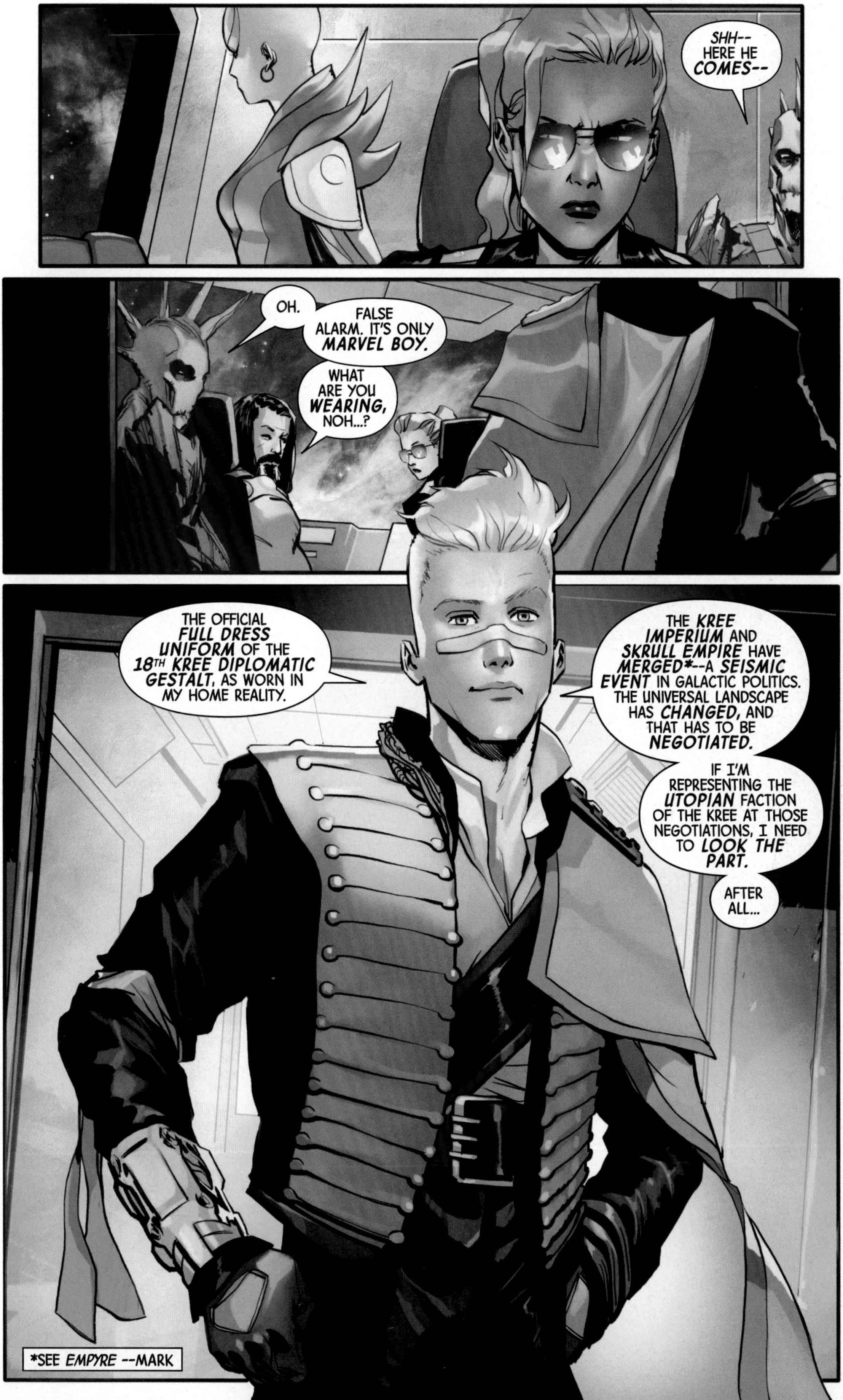
SHH-- HERE HE COMES--
OH.
FALSE ALARM. IT'S ONLY MARVEL BOY.
WHAT ARE YOU WEARING, NOH...?
THE OFFICIAL FULL DRESS UNIFORM OF THE 18TH KREE DIPLOMATIC GESTALT, AS WORN IN MY HOME REALITY.
THE KREE IMPERIUM AND SKRULL EMPIRE HAVE MERGED*--A SEISMIC EVENT IN GALACTIC POLITICS. THE UNIVERSAL LANDSCAPE HAS CHANGED, AND THAT HAS TO BE NEGOTIATED.
IF I'M REPRESENTING THE UTOPIAN FACTION OF THE KREE AT THOSE NEGOTIATIONS, I NEED TO LOOK THE PART.
AFTER ALL...
*SEE EMPYRE --MARK

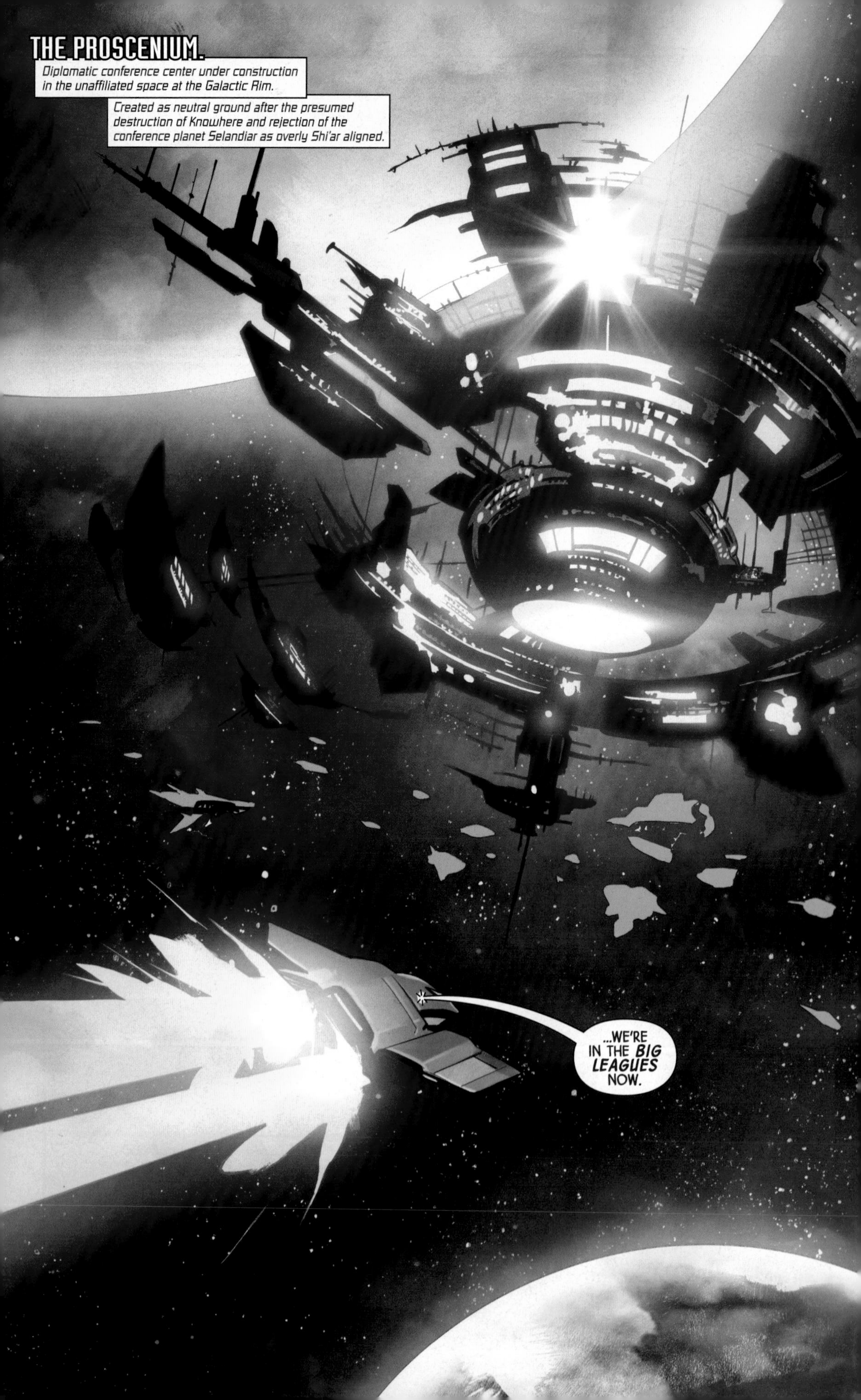
THE PROSCENIUM.
Diplomatic conference center under construction in the unaffiliated space at the Galactic Rim.
Created as neutral ground after the presumed destruction of Knowhere and rejection of the conference planet Selandiar as overly Shi'ar aligned.
...WE'RE IN THE BIG LEAGUES NOW.

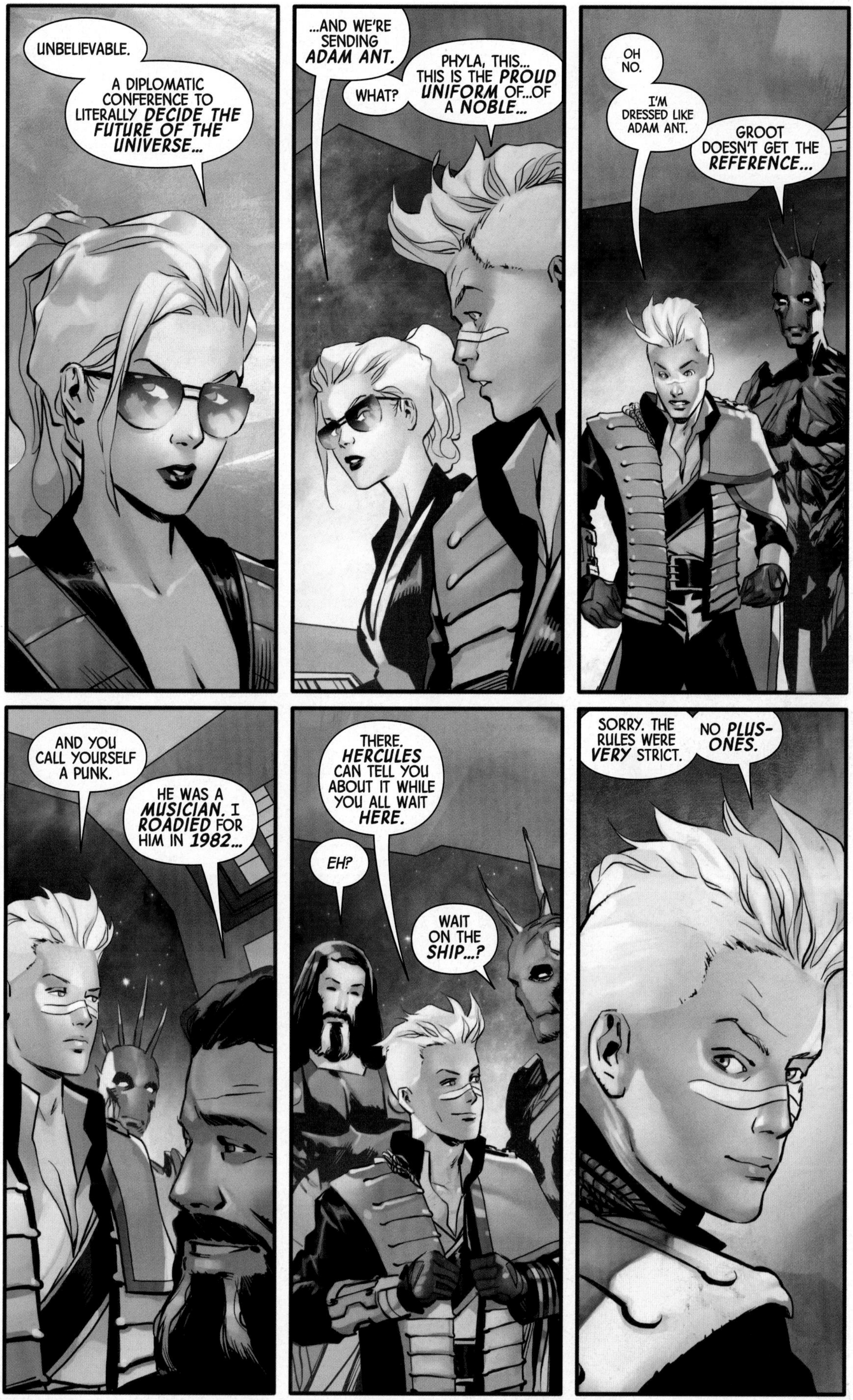
UNBELIEVABLE.
A DIPLOMATIC CONFERENCE TO LITERALLY DECIDE THE FUTURE OF THE UNIVERSE...
...AND WE'RE SENDING ADAM ANT.
WHAT?
PHYLA, THIS... THIS IS THE PROUD UNIFORM OF...OF A NOBLE...
OH NO.
I'M DRESSED LIKE ADAM ANT.
GROOT DOESN'T GET THE REFERENCE...
AND YOU CALL YOURSELF A PUNK.
HE WAS A MUSICIAN. I ROADIED FOR HIM IN 1982...
THERE. HERCULES CAN TELL YOU ABOUT IT WHILE YOU ALL WAIT HERE.
EH?
WAIT ON THE SHIP...?
SORRY. THE RULES WERE VERY STRICT.
NO PLUS-ONES.

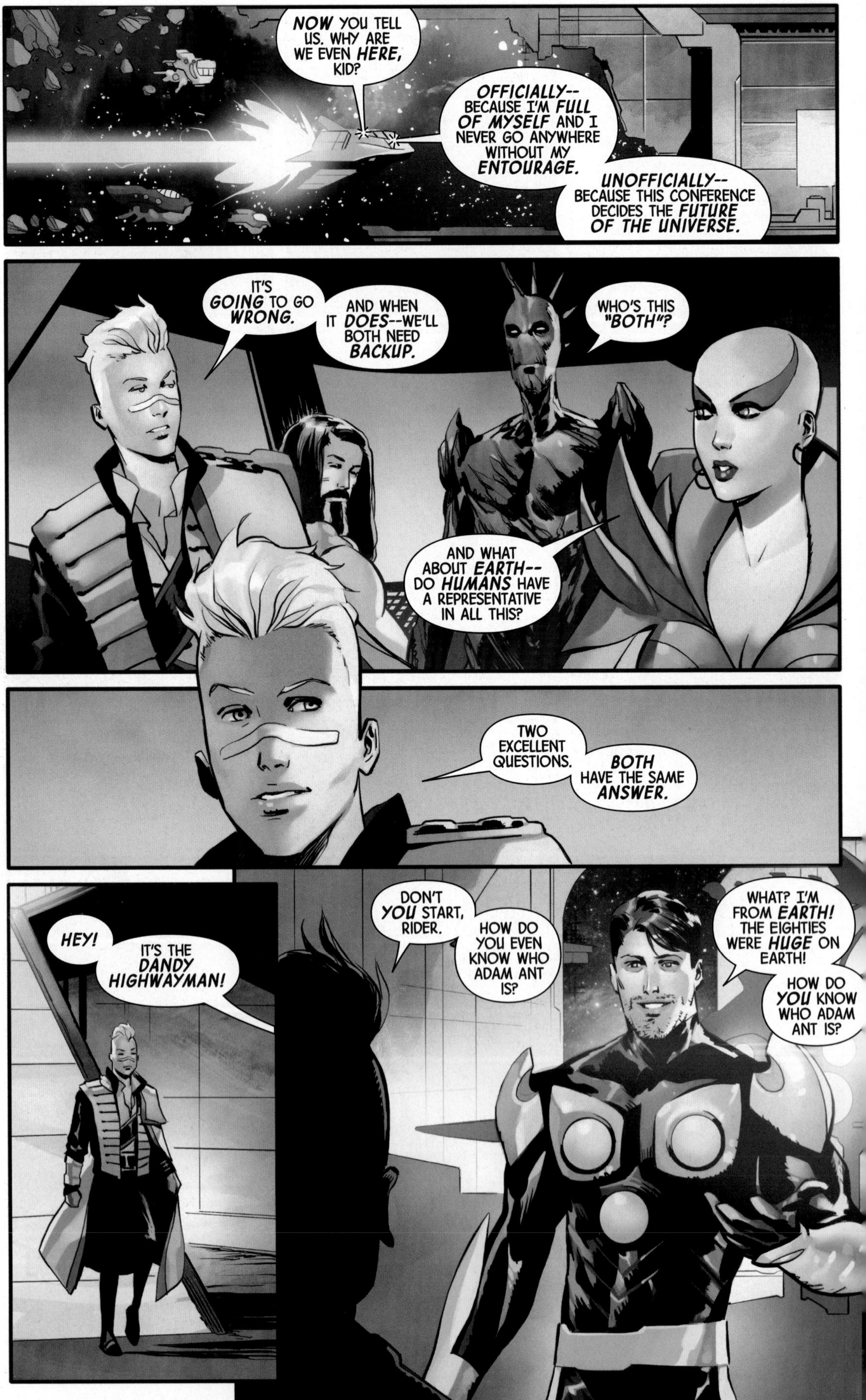

NOW YOU TELL US. WHY ARE WE EVEN HERE, KID?
OFFICIALLY-- BECAUSE I'M FULL OF MYSELF AND I NEVER GO ANYWHERE WITHOUT MY ENTOURAGE.
UNOFFICIALLY-- BECAUSE THIS CONFERENCE DECIDES THE FUTURE OF THE UNIVERSE.
IT'S GOING TO GO WRONG.
AND WHEN IT DOES--WE'LL BOTH NEED BACKUP.
WHO'S THIS "BOTH"?
AND WHAT ABOUT EARTH-- DO HUMANS HAVE A REPRESENTATIVE IN ALL THIS?
TWO EXCELLENT QUESTIONS.
BOTH HAVE THE SAME ANSWER.
HEY!
IT'S THE DANDY HIGHWAYMAN!
DON'T YOU START, RIDER.
HOW DO YOU EVEN KNOW WHO ADAM ANT IS?
WHAT? I'M FROM EARTH! THE EIGHTIES WERE HUGE ON EARTH!
HOW DO YOU KNOW WHO ADAM ANT IS?

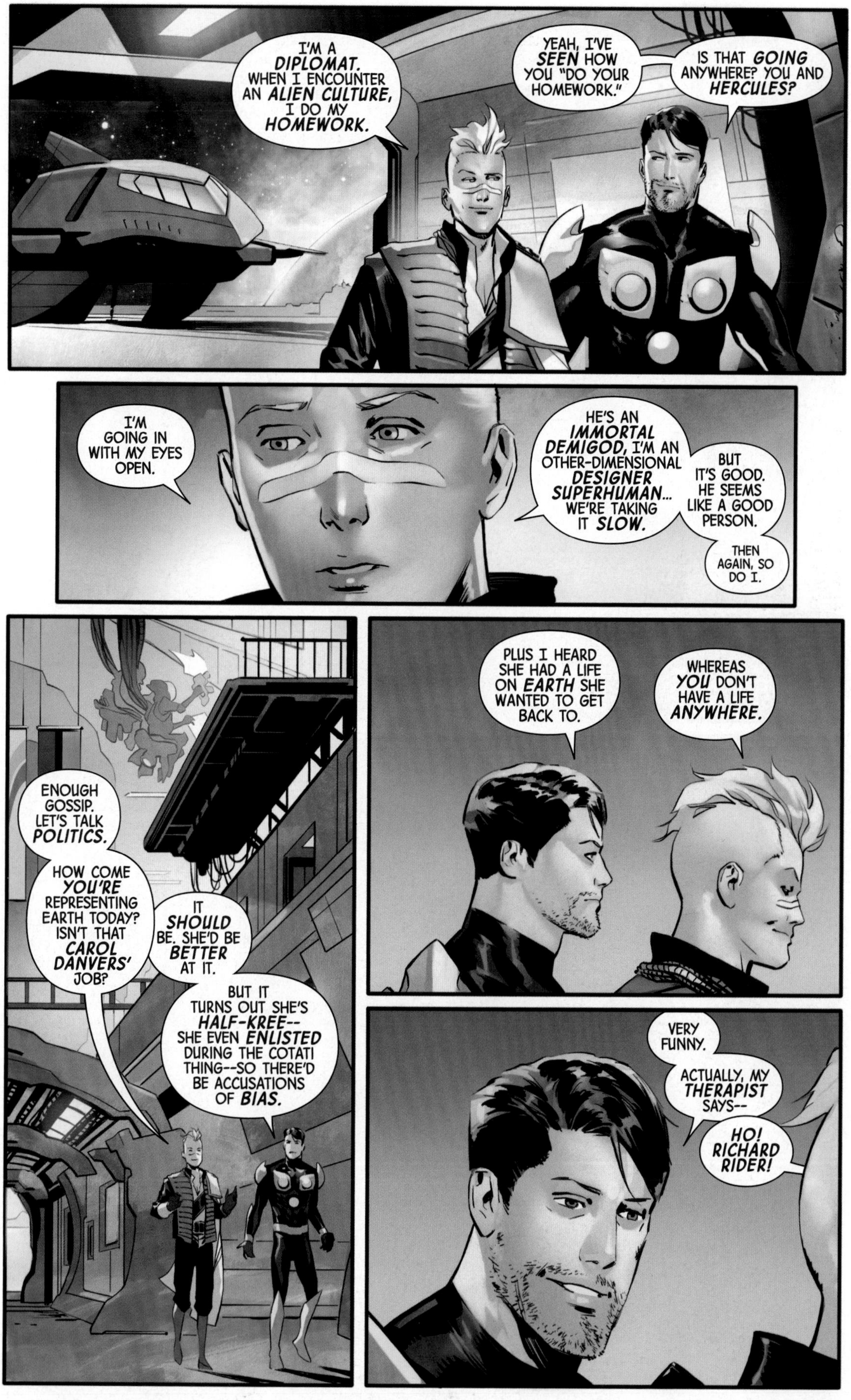
I'M A DIPLOMAT. WHEN I ENCOUNTER AN ALIEN CULTURE, I DO MY HOMEWORK.
YEAH, I'VE SEEN HOW YOU "DO YOUR HOMEWORK."
IS THAT GOING ANYWHERE? YOU AND HERCULES?
I'M GOING IN WITH MY EYES OPEN.
HE'S AN IMMORTAL DEMIGOD, I'M AN OTHER-DIMENSIONAL DESIGNER SUPERHUMAN... WE'RE TAKING IT SLOW.
BUT IT'S GOOD. HE SEEMS LIKE A GOOD PERSON.
THEN AGAIN, SO DO I.
ENOUGH GOSSIP. LET'S TALK POLITICS.
HOW COME YOU'RE REPRESENTING EARTH TODAY? ISN'T THAT CAROL DANVERS' JOB?
IT SHOULD BE. SHE'D BE BETTER AT IT.
BUT IT TURNS OUT SHE'S HALF-KREE-- SHE EVEN ENLISTED DURING THE COTATI THING--SO THERE'D BE ACCUSATIONS OF BIAS.
PLUS I HEARD SHE HAD A LIFE ON EARTH SHE WANTED TO GET BACK TO.
WHEREAS YOU DON'T HAVE A LIFE ANYWHERE.
VERY FUNNY.
ACTUALLY, MY THERAPIST SAYS--
HO! RICHARD RIDER!

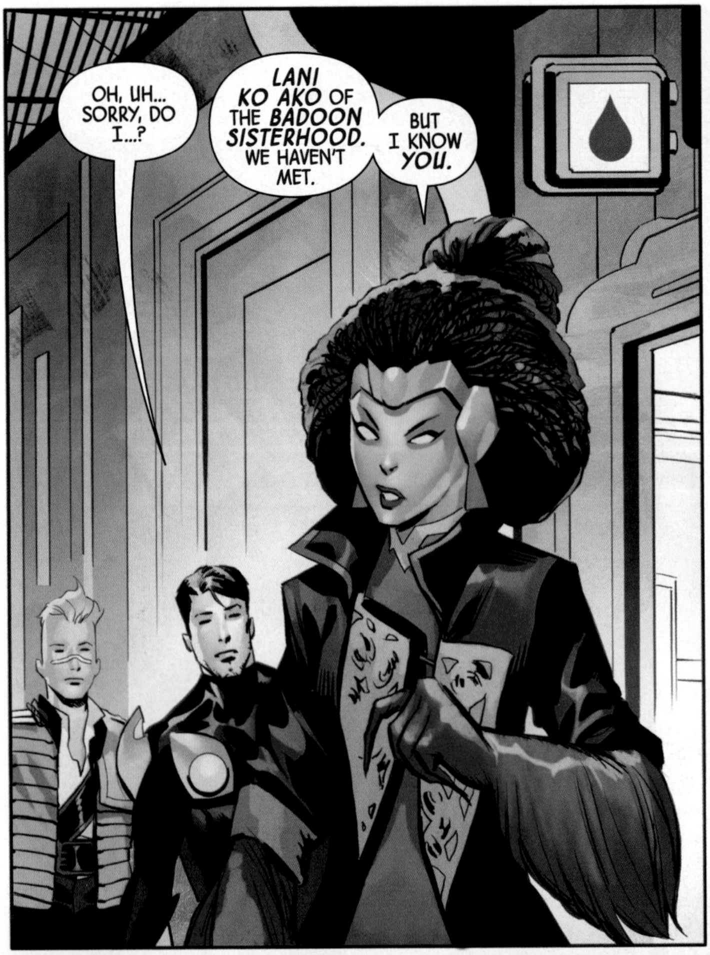
OH, UH... SORRY, DO I...?
LANI KO AKO OF THE BADOON SISTERHOOD. WE HAVEN'T MET.
BUT I KNOW YOU.

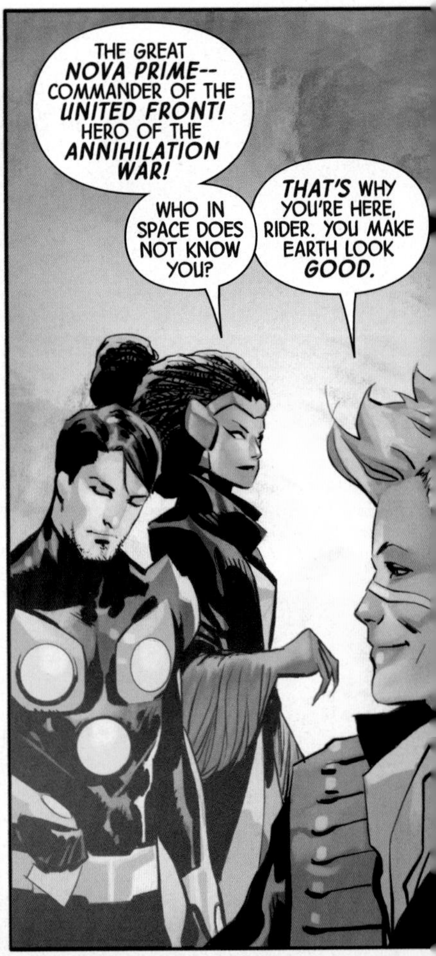
THE GREAT NOVA PRIME-- COMMANDER OF THE UNITED FRONT! HERO OF THE ANNIHILATION WAR!
WHO IN SPACE DOES NOT KNOW YOU?
THAT'S WHY YOU'RE HERE, RIDER. YOU MAKE EARTH LOOK GOOD.

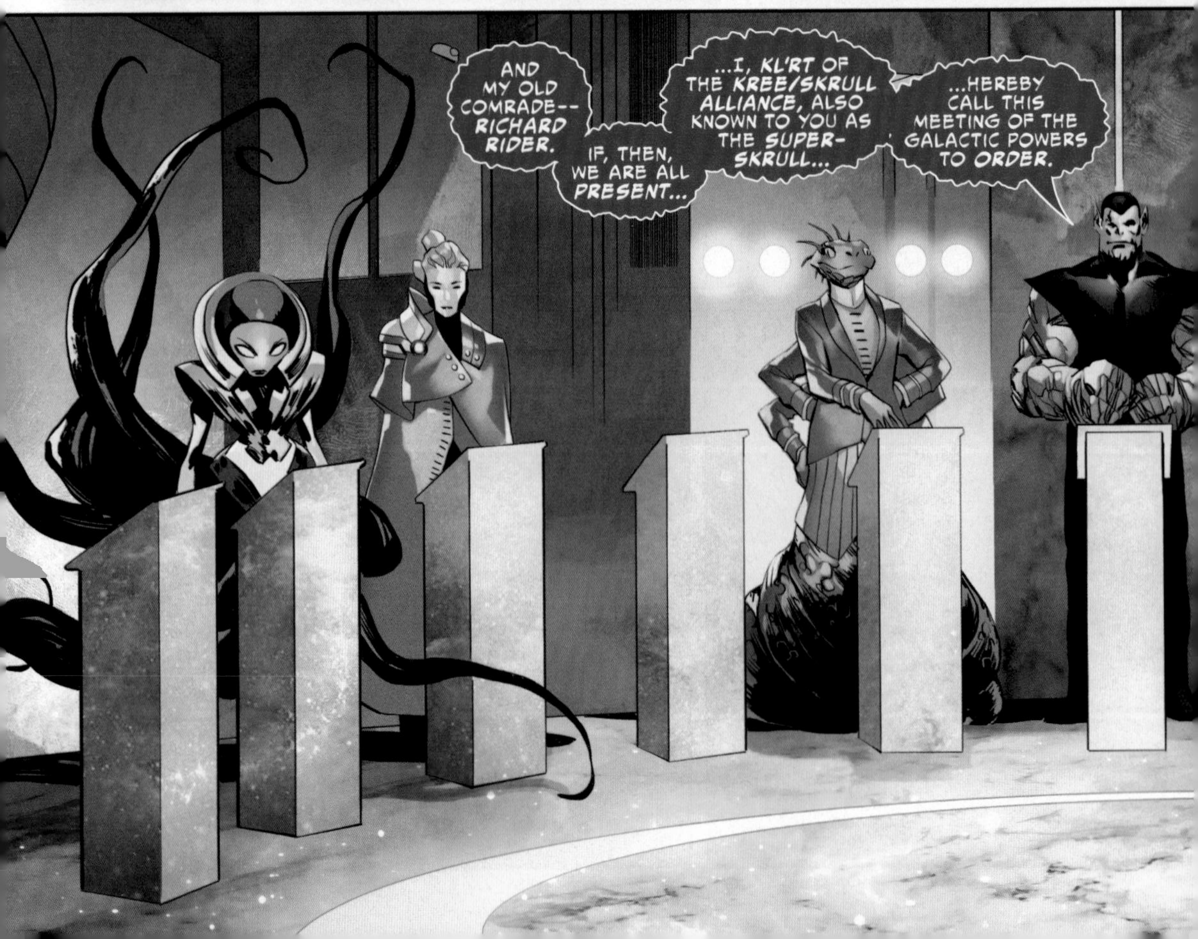
AND MY OLD COMRADE-- RICHARD RIDER.
IF, THEN, WE ARE ALL PRESENT...
...I, KL'RT OF THE KREE/SKRULL ALLIANCE, ALSO KNOWN TO YOU AS THE SUPER-SKRULL...
...HEREBY CALL THIS MEETING OF THE GALACTIC POWERS TO ORDER.

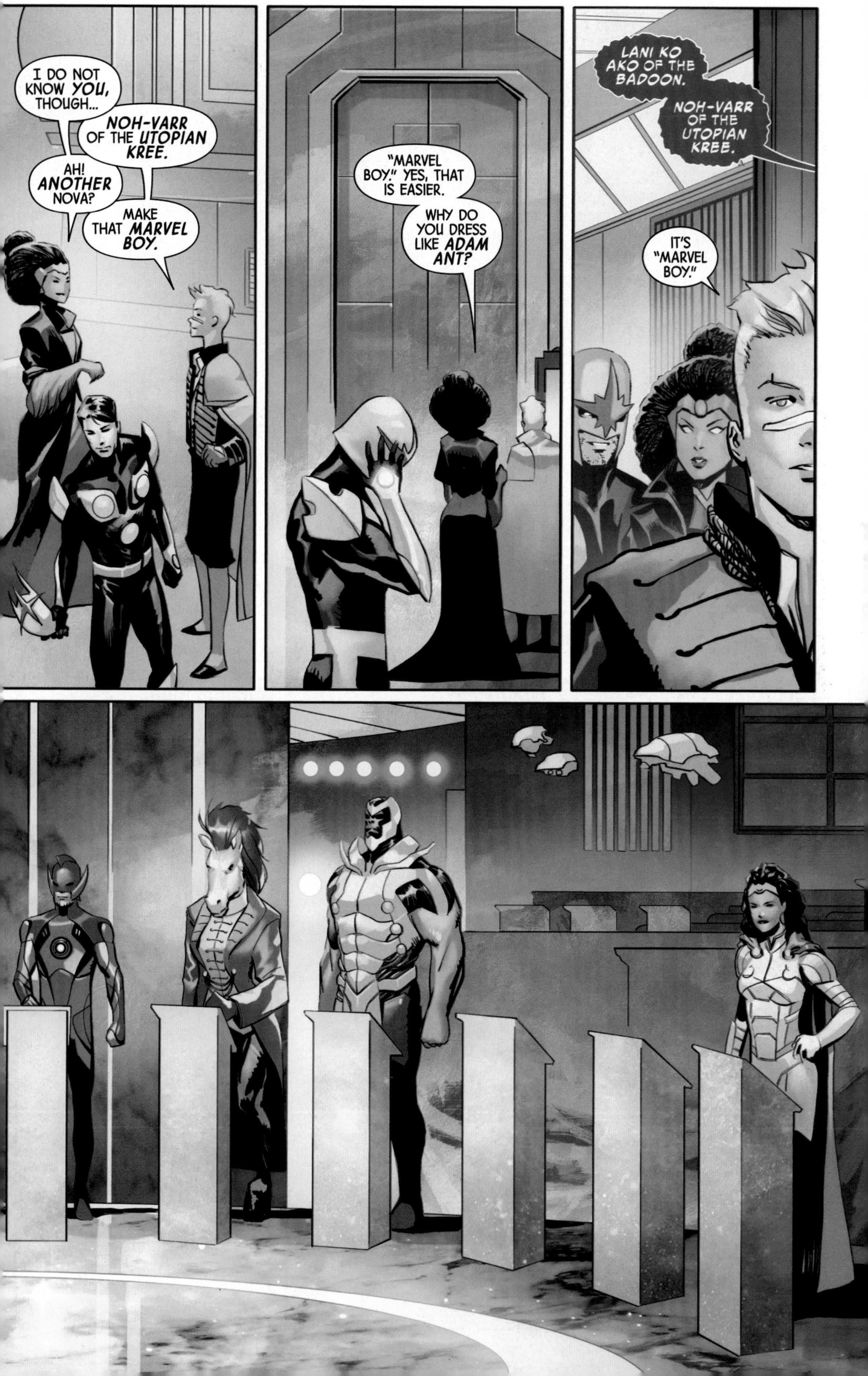
I DO NOT KNOW YOU, THOUGH...
NOH-VARR OF THE UTOPIAN KREE.
AH! ANOTHER NOVA?
MAKE THAT MARVEL BOY.
"MARVEL BOY." YES, THAT IS EASIER.
WHY DO YOU DRESS LIKE ADAM ANT?
LANI KO AKO OF THE BADOON.
NOH-VARR OF THE UTOPIAN KREE.
IT'S "MARVEL BOY."

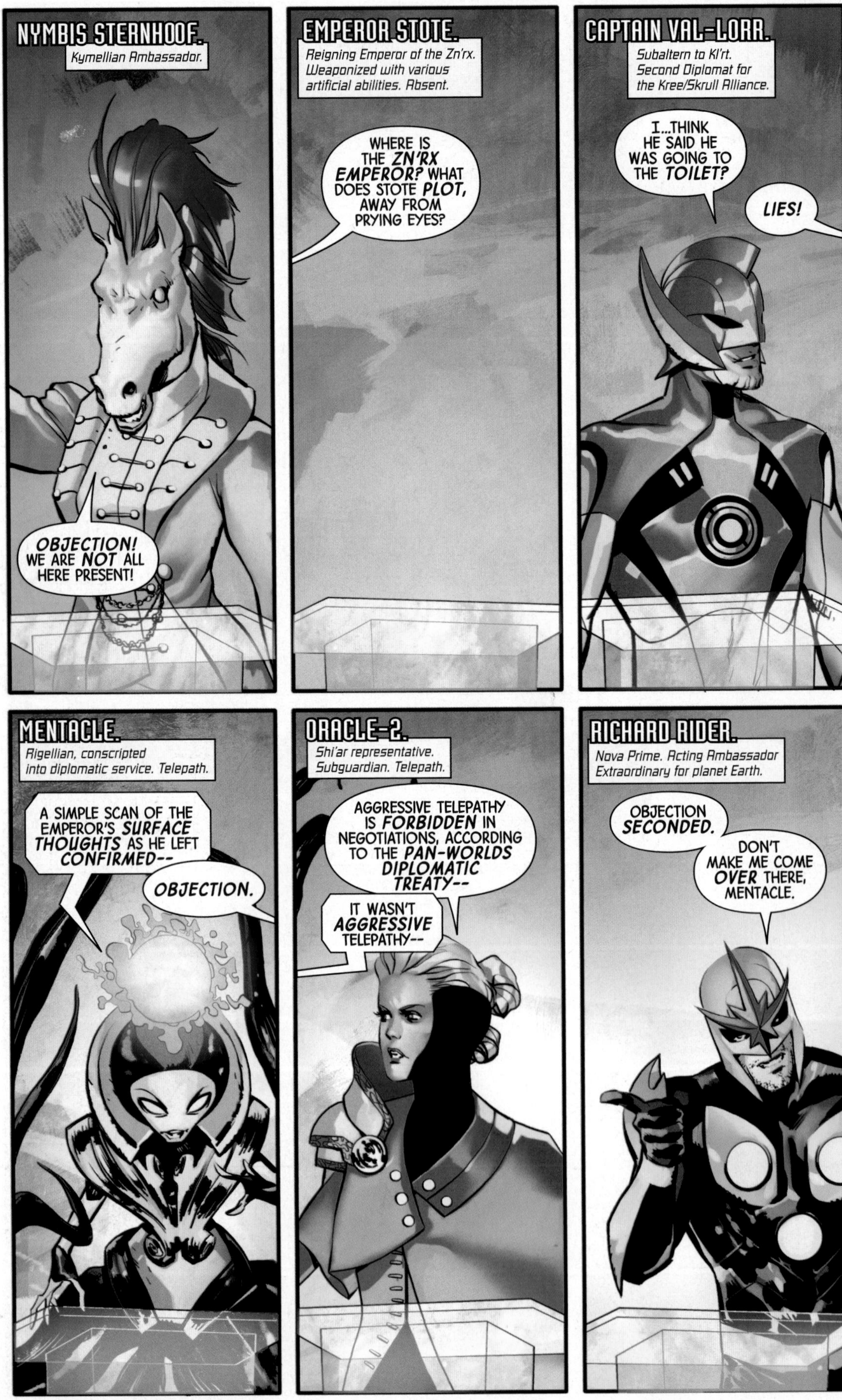
NYMBIS STERNHOOF.
Kymellian Ambassador.
OBJECTION! WE ARE NOT ALL HERE PRESENT!
EMPEROR STOTE.
Reigning Emperor of the Zn'rx. Weaponized with various artificial abilities. Absent.
WHERE IS THE ZN'RX EMPEROR? WHAT DOES STOTE PLOT, AWAY FROM PRYING EYES?
CAPTAIN VAL-LORR.
Subaltern to Kl'rt. Second Diplomat for the Kree/Skrull Alliance.
I...THINK HE SAID HE WAS GOING TO THE TOILET?
LIES!
MENTACLE.
Rigellian, conscripted into diplomatic service. Telepath.
A SIMPLE SCAN OF THE EMPEROR'S SURFACE THOUGHTS AS HE LEFT CONFIRMED--
OBJECTION.
ORACLE-2.
Shi'ar representative. Subguardian. Telepath.
AGGRESSIVE TELEPATHY IS FORBIDDEN IN NEGOTIATIONS, ACCORDING TO THE PAN-WORLDS DIPLOMATIC TREATY--
IT WASN'T AGGRESSIVE TELEPATHY--
RICHARD RIDER.
Nova Prime. Acting Ambassador Extraordinary for planet Earth.
OBJECTION SECONDED.
DON'T MAKE ME COME OVER THERE, MENTACLE.

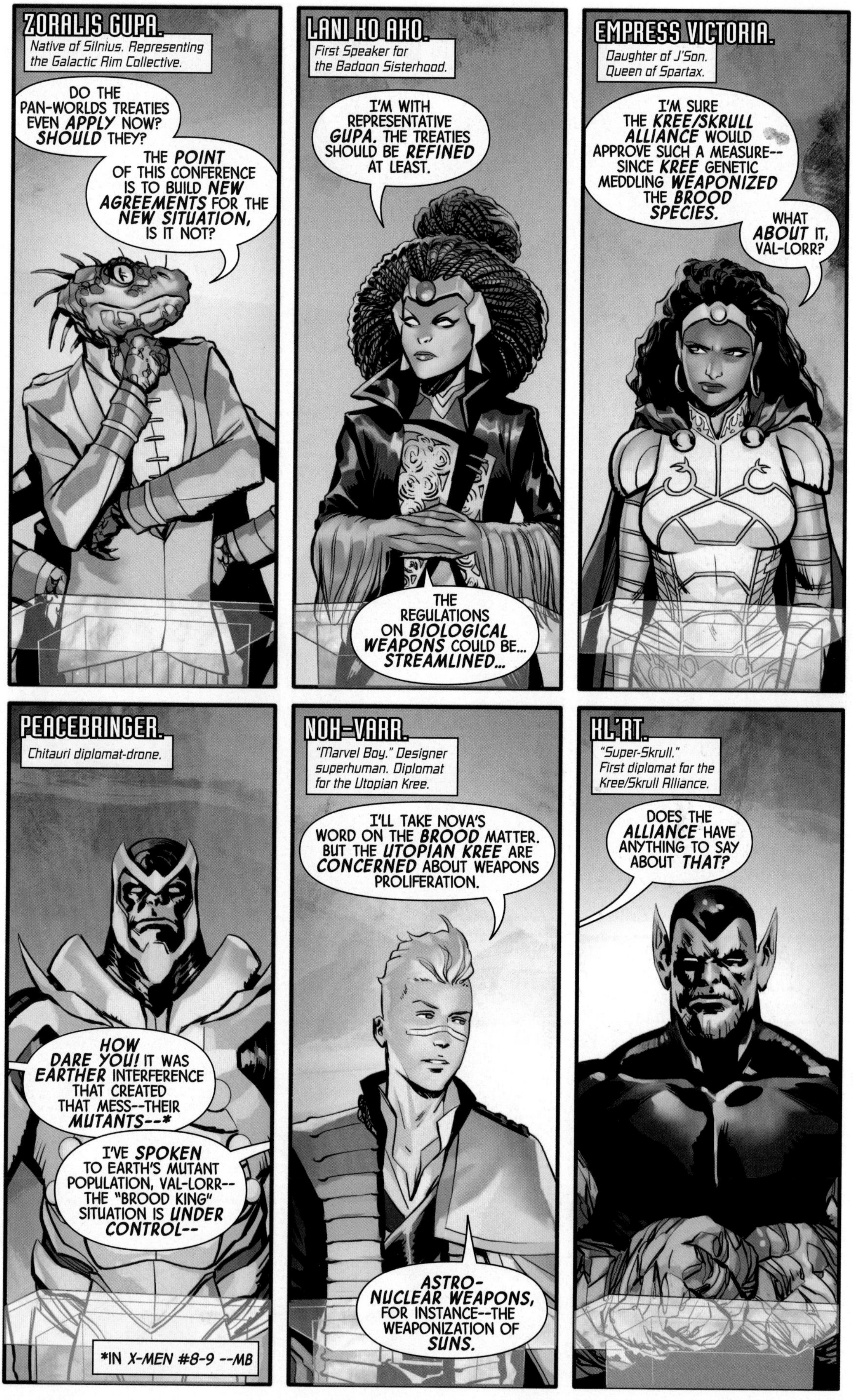
ZORALIS GUPA.
Native of Silnius. Representing the Galactic Rim Collective.
DO THE PAN-WORLDS TREATIES EVEN APPLY NOW? SHOULD THEY?
THE POINT OF THIS CONFERENCE IS TO BUILD NEW AGREEMENTS FOR THE NEW SITUATION, IS IT NOT?
LANI KO AKO.
First Speaker for the Badoon Sisterhood.
I'M WITH REPRESENTATIVE GUPA. THE TREATIES SHOULD BE REFINED AT LEAST.
THE REGULATIONS ON BIOLOGICAL WEAPONS COULD BE... STREAMLINED...
EMPRESS VICTORIA.
Daughter of J'Son. Queen of Spartax.
I'M SURE THE KREE/SKRULL ALLIANCE WOULD APPROVE SUCH A MEASURE-- SINCE KREE GENETIC MEDDLING WEAPONIZED THE BROOD SPECIES.
WHAT ABOUT IT, VAL-LORR?
PEACEBRINGER.
Chitauri diplomat-drone.
HOW DARE YOU! IT WAS EARTHER INTERFERENCE THAT CREATED THAT MESS--THEIR MUTANTS--*
I'VE SPOKEN TO EARTH'S MUTANT POPULATION, VAL-LORR-- THE "BROOD KING" SITUATION IS UNDER CONTROL--
*IN X-MEN #8-9 --MB
NOH-VARR.
"Marvel Boy." Designer superhuman. Diplomat for the Utopian Kree.
I'LL TAKE NOVA'S WORD ON THE BROOD MATTER. BUT THE UTOPIAN KREE ARE CONCERNED ABOUT WEAPONS PROLIFERATION.
ASTRO-NUCLEAR WEAPONS, FOR INSTANCE--THE WEAPONIZATION OF SUNS.
KL'RT.
"Super-Skrull." First diplomat for the Kree/Skrull Alliance.
DOES THE ALLIANCE HAVE ANYTHING TO SAY ABOUT THAT?

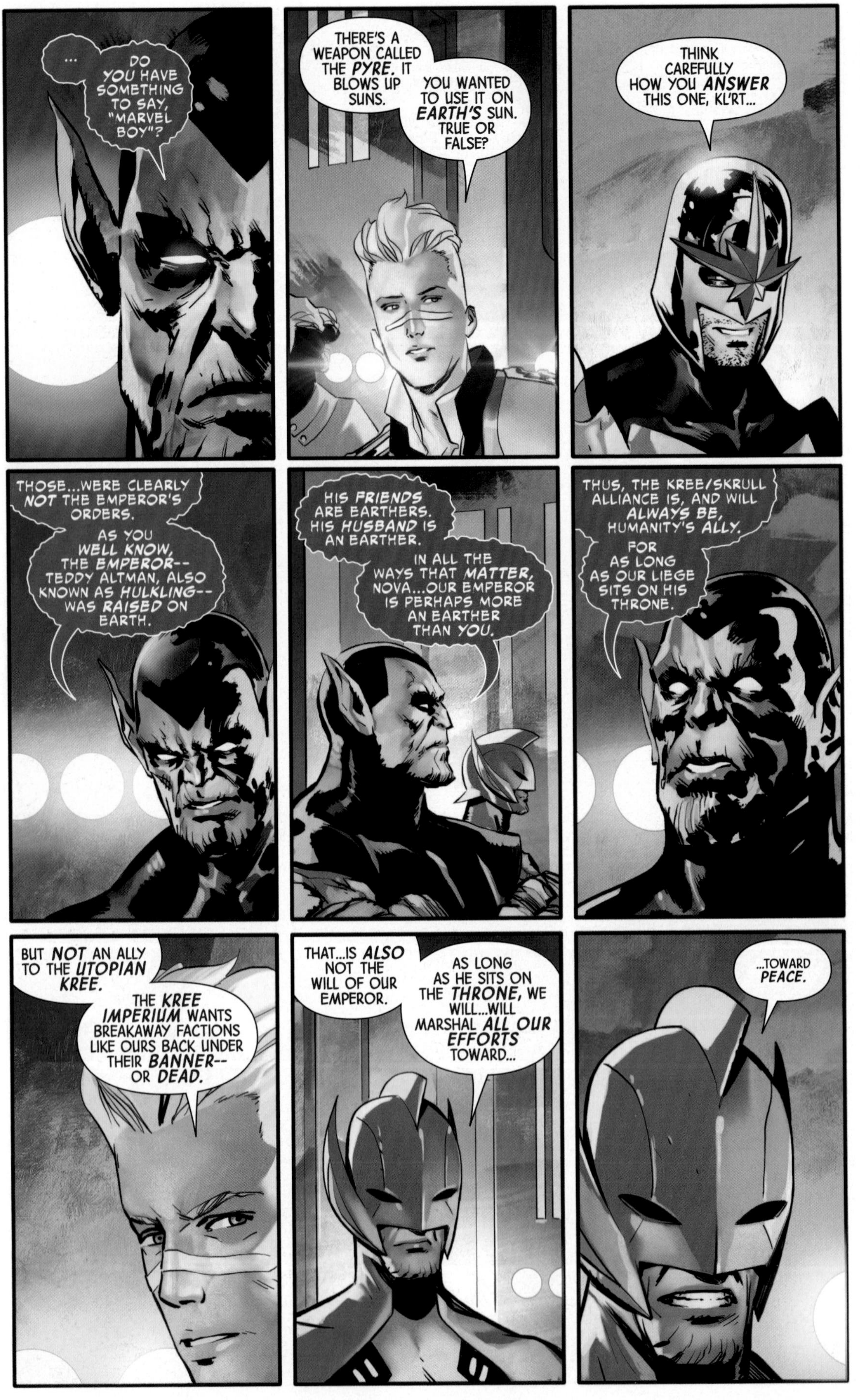
...
DO YOU HAVE SOMETHING TO SAY, "MARVEL BOY"?
THERE'S A WEAPON CALLED THE PYRE. IT BLOWS UP SUNS.
YOU WANTED TO USE IT ON EARTH'S SUN. TRUE OR FALSE?
THINK CAREFULLY HOW YOU ANSWER THIS ONE, KL'RT...
THOSE...WERE CLEARLY NOT THE EMPEROR'S ORDERS.
AS YOU WELL KNOW, THE EMPEROR-- TEDDY ALTMAN, ALSO KNOWN AS HULKLING-- WAS RAISED ON EARTH.
HIS FRIENDS ARE EARTHERS. HIS HUSBAND IS AN EARTHER.
IN ALL THE WAYS THAT MATTER, NOVA...OUR EMPEROR IS PERHAPS MORE AN EARTHER THAN YOU.
THUS, THE KREE/SKRULL ALLIANCE IS, AND WILL ALWAYS BE, HUMANITY'S ALLY.
FOR AS LONG AS OUR LIEGE SITS ON HIS THRONE.
BUT NOT AN ALLY TO THE UTOPIAN KREE.
THE KREE IMPERIUM WANTS BREAKAWAY FACTIONS LIKE OURS BACK UNDER THEIR BANNER-- OR DEAD.
THAT...IS ALSO NOT THE WILL OF OUR EMPEROR.
AS LONG AS HE SITS ON THE THRONE, WE WILL...WILL MARSHAL ALL OUR EFFORTS TOWARD...
...TOWARD PEACE.

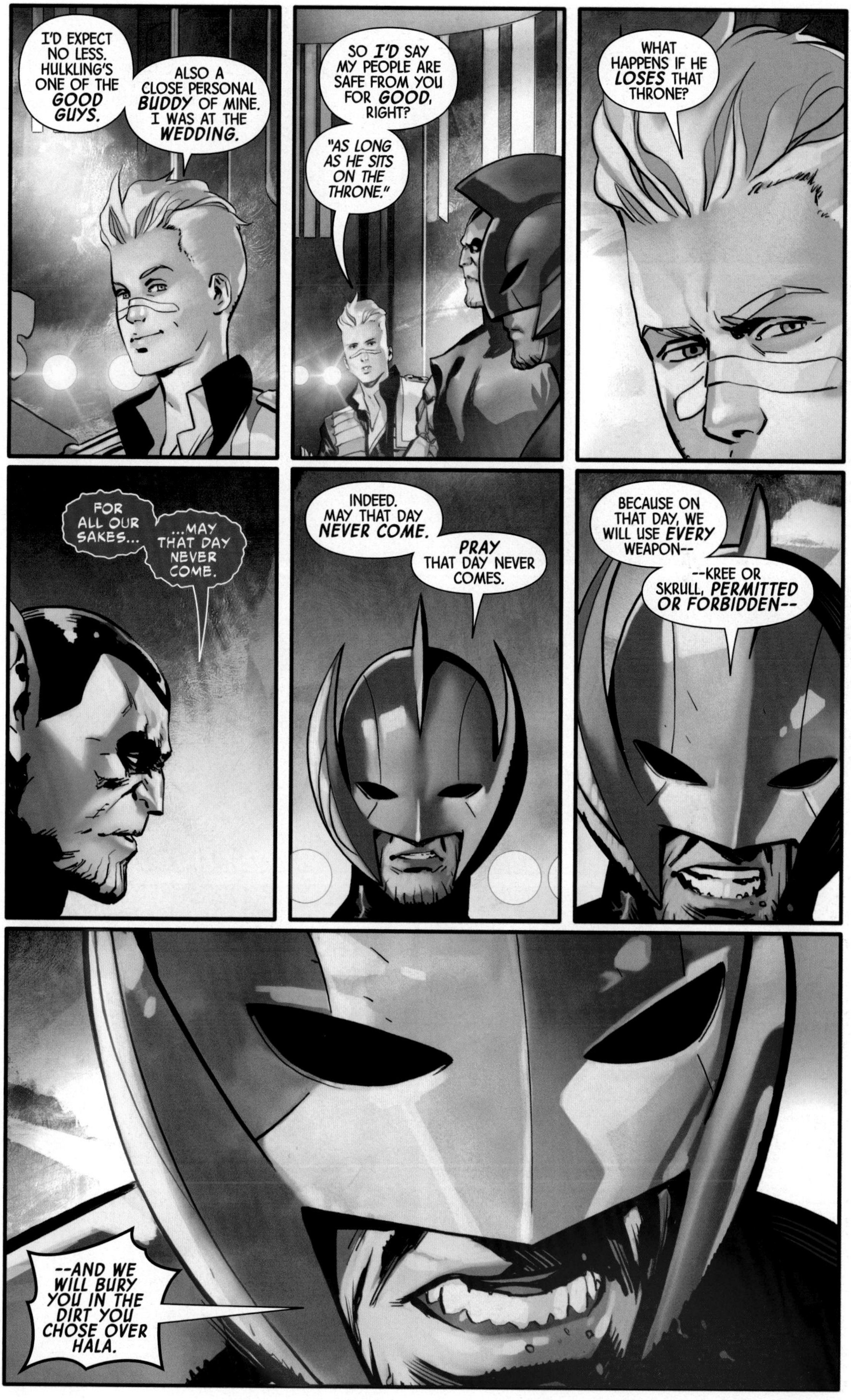
I'D EXPECT NO LESS. HULKLING'S ONE OF THE GOOD GUYS.
ALSO A CLOSE PERSONAL BUDDY OF MINE. I WAS AT THE WEDDING.
SO I'D SAY MY PEOPLE ARE SAFE FROM YOU FOR GOOD, RIGHT?
"AS LONG AS HE SITS ON THE THRONE."
WHAT HAPPENS IF HE LOSES THAT THRONE?
FOR ALL OUR SAKES...
...MAY THAT DAY NEVER COME.
INDEED. MAY THAT DAY NEVER COME.
PRAY THAT DAY NEVER COMES.
BECAUSE ON THAT DAY, WE WILL USE EVERY WEAPON--
--KREE OR SKRULL, PERMITTED OR FORBIDDEN--
--AND WE WILL BURY YOU IN THE DIRT YOU CHOSE OVER HALA.

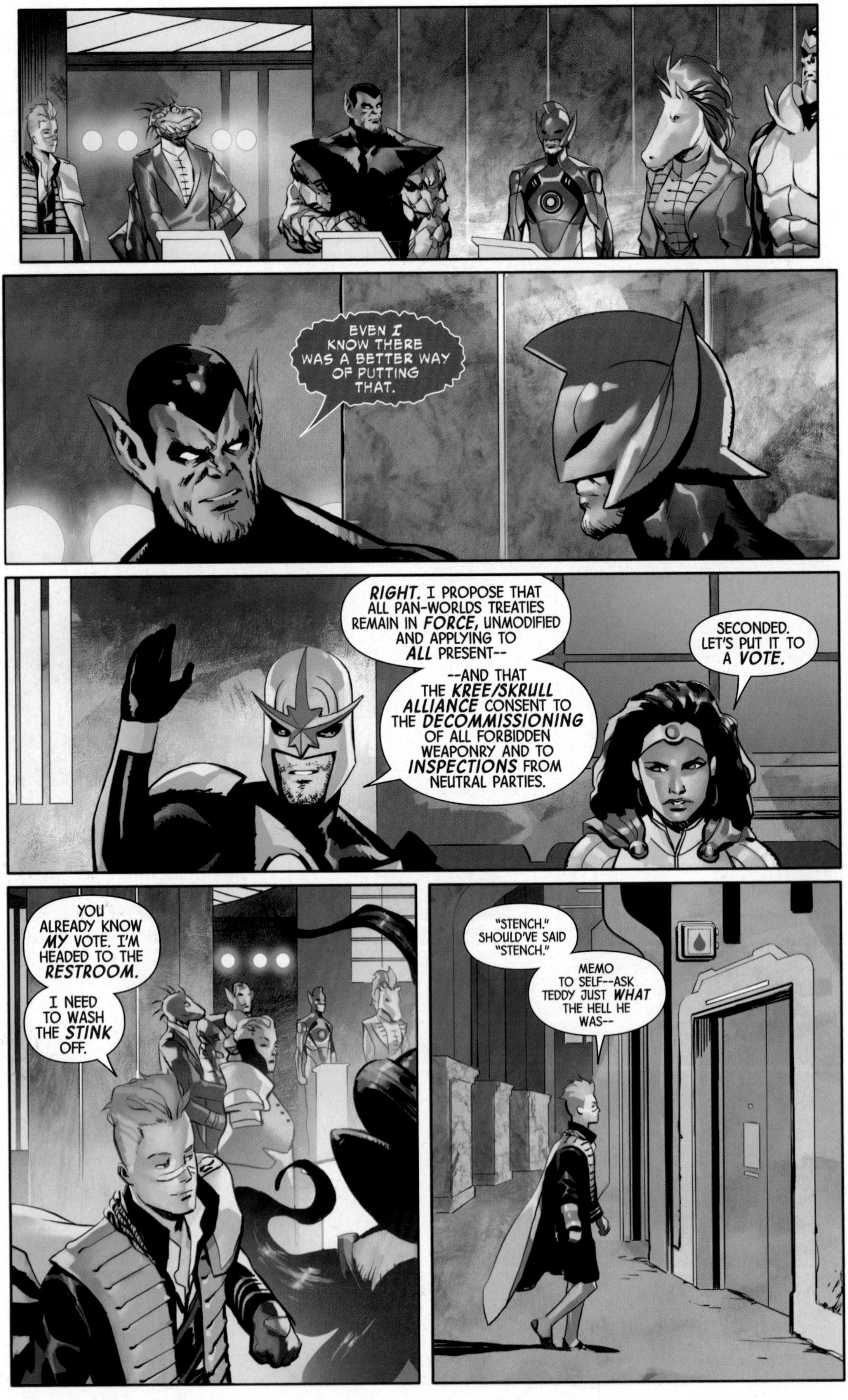
EVEN I KNOW THERE WAS A BETTER WAY OF PUTTING THAT.
RIGHT. I PROPOSE THAT ALL PAN-WORLDS TREATIES REMAIN IN FORCE, UNMODIFIED AND APPLYING TO ALL PRESENT--
--AND THAT THE KREE/SKRULL ALLIANCE CONSENT TO THE DECOMMISSIONING OF ALL FORBIDDEN WEAPONRY AND TO INSPECTIONS FROM NEUTRAL PARTIES.
SECONDED. LET'S PUT IT TO A VOTE.
YOU ALREADY KNOW MY VOTE. I'M HEADED TO THE RESTROOM.
I NEED TO WASH THE STINK OFF.
"STENCH." SHOULD'VE SAID "STENCH."
MEMO TO SELF--ASK TEDDY JUST WHAT THE HELL HE WAS--

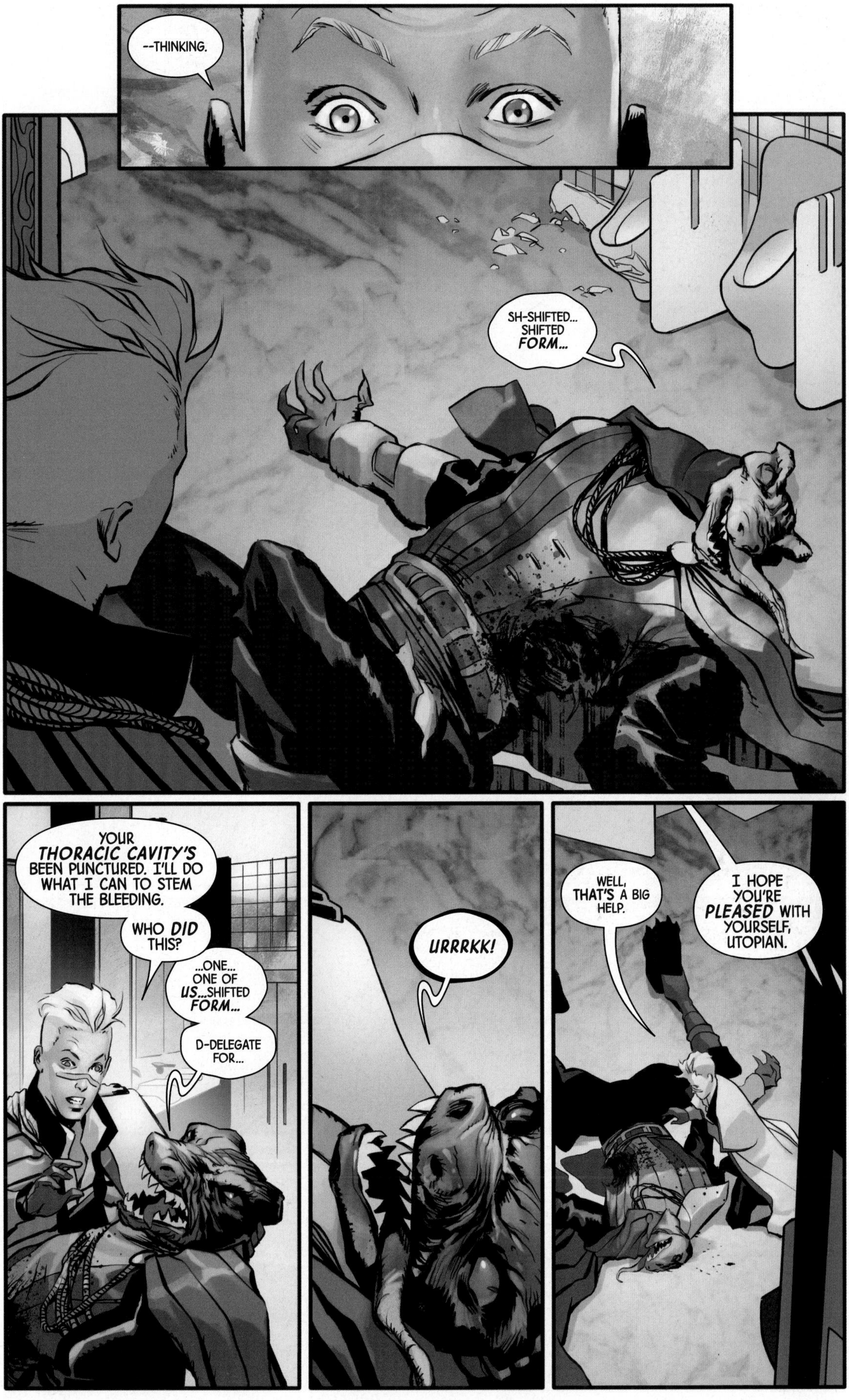
--THINKING.
SH-SHIFTED... SHIFTED FORM...
YOUR THORACIC CAVITY'S BEEN PUNCTURED. I'LL DO WHAT I CAN TO STEM THE BLEEDING.
WHO DID THIS?
...ONE... ONE OF US...SHIFTED FORM...
D-DELEGATE FOR...
URRRKK!
WELL, THAT'S A BIG HELP.
I HOPE YOU'RE PLEASED WITH YOURSELF, UTOPIAN.

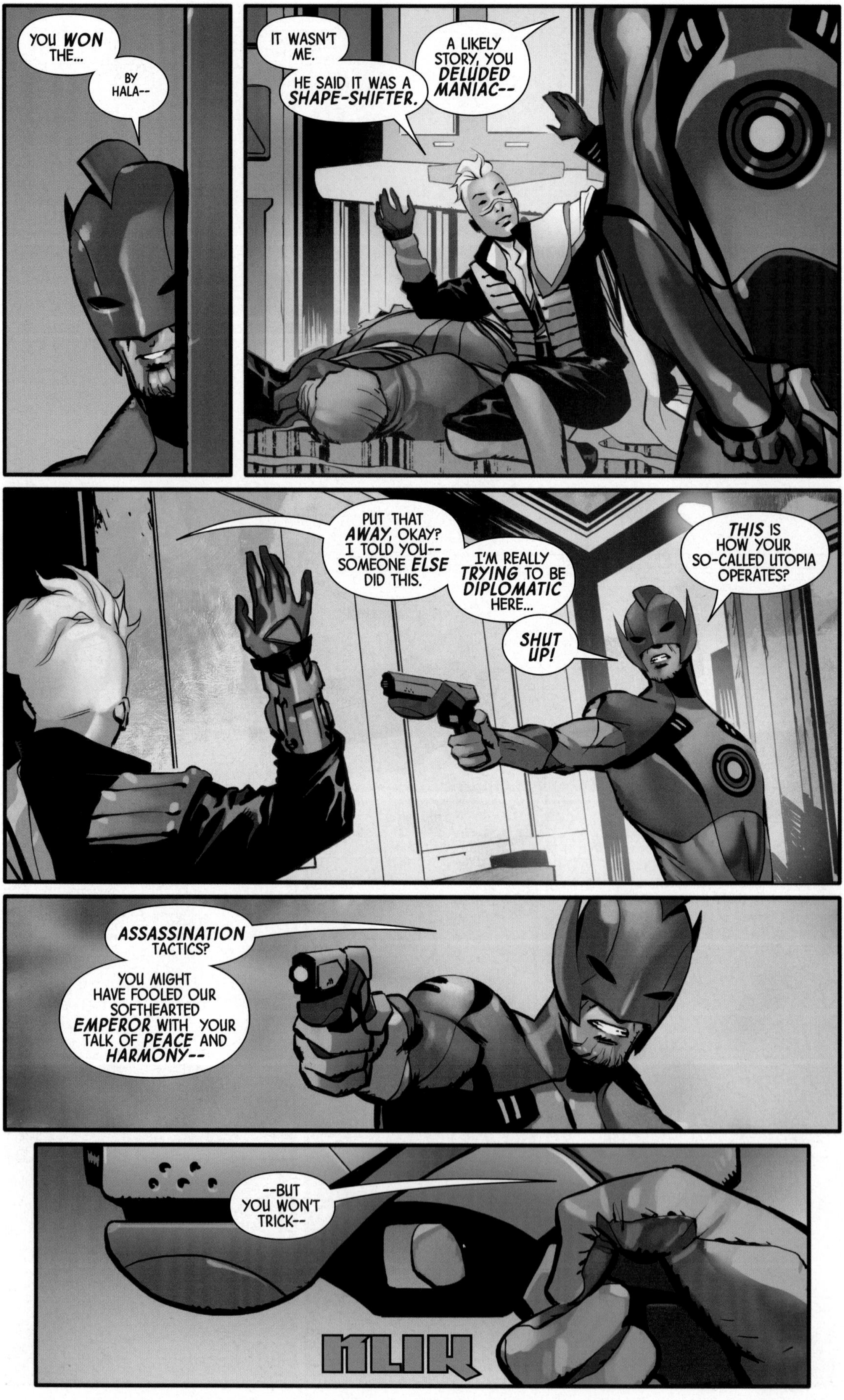

YOU WON THE...
BY HALA--
IT WASN'T ME.
HE SAID IT WAS A SHAPE-SHIFTER.
A LIKELY STORY, YOU DELUDED MANIAC--
PUT THAT AWAY, OKAY? I TOLD YOU-- SOMEONE ELSE DID THIS.
I'M REALLY TRYING TO BE DIPLOMATIC HERE...
THIS IS HOW YOUR SO-CALLED UTOPIA OPERATES?
SHUT UP!
ASSASSINATION TACTICS?
YOU MIGHT HAVE FOOLED OUR SOFTHEARTED EMPEROR WITH YOUR TALK OF PEACE AND HARMONY--
--BUT YOU WON'T TRICK--
KLIK

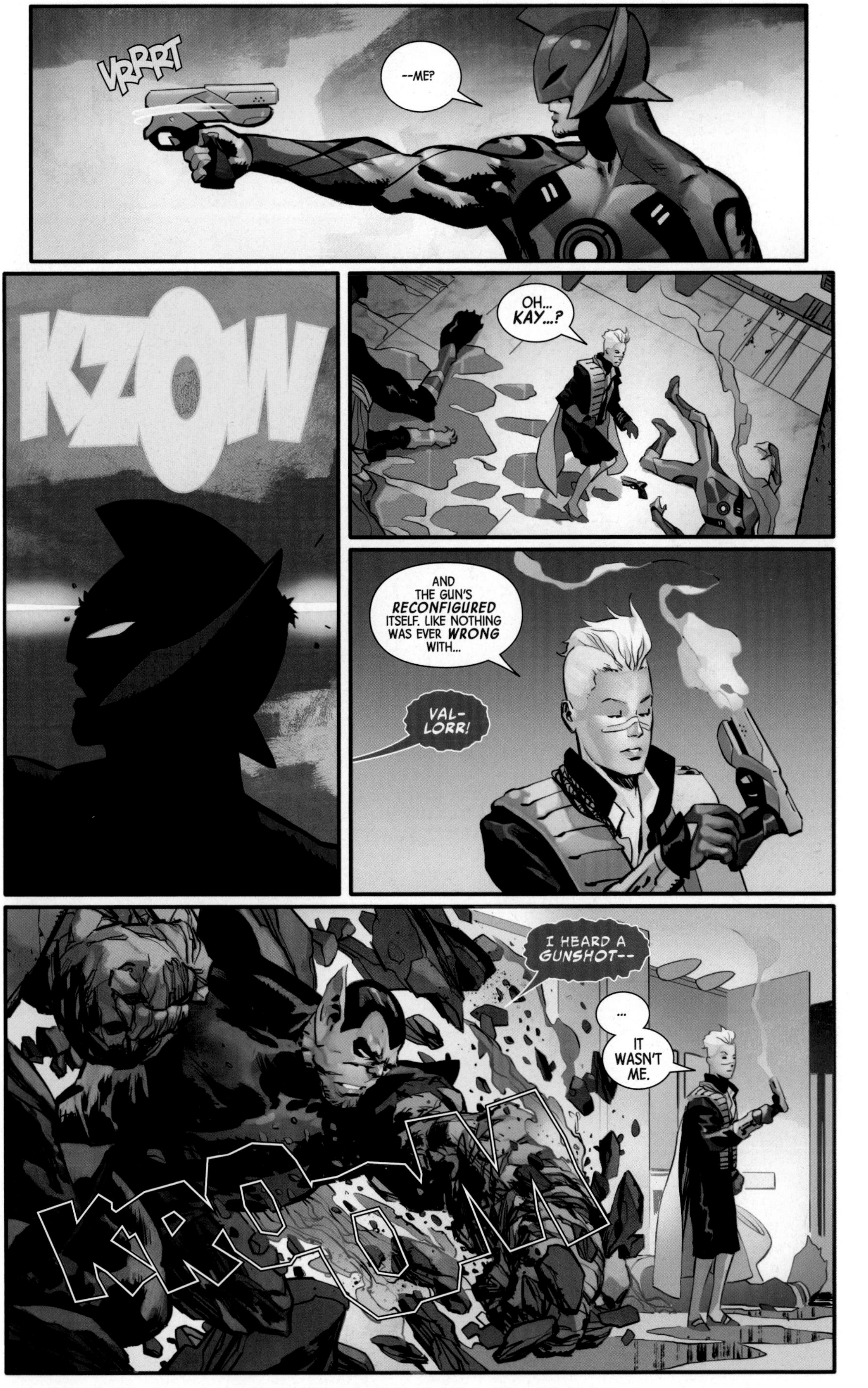
VRRRT
--ME?
KZOW
OH... KAY...?
AND THE GUN'S RECONFIGURED ITSELF. LIKE NOTHING WAS EVER WRONG WITH...
VAL-LORR!
I HEARD A GUNSHOT--
...
IT WASN'T ME.
KROOM

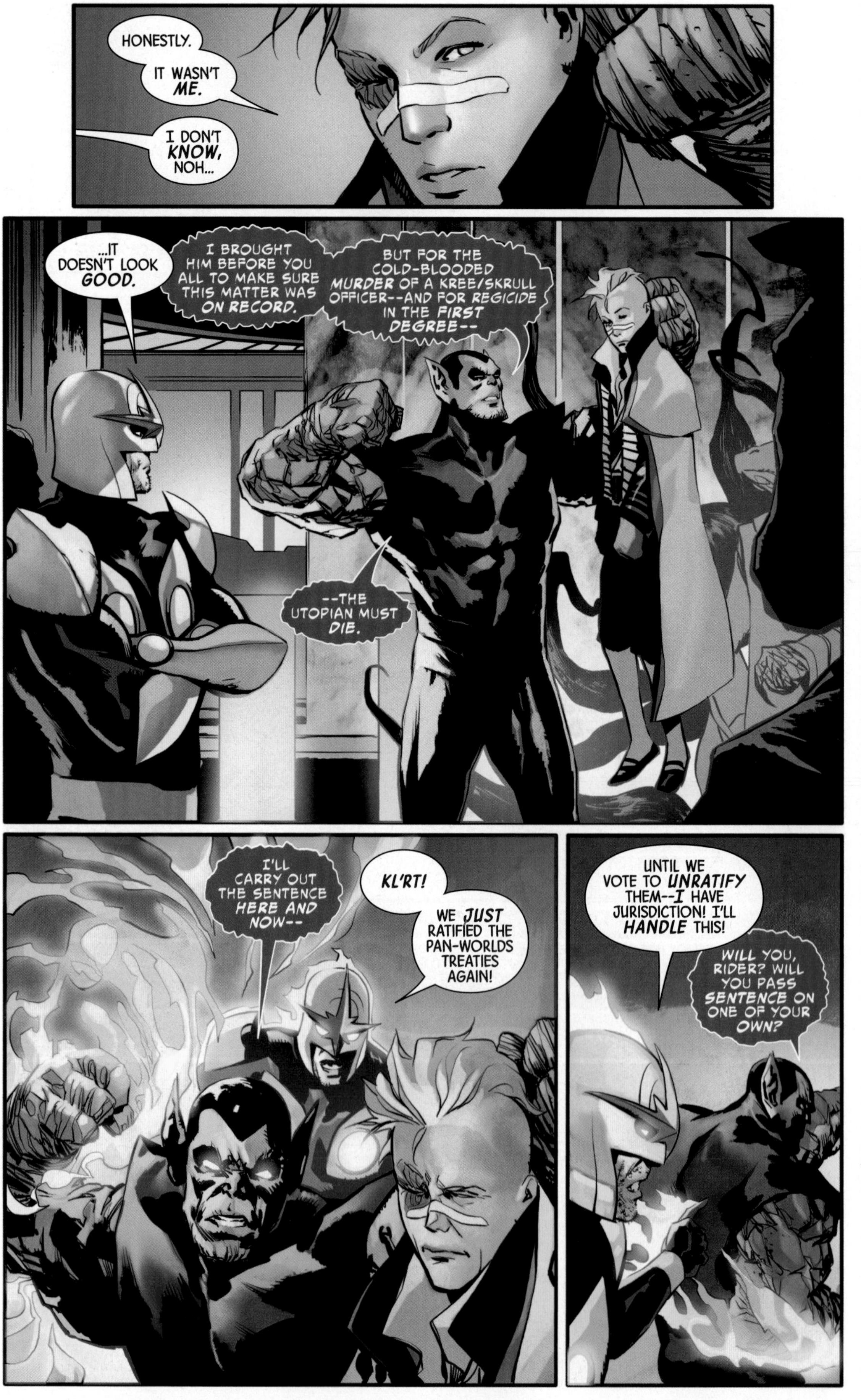
HONESTLY.
IT WASN'T ME.
I DON'T KNOW, NOH...
...IT DOESN'T LOOK GOOD.
I BROUGHT HIM BEFORE YOU ALL TO MAKE SURE THIS MATTER WAS ON RECORD.
BUT FOR THE COLD-BLOODED MURDER OF A KREE/SKRULL OFFICER--AND FOR REGICIDE IN THE FIRST DEGREE--
--THE UTOPIAN MUST DIE.
I'LL CARRY OUT THE SENTENCE HERE AND NOW--
KL'RT!
WE JUST RATIFIED THE PAN-WORLDS TREATIES AGAIN!
UNTIL WE VOTE TO UNRATIFY THEM--I HAVE JURISDICTION! I'LL HANDLE THIS!
WILL YOU, RIDER? WILL YOU PASS SENTENCE ON ONE OF YOUR OWN?

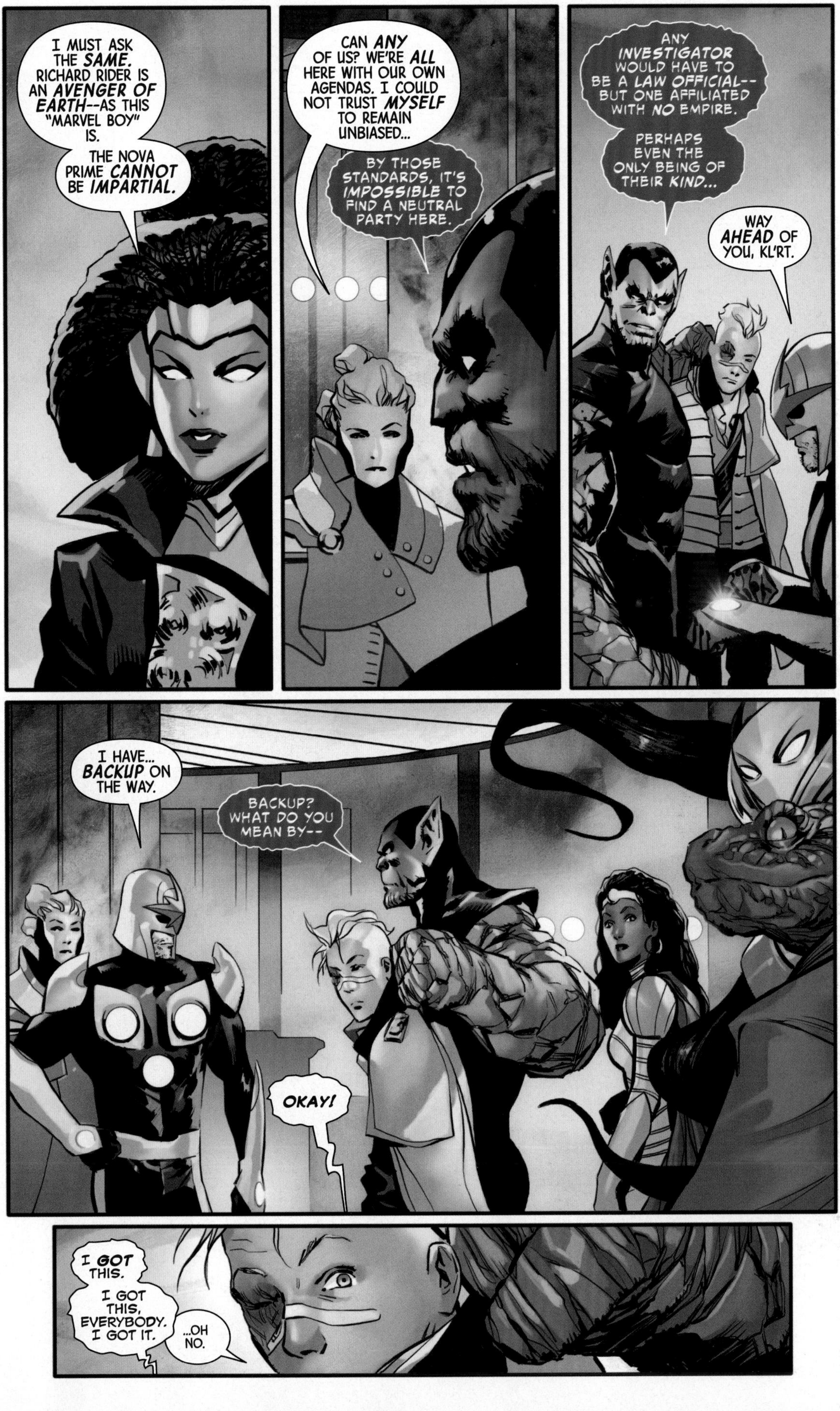
I MUST ASK THE SAME. RICHARD RIDER IS AN AVENGER OF EARTH--AS THIS "MARVEL BOY" IS.
THE NOVA PRIME CANNOT BE IMPARTIAL.
CAN ANY OF US? WE'RE ALL HERE WITH OUR OWN AGENDAS. I COULD NOT TRUST MYSELF TO REMAIN UNBIASED...
BY THOSE STANDARDS, IT'S IMPOSSIBLE TO FIND A NEUTRAL PARTY HERE.
ANY INVESTIGATOR WOULD HAVE TO BE A LAW OFFICIAL--BUT ONE AFFILIATED WITH NO EMPIRE.
PERHAPS EVEN THE ONLY BEING OF THEIR KIND...
WAY AHEAD OF YOU, KL'RT.
I HAVE... BACKUP ON THE WAY.
BACKUP? WHAT DO YOU MEAN BY--
OKAY!
I GOT THIS.
I GOT THIS, EVERYBODY. I GOT IT.
...OH NO.

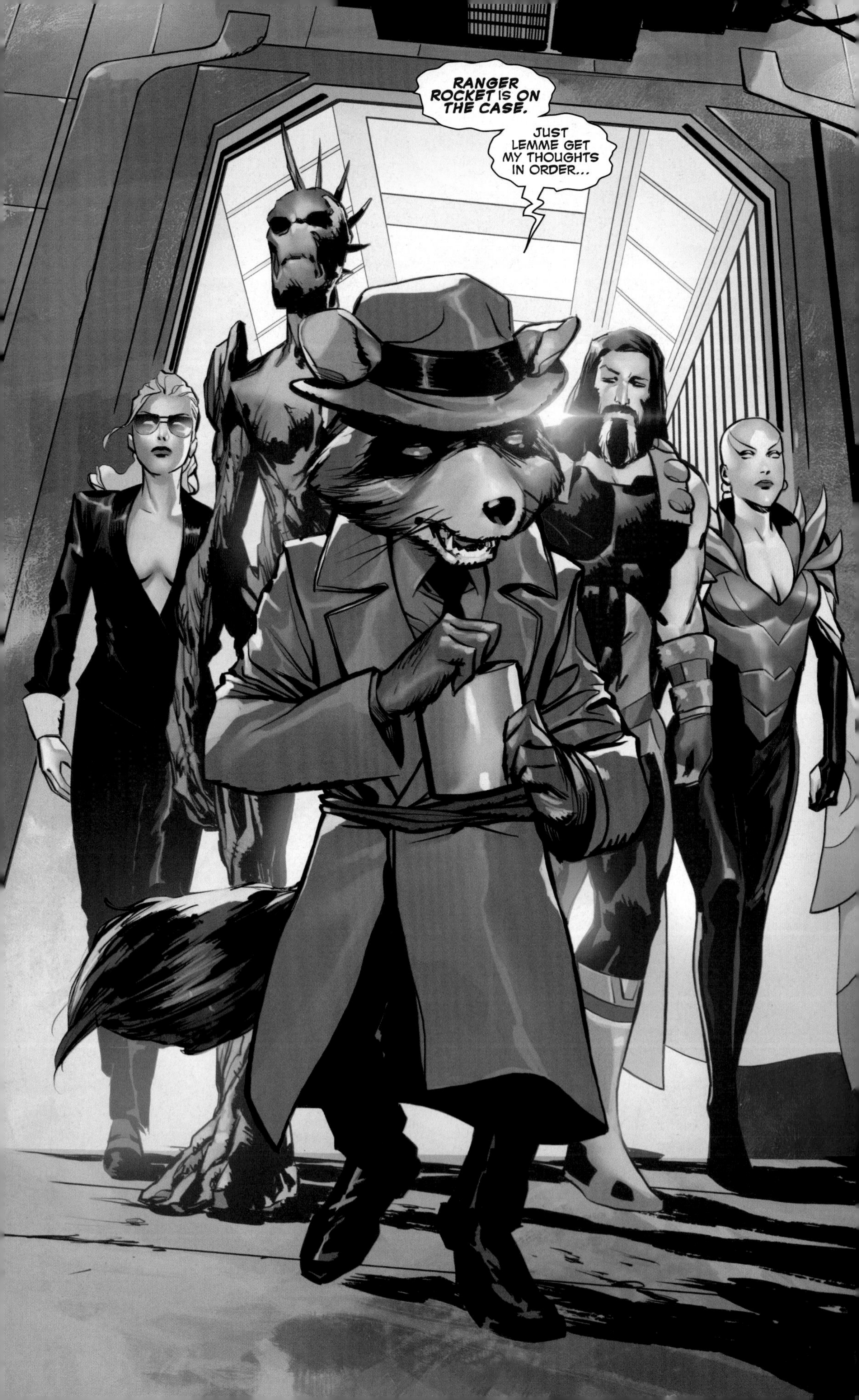
RANGER ROCKET IS ON THE CASE.
JUST LEMME GET MY THOUGHTS IN ORDER...

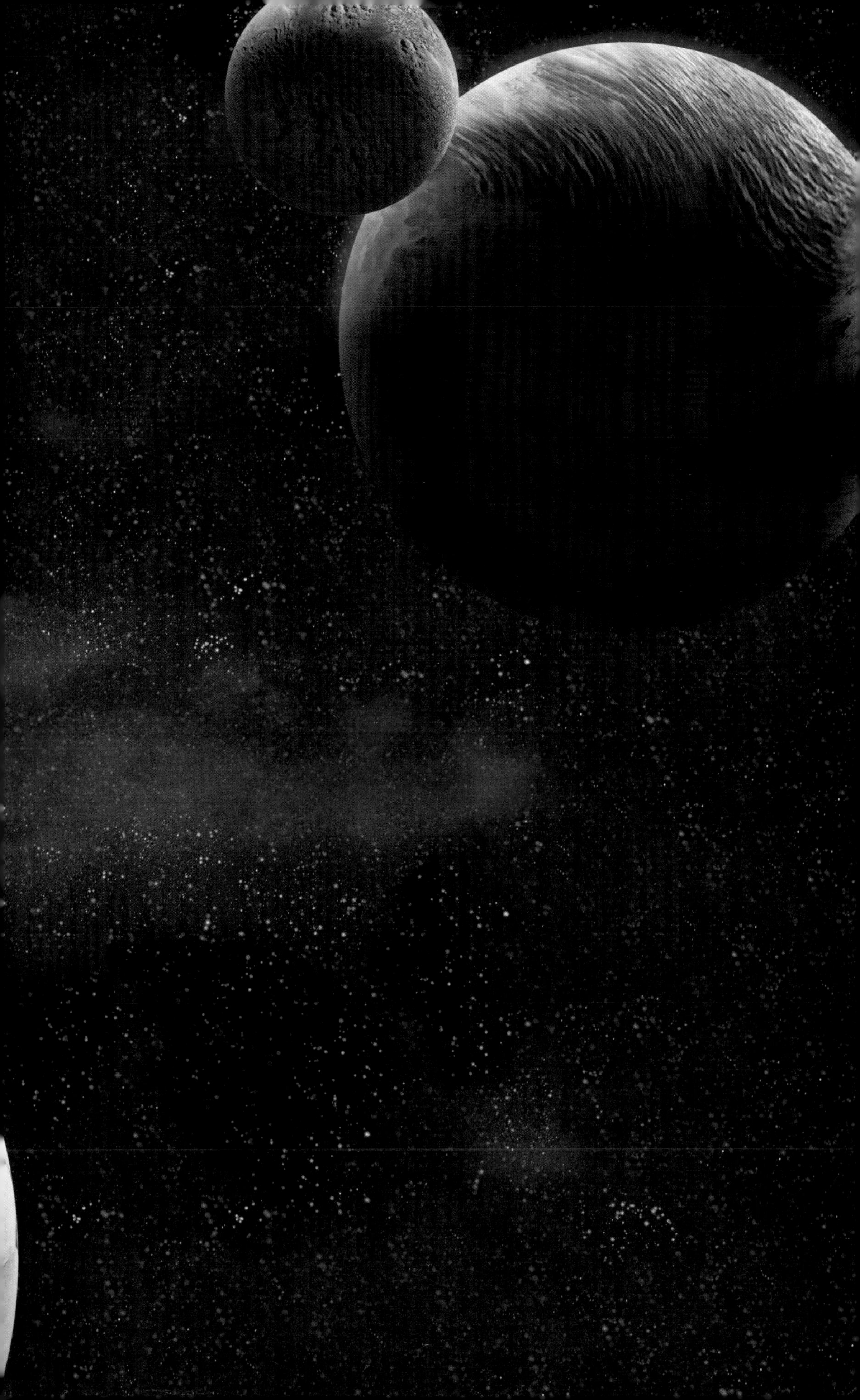

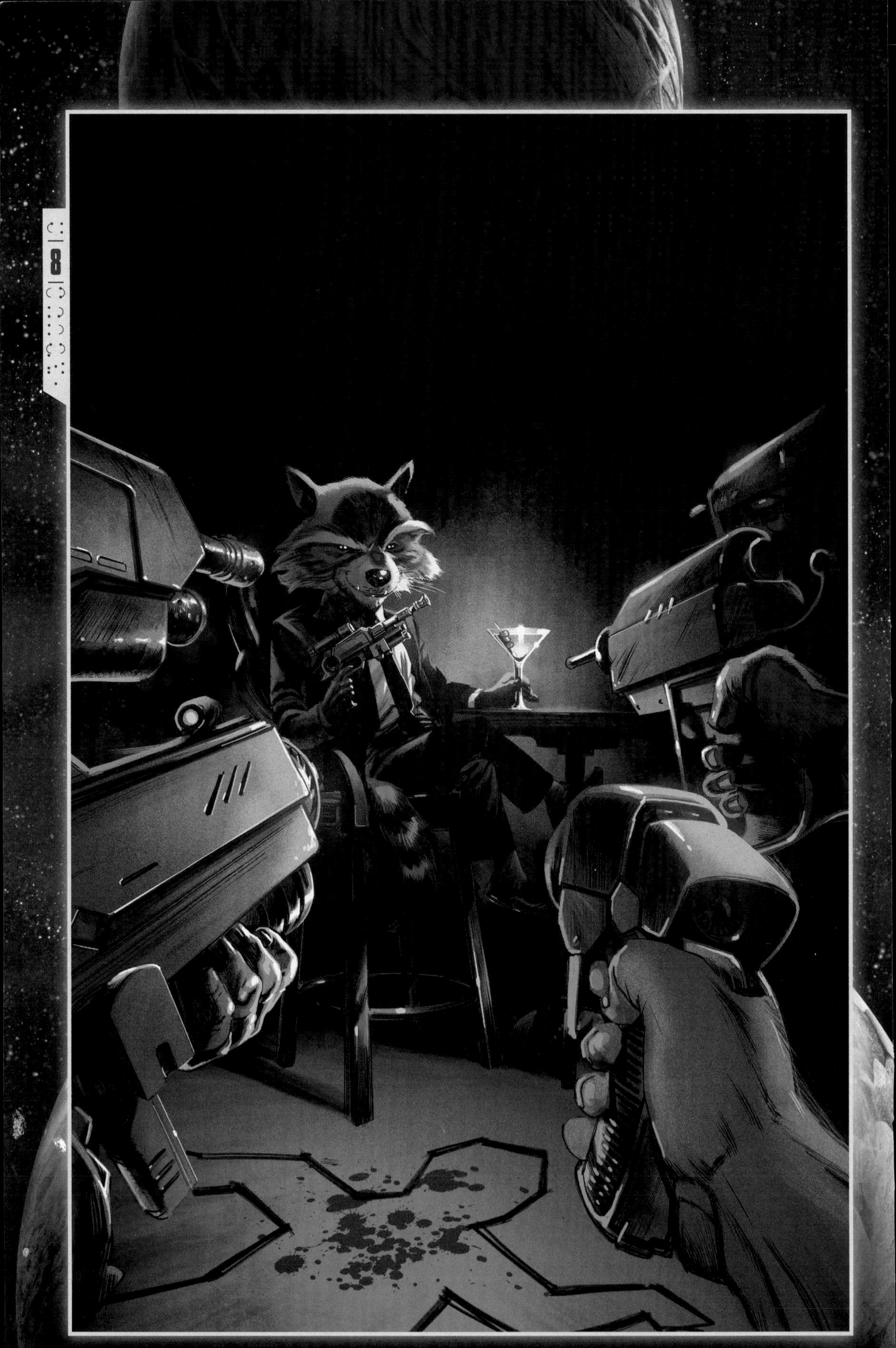

"Business as usual."

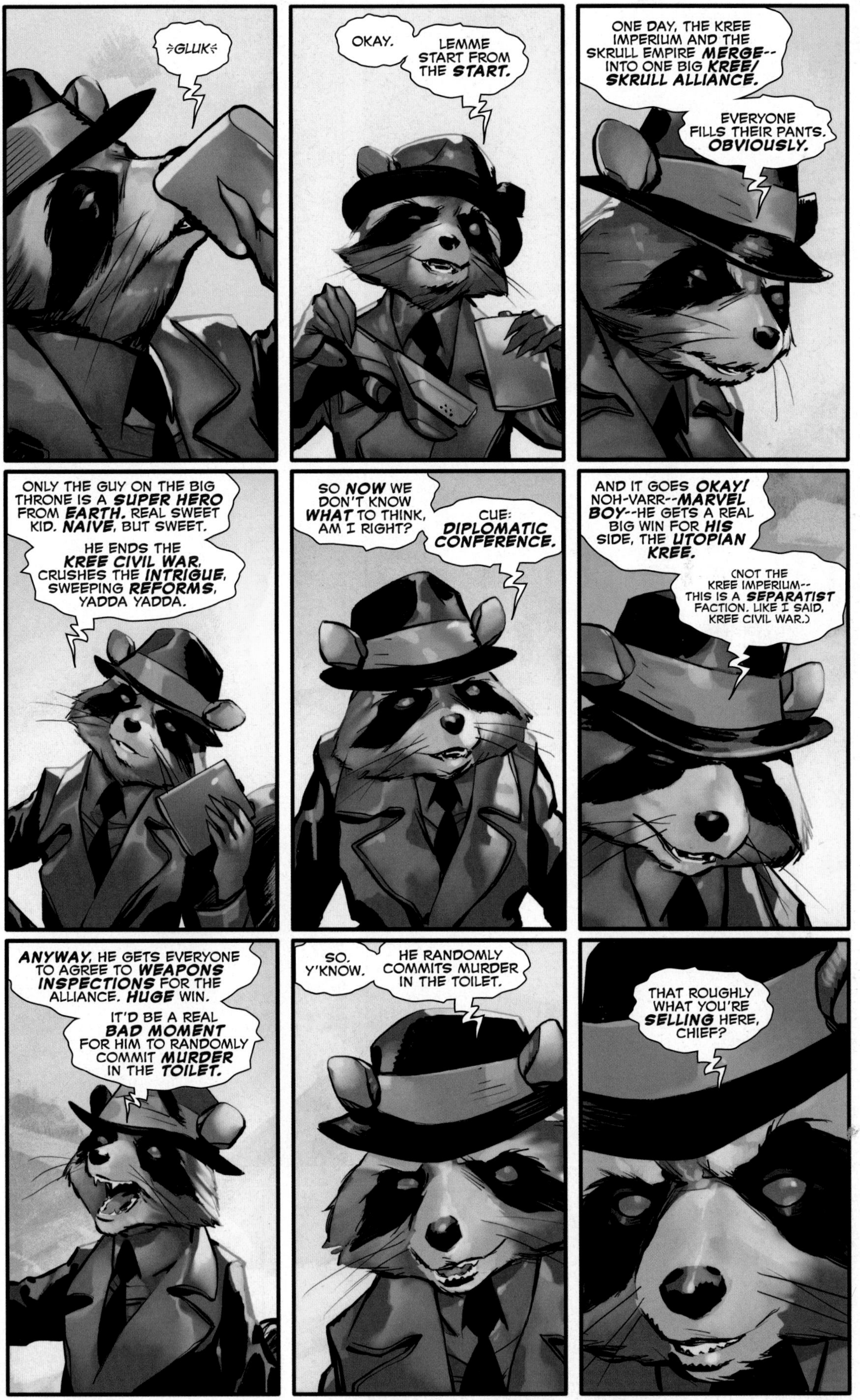

GLUK
OKAY.
LEMME START FROM THE START.
ONE DAY, THE KREE IMPERIUM AND THE SKRULL EMPIRE MERGE-- INTO ONE BIG KREE/ SKRULL ALLIANCE.
EVERYONE FILLS THEIR PANTS. OBVIOUSLY.
ONLY THE GUY ON THE BIG THRONE IS A SUPER HERO FROM EARTH. REAL SWEET KID. NAIVE, BUT SWEET.
HE ENDS THE KREE CIVIL WAR, CRUSHES THE INTRIGUE, SWEEPING REFORMS, YADDA YADDA.
SO NOW WE DON'T KNOW WHAT TO THINK, AM I RIGHT?
CUE: DIPLOMATIC CONFERENCE.
AND IT GOES OKAY! NOH-VARR--MARVEL BOY--HE GETS A REAL BIG WIN FOR HIS SIDE, THE UTOPIAN KREE.
(NOT THE KREE IMPERIUM-- THIS IS A SEPARATIST FACTION. LIKE I SAID, KREE CIVIL WAR.)
ANYWAY, HE GETS EVERYONE TO AGREE TO WEAPONS INSPECTIONS FOR THE ALLIANCE. HUGE WIN.
IT'D BE A REAL BAD MOMENT FOR HIM TO RANDOMLY COMMIT MURDER IN THE TOILET.
SO. Y'KNOW.
HE RANDOMLY COMMITS MURDER IN THE TOILET.
THAT ROUGHLY WHAT YOU'RE SELLING HERE, CHIEF?

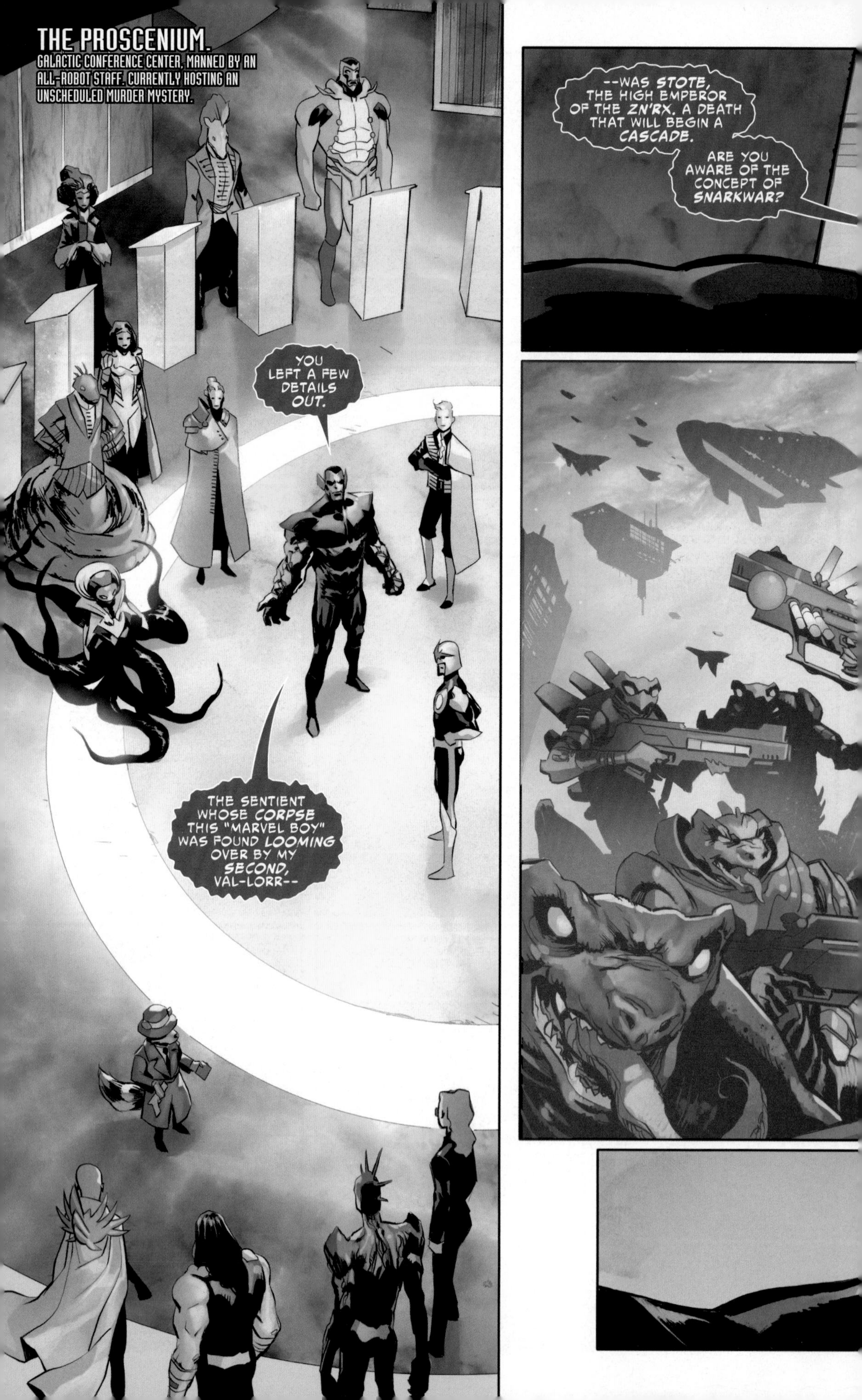
THE PROSCENIUM.
GALACTIC CONFERENCE CENTER, MANNED BY AN ALL-ROBOT STAFF. CURRENTLY HOSTING AN UNSCHEDULED MURDER MYSTERY.
YOU LEFT A FEW DETAILS OUT.
THE SENTIENT WHOSE CORPSE THIS "MARVEL BOY" WAS FOUND LOOMING OVER BY MY SECOND, VAL-LORR--
--WAS STOTE, THE HIGH EMPEROR OF THE ZN'RX. A DEATH THAT WILL BEGIN A CASCADE.
ARE YOU AWARE OF THE CONCEPT OF SNARKWAR?

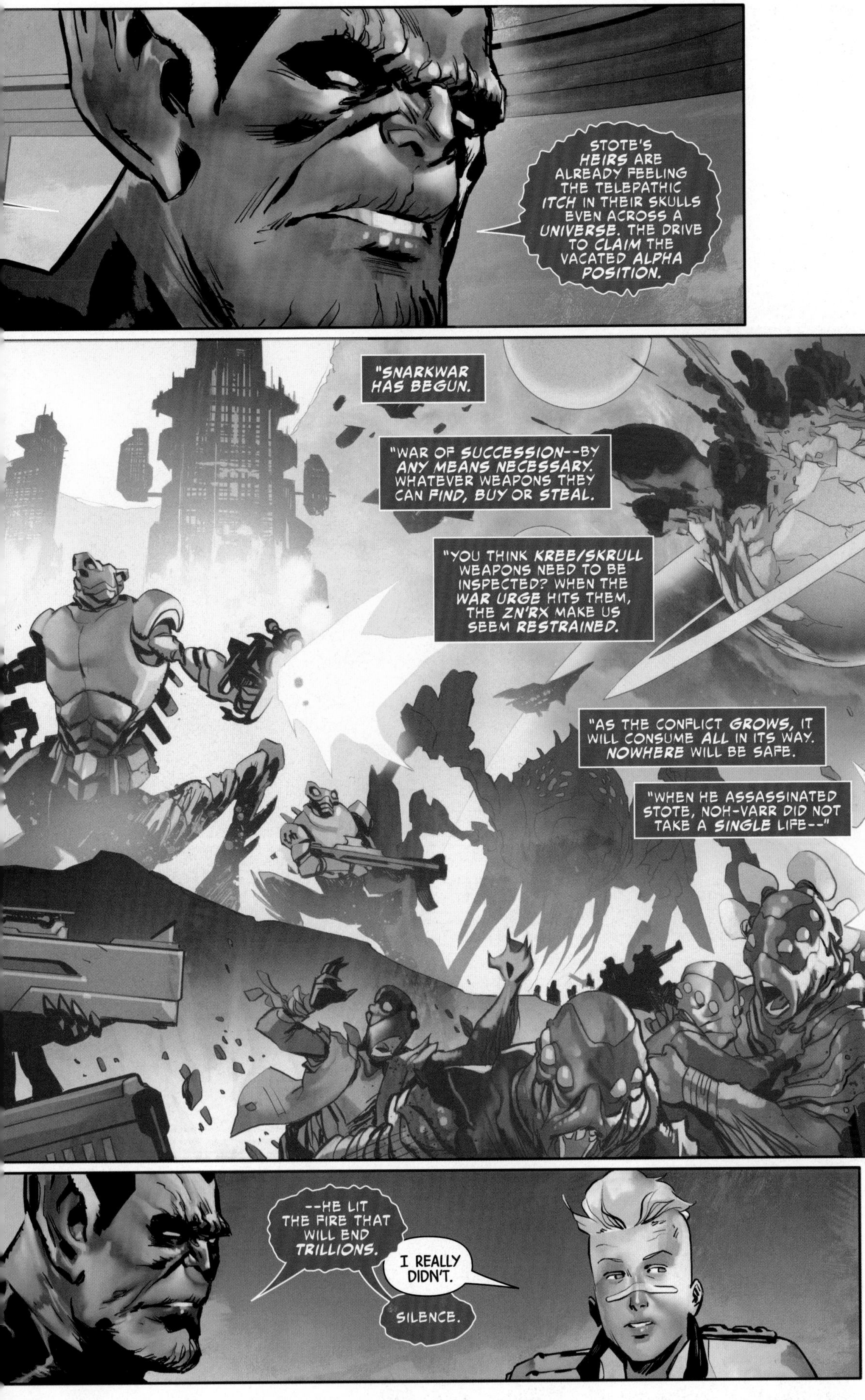
STOTE'S HEIRS ARE ALREADY FEELING THE TELEPATHIC ITCH IN THEIR SKULLS EVEN ACROSS A UNIVERSE. THE DRIVE TO CLAIM THE VACATED ALPHA POSITION.
"SNARKWAR HAS BEGUN.
"WAR OF SUCCESSION--BY ANY MEANS NECESSARY. WHATEVER WEAPONS THEY CAN FIND, BUY OR STEAL.
"YOU THINK KREE/SKRULL WEAPONS NEED TO BE INSPECTED? WHEN THE WAR URGE HITS THEM, THE ZN'RX MAKE US SEEM RESTRAINED.
"AS THE CONFLICT GROWS, IT WILL CONSUME ALL IN ITS WAY. NOWHERE WILL BE SAFE.
"WHEN HE ASSASSINATED STOTE, NOH-VARR DID NOT TAKE A SINGLE LIFE--"
--HE LIT THE FIRE THAT WILL END TRILLIONS.
I REALLY DIDN'T.
SILENCE.

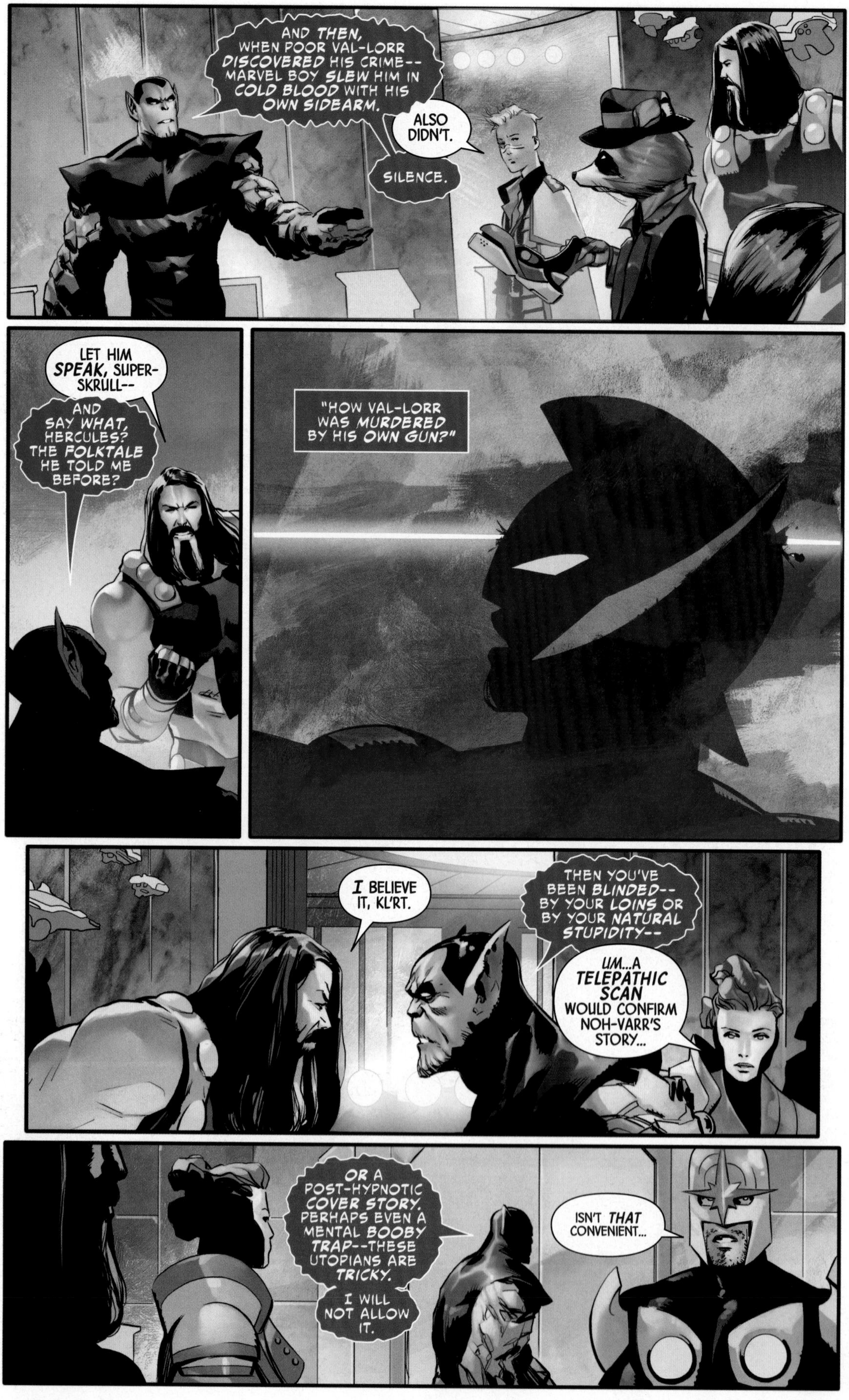
AND THEN, WHEN POOR VAL-LORR DISCOVERED HIS CRIME-- MARVEL BOY SLEW HIM IN COLD BLOOD WITH HIS OWN SIDEARM.
ALSO DIDN'T.
SILENCE.
LET HIM SPEAK, SUPER-SKRULL--
AND SAY WHAT, HERCULES? THE FOLKTALE HE TOLD ME BEFORE?
"HOW VAL-LORR WAS MURDERED BY HIS OWN GUN?"
I BELIEVE IT, KL'RT.
THEN YOU'VE BEEN BLINDED-- BY YOUR LOINS OR BY YOUR NATURAL STUPIDITY--
UM...A TELEPATHIC SCAN WOULD CONFIRM NOH-VARR'S STORY...
OR A POST-HYPNOTIC COVER STORY. PERHAPS EVEN A MENTAL BOOBY TRAP--THESE UTOPIANS ARE TRICKY.
I WILL NOT ALLOW IT.
ISN'T THAT CONVENIENT...

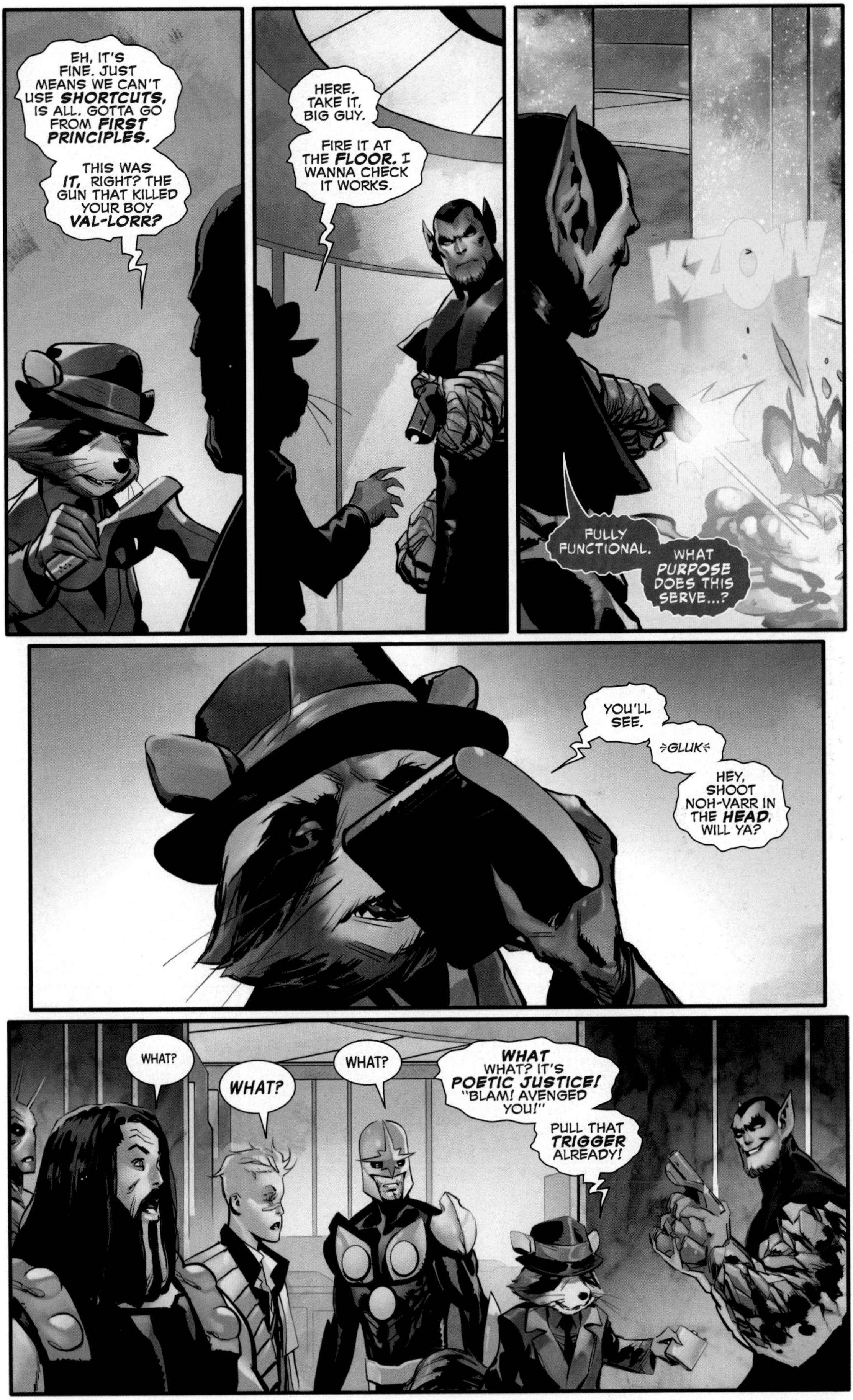
EH, IT'S FINE. JUST MEANS WE CAN'T USE SHORTCUTS, IS ALL. GOTTA GO FROM FIRST PRINCIPLES.
THIS WAS IT, RIGHT? THE GUN THAT KILLED YOUR BOY VAL-LORR?
HERE. TAKE IT, BIG GUY.
FIRE IT AT THE FLOOR. I WANNA CHECK IT WORKS.
KZOW
FULLY FUNCTIONAL.
WHAT PURPOSE DOES THIS SERVE...?
YOU'LL SEE.
GLUK
HEY, SHOOT NOH-VARR IN THE HEAD, WILL YA?
WHAT?
WHAT?
WHAT?
WHAT WHAT? IT'S POETIC JUSTICE! "BLAM! AVENGED YOU!"
PULL THAT TRIGGER ALREADY!

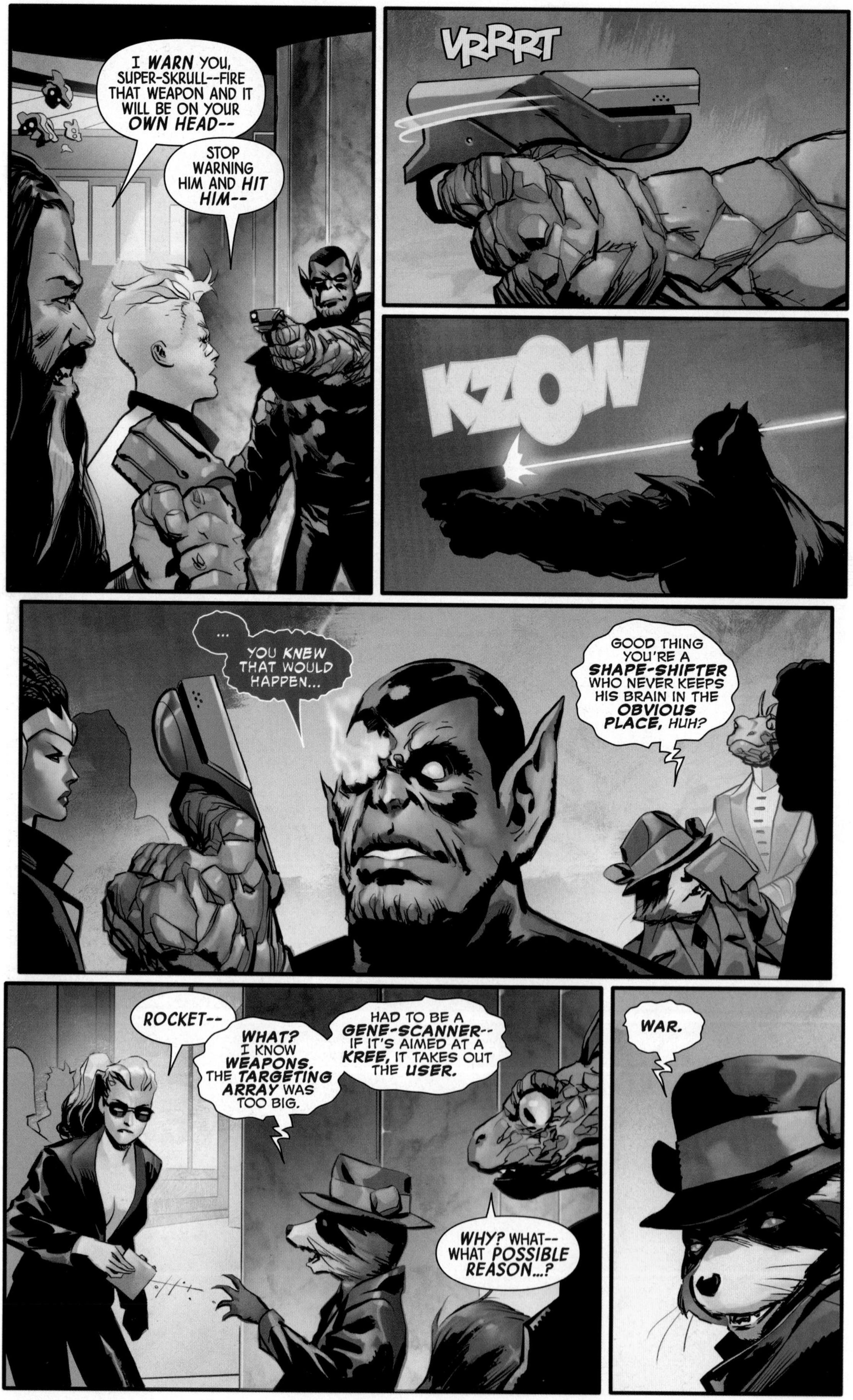
I WARN YOU, SUPER-SKRULL--FIRE THAT WEAPON AND IT WILL BE ON YOUR OWN HEAD--
STOP WARNING HIM AND HIT HIM--
VRRRT
KZOW
... YOU KNEW THAT WOULD HAPPEN...
GOOD THING YOU'RE A SHAPE-SHIFTER WHO NEVER KEEPS HIS BRAIN IN THE OBVIOUS PLACE, HUH?
ROCKET--
WHAT? I KNOW WEAPONS. THE TARGETING ARRAY WAS TOO BIG.
HAD TO BE A GENE-SCANNER--IF IT'S AIMED AT A KREE, IT TAKES OUT THE USER.
WHY? WHAT--WHAT POSSIBLE REASON...?
WAR.

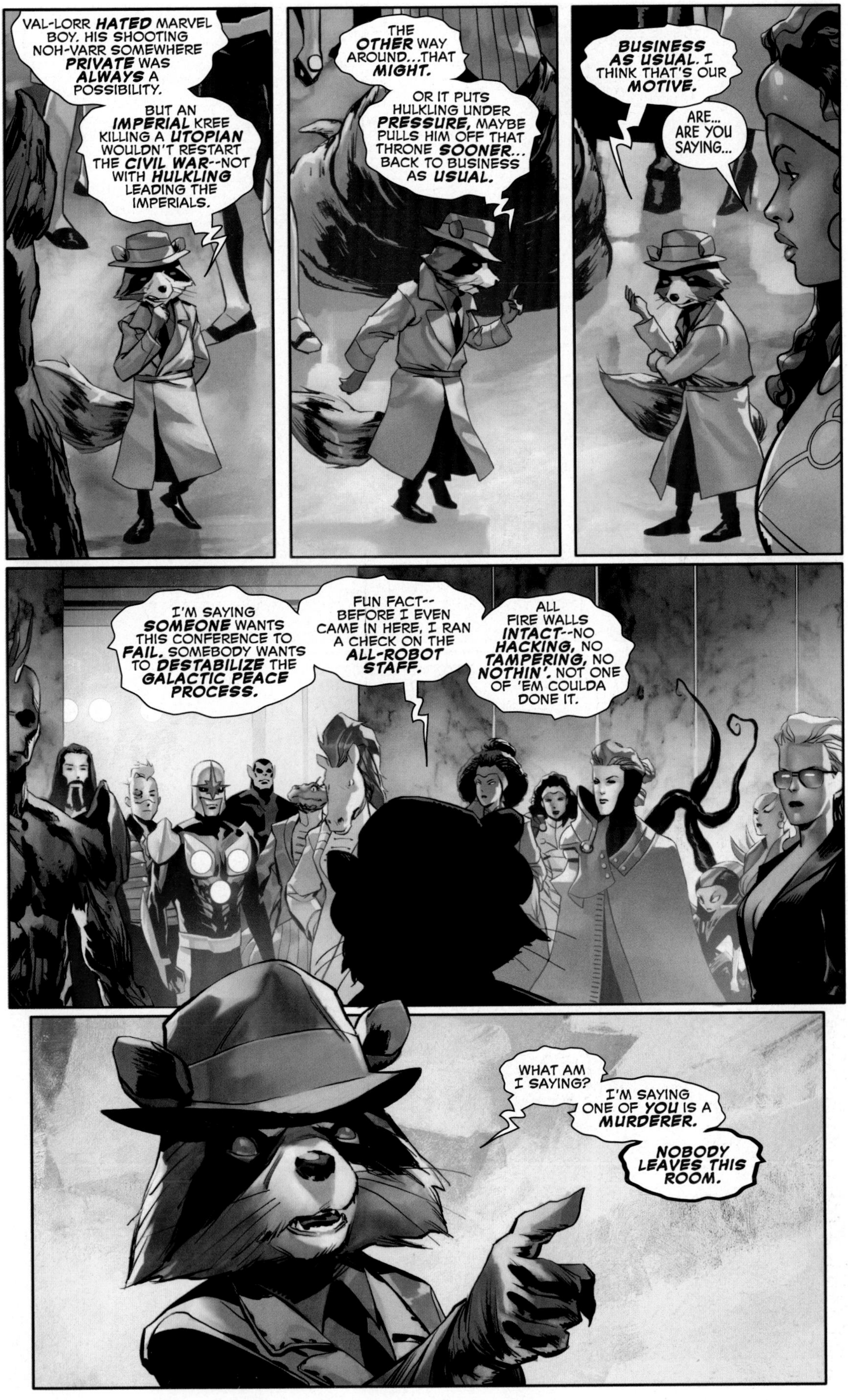
VAL-LORR HATED MARVEL BOY. HIS SHOOTING NOH-VARR SOMEWHERE PRIVATE WAS ALWAYS A POSSIBILITY.
BUT AN IMPERIAL KREE KILLING A UTOPIAN WOULDN'T RESTART THE CIVIL WAR--NOT WITH HULKLING LEADING THE IMPERIALS.
THE OTHER WAY AROUND...THAT MIGHT.
OR IT PUTS HULKLING UNDER PRESSURE, MAYBE PULLS HIM OFF THAT THRONE SOONER... BACK TO BUSINESS AS USUAL.
BUSINESS AS USUAL. I THINK THAT'S OUR MOTIVE.
ARE... ARE YOU SAYING...
I'M SAYING SOMEONE WANTS THIS CONFERENCE TO FAIL. SOMEBODY WANTS TO DESTABILIZE THE GALACTIC PEACE PROCESS.
FUN FACT--BEFORE I EVEN CAME IN HERE, I RAN A CHECK ON THE ALL-ROBOT STAFF.
ALL FIRE WALLS INTACT--NO HACKING, NO TAMPERING, NO NOTHIN'. NOT ONE OF 'EM COULDA DONE IT.
WHAT AM I SAYING?
I'M SAYING ONE OF YOU IS A MURDERER.
NOBODY LEAVES THIS ROOM.

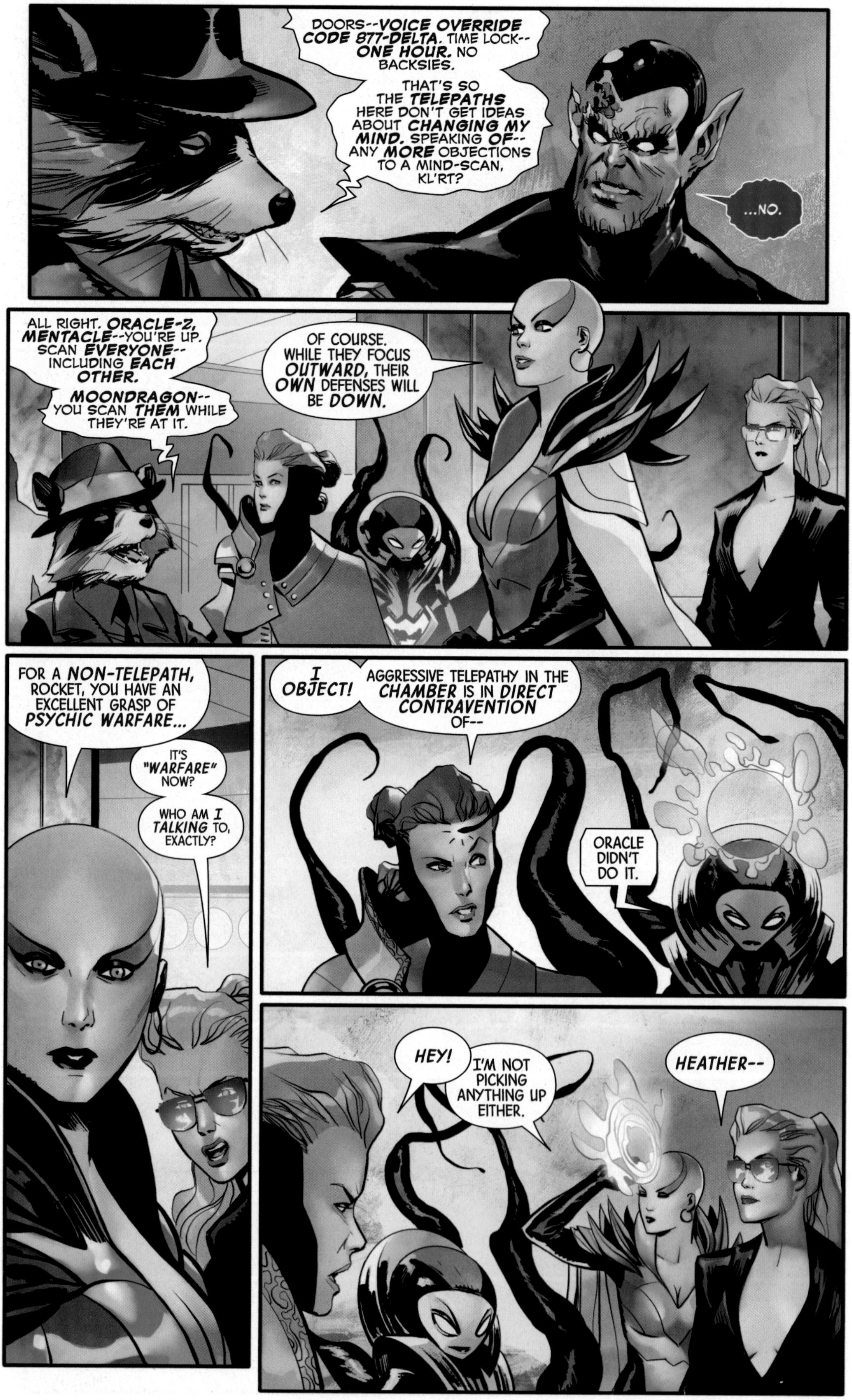
DOORS--VOICE OVERRIDE CODE 877-DELTA. TIME LOCK--ONE HOUR. NO BACKSIES.
THAT'S SO THE TELEPATHS HERE DON'T GET IDEAS ABOUT CHANGING MY MIND. SPEAKING OF--ANY MORE OBJECTIONS TO A MIND-SCAN, KL'RT?
...NO.
ALL RIGHT. ORACLE-2, MENTACLE--YOU'RE UP. SCAN EVERYONE--INCLUDING EACH OTHER.
MOONDRAGON--YOU SCAN THEM WHILE THEY'RE AT IT.
OF COURSE. WHILE THEY FOCUS OUTWARD, THEIR OWN DEFENSES WILL BE DOWN.
FOR A NON-TELEPATH, ROCKET, YOU HAVE AN EXCELLENT GRASP OF PSYCHIC WARFARE...
IT'S "WARFARE" NOW?
WHO AM I TALKING TO, EXACTLY?
I OBJECT!
AGGRESSIVE TELEPATHY IN THE CHAMBER IS IN DIRECT CONTRAVENTION OF--
ORACLE DIDN'T DO IT.
HEY!
I'M NOT PICKING ANYTHING UP EITHER.
HEATHER--

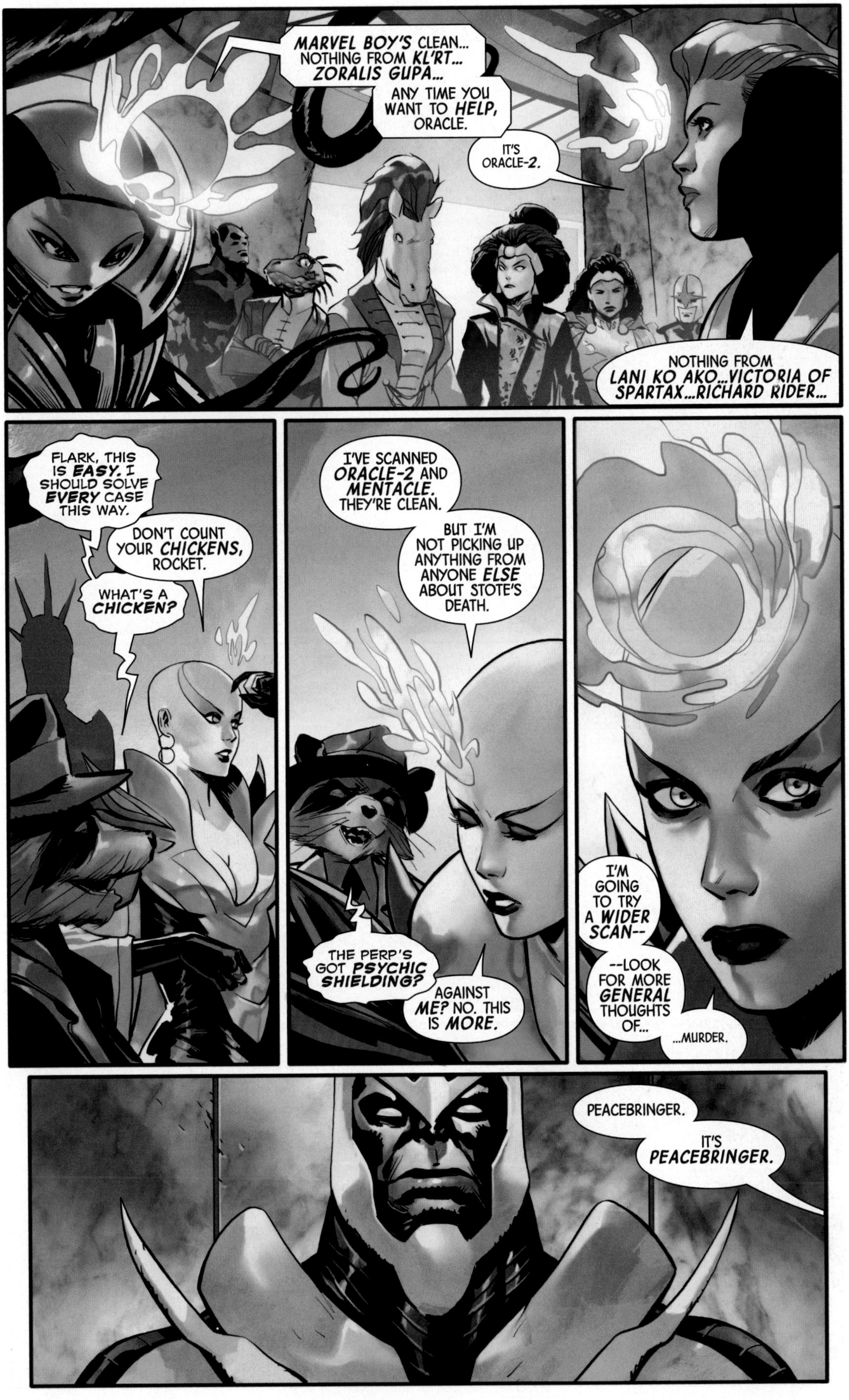
MARVEL BOY'S CLEAN... NOTHING FROM KL'RT... ZORALIS GUPA...
ANY TIME YOU WANT TO HELP, ORACLE.
IT'S ORACLE-2.
NOTHING FROM LANI KO AKO...VICTORIA OF SPARTAX...RICHARD RIDER...
FLARK, THIS IS EASY. I SHOULD SOLVE EVERY CASE THIS WAY.
DON'T COUNT YOUR CHICKENS, ROCKET.
WHAT'S A CHICKEN?
I'VE SCANNED ORACLE-2 AND MENTACLE. THEY'RE CLEAN.
BUT I'M NOT PICKING UP ANYTHING FROM ANYONE ELSE ABOUT STOTE'S DEATH.
THE PERP'S GOT PSYCHIC SHIELDING?
AGAINST ME? NO. THIS IS MORE.
I'M GOING TO TRY A WIDER SCAN--
--LOOK FOR MORE GENERAL THOUGHTS OF...
...MURDER.
PEACEBRINGER.
IT'S PEACEBRINGER.

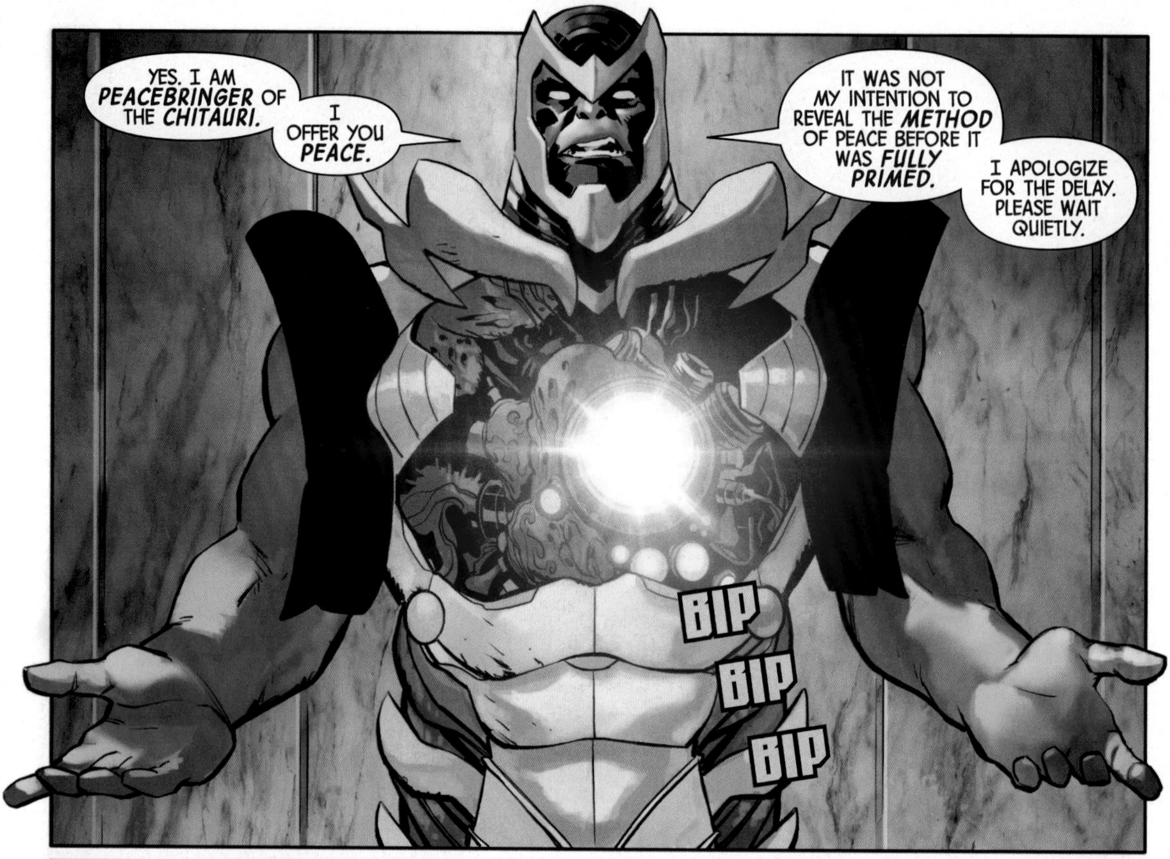
YES. I AM PEACEBRINGER OF THE CHITAURI.
I OFFER YOU PEACE.
IT WAS NOT MY INTENTION TO REVEAL THE METHOD OF PEACE BEFORE IT WAS FULLY PRIMED.
I APOLOGIZE FOR THE DELAY. PLEASE WAIT QUIETLY.
BIP
BIP
BIP

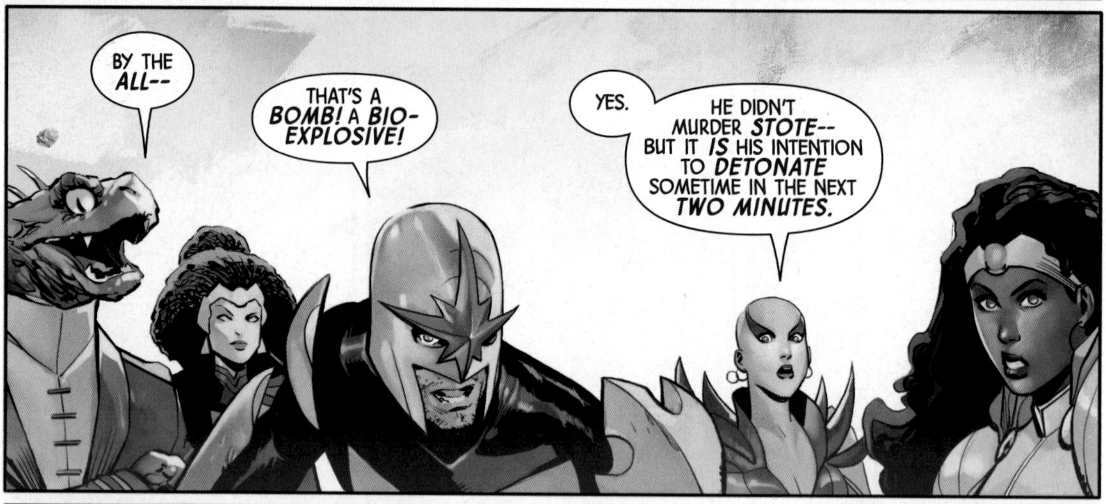
BY THE ALL--
THAT'S A BOMB! A BIO-EXPLOSIVE!
YES.
HE DIDN'T MURDER STOTE-- BUT IT IS HIS INTENTION TO DETONATE SOMETIME IN THE NEXT TWO MINUTES.

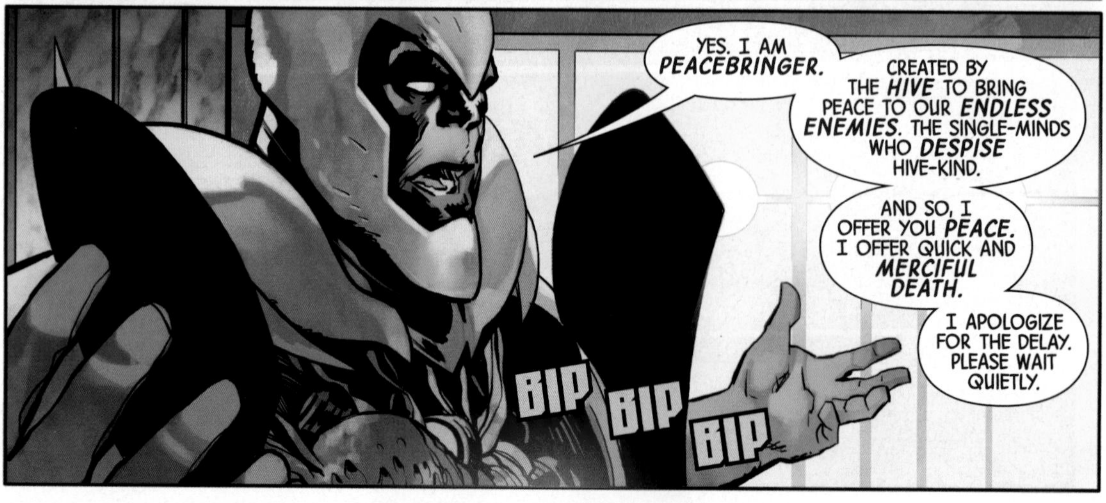
YES. I AM PEACEBRINGER.
CREATED BY THE HIVE TO BRING PEACE TO OUR ENDLESS ENEMIES. THE SINGLE-MINDS WHO DESPISE HIVE-KIND.
AND SO, I OFFER YOU PEACE. I OFFER QUICK AND MERCIFUL DEATH.
I APOLOGIZE FOR THE DELAY. PLEASE WAIT QUIETLY.
BIP
BIP
BIP

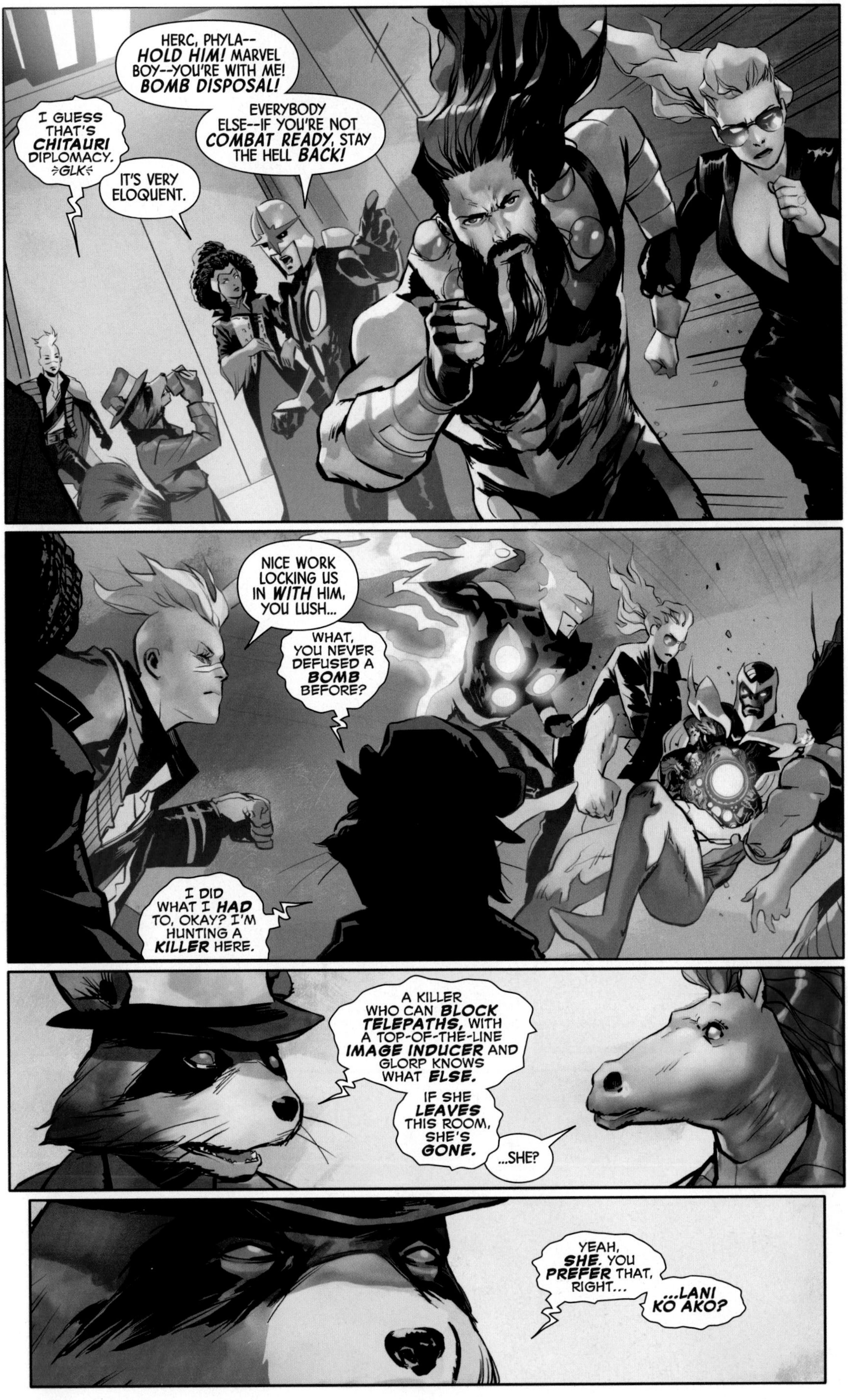
HERC, PHYLA--
HOLD HIM! MARVEL BOY--YOU'RE WITH ME! BOMB DISPOSAL!
I GUESS THAT'S CHITAURI DIPLOMACY. ≯GLK≮
EVERYBODY ELSE--IF YOU'RE NOT COMBAT READY, STAY THE HELL BACK!
IT'S VERY ELOQUENT.
NICE WORK LOCKING US IN WITH HIM, YOU LUSH...
WHAT, YOU NEVER DEFUSED A BOMB BEFORE?
I DID WHAT I HAD TO, OKAY? I'M HUNTING A KILLER HERE.
A KILLER WHO CAN BLOCK TELEPATHS, WITH A TOP-OF-THE-LINE IMAGE INDUCER AND GLORP KNOWS WHAT ELSE.
IF SHE LEAVES THIS ROOM, SHE'S GONE.
...SHE?
YEAH, SHE. YOU PREFER THAT, RIGHT...
...LANI KO AKO?

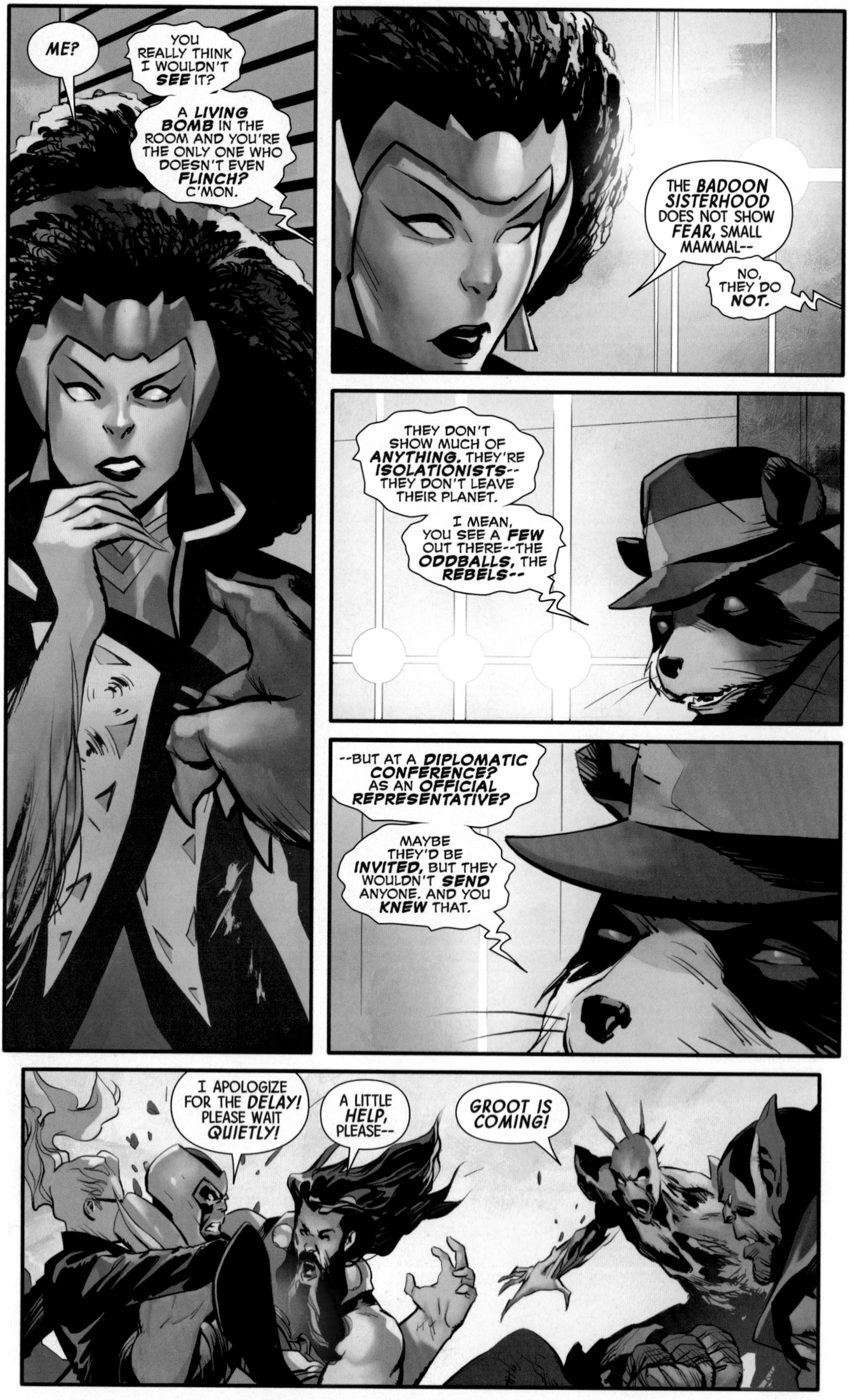
ME?
YOU REALLY THINK I WOULDN'T SEE IT?
A LIVING BOMB IN THE ROOM AND YOU'RE THE ONLY ONE WHO DOESN'T EVEN FLINCH? C'MON.
THE BADOON SISTERHOOD DOES NOT SHOW FEAR, SMALL MAMMAL--
NO, THEY DO NOT.
THEY DON'T SHOW MUCH OF ANYTHING. THEY'RE ISOLATIONISTS-- THEY DON'T LEAVE THEIR PLANET.
I MEAN, YOU SEE A FEW OUT THERE--THE ODDBALLS, THE REBELS--
--BUT AT A DIPLOMATIC CONFERENCE? AS AN OFFICIAL REPRESENTATIVE?
MAYBE THEY'D BE INVITED, BUT THEY WOULDN'T SEND ANYONE. AND YOU KNEW THAT.
I APOLOGIZE FOR THE DELAY! PLEASE WAIT QUIETLY!
A LITTLE HELP, PLEASE--
GROOT IS COMING!

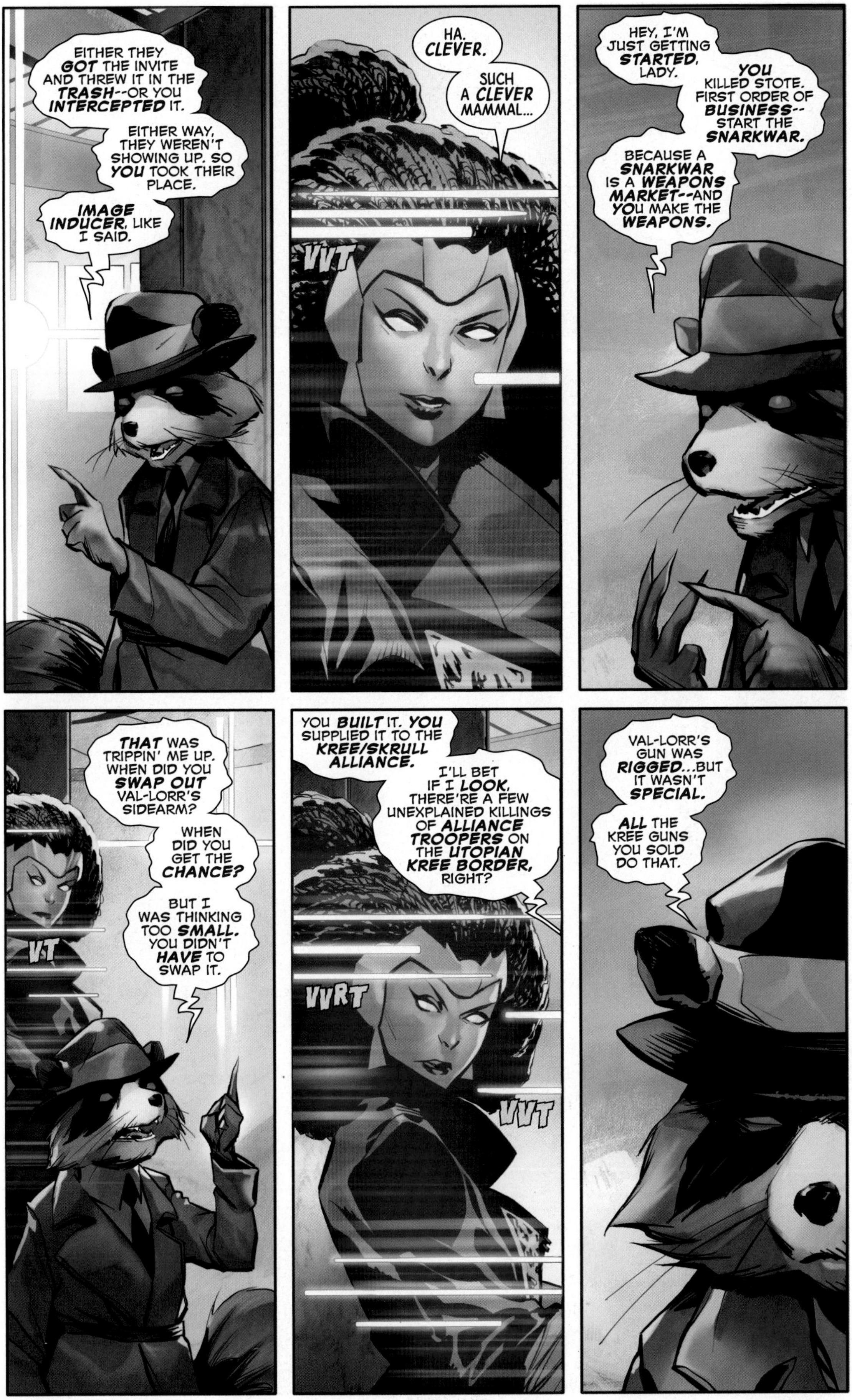
EITHER THEY GOT THE INVITE AND THREW IT IN THE TRASH--OR YOU INTERCEPTED IT.
EITHER WAY, THEY WEREN'T SHOWING UP. SO YOU TOOK THEIR PLACE.
IMAGE INDUCER, LIKE I SAID.
HA. CLEVER.
SUCH A CLEVER MAMMAL...
VVT
HEY, I'M JUST GETTING STARTED, LADY.
YOU KILLED STOTE. FIRST ORDER OF BUSINESS-- START THE SNARKWAR.
BECAUSE A SNARKWAR IS A WEAPONS MARKET--AND YOU MAKE THE WEAPONS.
THAT WAS TRIPPIN' ME UP. WHEN DID YOU SWAP OUT VAL-LORR'S SIDEARM?
WHEN DID YOU GET THE CHANCE?
BUT I WAS THINKING TOO SMALL. YOU DIDN'T HAVE TO SWAP IT.
VT
YOU BUILT IT. YOU SUPPLIED IT TO THE KREE/SKRULL ALLIANCE.
I'LL BET IF I LOOK, THERE'RE A FEW UNEXPLAINED KILLINGS OF ALLIANCE TROOPERS ON THE UTOPIAN KREE BORDER, RIGHT?
VVRT
VVT
VAL-LORR'S GUN WAS RIGGED...BUT IT WASN'T SPECIAL.
ALL THE KREE GUNS YOU SOLD DO THAT.

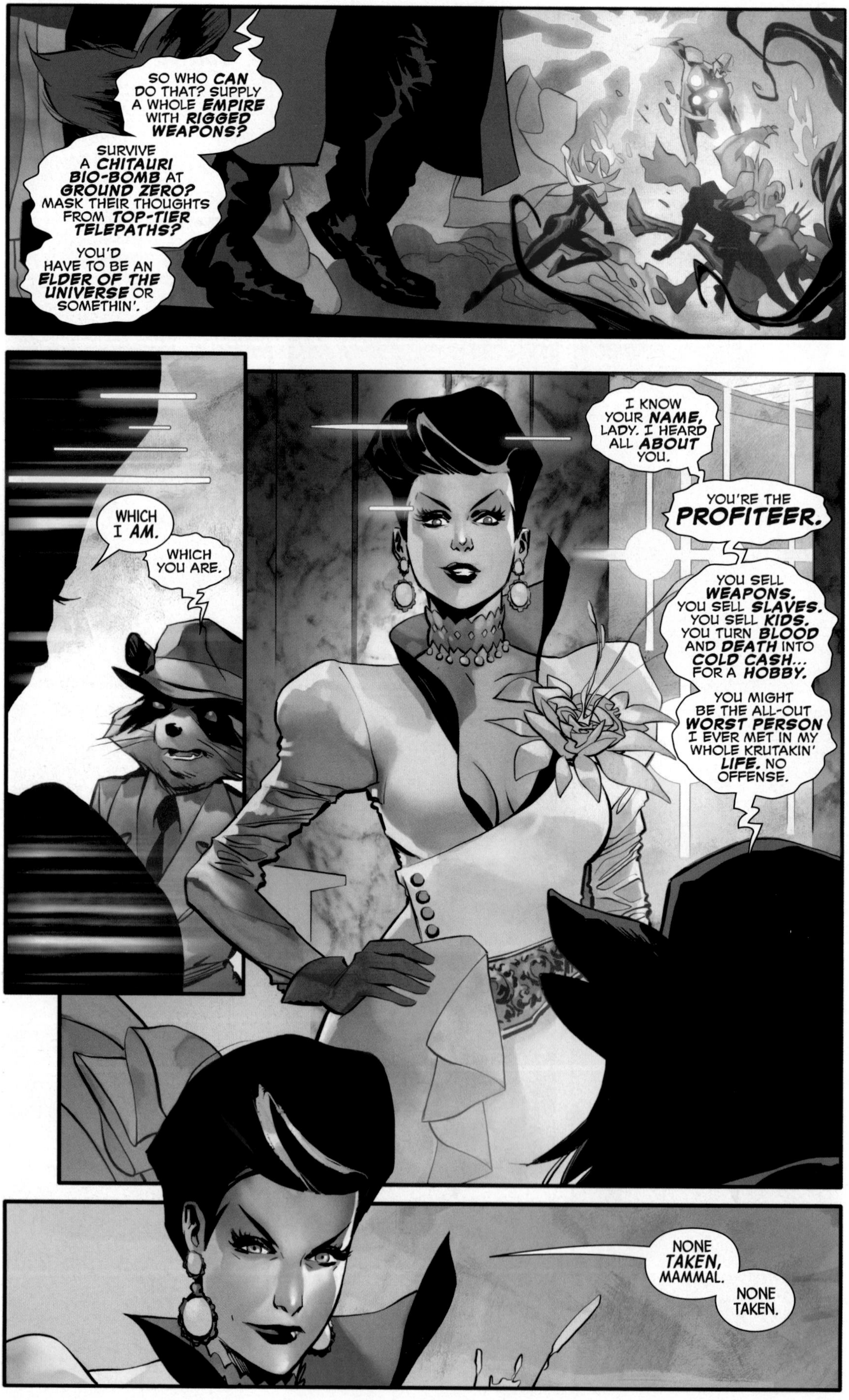

SO WHO CAN DO THAT? SUPPLY A WHOLE EMPIRE WITH RIGGED WEAPONS?
SURVIVE A CHITAURI BIO-BOMB AT GROUND ZERO? MASK THEIR THOUGHTS FROM TOP-TIER TELEPATHS?
YOU'D HAVE TO BE AN ELDER OF THE UNIVERSE OR SOMETHIN'.
I KNOW YOUR NAME, LADY. I HEARD ALL ABOUT YOU.
YOU'RE THE PROFITEER.
WHICH I AM.
WHICH YOU ARE.
YOU SELL WEAPONS. YOU SELL SLAVES. YOU SELL KIDS. YOU TURN BLOOD AND DEATH INTO COLD CASH... FOR A HOBBY.
YOU MIGHT BE THE ALL-OUT WORST PERSON I EVER MET IN MY WHOLE KRUTAKIN' LIFE. NO OFFENSE.
NONE TAKEN, MAMMAL.
NONE TAKEN.

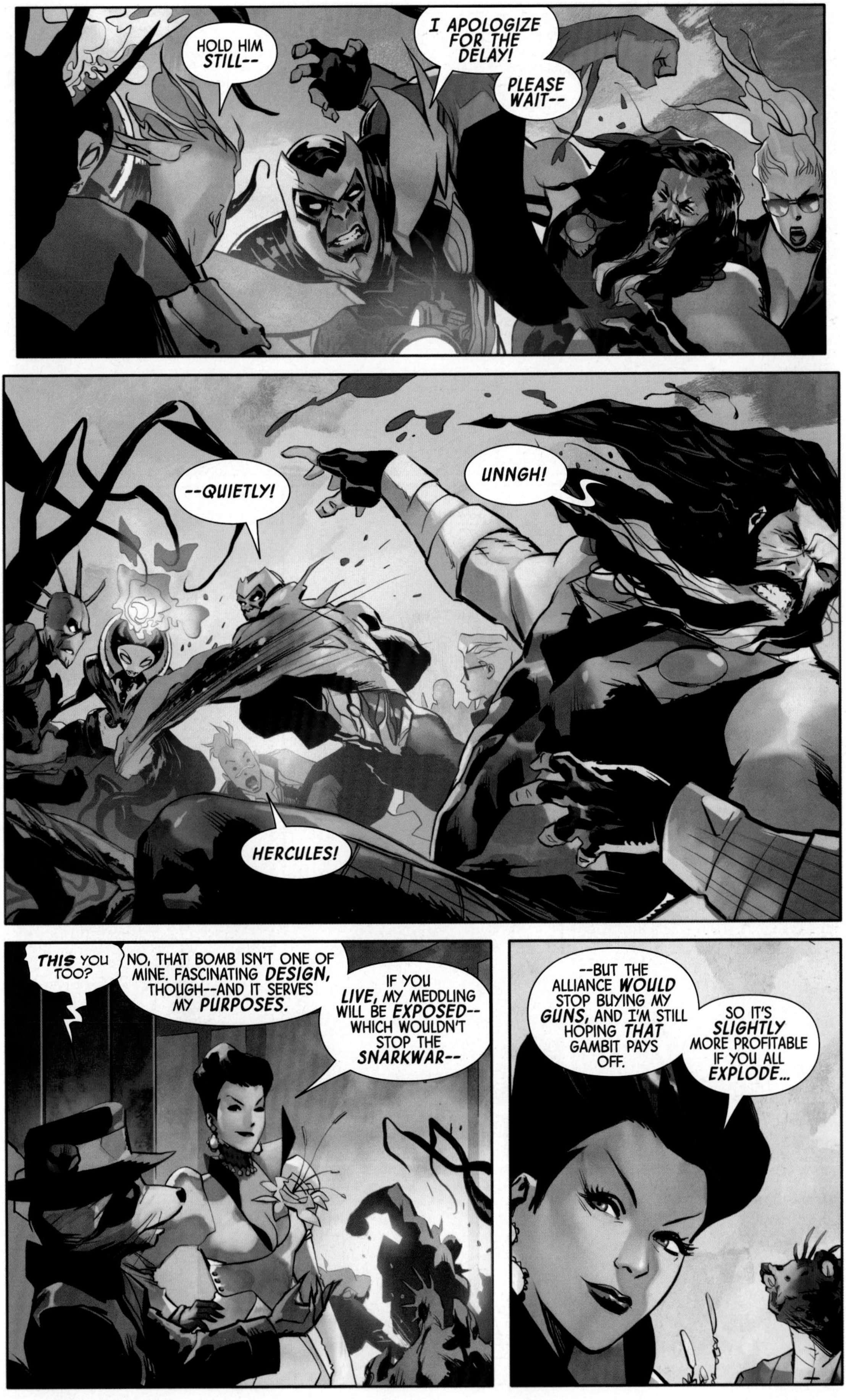
HOLD HIM STILL--
I APOLOGIZE FOR THE DELAY!
PLEASE WAIT--
--QUIETLY!
UNNGH!
HERCULES!
THIS YOU TOO?
NO, THAT BOMB ISN'T ONE OF MINE. FASCINATING DESIGN, THOUGH--AND IT SERVES MY PURPOSES.
IF YOU LIVE, MY MEDDLING WILL BE EXPOSED--WHICH WOULDN'T STOP THE SNARKWAR--
--BUT THE ALLIANCE WOULD STOP BUYING MY GUNS, AND I'M STILL HOPING THAT GAMBIT PAYS OFF.
SO IT'S SLIGHTLY MORE PROFITABLE IF YOU ALL EXPLODE...

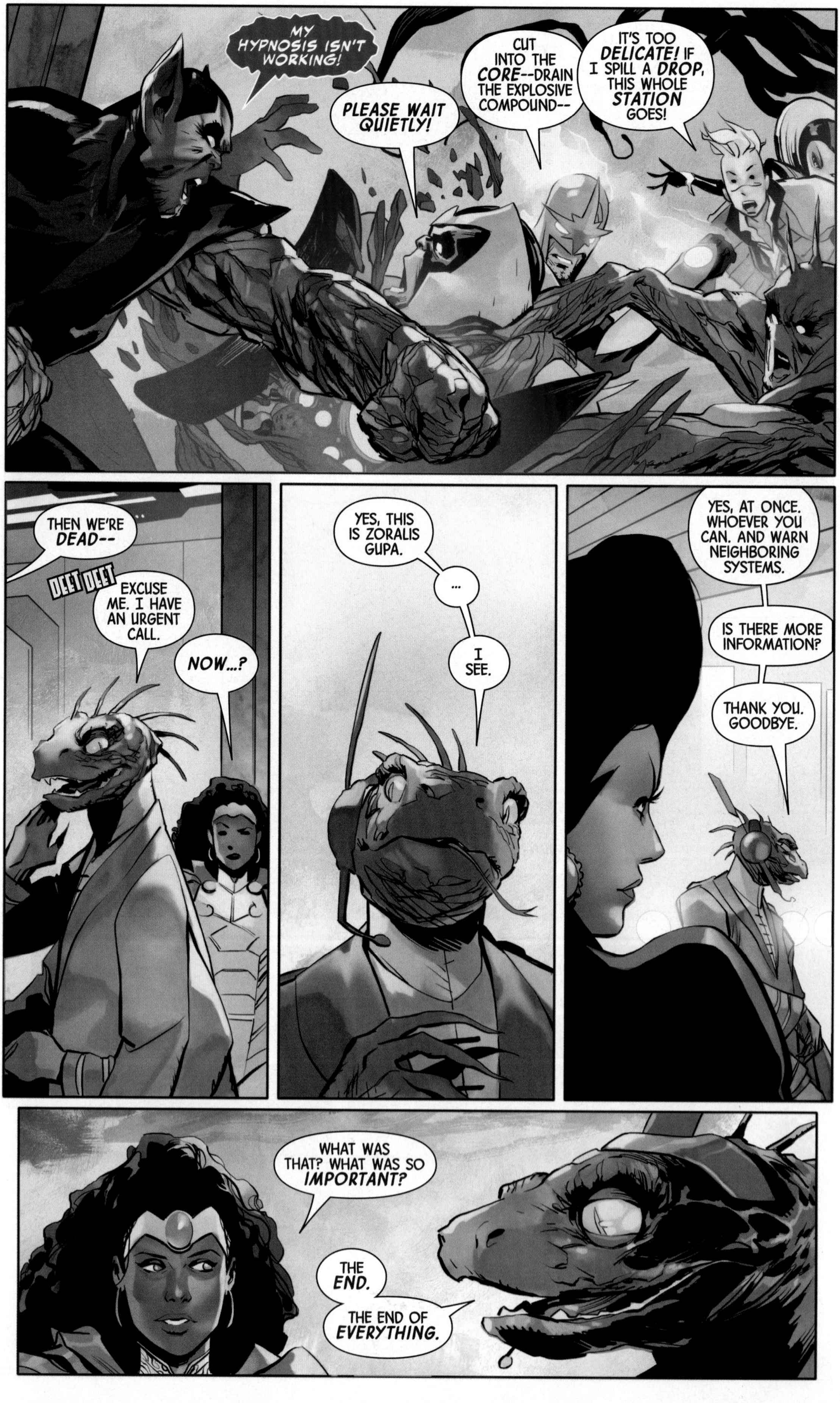
MY HYPNOSIS ISN'T WORKING!
PLEASE WAIT QUIETLY!
CUT INTO THE CORE--DRAIN THE EXPLOSIVE COMPOUND--
IT'S TOO DELICATE! IF I SPILL A DROP, THIS WHOLE STATION GOES!
THEN WE'RE DEAD--
DEET DEET
EXCUSE ME. I HAVE AN URGENT CALL.
NOW...?
YES, THIS IS ZORALIS GUPA.
...
I SEE.
YES, AT ONCE. WHOEVER YOU CAN. AND WARN NEIGHBORING SYSTEMS.
IS THERE MORE INFORMATION?
THANK YOU. GOODBYE.
WHAT WAS THAT? WHAT WAS SO IMPORTANT?
THE END.
THE END OF EVERYTHING.

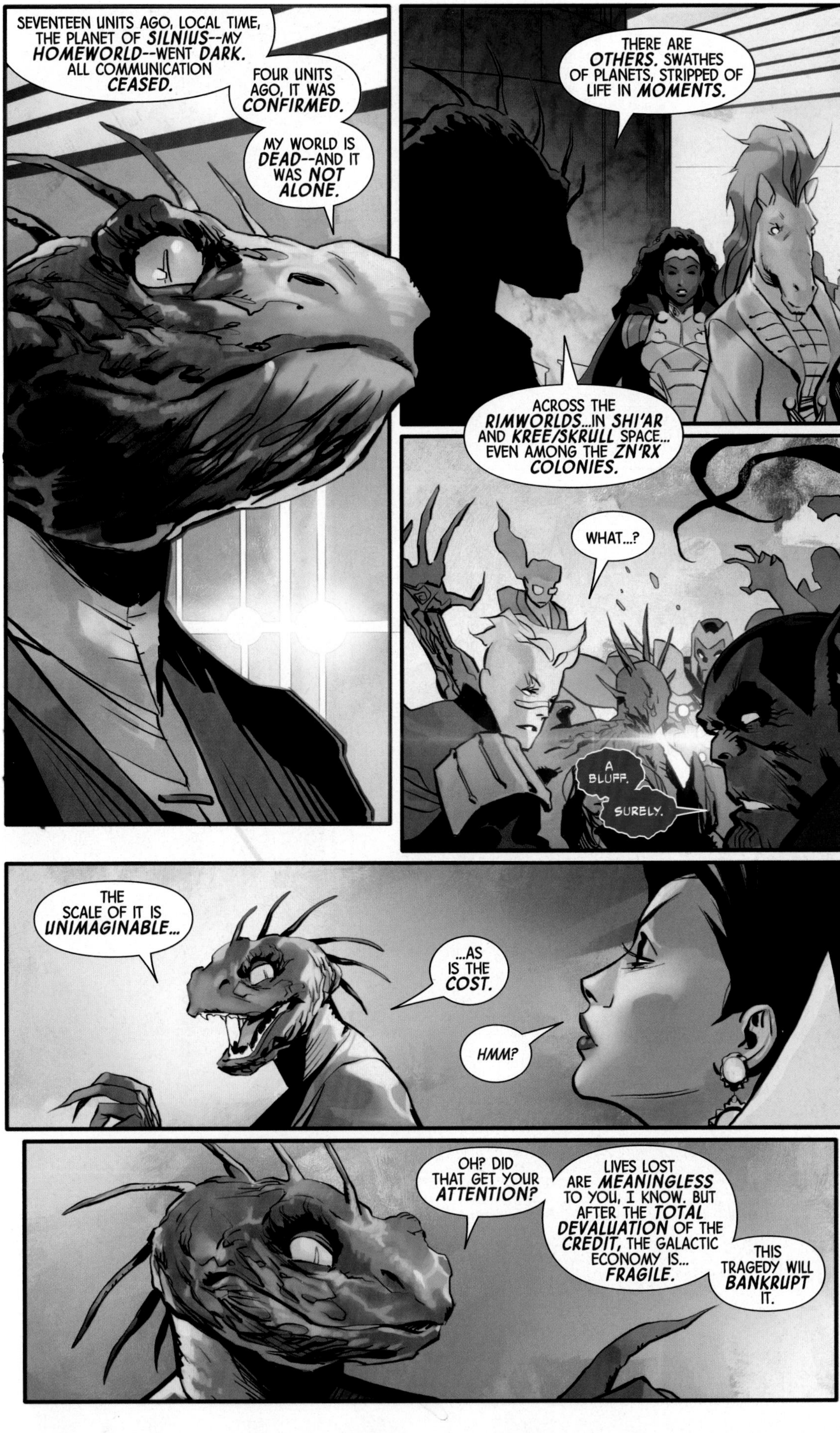
SEVENTEEN UNITS AGO, LOCAL TIME, THE PLANET OF SILNIUS--MY HOMEWORLD--WENT DARK. ALL COMMUNICATION CEASED.
FOUR UNITS AGO, IT WAS CONFIRMED.
MY WORLD IS DEAD--AND IT WAS NOT ALONE.
THERE ARE OTHERS. SWATHES OF PLANETS, STRIPPED OF LIFE IN MOMENTS.
ACROSS THE RIMWORLDS...IN SHI'AR AND KREE/SKRULL SPACE... EVEN AMONG THE ZN'RX COLONIES.
WHAT...?
A BLUFF.
SURELY.
THE SCALE OF IT IS UNIMAGINABLE...
...AS IS THE COST.
HMM?
OH? DID THAT GET YOUR ATTENTION?
LIVES LOST ARE MEANINGLESS TO YOU, I KNOW. BUT AFTER THE TOTAL DEVALUATION OF THE CREDIT, THE GALACTIC ECONOMY IS... FRAGILE.
THIS TRAGEDY WILL BANKRUPT IT.

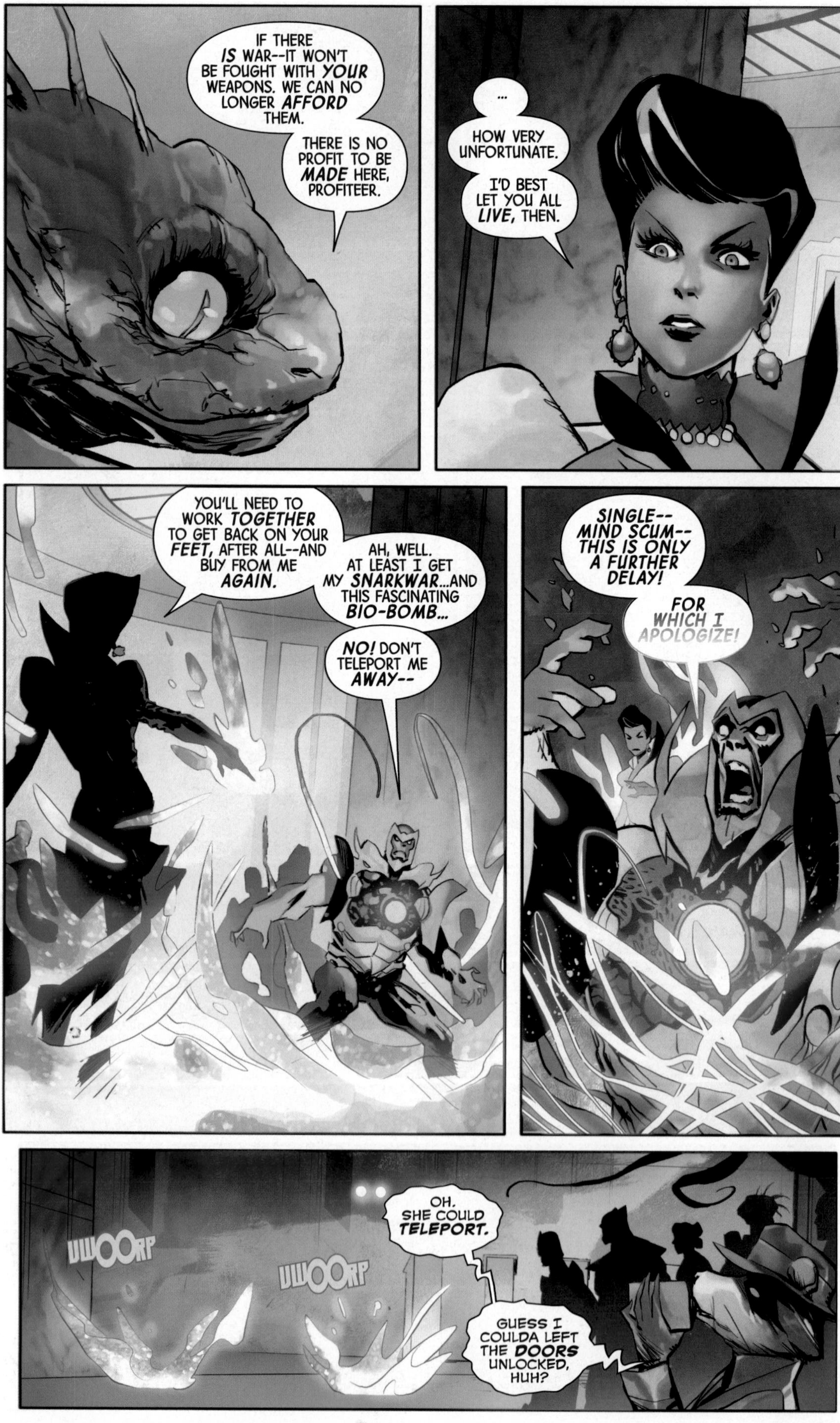
IF THERE IS WAR--IT WON'T BE FOUGHT WITH YOUR WEAPONS. WE CAN NO LONGER AFFORD THEM.
THERE IS NO PROFIT TO BE MADE HERE, PROFITEER.
...
HOW VERY UNFORTUNATE.
I'D BEST LET YOU ALL LIVE, THEN.
YOU'LL NEED TO WORK TOGETHER TO GET BACK ON YOUR FEET, AFTER ALL--AND BUY FROM ME AGAIN.
AH, WELL. AT LEAST I GET MY SNARKWAR...AND THIS FASCINATING BIO-BOMB...
NO! DON'T TELEPORT ME AWAY--
SINGLE--MIND SCUM--THIS IS ONLY A FURTHER DELAY!
FOR WHICH I APOLOGIZE!
UWOORP
UWOORP
OH. SHE COULD TELEPORT.
GUESS I COULDA LEFT THE DOORS UNLOCKED, HUH?

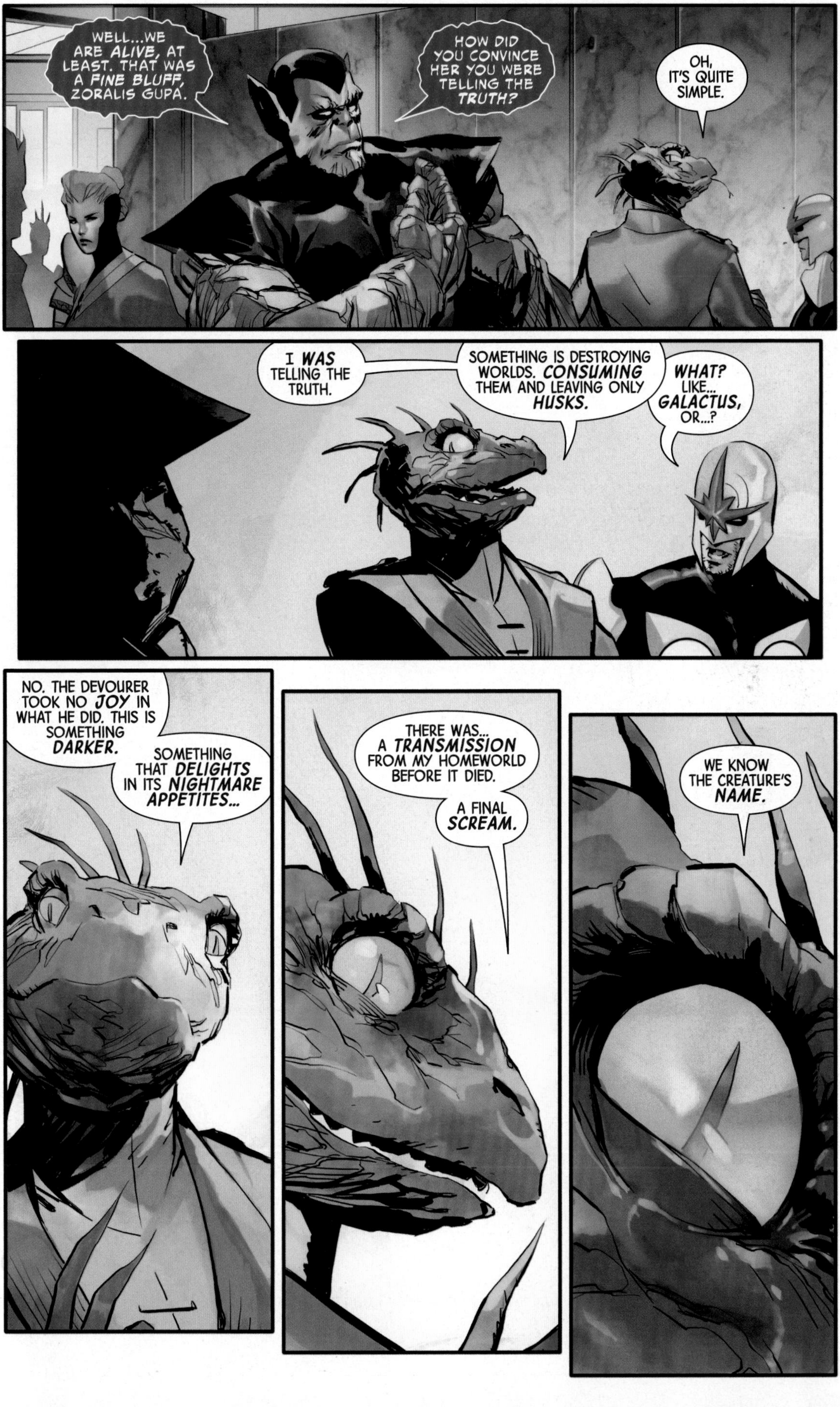
WELL...WE ARE ALIVE, AT LEAST. THAT WAS A FINE BLUFF, ZORALIS GUPA.
HOW DID YOU CONVINCE HER YOU WERE TELLING THE TRUTH?
OH, IT'S QUITE SIMPLE.
I WAS TELLING THE TRUTH.
SOMETHING IS DESTROYING WORLDS. CONSUMING THEM AND LEAVING ONLY HUSKS.
WHAT? LIKE... GALACTUS, OR...?
NO. THE DEVOURER TOOK NO JOY IN WHAT HE DID. THIS IS SOMETHING DARKER.
SOMETHING THAT DELIGHTS IN ITS NIGHTMARE APPETITES...
THERE WAS... A TRANSMISSION FROM MY HOMEWORLD BEFORE IT DIED.
A FINAL SCREAM.
WE KNOW THE CREATURE'S NAME.

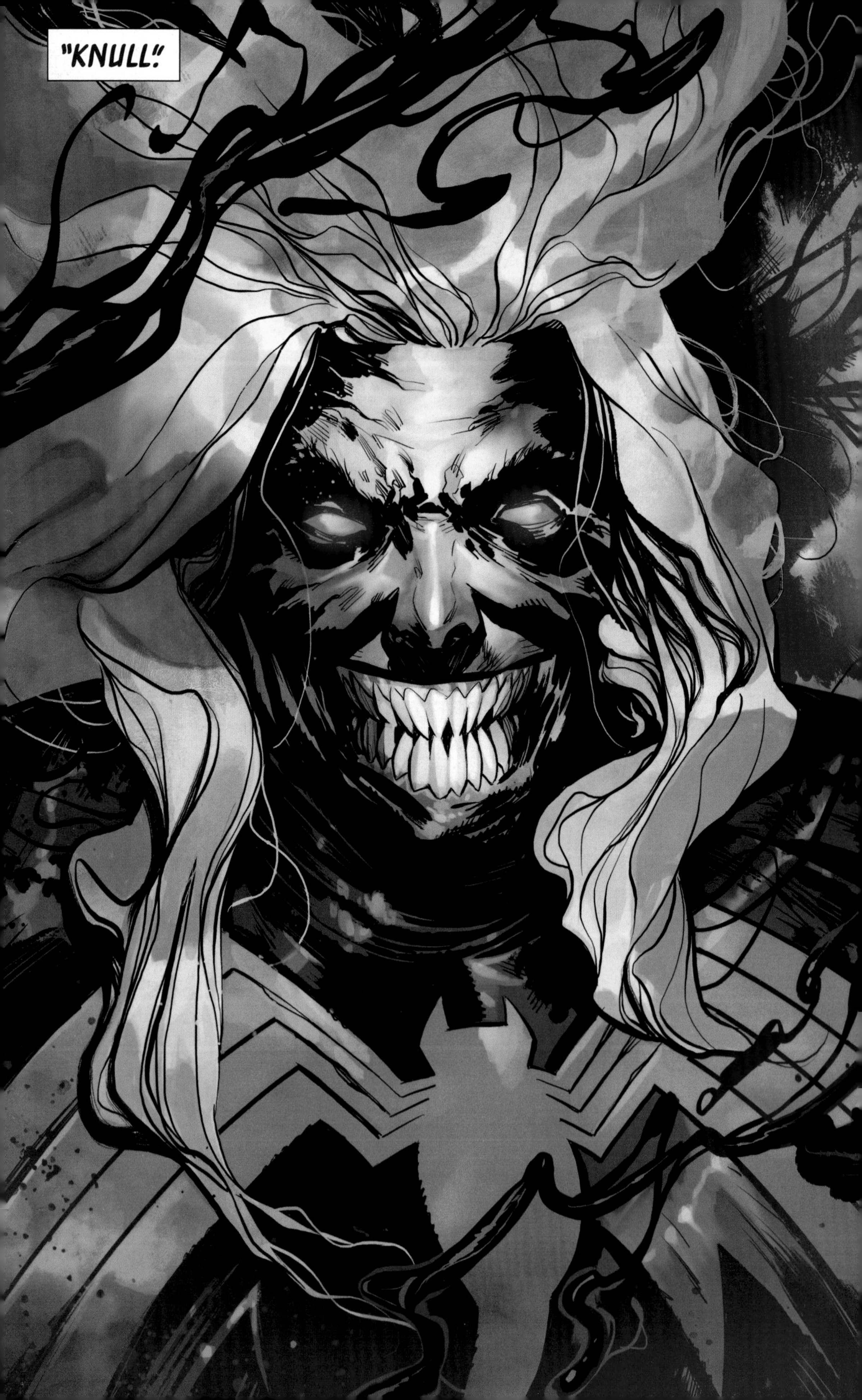
"KNULL!"

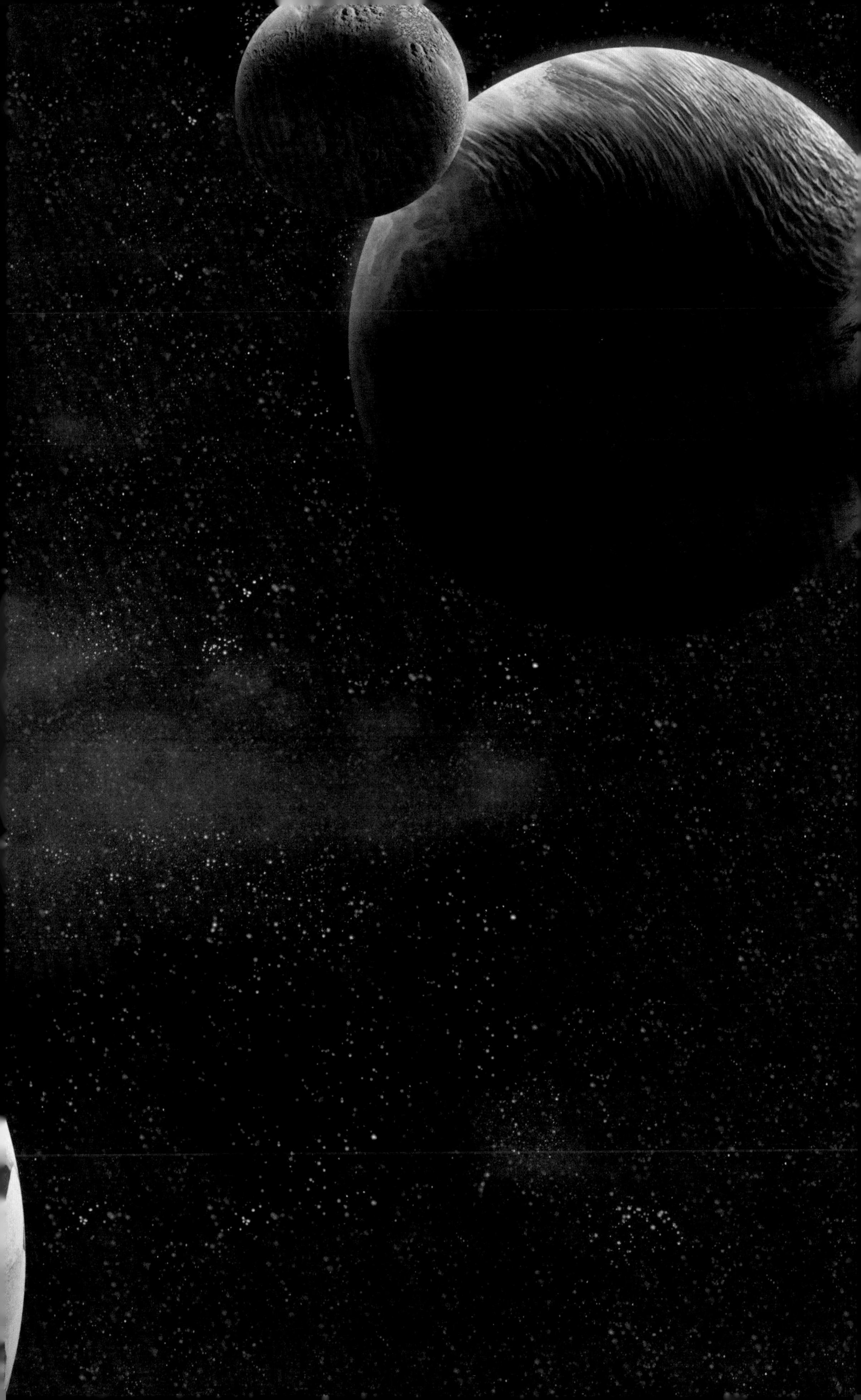

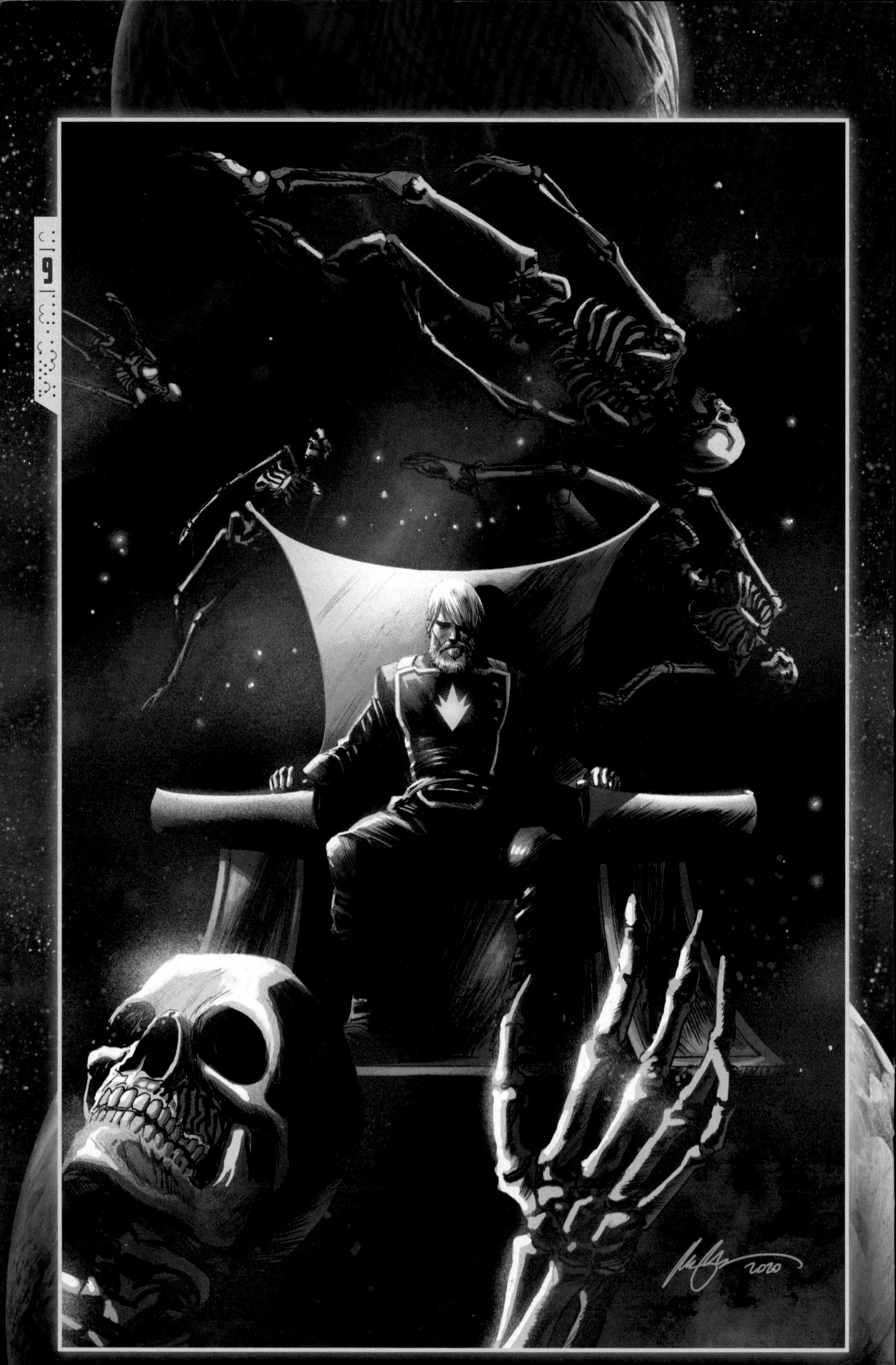
9

"I shall make you a Star-Lord."

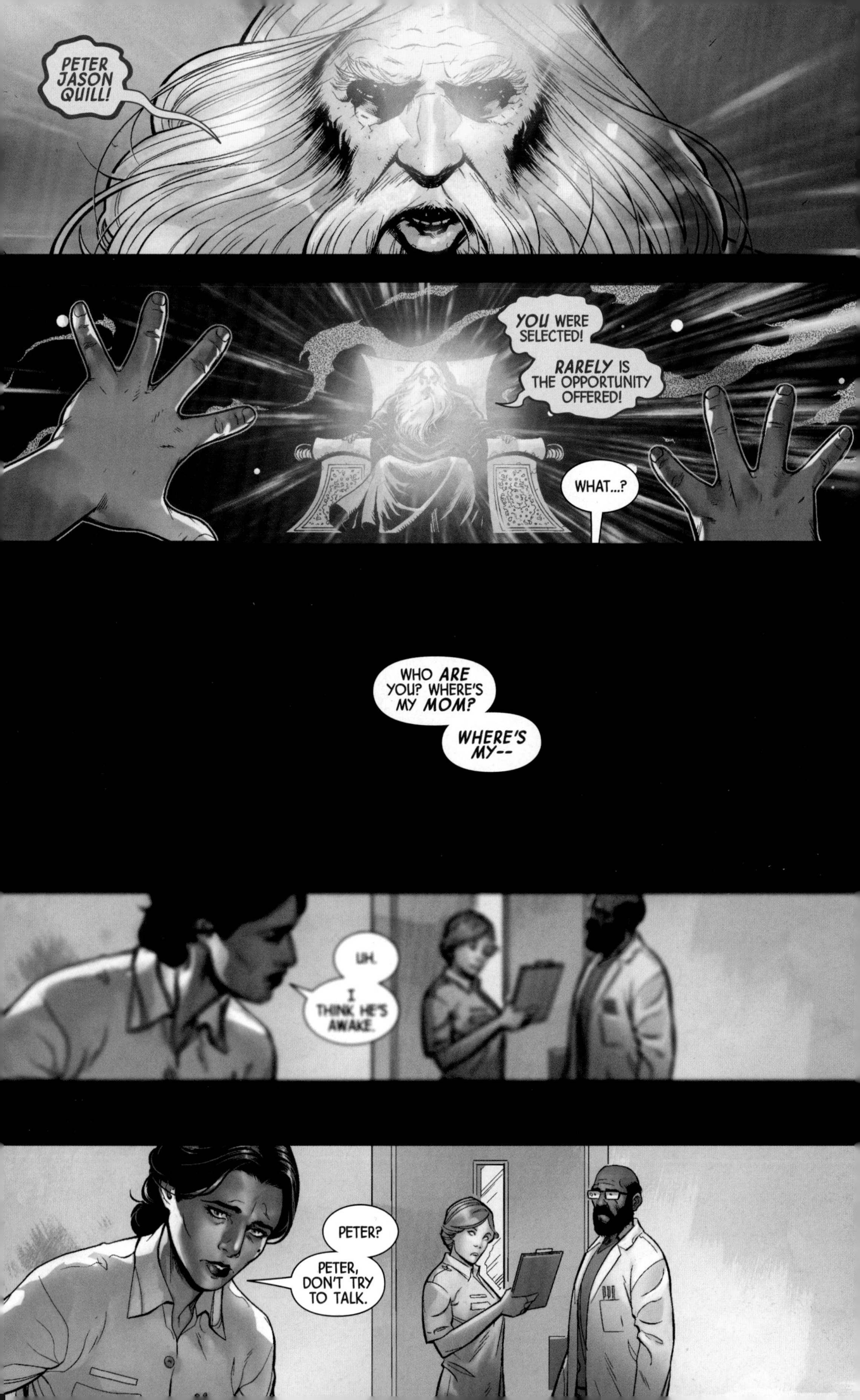
PETER JASON QUILL!
YOU WERE SELECTED!
RARELY IS THE OPPORTUNITY OFFERED!
WHAT...?
WHO ARE YOU? WHERE'S MY MOM?
WHERE'S MY--
UH.
I THINK HE'S AWAKE.
PETER?
PETER, DON'T TRY TO TALK.

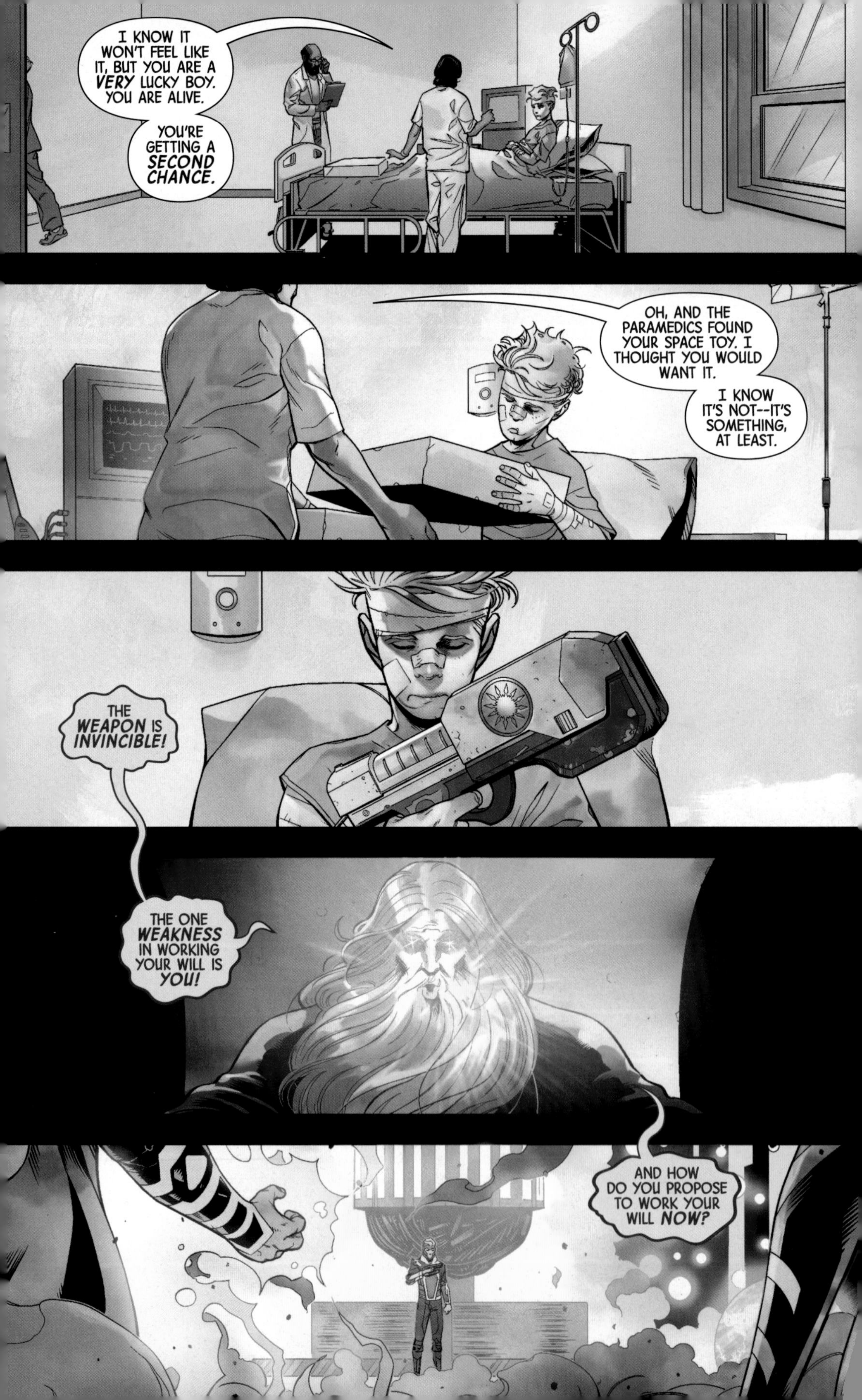
I KNOW IT WON'T FEEL LIKE IT, BUT YOU ARE A VERY LUCKY BOY. YOU ARE ALIVE.
YOU'RE GETTING A SECOND CHANCE.
OH, AND THE PARAMEDICS FOUND YOUR SPACE TOY. I THOUGHT YOU WOULD WANT IT.
I KNOW IT'S NOT--IT'S SOMETHING, AT LEAST.
THE WEAPON IS INVINCIBLE!
THE ONE WEAKNESS IN WORKING YOUR WILL IS YOU!
AND HOW DO YOU PROPOSE TO WORK YOUR WILL NOW?

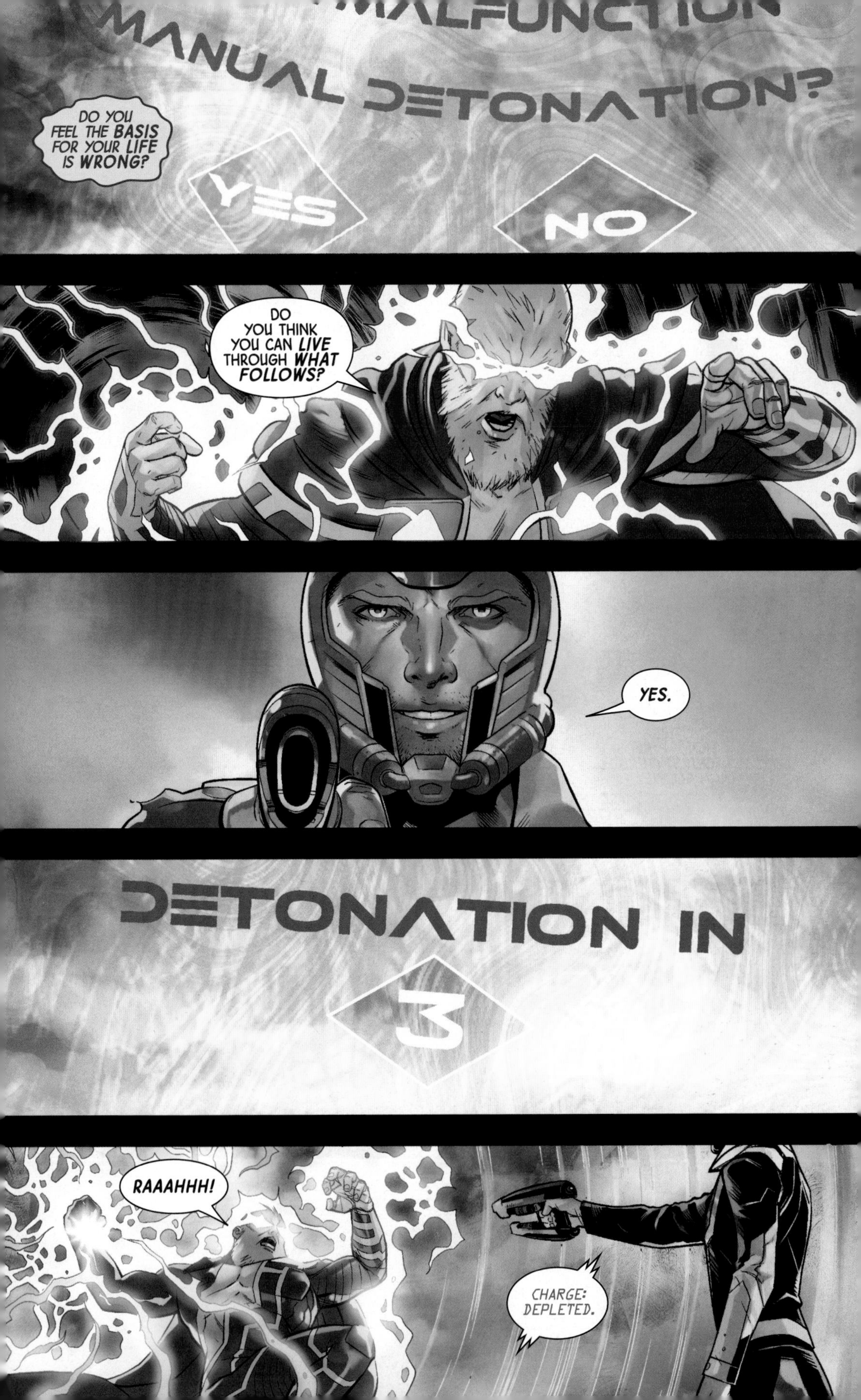
MALFUNCTION
MANUAL DETONATION?
DO YOU FEEL THE BASIS FOR YOUR LIFE IS WRONG?
YES
NO
DO YOU THINK YOU CAN LIVE THROUGH WHAT FOLLOWS?
YES.
DETONATION IN
3
RAAAHHH!
CHARGE: DEPLETED.

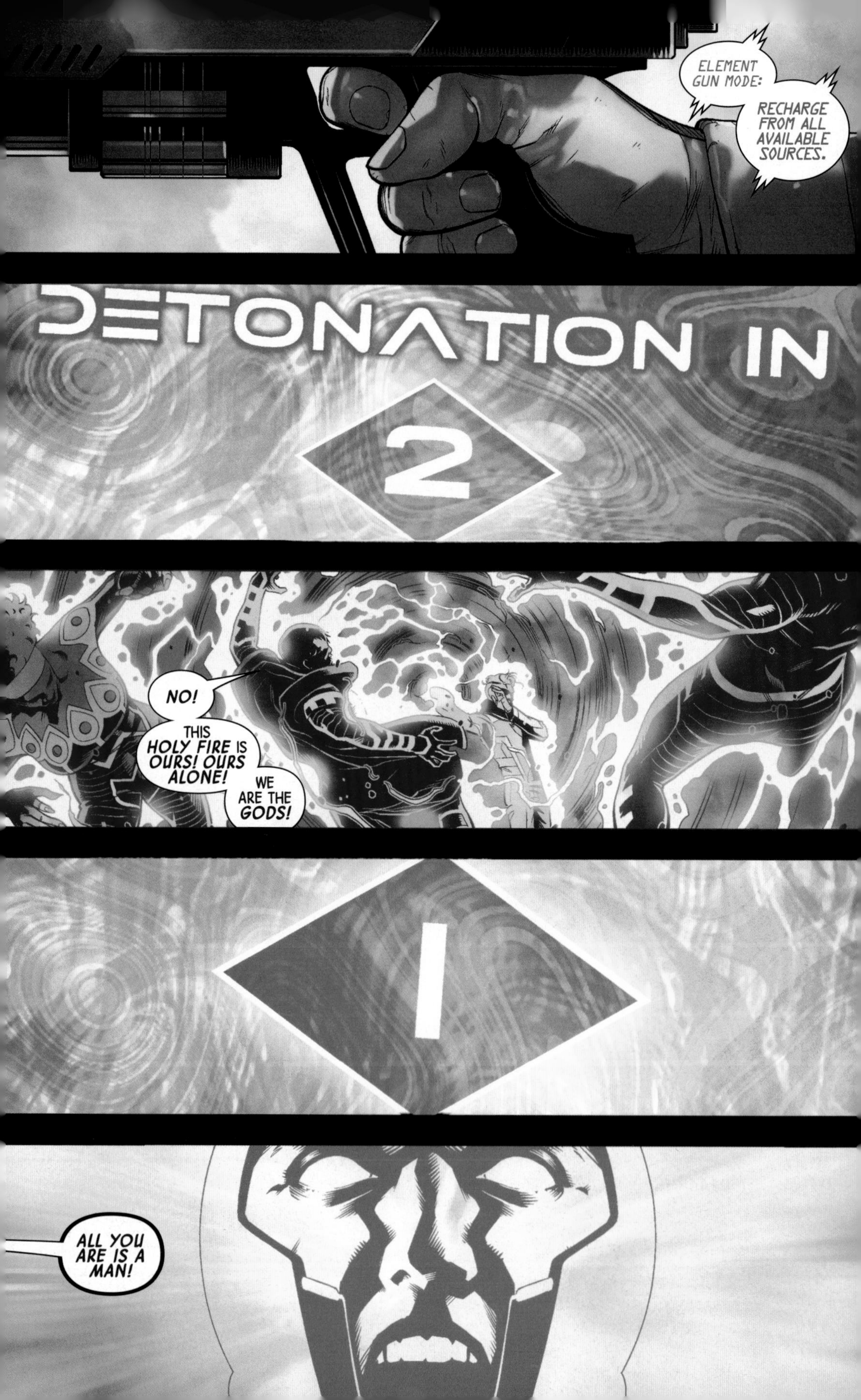
ELEMENT GUN MODE:
RECHARGE FROM ALL AVAILABLE SOURCES.
DETONATION IN
2
NO!
THIS HOLY FIRE IS OURS! OURS ALONE!
WE ARE THE GODS!
1
ALL YOU ARE IS A MAN!

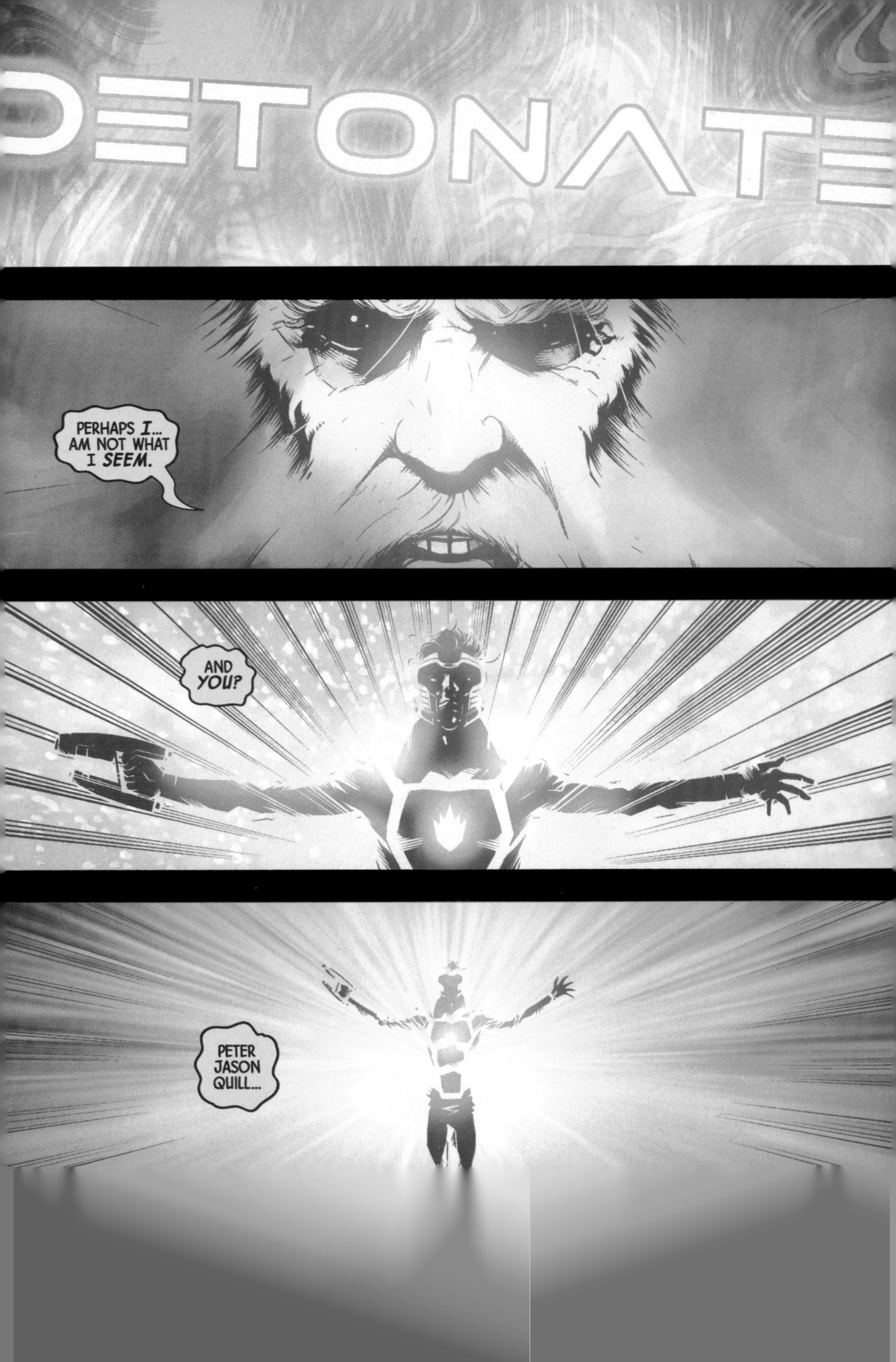
DETONATE
PERHAPS I... AM NOT WHAT I SEEM.
AND YOU?
PETER JASON QUILL...

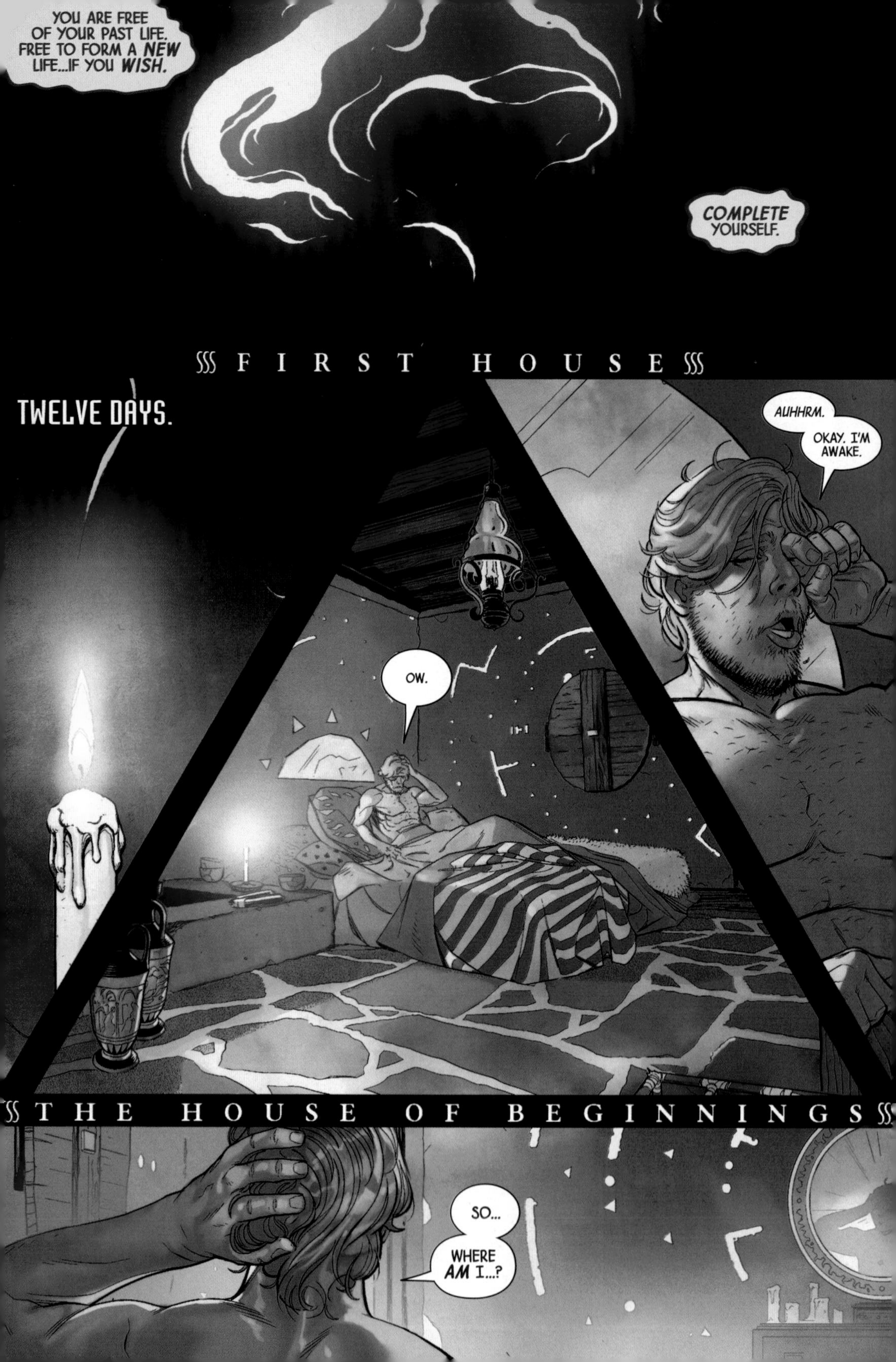
YOU ARE FREE OF YOUR PAST LIFE. FREE TO FORM A NEW LIFE...IF YOU WISH.
COMPLETE YOURSELF.
FIRST HOUSE
TWELVE DAYS.
OW.
AUHHRM.
OKAY. I'M AWAKE.
THE HOUSE OF BEGINNINGS
SO...
WHERE AM I...?

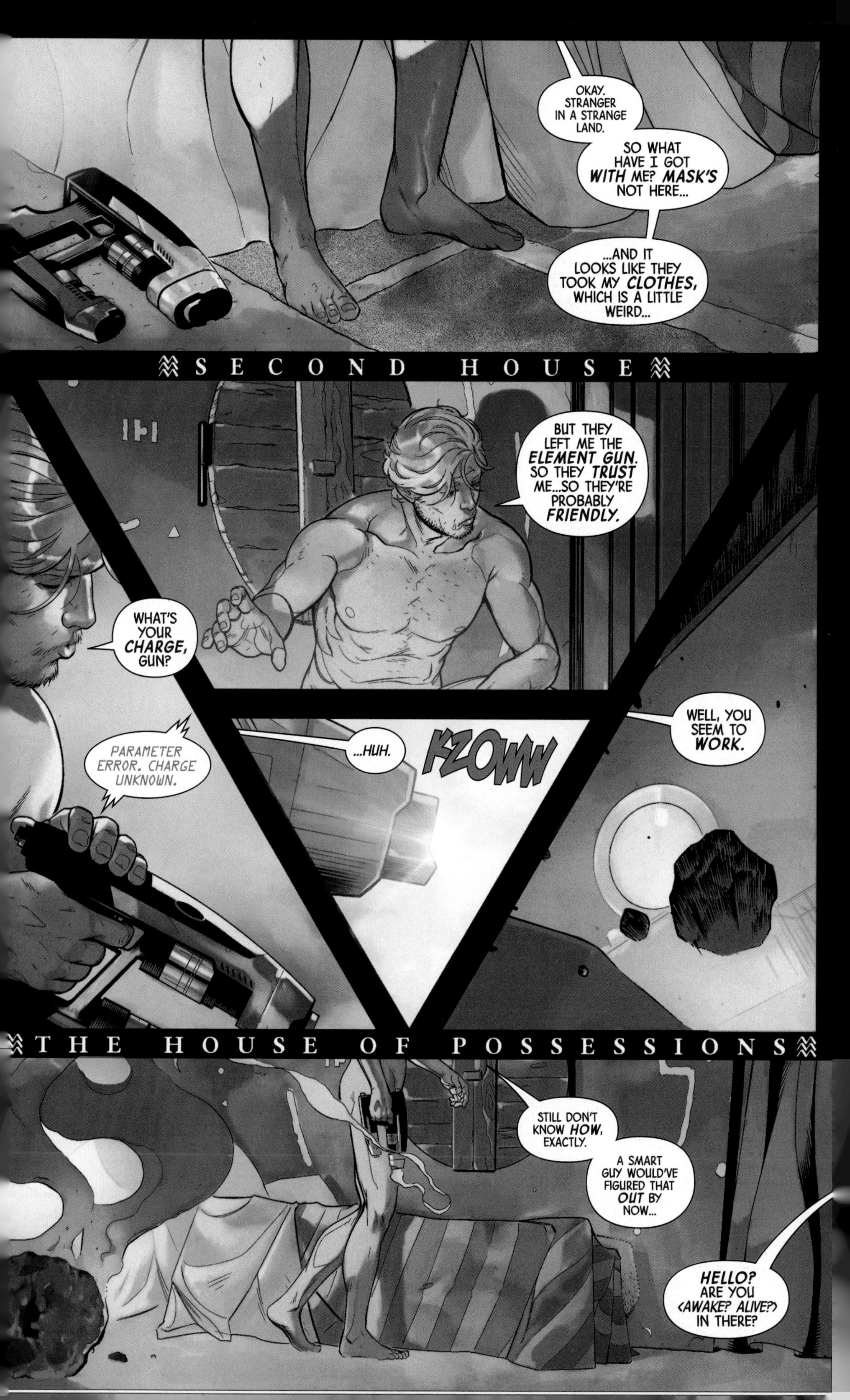

OKAY. STRANGER IN A STRANGE LAND.
SO WHAT HAVE I GOT WITH ME? MASK'S NOT HERE...
...AND IT LOOKS LIKE THEY TOOK MY CLOTHES, WHICH IS A LITTLE WEIRD...
SECOND HOUSE
BUT THEY LEFT ME THE ELEMENT GUN. SO THEY TRUST ME...SO THEY'RE PROBABLY FRIENDLY.
WHAT'S YOUR CHARGE, GUN?
PARAMETER ERROR. CHARGE UNKNOWN.
...HUH.
KZOWW
WELL, YOU SEEM TO WORK.
THE HOUSE OF POSSESSIONS
STILL DON'T KNOW HOW, EXACTLY.
A SMART GUY WOULD'VE FIGURED THAT OUT BY NOW...
HELLO? ARE YOU <AWAKE? ALIVE?> IN THERE?

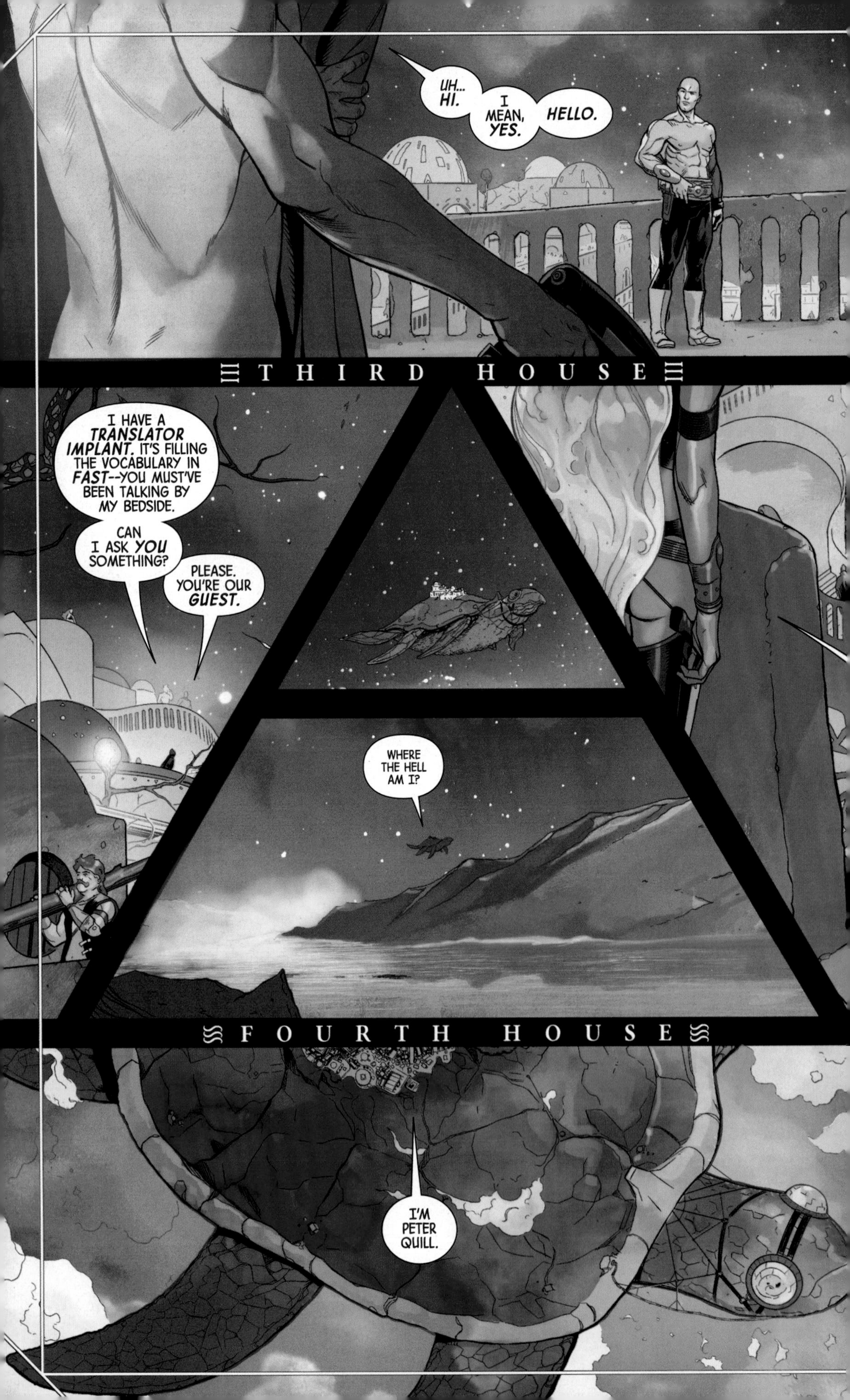
UH... HI.
I MEAN, YES.
HELLO.
THIRD HOUSE
I HAVE A TRANSLATOR IMPLANT. IT'S FILLING THE VOCABULARY IN FAST--YOU MUST'VE BEEN TALKING BY MY BEDSIDE.
CAN I ASK YOU SOMETHING?
PLEASE. YOU'RE OUR GUEST.
WHERE THE HELL AM I?
FOURTH HOUSE
I'M PETER QUILL.

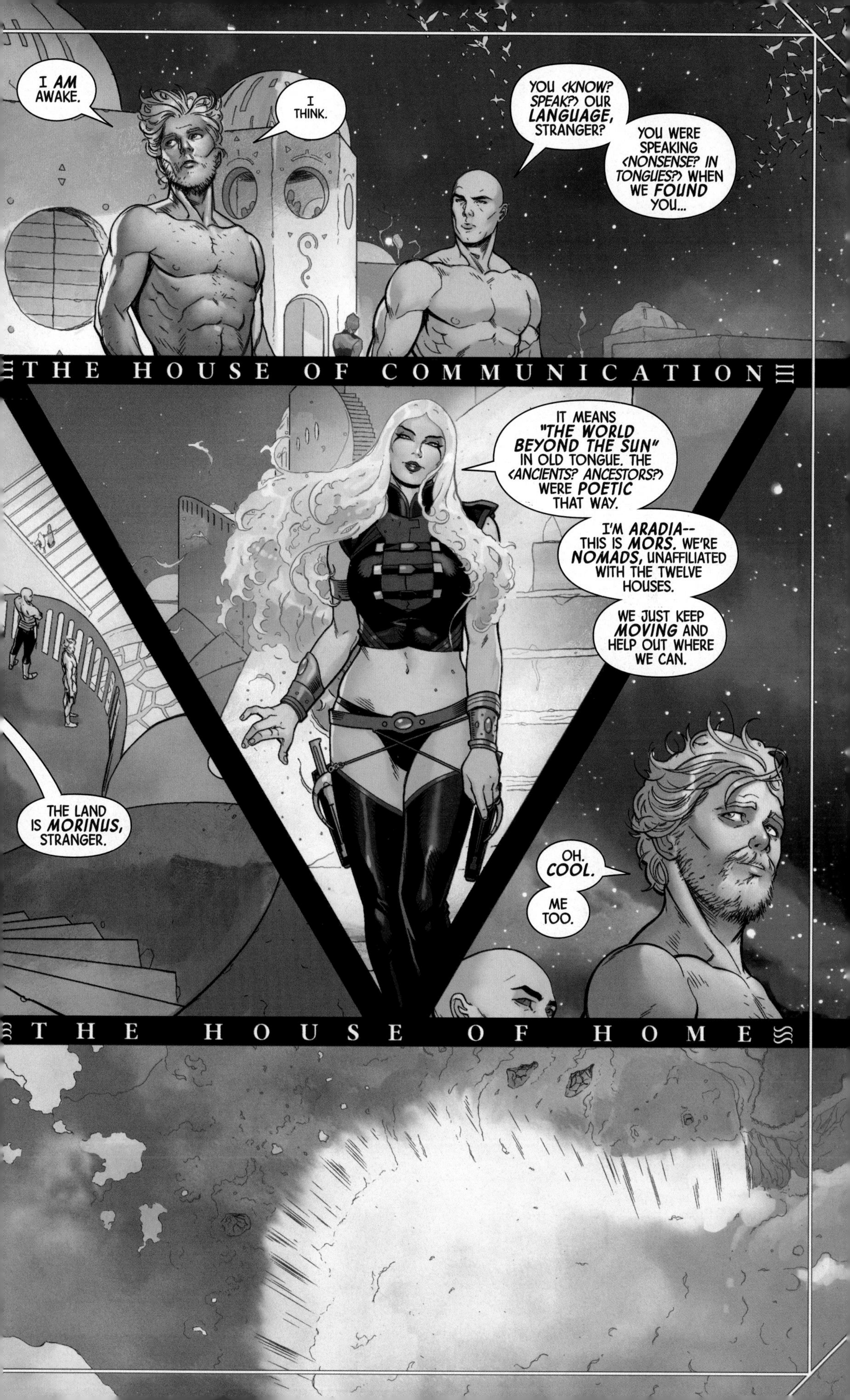
I AM AWAKE.
I THINK.
YOU <KNOW? SPEAK?> OUR LANGUAGE, STRANGER?
YOU WERE SPEAKING <NONSENSE? IN TONGUES?> WHEN WE FOUND YOU...
THE HOUSE OF COMMUNICATION
THE LAND IS MORINUS, STRANGER.
IT MEANS "THE WORLD BEYOND THE SUN" IN OLD TONGUE. THE <ANCIENTS? ANCESTORS?> WERE POETIC THAT WAY.
I'M ARADIA-- THIS IS MORS. WE'RE NOMADS, UNAFFILIATED WITH THE TWELVE HOUSES.
WE JUST KEEP MOVING AND HELP OUT WHERE WE CAN.
OH. COOL.
ME TOO.
THE HOUSE OF HOME

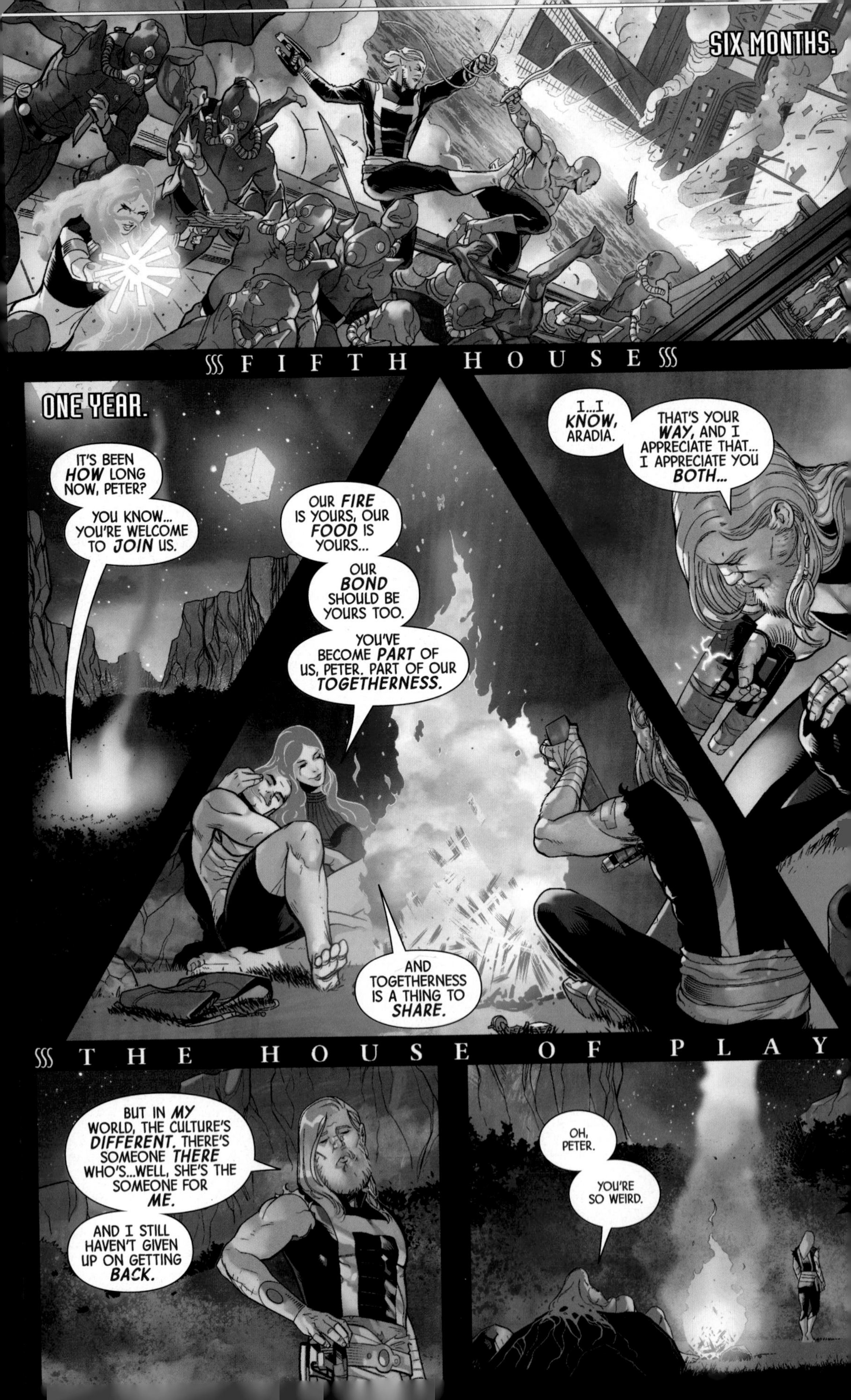
SIX MONTHS.
FIFTH HOUSE
ONE YEAR.
IT'S BEEN HOW LONG NOW, PETER?
YOU KNOW... YOU'RE WELCOME TO JOIN US.
OUR FIRE IS YOURS, OUR FOOD IS YOURS...
OUR BOND SHOULD BE YOURS TOO.
YOU'VE BECOME PART OF US, PETER. PART OF OUR TOGETHERNESS.
AND TOGETHERNESS IS A THING TO SHARE.
I...I KNOW, ARADIA.
THAT'S YOUR WAY, AND I APPRECIATE THAT... I APPRECIATE YOU BOTH...
THE HOUSE OF PLAY
BUT IN MY WORLD, THE CULTURE'S DIFFERENT. THERE'S SOMEONE THERE WHO'S...WELL, SHE'S THE SOMEONE FOR ME.
AND I STILL HAVEN'T GIVEN UP ON GETTING BACK.
OH, PETER.
YOU'RE SO WEIRD.

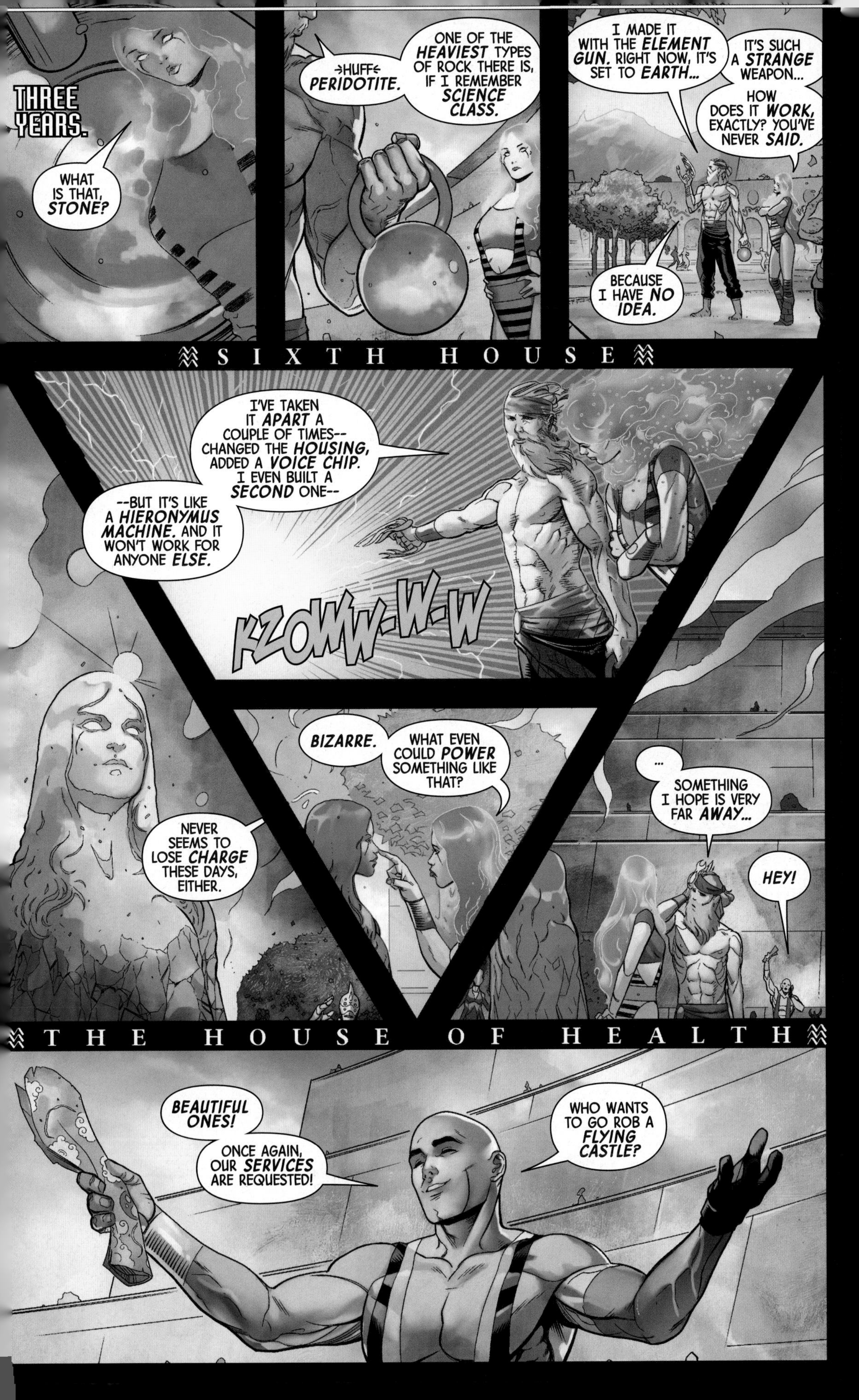
THREE YEARS.
WHAT IS THAT, STONE?
→HUFF← PERIDOTITE.
ONE OF THE HEAVIEST TYPES OF ROCK THERE IS, IF I REMEMBER SCIENCE CLASS.
I MADE IT WITH THE ELEMENT GUN. RIGHT NOW, IT'S SET TO EARTH...
IT'S SUCH A STRANGE WEAPON...
HOW DOES IT WORK, EXACTLY? YOU'VE NEVER SAID.
BECAUSE I HAVE NO IDEA.
SIXTH HOUSE
I'VE TAKEN IT APART A COUPLE OF TIMES-- CHANGED THE HOUSING, ADDED A VOICE CHIP. I EVEN BUILT A SECOND ONE--
--BUT IT'S LIKE A HIERONYMUS MACHINE. AND IT WON'T WORK FOR ANYONE ELSE.
KZOWW-W-W
NEVER SEEMS TO LOSE CHARGE THESE DAYS, EITHER.
BIZARRE.
WHAT EVEN COULD POWER SOMETHING LIKE THAT?
...
SOMETHING I HOPE IS VERY FAR AWAY...
HEY!
THE HOUSE OF HEALTH
BEAUTIFUL ONES!
ONCE AGAIN, OUR SERVICES ARE REQUESTED!
WHO WANTS TO GO ROB A FLYING CASTLE?

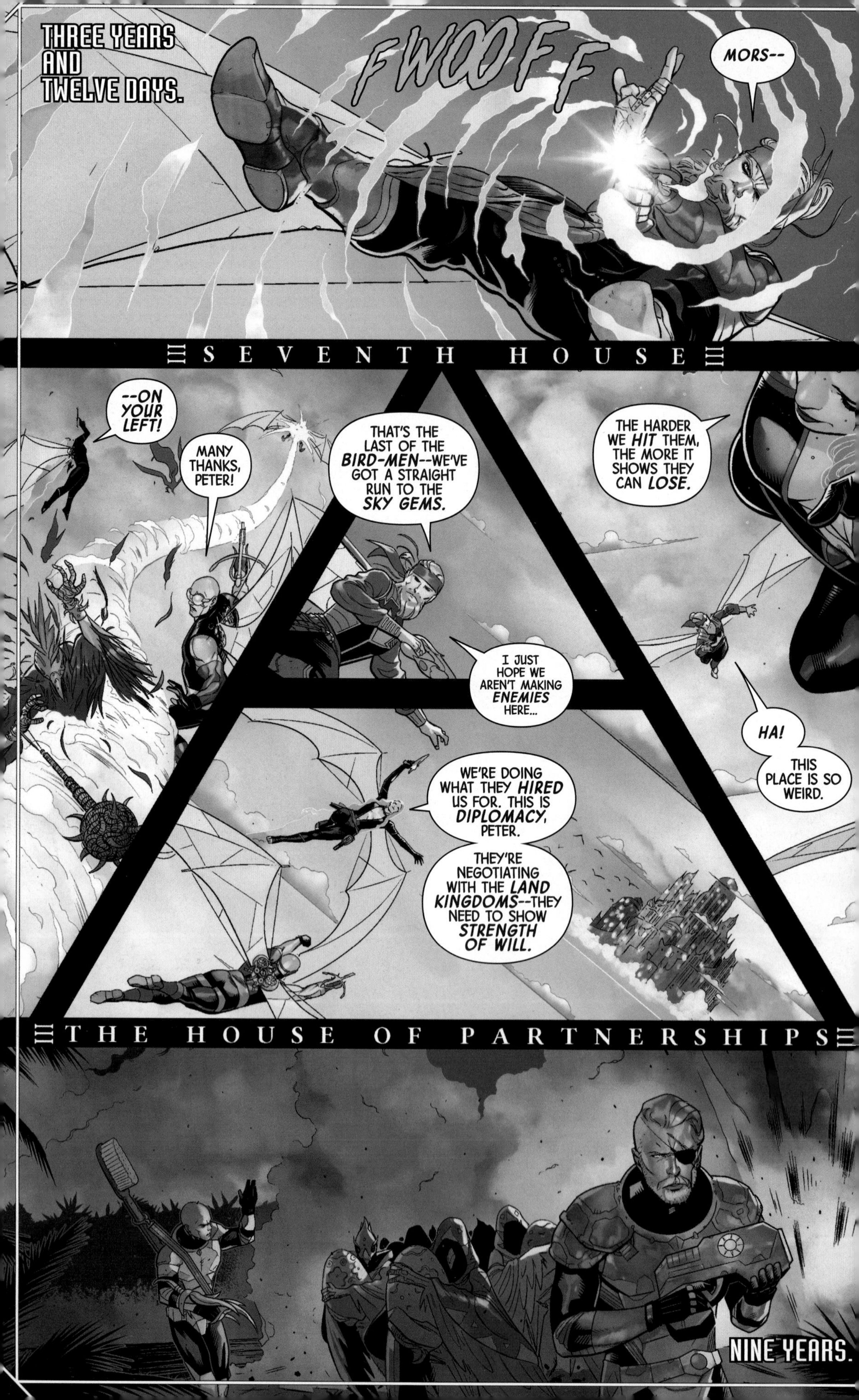
THREE YEARS AND TWELVE DAYS.
FWOOFFF
MORS--
SEVENTH HOUSE
--ON YOUR LEFT!
MANY THANKS, PETER!
THAT'S THE LAST OF THE BIRD-MEN--WE'VE GOT A STRAIGHT RUN TO THE SKY GEMS.
THE HARDER WE HIT THEM, THE MORE IT SHOWS THEY CAN LOSE.
I JUST HOPE WE AREN'T MAKING ENEMIES HERE...
WE'RE DOING WHAT THEY HIRED US FOR. THIS IS DIPLOMACY, PETER.
THEY'RE NEGOTIATING WITH THE LAND KINGDOMS--THEY NEED TO SHOW STRENGTH OF WILL.
HA!
THIS PLACE IS SO WEIRD.
THE HOUSE OF PARTNERSHIPS
NINE YEARS.

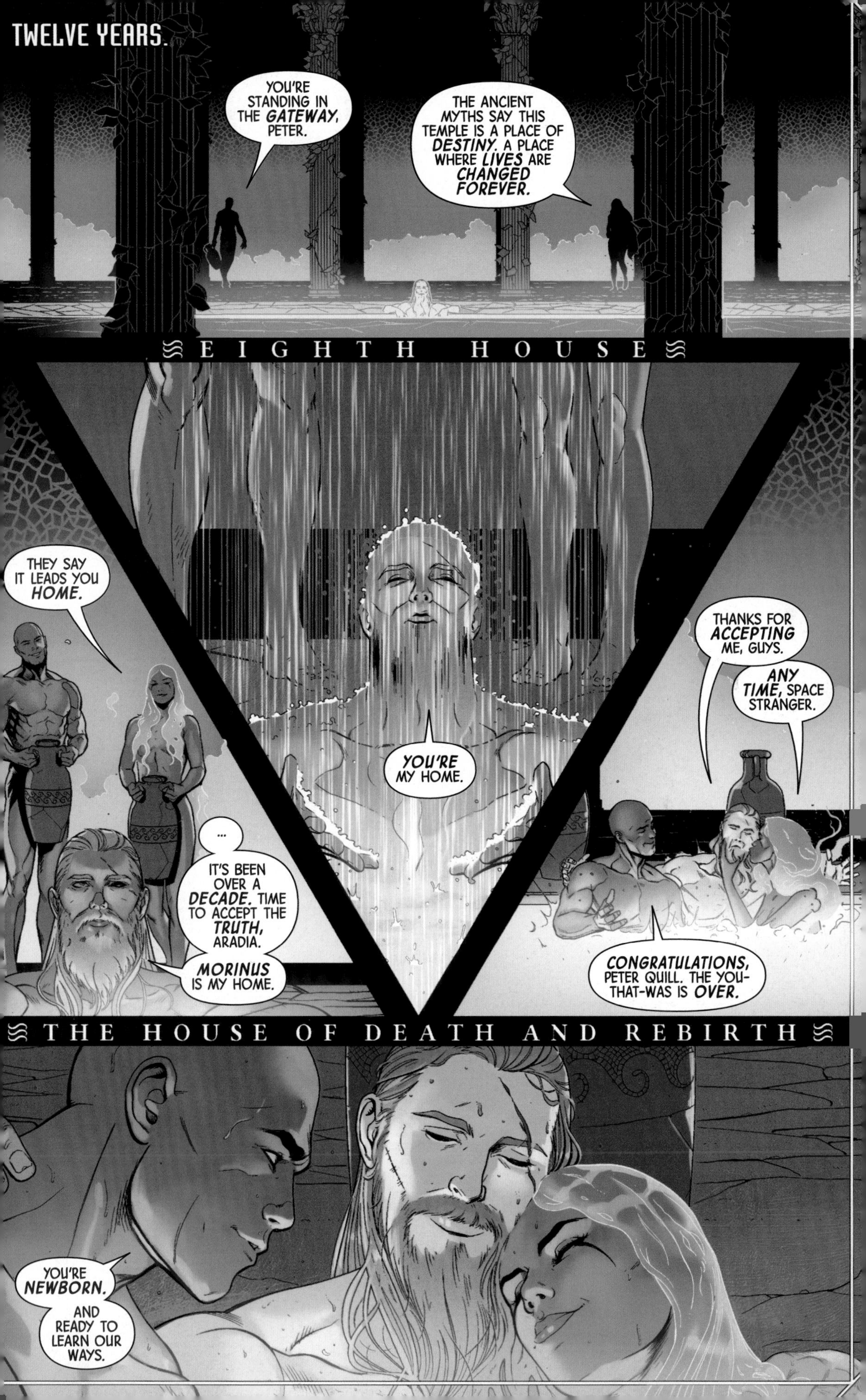
TWELVE YEARS.
YOU'RE STANDING IN THE GATEWAY, PETER.
THE ANCIENT MYTHS SAY THIS TEMPLE IS A PLACE OF DESTINY. A PLACE WHERE LIVES ARE CHANGED FOREVER.
EIGHTH HOUSE
THEY SAY IT LEADS YOU HOME.
...
IT'S BEEN OVER A DECADE. TIME TO ACCEPT THE TRUTH, ARADIA.
MORINUS IS MY HOME.
YOU'RE MY HOME.
THANKS FOR ACCEPTING ME, GUYS.
ANY TIME, SPACE STRANGER.
CONGRATULATIONS, PETER QUILL. THE YOU-THAT-WAS IS OVER.
THE HOUSE OF DEATH AND REBIRTH
YOU'RE NEWBORN.
AND READY TO LEARN OUR WAYS.

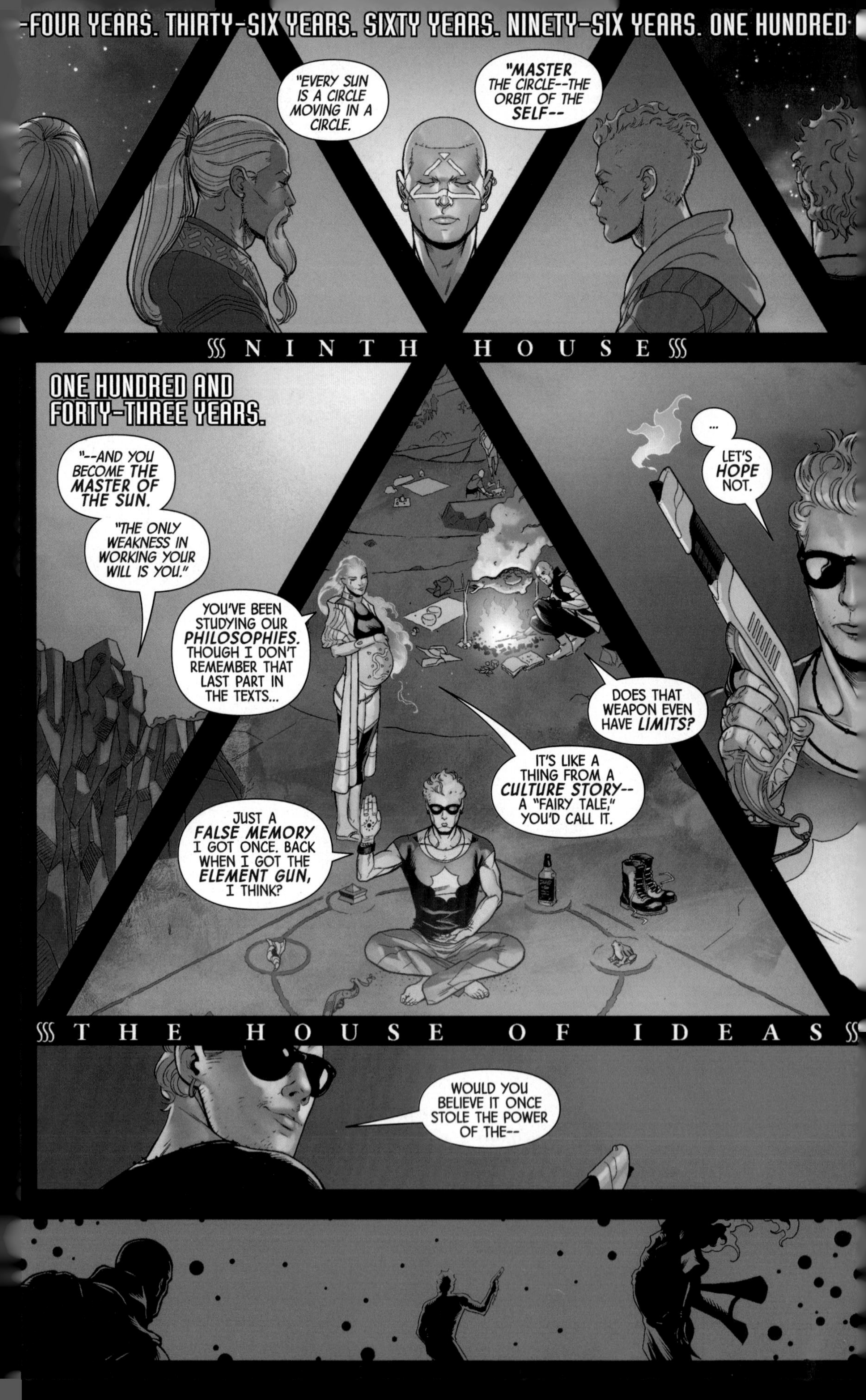
-FOUR YEARS. THIRTY-SIX YEARS. SIXTY YEARS. NINETY-SIX YEARS. ONE HUNDRED
"EVERY SUN IS A CIRCLE MOVING IN A CIRCLE.
"MASTER THE CIRCLE--THE ORBIT OF THE SELF--
NINTH HOUSE
ONE HUNDRED AND FORTY-THREE YEARS.
"--AND YOU BECOME THE MASTER OF THE SUN.
"THE ONLY WEAKNESS IN WORKING YOUR WILL IS YOU."
YOU'VE BEEN STUDYING OUR PHILOSOPHIES. THOUGH I DON'T REMEMBER THAT LAST PART IN THE TEXTS...
JUST A FALSE MEMORY I GOT ONCE. BACK WHEN I GOT THE ELEMENT GUN, I THINK?
IT'S LIKE A THING FROM A CULTURE STORY-- A "FAIRY TALE," YOU'D CALL IT.
DOES THAT WEAPON EVEN HAVE LIMITS?
...
LET'S HOPE NOT.
THE HOUSE OF IDEAS
WOULD YOU BELIEVE IT ONCE STOLE THE POWER OF THE--

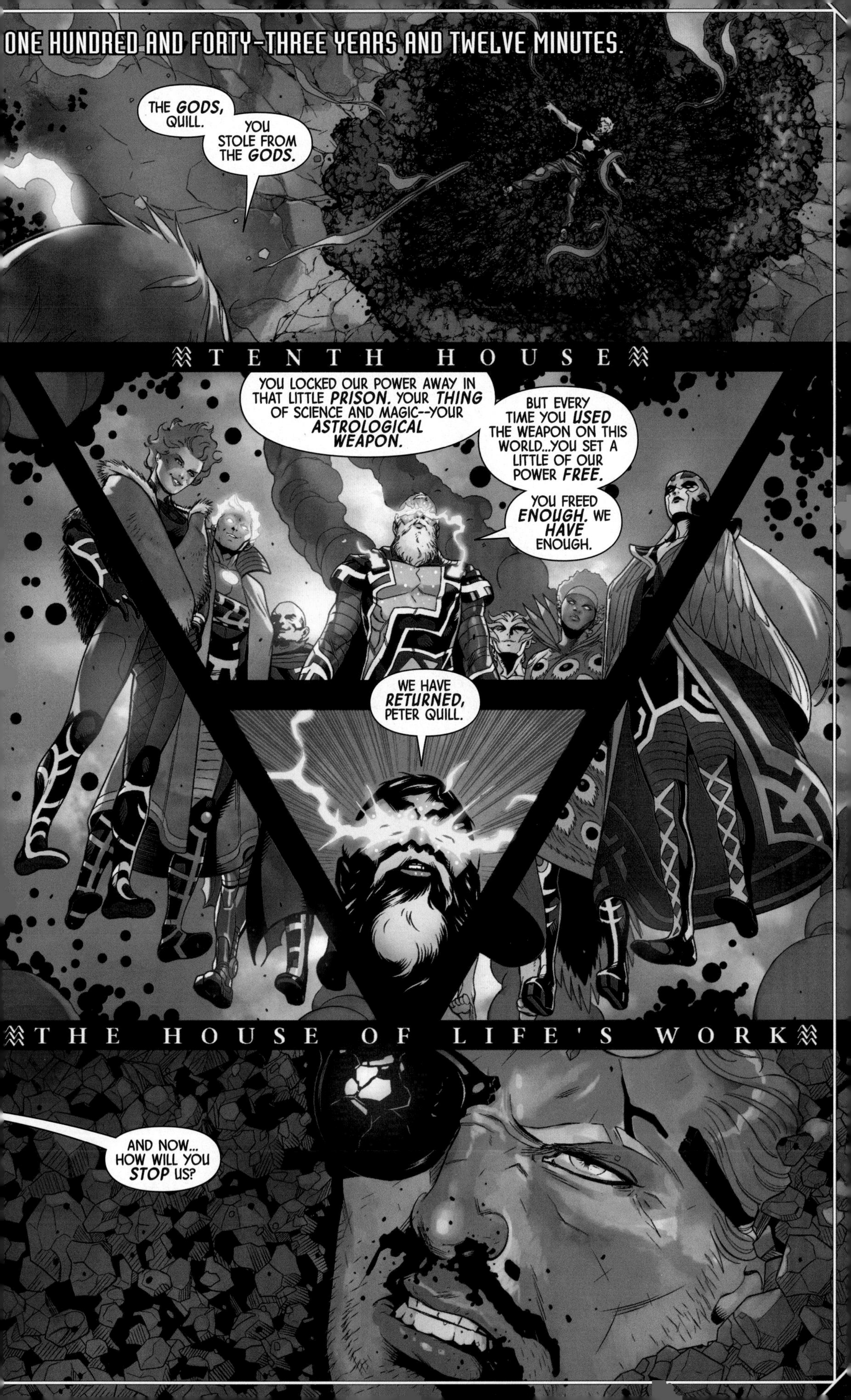
ONE HUNDRED AND FORTY-THREE YEARS AND TWELVE MINUTES.
THE GODS, QUILL.
YOU STOLE FROM THE GODS.
TENTH HOUSE
YOU LOCKED OUR POWER AWAY IN THAT LITTLE PRISON. YOUR THING OF SCIENCE AND MAGIC--YOUR ASTROLOGICAL WEAPON.
BUT EVERY TIME YOU USED THE WEAPON ON THIS WORLD...YOU SET A LITTLE OF OUR POWER FREE.
YOU FREED ENOUGH. WE HAVE ENOUGH.
WE HAVE RETURNED, PETER QUILL.
THE HOUSE OF LIFE'S WORK
AND NOW... HOW WILL YOU STOP US?

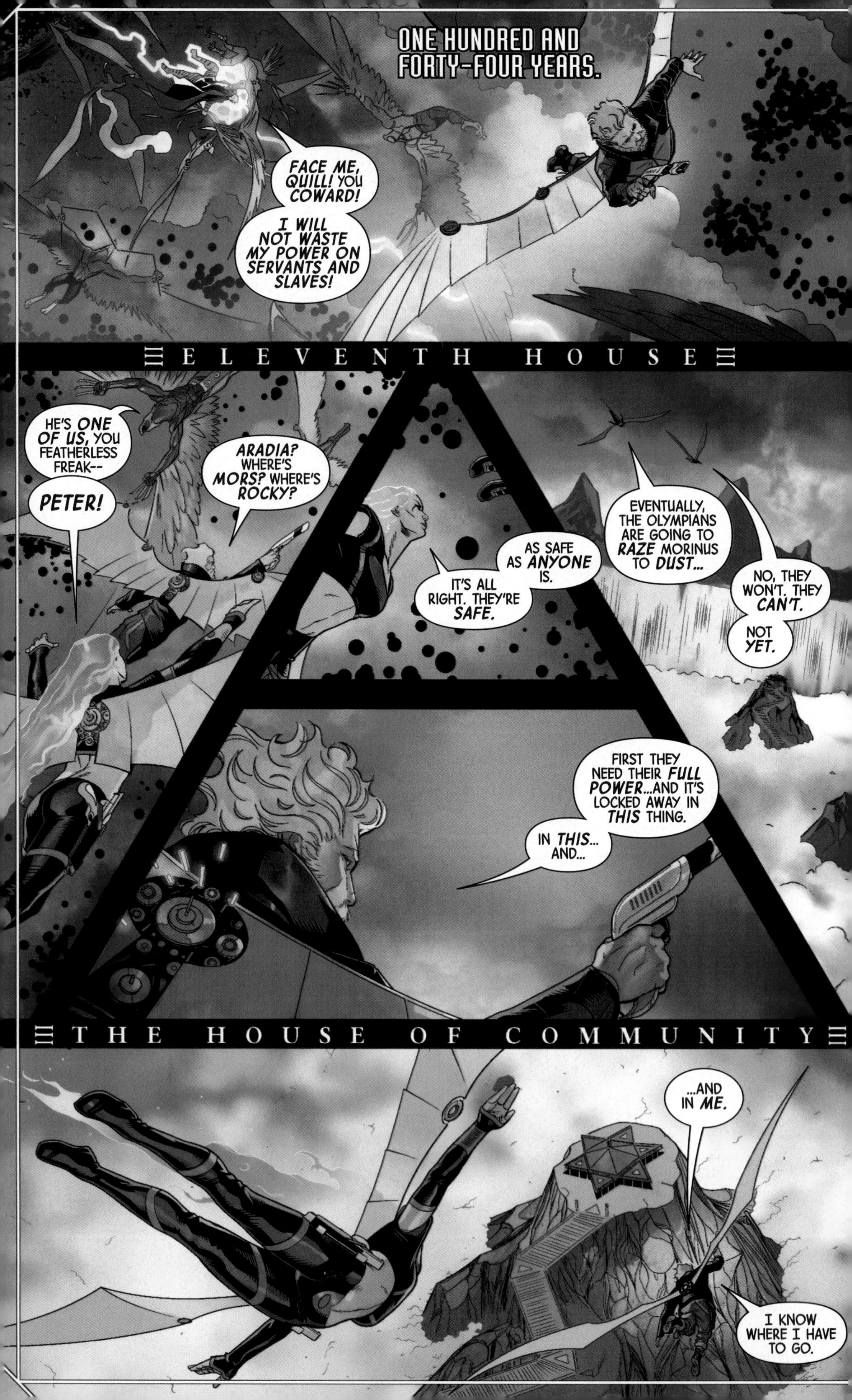
ONE HUNDRED AND FORTY-FOUR YEARS.
FACE ME, QUILL! YOU COWARD!
I WILL NOT WASTE MY POWER ON SERVANTS AND SLAVES!
ELEVENTH HOUSE
HE'S ONE OF US, YOU FEATHERLESS FREAK--
PETER!
ARADIA? WHERE'S MORS? WHERE'S ROCKY?
IT'S ALL RIGHT. THEY'RE SAFE.
AS SAFE AS ANYONE IS.
EVENTUALLY, THE OLYMPIANS ARE GOING TO RAZE MORINUS TO DUST...
NO, THEY WON'T. THEY CAN'T.
NOT YET.
FIRST THEY NEED THEIR FULL POWER...AND IT'S LOCKED AWAY IN THIS THING.
IN THIS... AND...
THE HOUSE OF COMMUNITY
...AND IN ME.
I KNOW WHERE I HAVE TO GO.

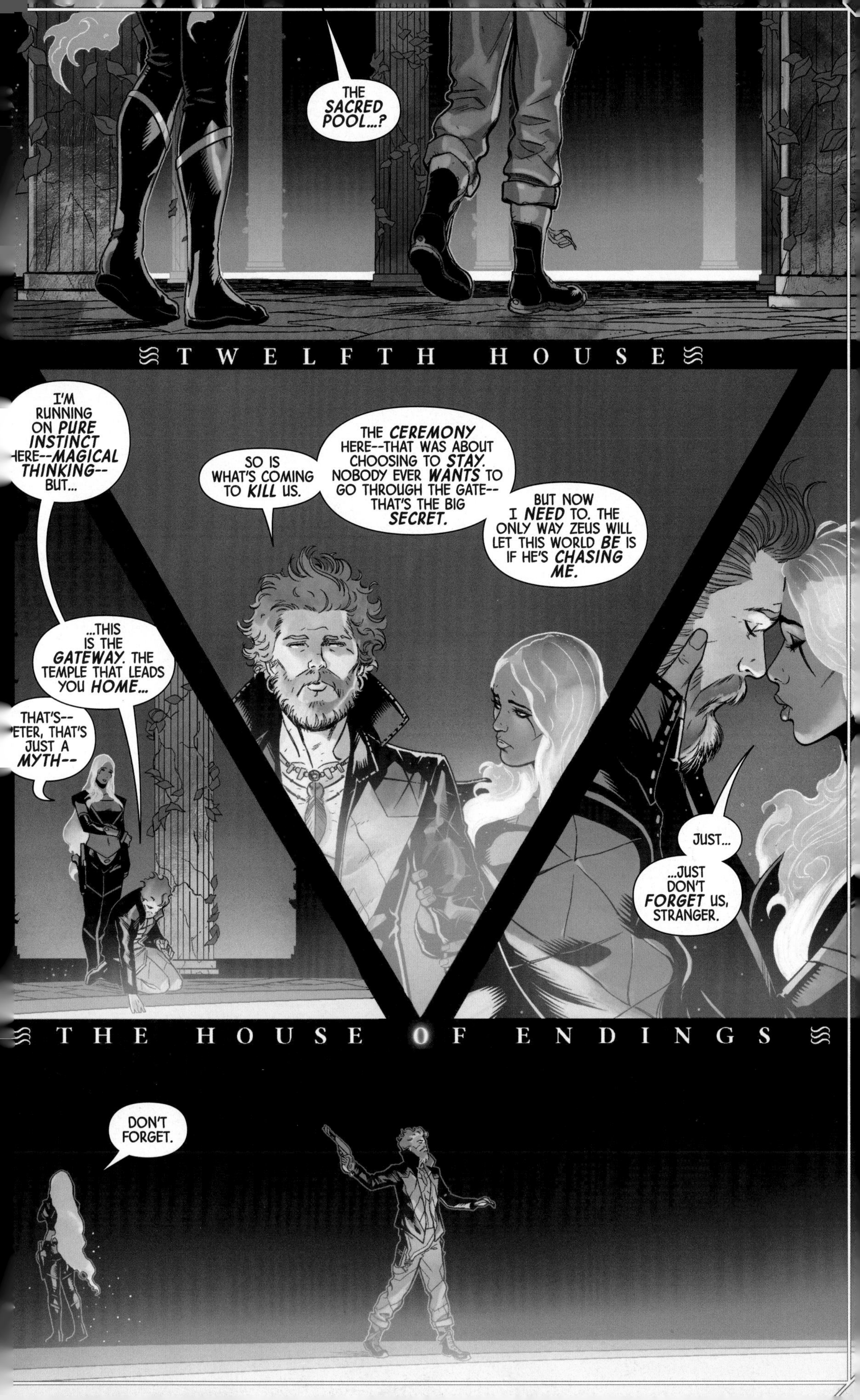

THE SACRED POOL...?
TWELFTH HOUSE
I'M RUNNING ON PURE INSTINCT ERE--MAGICAL THINKING-- BUT...
...THIS IS THE GATEWAY. THE TEMPLE THAT LEADS YOU HOME...
THAT'S-- ETER, THAT'S JUST A MYTH--
SO IS WHAT'S COMING TO KILL US.
THE CEREMONY HERE--THAT WAS ABOUT CHOOSING TO STAY. NOBODY EVER WANTS TO GO THROUGH THE GATE-- THAT'S THE BIG SECRET.
BUT NOW I NEED TO. THE ONLY WAY ZEUS WILL LET THIS WORLD BE IS IF HE'S CHASING ME.
JUST...
...JUST DON'T FORGET US, STRANGER.
THE HOUSE OF ENDINGS
DON'T FORGET.

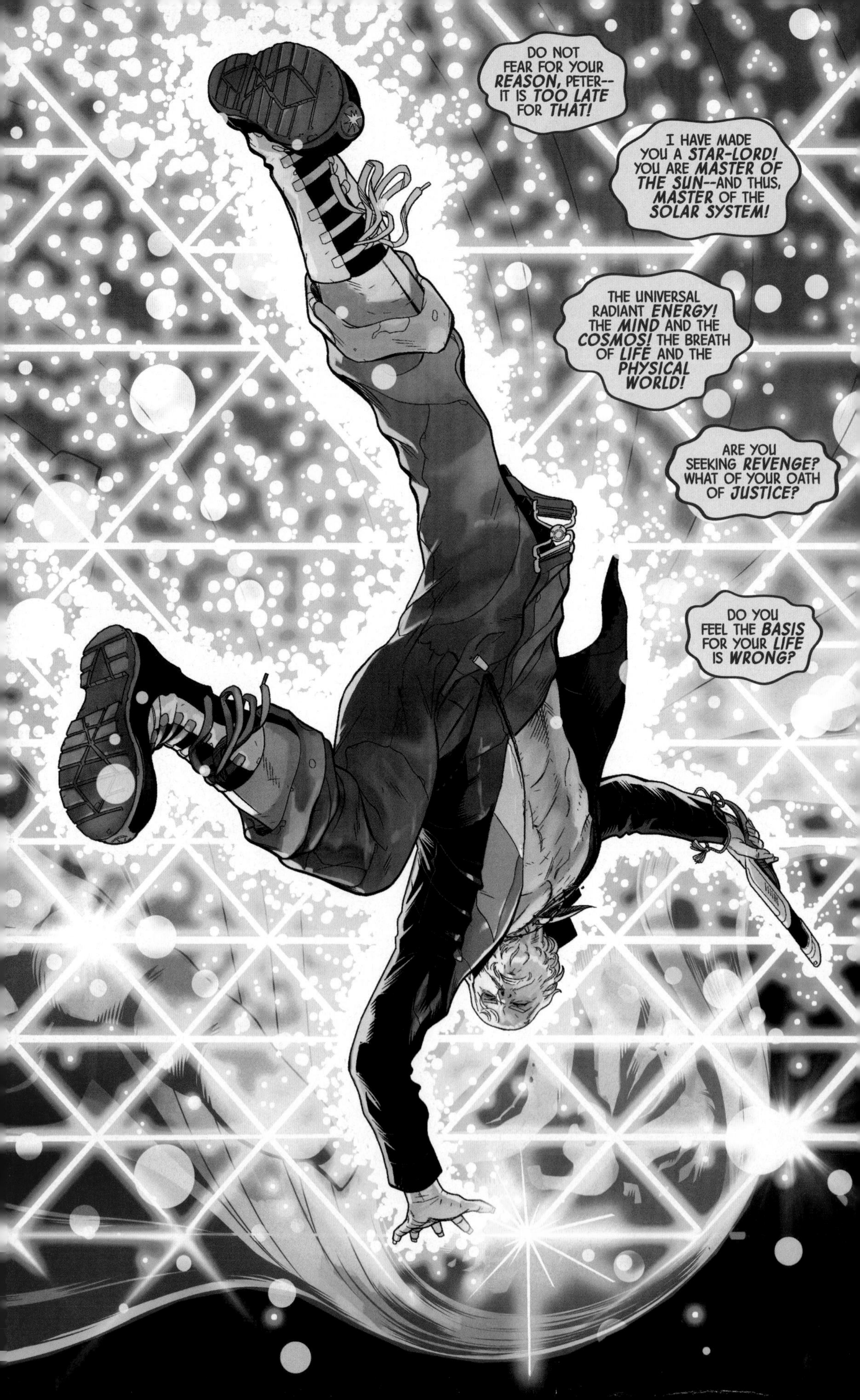
DO NOT FEAR FOR YOUR REASON, PETER-- IT IS TOO LATE FOR THAT!
I HAVE MADE YOU A STAR-LORD! YOU ARE MASTER OF THE SUN--AND THUS, MASTER OF THE SOLAR SYSTEM!
THE UNIVERSAL RADIANT ENERGY! THE MIND AND THE COSMOS! THE BREATH OF LIFE AND THE PHYSICAL WORLD!
ARE YOU SEEKING REVENGE? WHAT OF YOUR OATH OF JUSTICE?
DO YOU FEEL THE BASIS FOR YOUR LIFE IS WRONG?

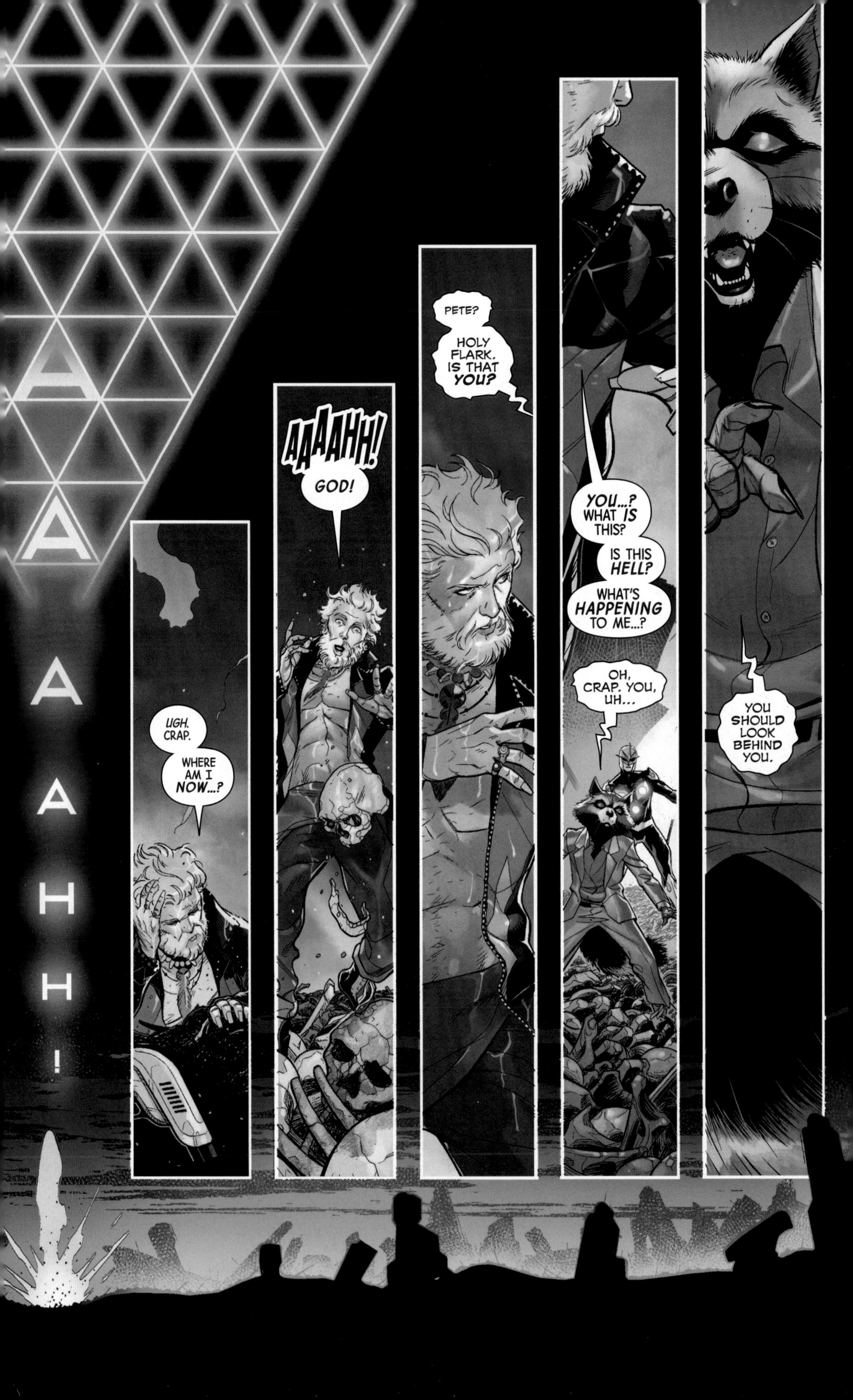
AAAHH!
UGH. CRAP.
WHERE AM I NOW...?
AAAAHH!
GOD!
PETE?
HOLY FLARK. IS THAT YOU?
YOU...? WHAT IS THIS?
IS THIS HELL?
WHAT'S HAPPENING TO ME...?
OH, CRAP. YOU, UH...
YOU SHOULD LOOK BEHIND YOU.

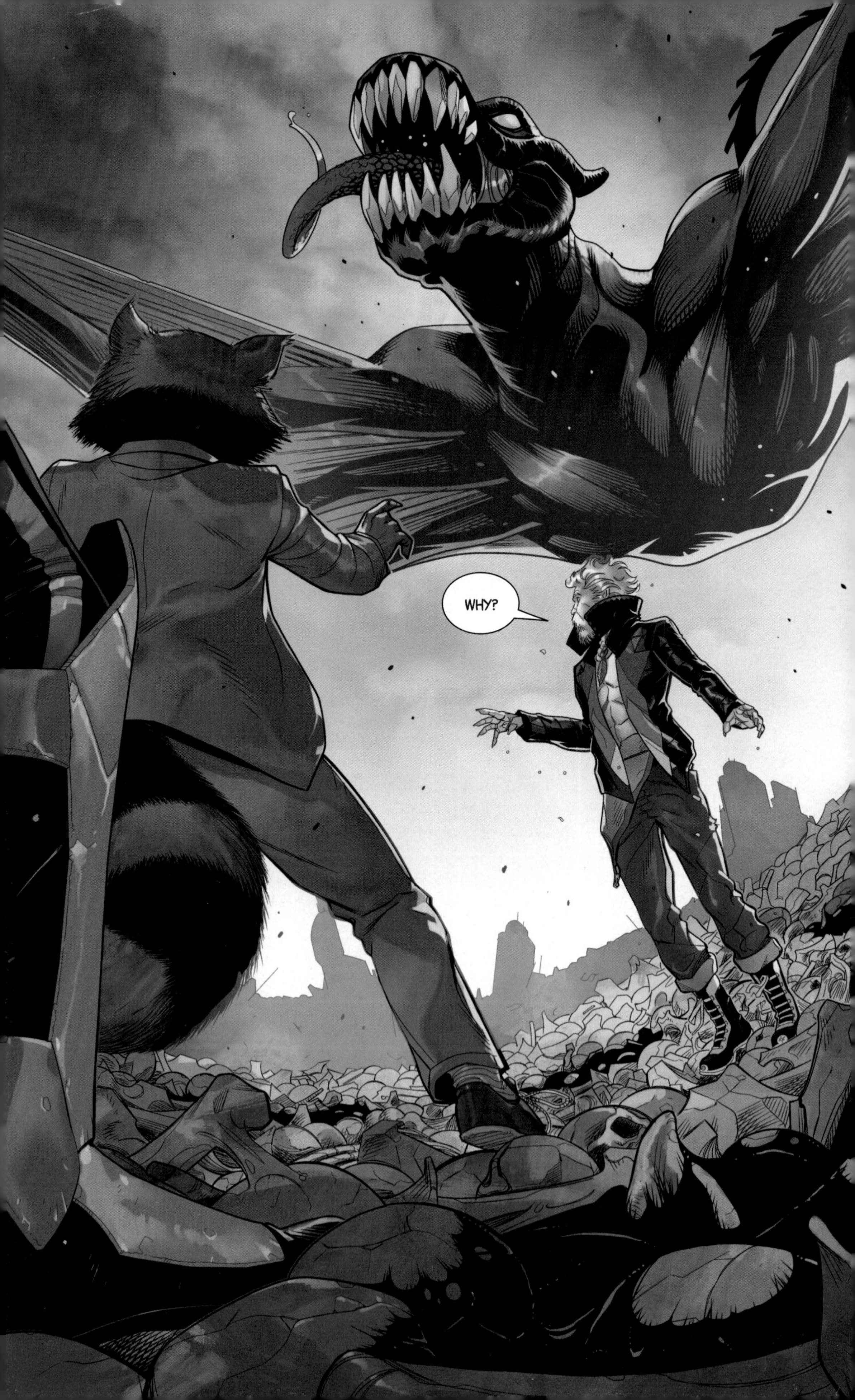
WHY?

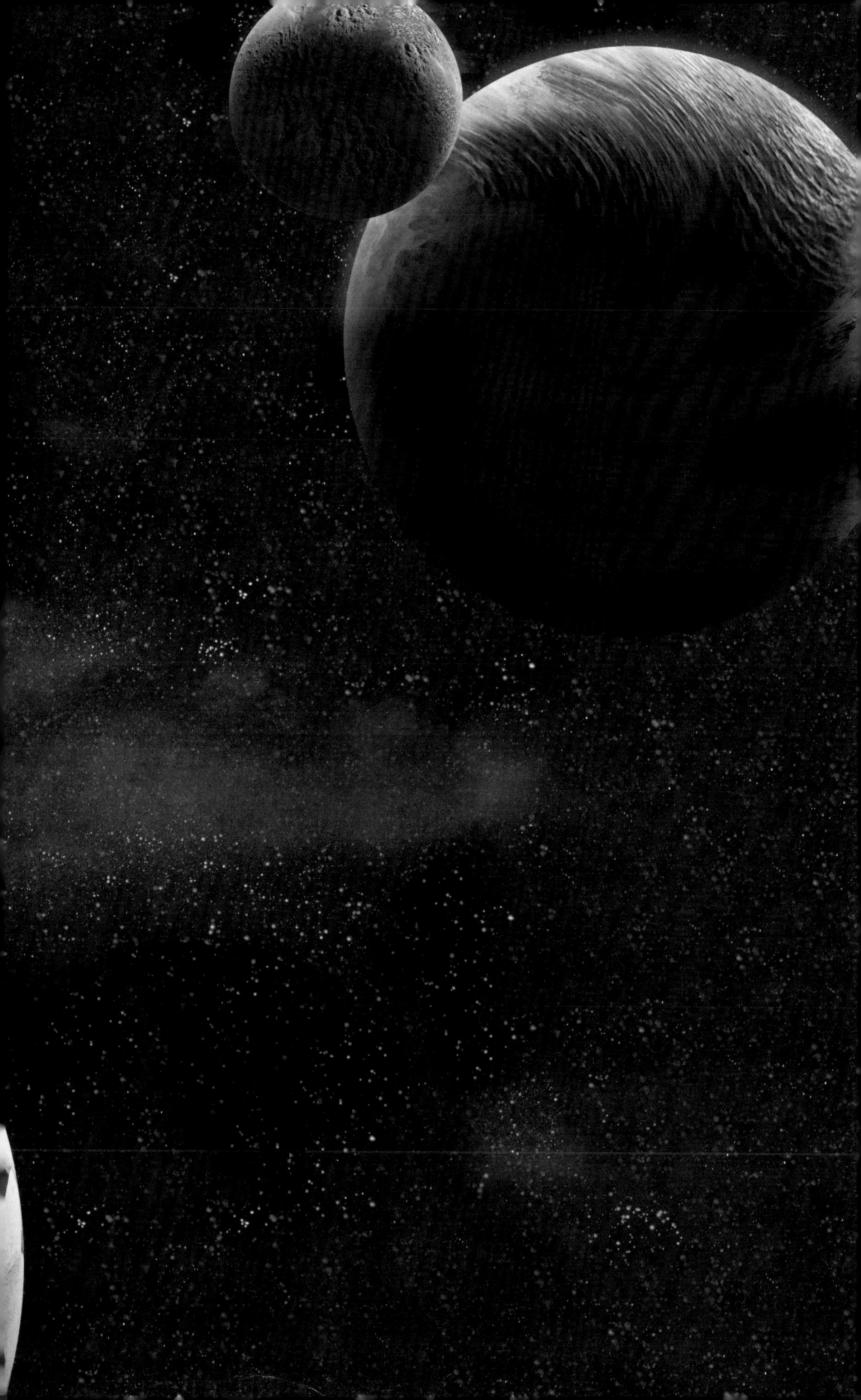

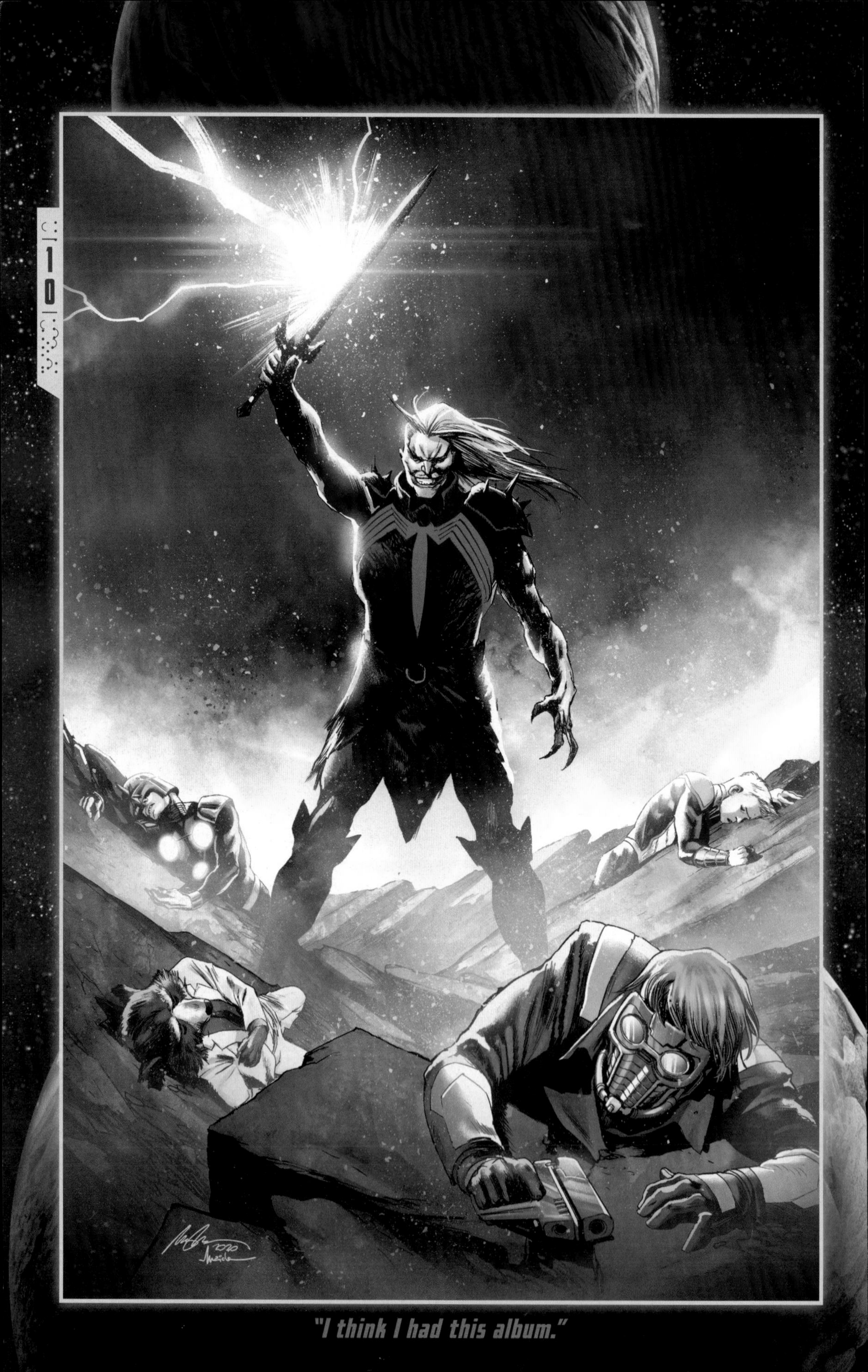
10

"I think I had this album."

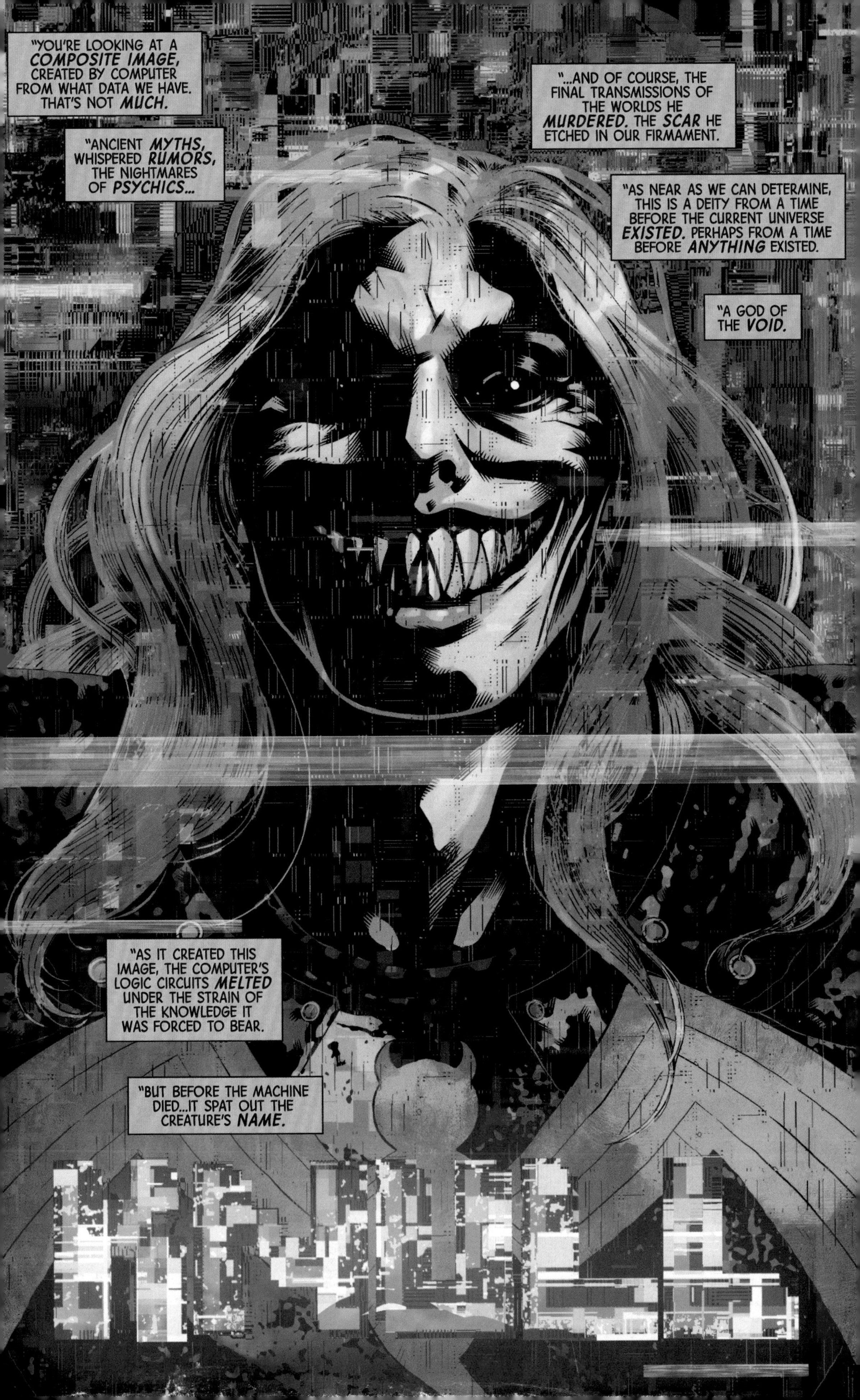
"YOU'RE LOOKING AT A COMPOSITE IMAGE, CREATED BY COMPUTER FROM WHAT DATA WE HAVE. THAT'S NOT MUCH.
"ANCIENT MYTHS, WHISPERED RUMORS, THE NIGHTMARES OF PSYCHICS...
"...AND OF COURSE, THE FINAL TRANSMISSIONS OF THE WORLDS HE MURDERED. THE SCAR HE ETCHED IN OUR FIRMAMENT.
"AS NEAR AS WE CAN DETERMINE, THIS IS A DEITY FROM A TIME BEFORE THE CURRENT UNIVERSE EXISTED. PERHAPS FROM A TIME BEFORE ANYTHING EXISTED.
"A GOD OF THE VOID.
"AS IT CREATED THIS IMAGE, THE COMPUTER'S LOGIC CIRCUITS MELTED UNDER THE STRAIN OF THE KNOWLEDGE IT WAS FORCED TO BEAR.
"BUT BEFORE THE MACHINE DIED...IT SPAT OUT THE CREATURE'S NAME.

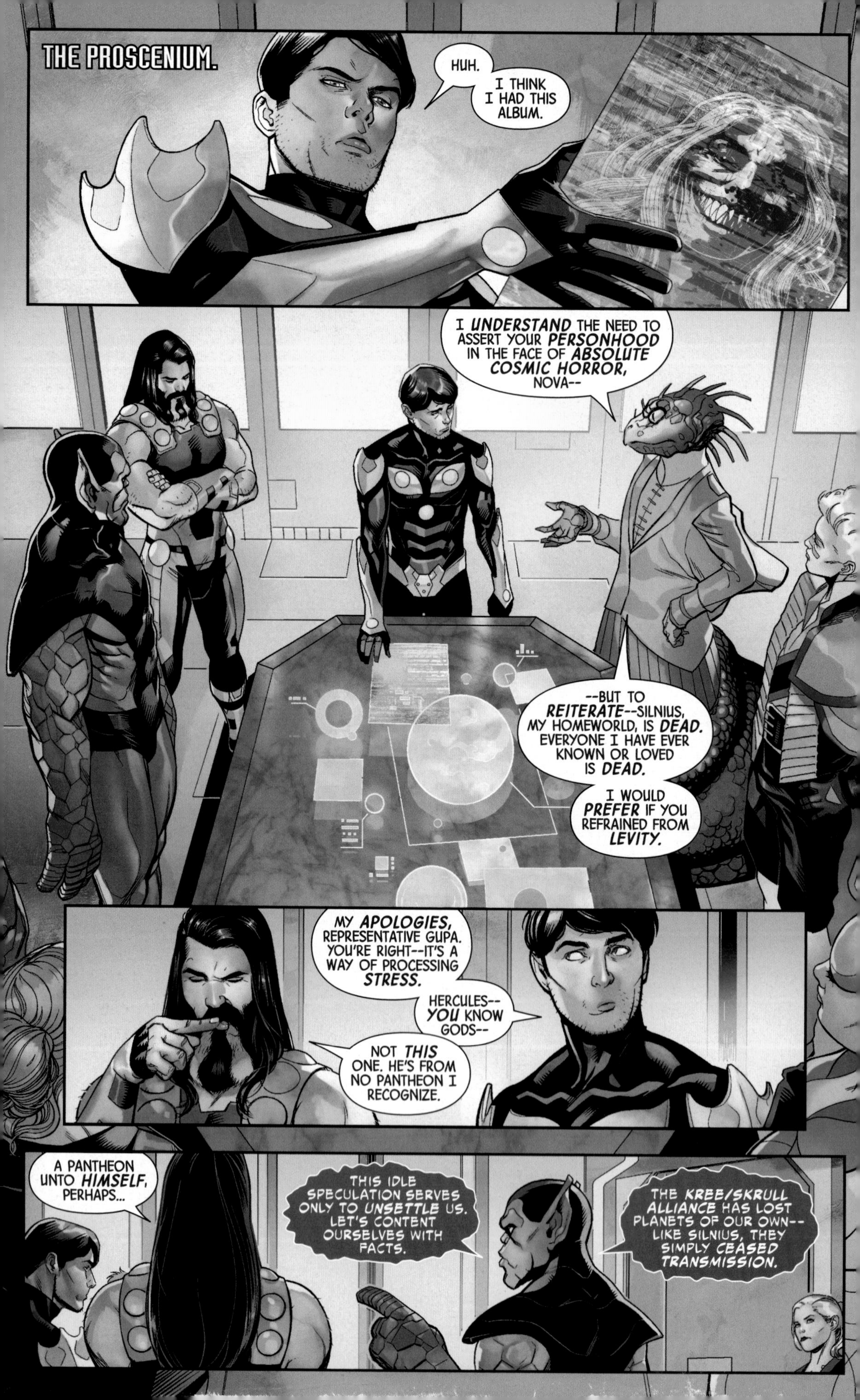
THE PROSCENIUM.
HUH. I THINK I HAD THIS ALBUM.
I UNDERSTAND THE NEED TO ASSERT YOUR PERSONHOOD IN THE FACE OF ABSOLUTE COSMIC HORROR, NOVA--
--BUT TO REITERATE--SILNIUS, MY HOMEWORLD, IS DEAD. EVERYONE I HAVE EVER KNOWN OR LOVED IS DEAD.
I WOULD PREFER IF YOU REFRAINED FROM LEVITY.
MY APOLOGIES, REPRESENTATIVE GUPA. YOU'RE RIGHT--IT'S A WAY OF PROCESSING STRESS.
HERCULES--YOU KNOW GODS--
NOT THIS ONE. HE'S FROM NO PANTHEON I RECOGNIZE.
A PANTHEON UNTO HIMSELF, PERHAPS...
THIS IDLE SPECULATION SERVES ONLY TO UNSETTLE US. LET'S CONTENT OURSELVES WITH FACTS.
THE KREE/SKRULL ALLIANCE HAS LOST PLANETS OF OUR OWN--LIKE SILNIUS, THEY SIMPLY CEASED TRANSMISSION.

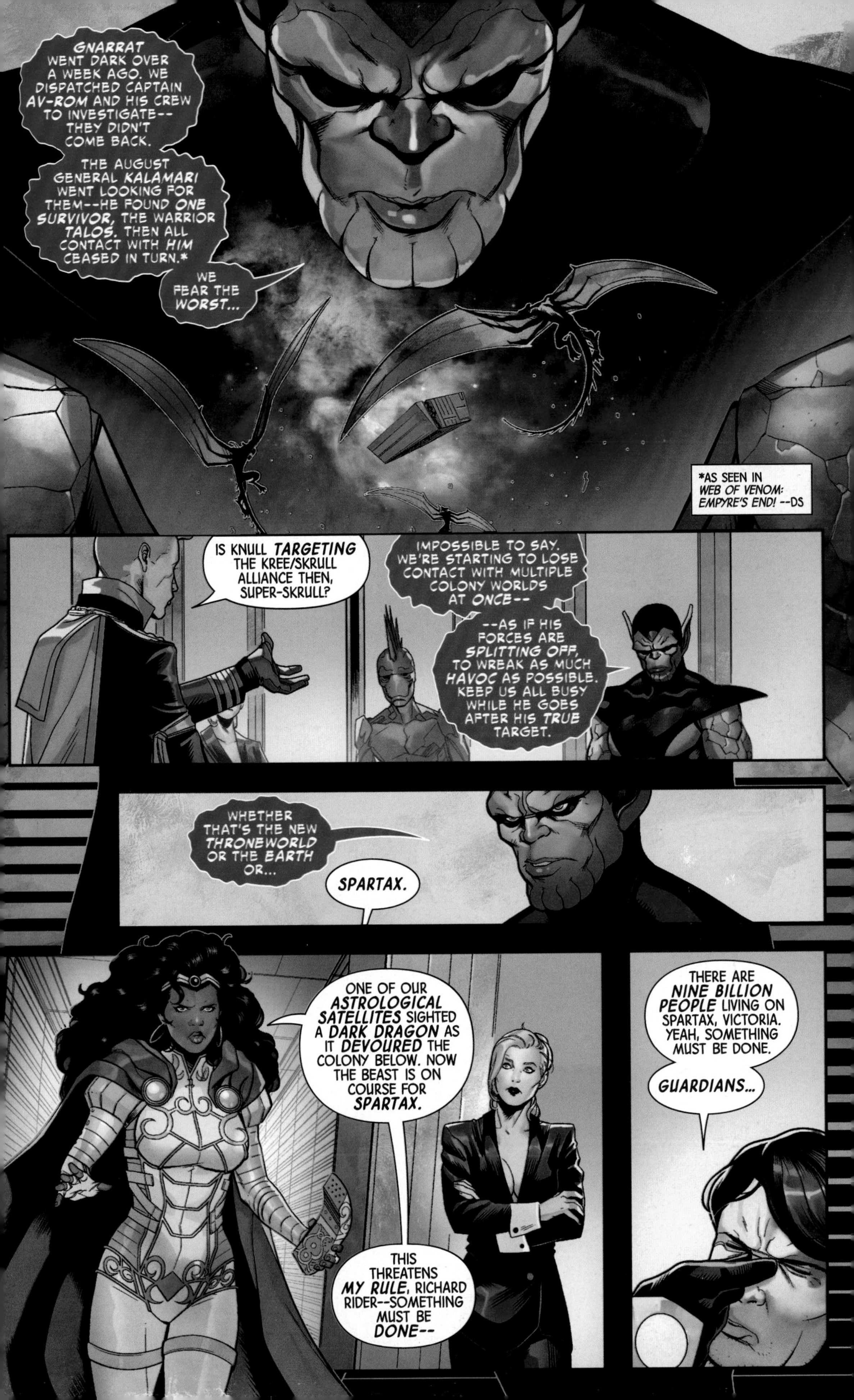
GNARRAT WENT DARK OVER A WEEK AGO. WE DISPATCHED CAPTAIN AV-ROM AND HIS CREW TO INVESTIGATE-- THEY DIDN'T COME BACK.
THE AUGUST GENERAL KALAMARI WENT LOOKING FOR THEM--HE FOUND ONE SURVIVOR, THE WARRIOR TALOS. THEN ALL CONTACT WITH HIM CEASED IN TURN.*
WE FEAR THE WORST...
*AS SEEN IN WEB OF VENOM: EMPYRE'S END! --DS
IS KNULL TARGETING THE KREE/SKRULL ALLIANCE THEN, SUPER-SKRULL?
IMPOSSIBLE TO SAY. WE'RE STARTING TO LOSE CONTACT WITH MULTIPLE COLONY WORLDS AT ONCE--
--AS IF HIS FORCES ARE SPLITTING OFF, TO WREAK AS MUCH HAVOC AS POSSIBLE. KEEP US ALL BUSY WHILE HE GOES AFTER HIS TRUE TARGET.
WHETHER THAT'S THE NEW THRONEWORLD OR THE EARTH OR...
SPARTAX.
ONE OF OUR ASTROLOGICAL SATELLITES SIGHTED A DARK DRAGON AS IT DEVOURED THE COLONY BELOW. NOW THE BEAST IS ON COURSE FOR SPARTAX.
THIS THREATENS MY RULE, RICHARD RIDER--SOMETHING MUST BE DONE--
THERE ARE NINE BILLION PEOPLE LIVING ON SPARTAX, VICTORIA. YEAH, SOMETHING MUST BE DONE.
GUARDIANS...

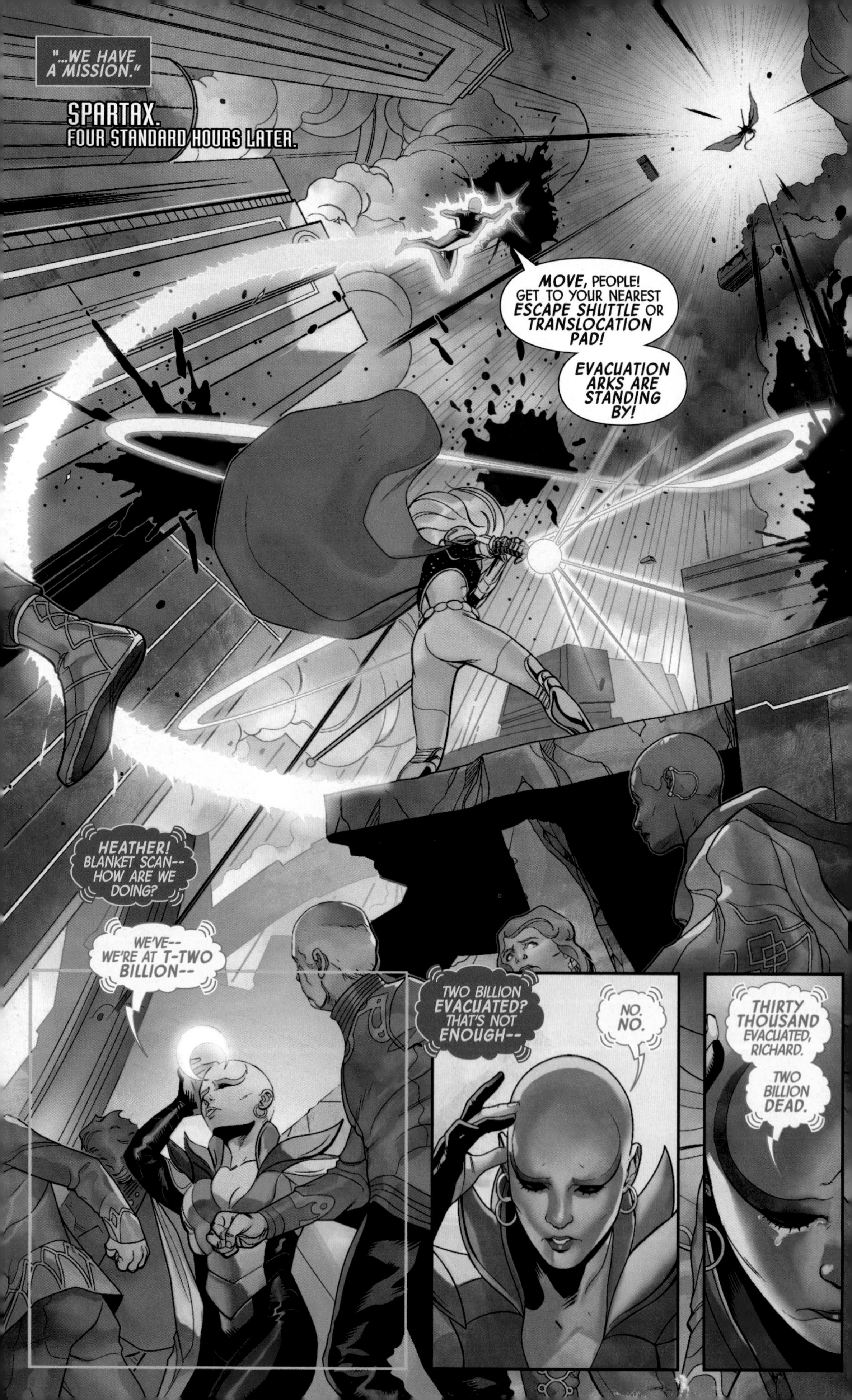

"...WE HAVE A MISSION."
SPARTAX.
FOUR STANDARD HOURS LATER.
MOVE, PEOPLE! GET TO YOUR NEAREST ESCAPE SHUTTLE OR TRANSLOCATION PAD!
EVACUATION ARKS ARE STANDING BY!
HEATHER! BLANKET SCAN-- HOW ARE WE DOING?
WE'VE-- WE'RE AT T-TWO BILLION--
TWO BILLION EVACUATED? THAT'S NOT ENOUGH--
NO. NO.
THIRTY THOUSAND EVACUATED, RICHARD.
TWO BILLION DEAD.

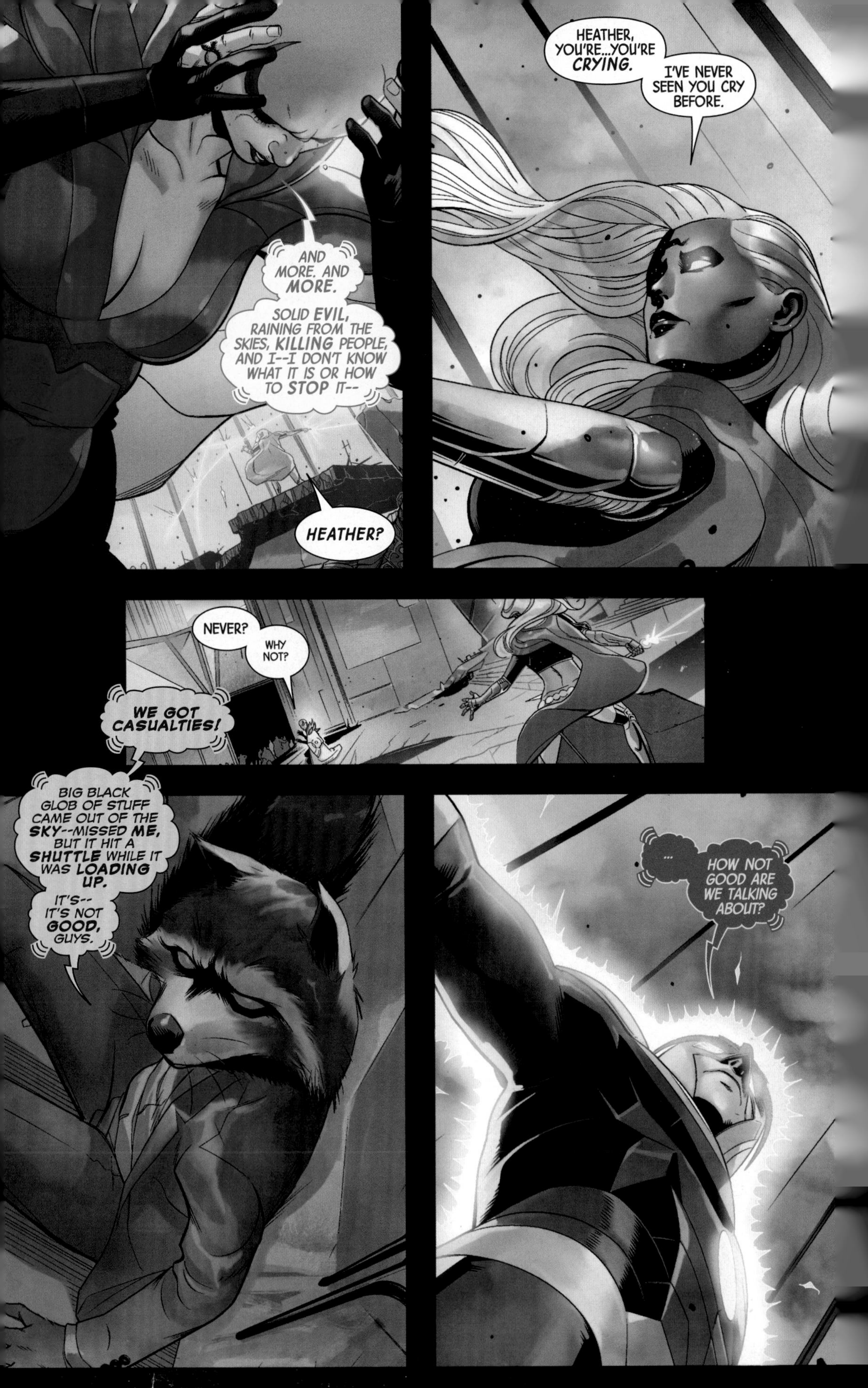
AND MORE. AND MORE.
SOLID EVIL, RAINING FROM THE SKIES, KILLING PEOPLE, AND I--I DON'T KNOW WHAT IT IS OR HOW TO STOP IT--
HEATHER?
HEATHER, YOU'RE...YOU'RE CRYING.
I'VE NEVER SEEN YOU CRY BEFORE.
NEVER?
WHY NOT?
WE GOT CASUALTIES!
BIG BLACK GLOB OF STUFF CAME OUT OF THE SKY--MISSED ME, BUT IT HIT A SHUTTLE WHILE IT WAS LOADING UP.
IT'S-- IT'S NOT GOOD, GUYS.
...
HOW NOT GOOD ARE WE TALKING ABOUT?

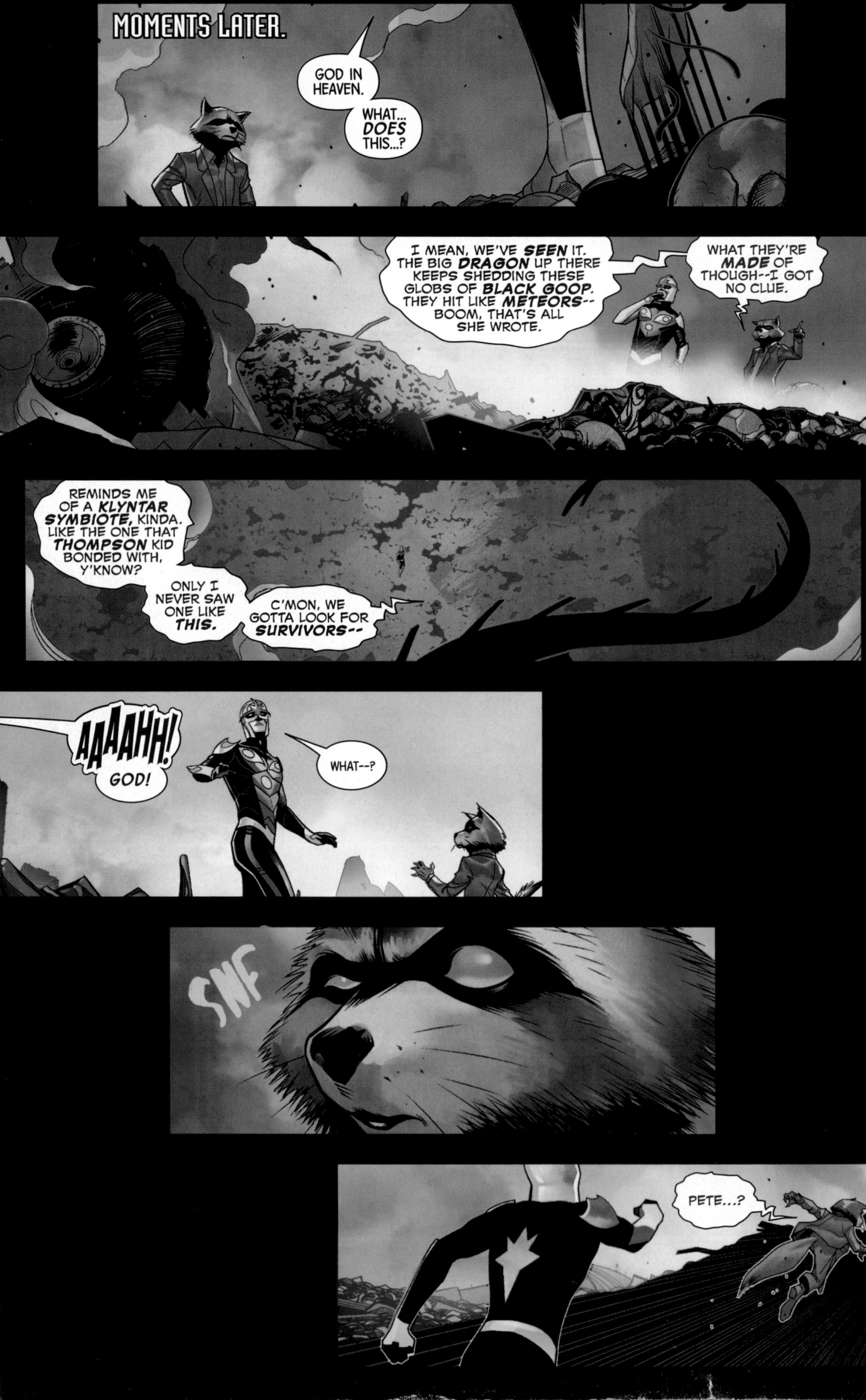
MOMENTS LATER.
GOD IN HEAVEN.
WHAT... DOES THIS...?
I MEAN, WE'VE SEEN IT. THE BIG DRAGON UP THERE KEEPS SHEDDING THESE GLOBS OF BLACK GOOP. THEY HIT LIKE METEORS-- BOOM, THAT'S ALL SHE WROTE.
WHAT THEY'RE MADE OF THOUGH--I GOT NO CLUE.
REMINDS ME OF A KLYNTAR SYMBIOTE, KINDA. LIKE THE ONE THAT THOMPSON KID BONDED WITH, Y'KNOW?
ONLY I NEVER SAW ONE LIKE THIS.
C'MON, WE GOTTA LOOK FOR SURVIVORS--
AAAAHH! GOD!
WHAT--?
SNF
PETE...?

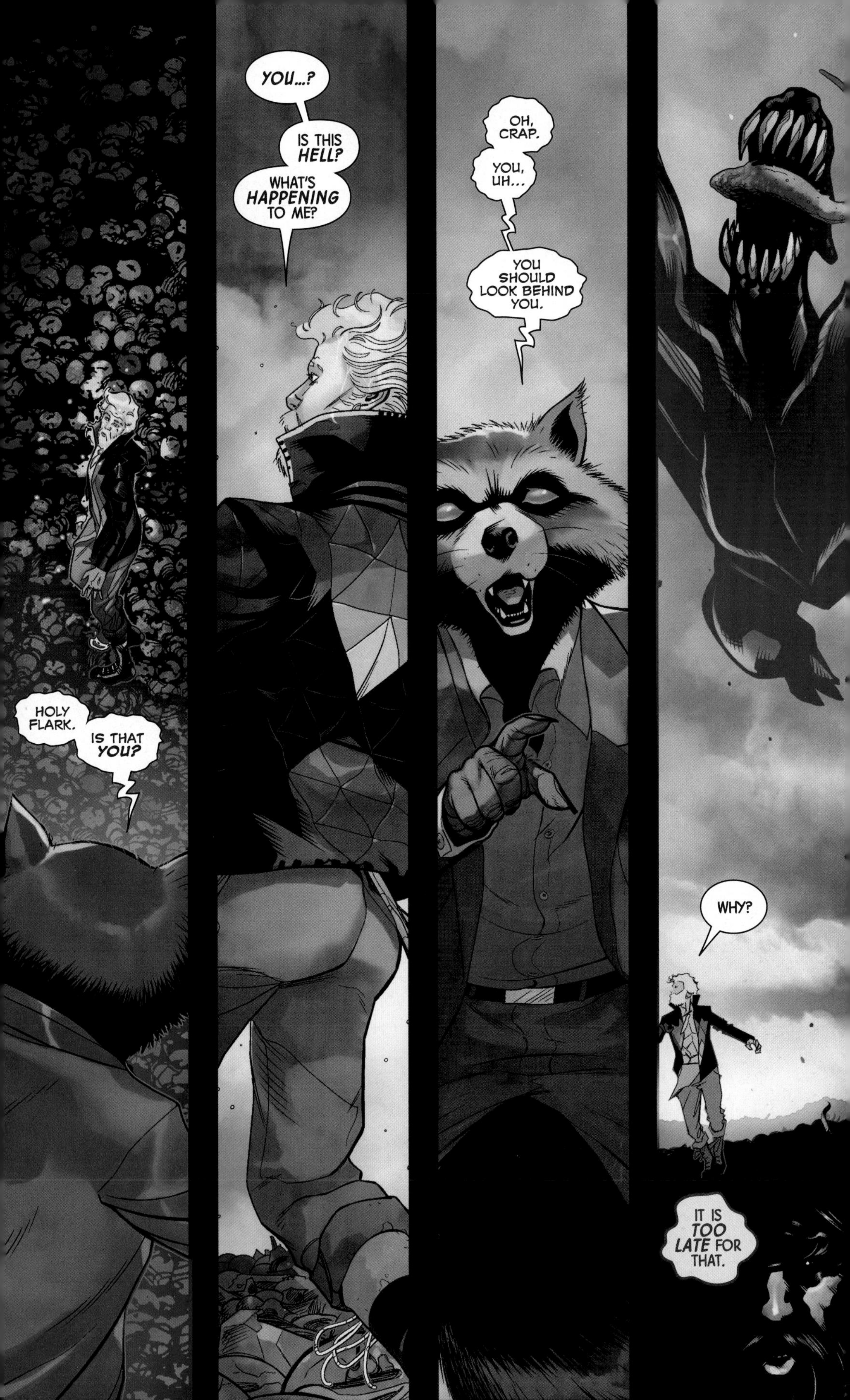
HOLY FLARK.
IS THAT YOU?
YOU...?
IS THIS HELL?
WHAT'S HAPPENING TO ME?
OH, CRAP.
YOU, UH...
YOU SHOULD LOOK BEHIND YOU.
WHY?
IT IS TOO LATE FOR THAT.

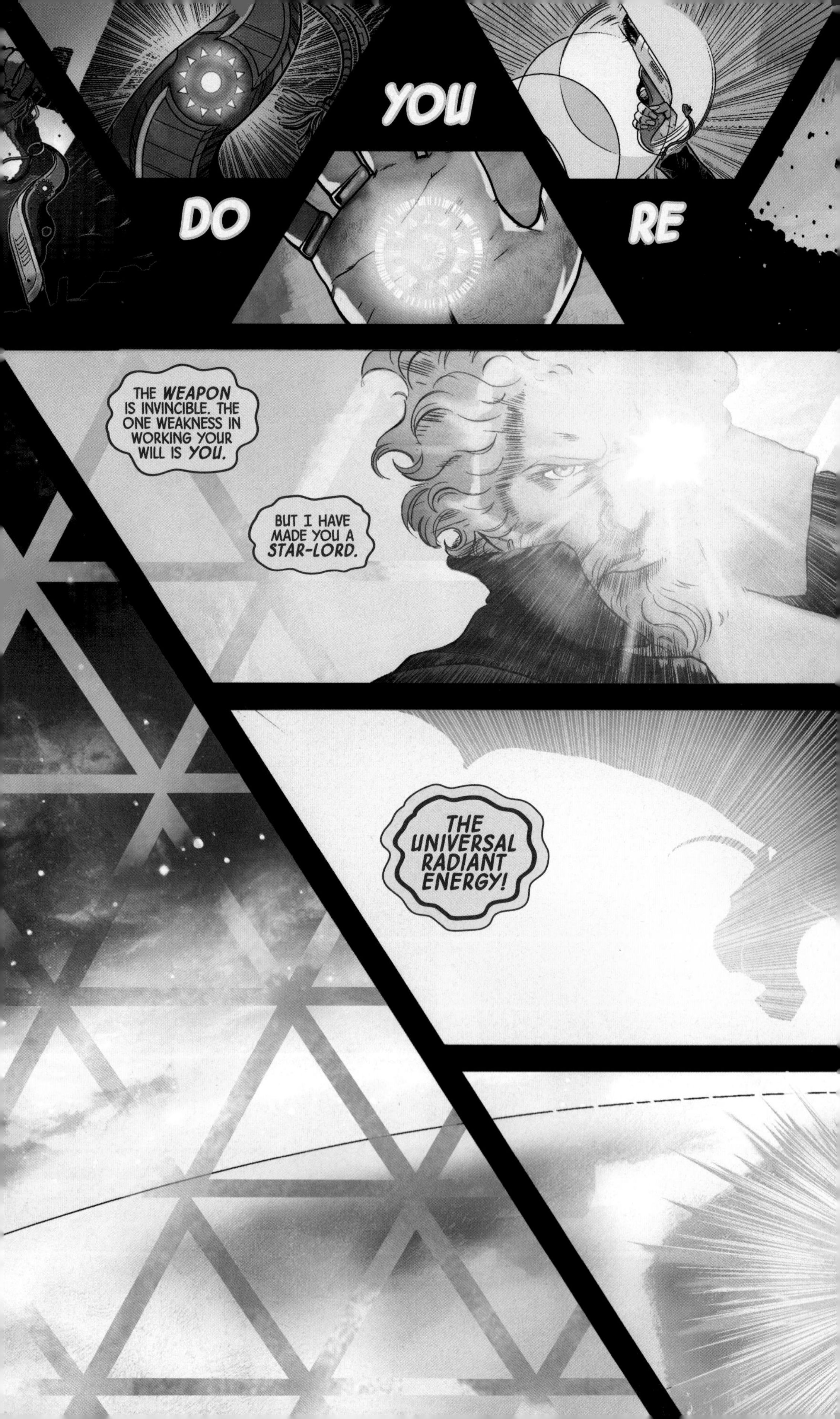
YOU
DO
RE
THE WEAPON IS INVINCIBLE. THE ONE WEAKNESS IN WORKING YOUR WILL IS YOU.
BUT I HAVE MADE YOU A STAR-LORD.
THE UNIVERSAL RADIANT ENERGY!

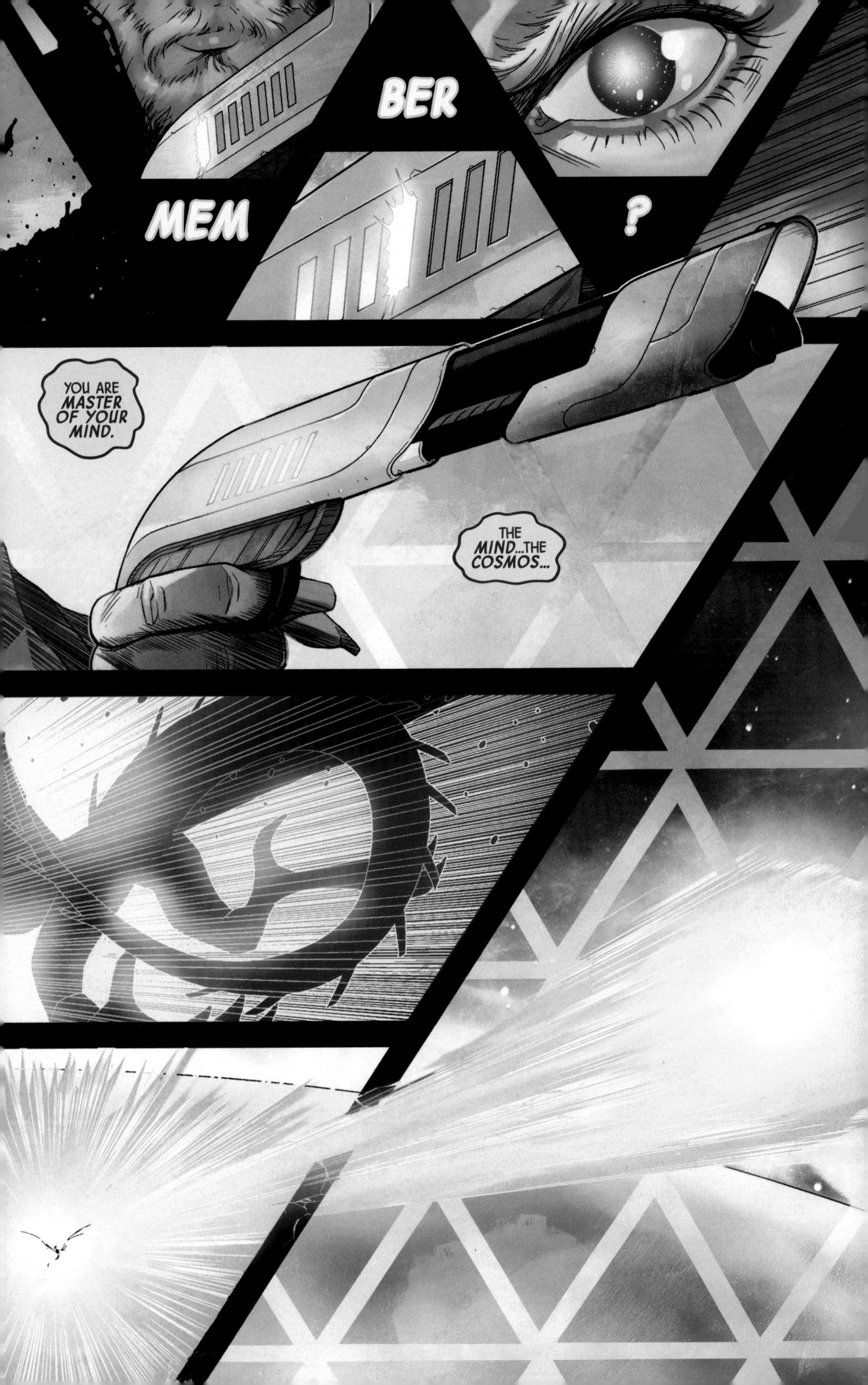
MEM
BER
?
YOU ARE MASTER OF YOUR MIND.
THE MIND...THE COSMOS...

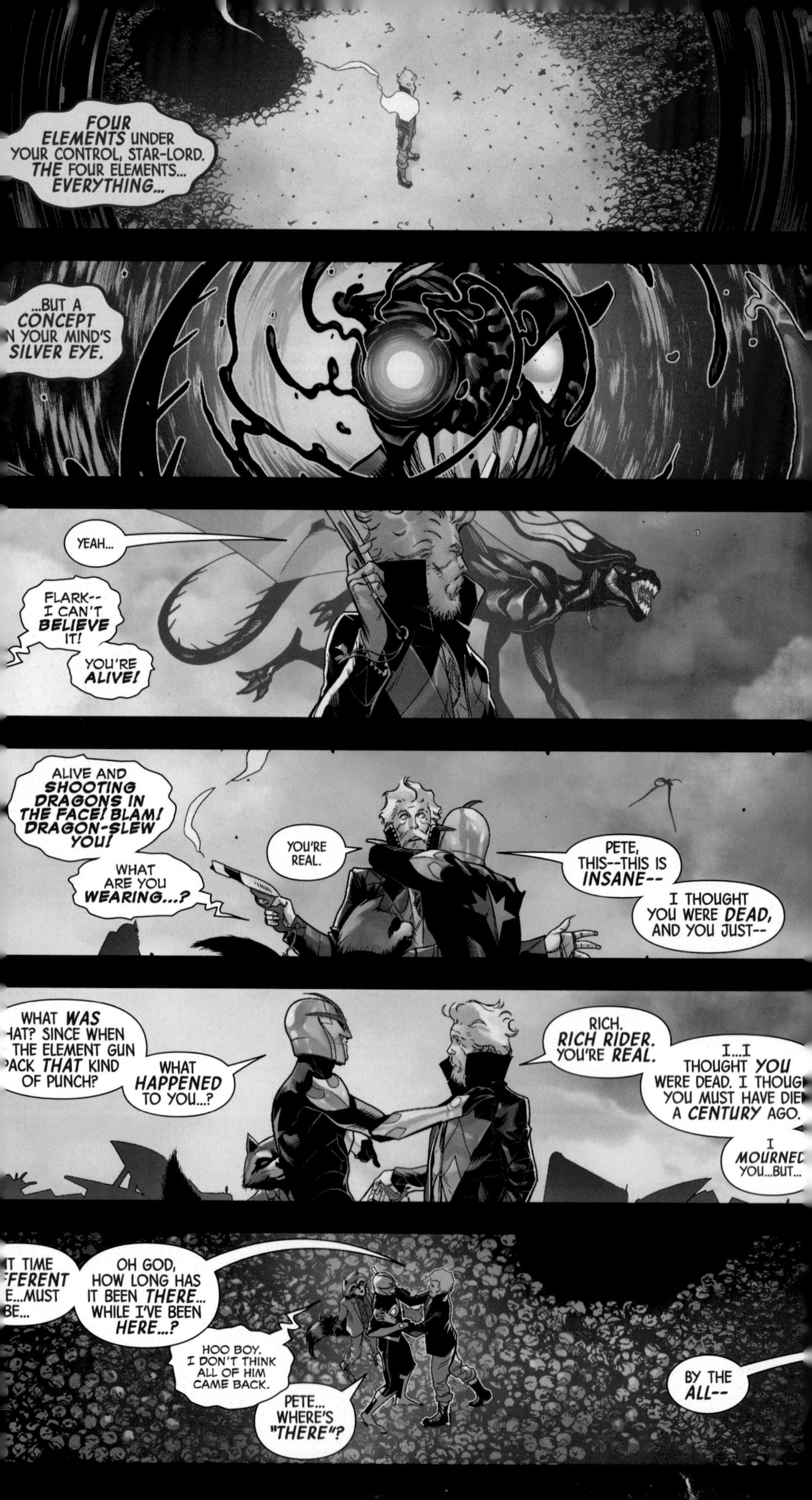
FOUR ELEMENTS UNDER YOUR CONTROL, STAR-LORD. THE FOUR ELEMENTS... EVERYTHING...
...BUT A CONCEPT IN YOUR MIND'S SILVER EYE.
YEAH...
FLARK-- I CAN'T BELIEVE IT!
YOU'RE ALIVE!
ALIVE AND SHOOTING DRAGONS IN THE FACE! BLAM! DRAGON-SLEW YOU!
WHAT ARE YOU WEARING...?
YOU'RE REAL.
PETE, THIS--THIS IS INSANE--
I THOUGHT YOU WERE DEAD, AND YOU JUST--
WHAT WAS THAT? SINCE WHEN THE ELEMENT GUN PACK THAT KIND OF PUNCH?
WHAT HAPPENED TO YOU...?
RICH. RICH RIDER. YOU'RE REAL.
I...I THOUGHT YOU WERE DEAD. I THOUG YOU MUST HAVE DIE A CENTURY AGO.
I MOURNED YOU...BUT...
IT TIME FFERENT E...MUST BE...
OH GOD, HOW LONG HAS IT BEEN THERE... WHILE I'VE BEEN HERE...?
HOO BOY. I DON'T THINK ALL OF HIM CAME BACK.
PETE... WHERE'S "THERE"?
BY THE ALL--

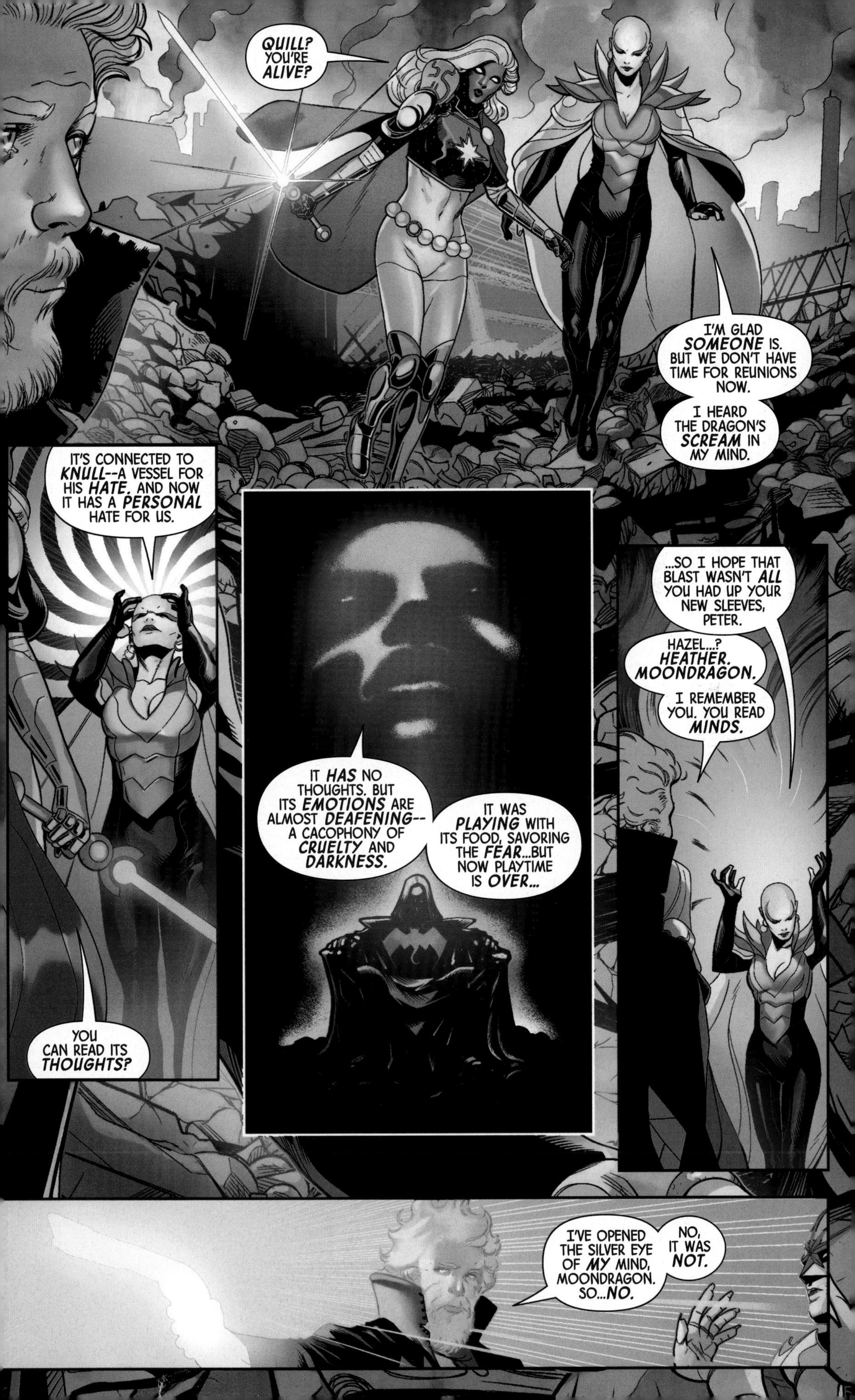
QUILL? YOU'RE ALIVE?
I'M GLAD SOMEONE IS. BUT WE DON'T HAVE TIME FOR REUNIONS NOW.
I HEARD THE DRAGON'S SCREAM IN MY MIND.
IT'S CONNECTED TO KNULL--A VESSEL FOR HIS HATE. AND NOW IT HAS A PERSONAL HATE FOR US.
YOU CAN READ ITS THOUGHTS?
IT HAS NO THOUGHTS. BUT ITS EMOTIONS ARE ALMOST DEAFENING--A CACOPHONY OF CRUELTY AND DARKNESS.
IT WAS PLAYING WITH ITS FOOD, SAVORING THE FEAR...BUT NOW PLAYTIME IS OVER...
...SO I HOPE THAT BLAST WASN'T ALL YOU HAD UP YOUR NEW SLEEVES, PETER.
HAZEL...? HEATHER. MOONDRAGON.
I REMEMBER YOU. YOU READ MINDS.
I'VE OPENED THE SILVER EYE OF MY MIND, MOONDRAGON. SO...NO.
NO, IT WAS NOT.

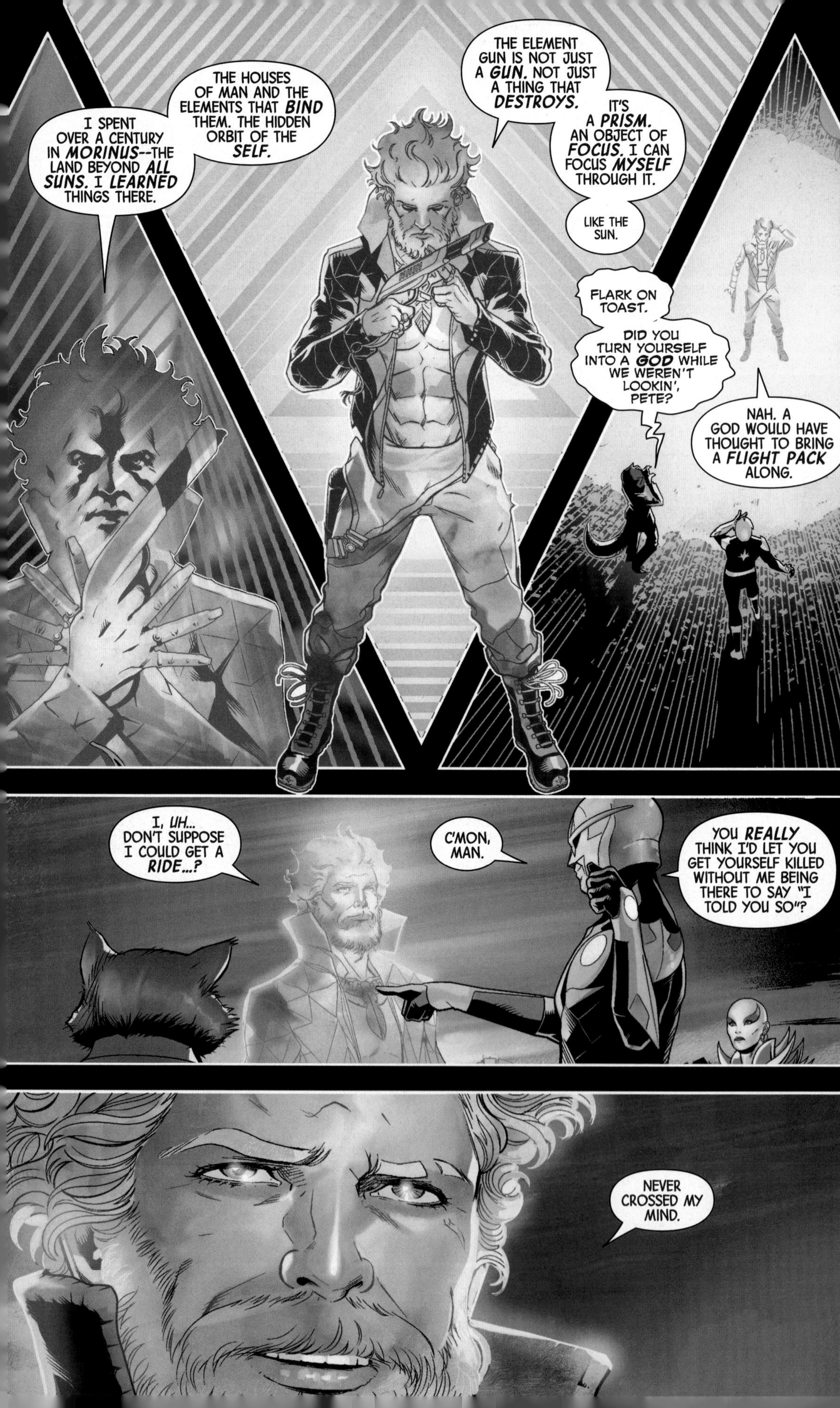
I SPENT OVER A CENTURY IN MORINUS--THE LAND BEYOND ALL SUNS. I LEARNED THINGS THERE.
THE HOUSES OF MAN AND THE ELEMENTS THAT BIND THEM. THE HIDDEN ORBIT OF THE SELF.
THE ELEMENT GUN IS NOT JUST A GUN. NOT JUST A THING THAT DESTROYS.
IT'S A PRISM. AN OBJECT OF FOCUS. I CAN FOCUS MYSELF THROUGH IT.
LIKE THE SUN.
FLARK ON TOAST.
DID YOU TURN YOURSELF INTO A GOD WHILE WE WEREN'T LOOKIN', PETE?
NAH. A GOD WOULD HAVE THOUGHT TO BRING A FLIGHT PACK ALONG.
I, UH... DON'T SUPPOSE I COULD GET A RIDE...?
C'MON, MAN.
YOU REALLY THINK I'D LET YOU GET YOURSELF KILLED WITHOUT ME BEING THERE TO SAY "I TOLD YOU SO"?
NEVER CROSSED MY MIND.

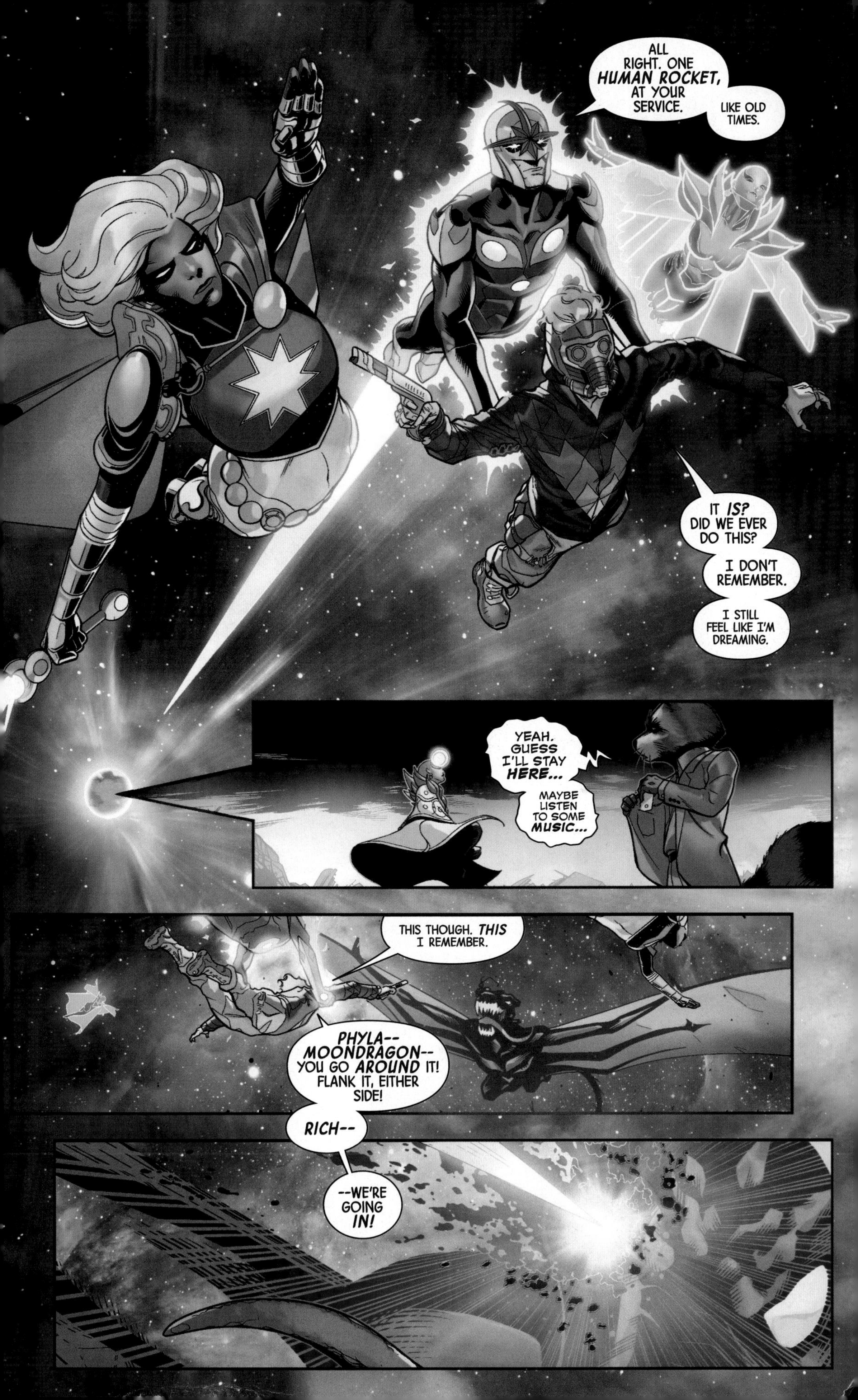

ALL RIGHT. ONE HUMAN ROCKET, AT YOUR SERVICE.
LIKE OLD TIMES.
IT IS? DID WE EVER DO THIS?
I DON'T REMEMBER.
I STILL FEEL LIKE I'M DREAMING.
YEAH. GUESS I'LL STAY HERE...
MAYBE LISTEN TO SOME MUSIC...
THIS THOUGH. THIS I REMEMBER.
PHYLA-- MOONDRAGON-- YOU GO AROUND IT! FLANK IT, EITHER SIDE!
RICH--
--WE'RE GOING IN!

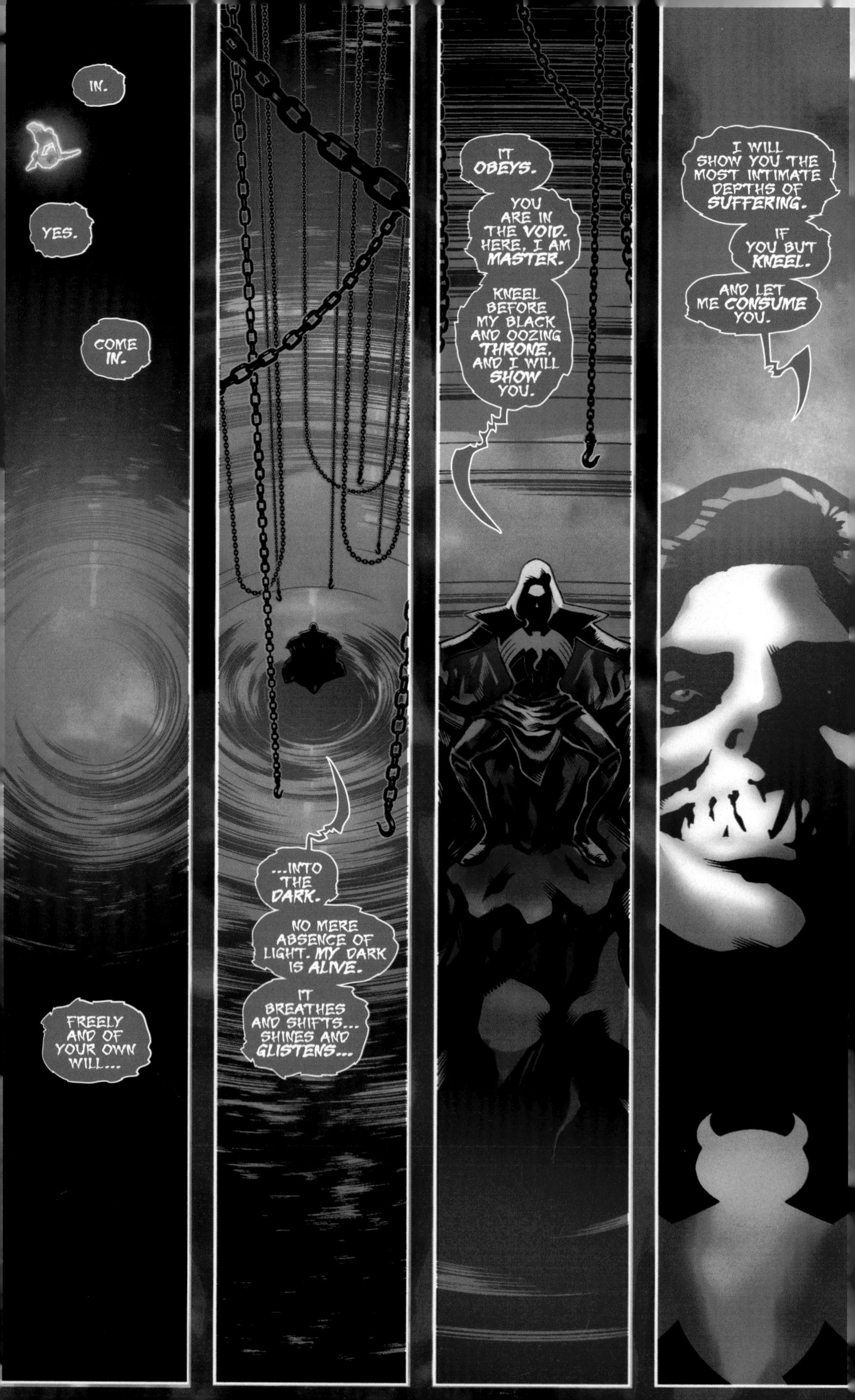
IN.
YES.
COME IN.
FREELY AND OF YOUR OWN WILL...
...INTO THE DARK.
NO MERE ABSENCE OF LIGHT. MY DARK IS ALIVE.
IT BREATHES AND SHIFTS... SHINES AND GLISTENS...
IT OBEYS.
YOU ARE IN THE VOID. HERE, I AM MASTER.
KNEEL BEFORE MY BLACK AND OOZING THRONE, AND I WILL SHOW YOU.
I WILL SHOW YOU THE MOST INTIMATE DEPTHS OF SUFFERING.
IF YOU BUT KNEEL.
AND LET ME CONSUME YOU.

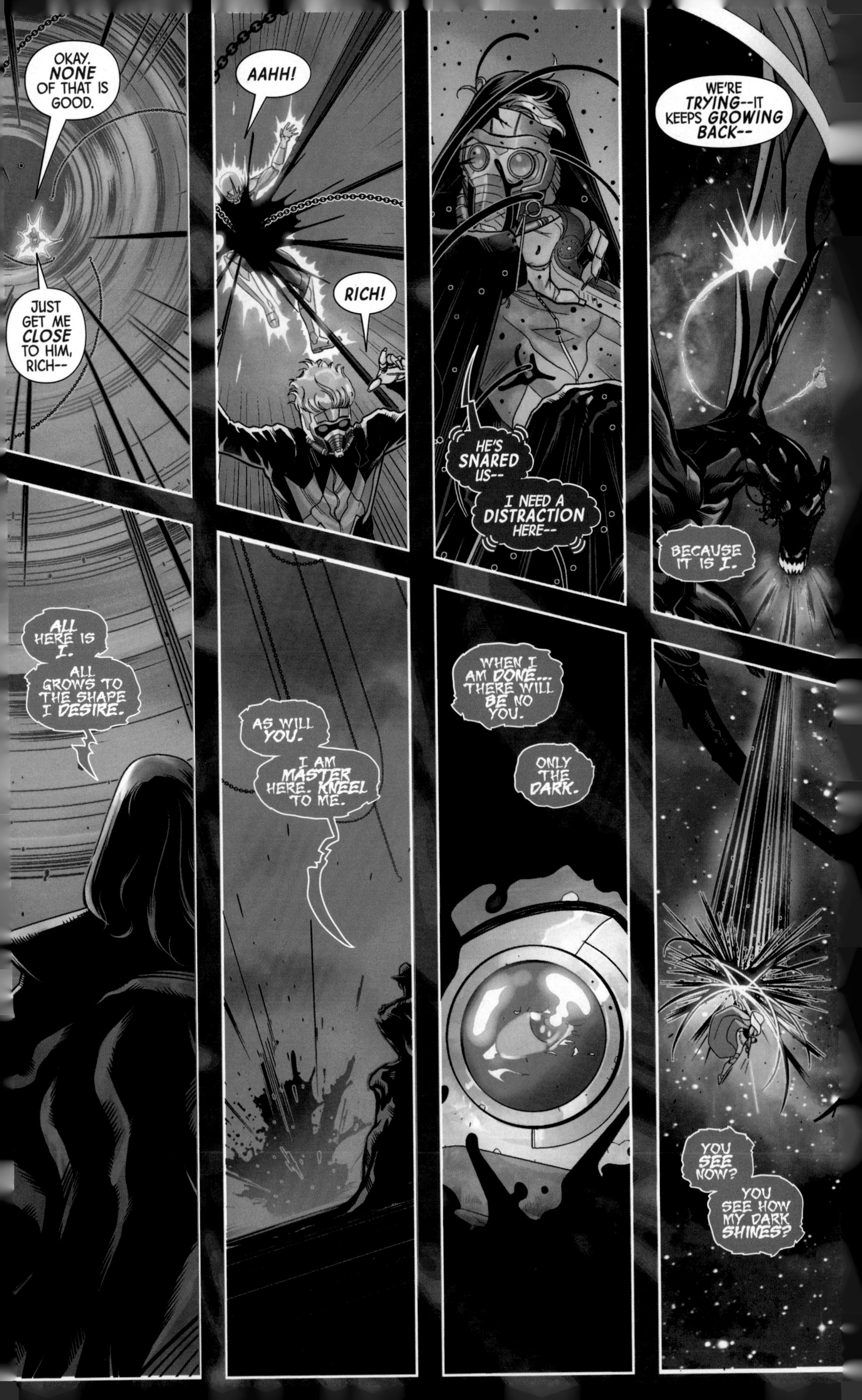
OKAY. NONE OF THAT IS GOOD.
JUST GET ME CLOSE TO HIM, RICH--
AAHH!
RICH!
HE'S SNARED US--
I NEED A DISTRACTION HERE--
WE'RE TRYING--IT KEEPS GROWING BACK--
BECAUSE IT IS I.
ALL HERE IS I.
ALL GROWS TO THE SHAPE I DESIRE.
AS WILL YOU.
I AM MASTER HERE. KNEEL TO ME.
WHEN I AM DONE... THERE WILL BE NO YOU.
ONLY THE DARK.
YOU SEE NOW?
YOU SEE HOW MY DARK SHINES?

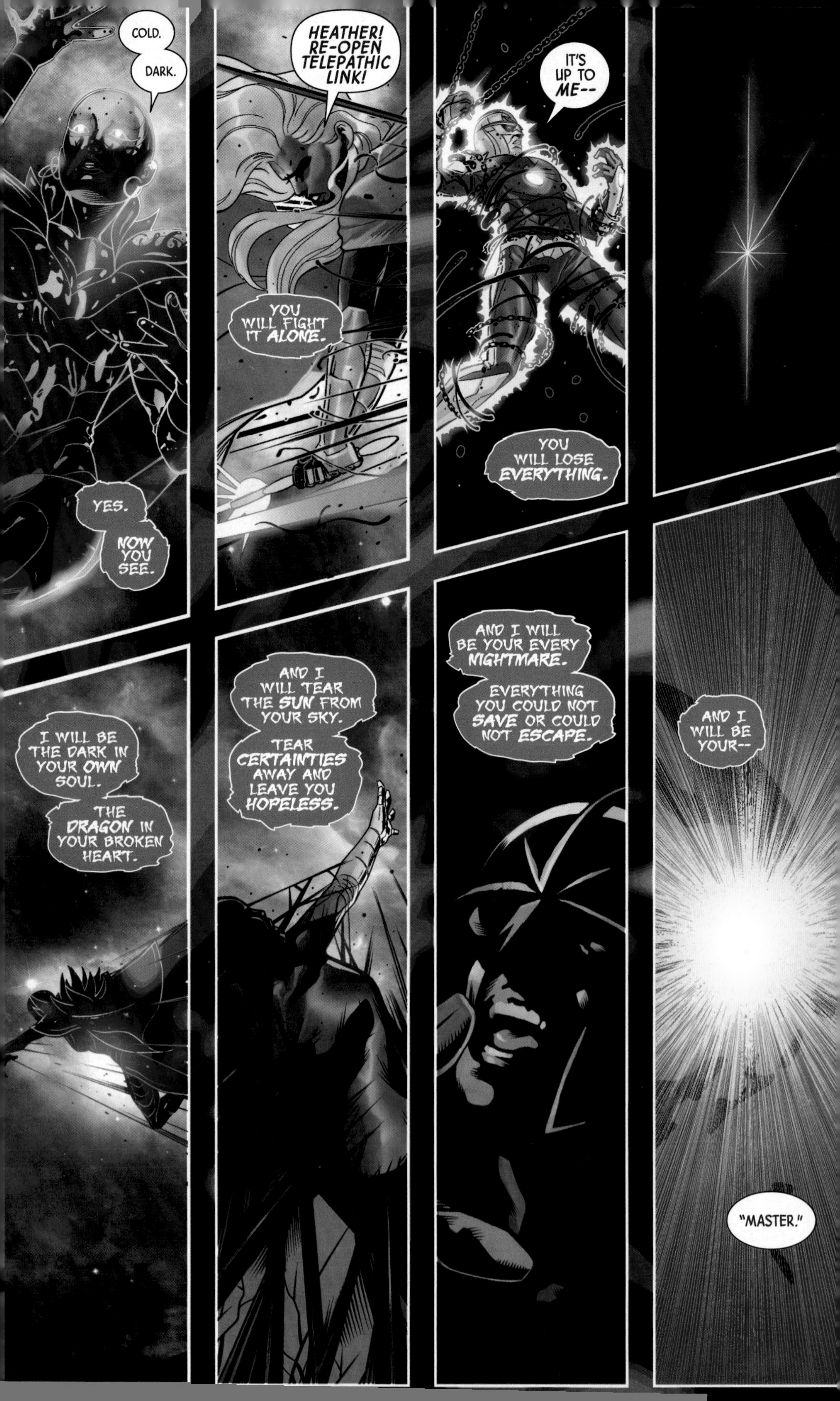

COLD.
DARK.
YES.
NOW YOU SEE.
HEATHER! RE-OPEN TELEPATHIC LINK!
YOU WILL FIGHT IT ALONE.
IT'S UP TO ME--
YOU WILL LOSE EVERYTHING.
I WILL BE THE DARK IN YOUR OWN SOUL.
THE DRAGON IN YOUR BROKEN HEART.
AND I WILL TEAR THE SUN FROM YOUR SKY.
TEAR CERTAINTIES AWAY AND LEAVE YOU HOPELESS.
AND I WILL BE YOUR EVERY NIGHTMARE.
EVERYTHING YOU COULD NOT SAVE OR COULD NOT ESCAPE.
AND I WILL BE YOUR--
"MASTER."

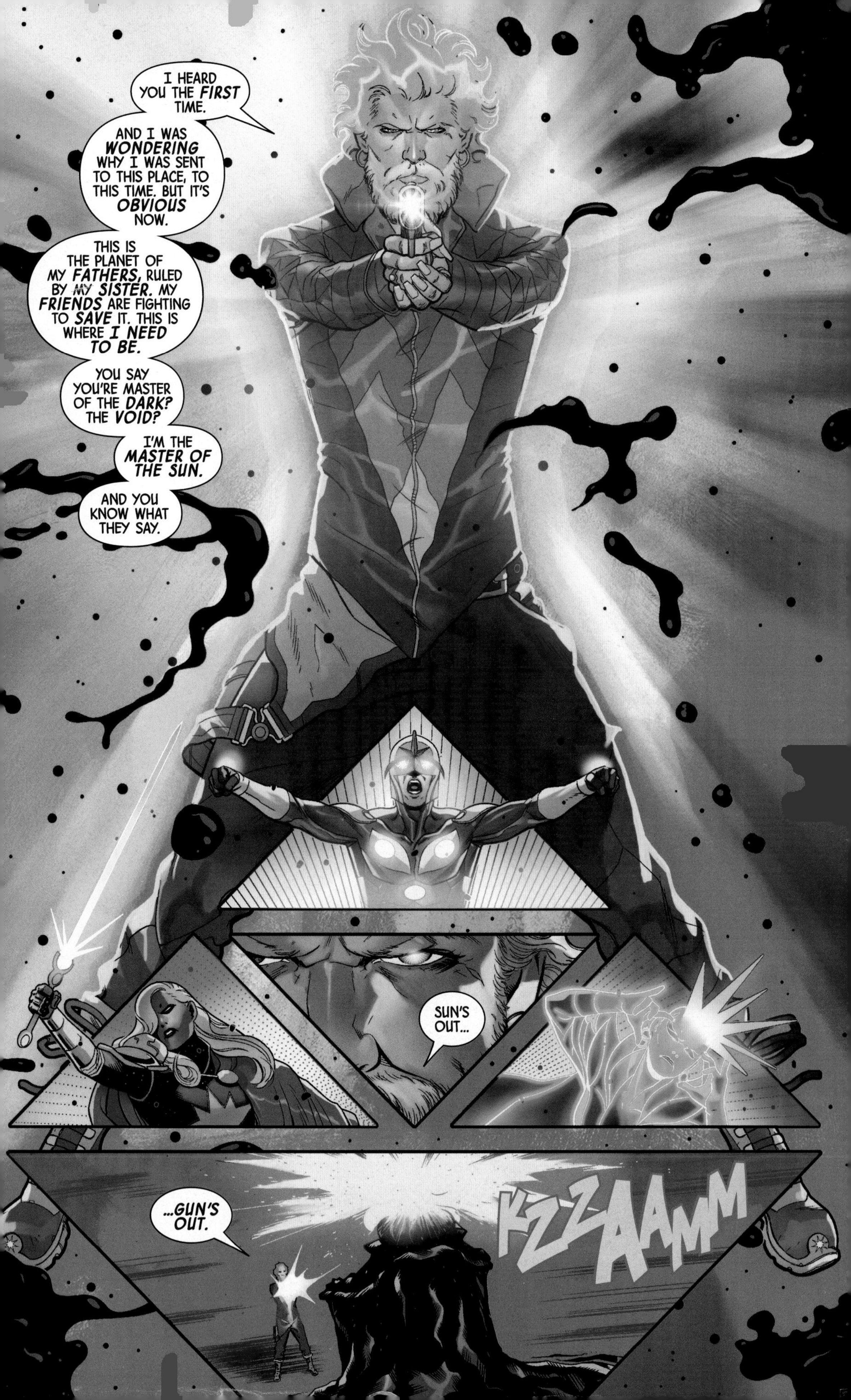
I HEARD YOU THE FIRST TIME.
AND I WAS WONDERING WHY I WAS SENT TO THIS PLACE, TO THIS TIME. BUT IT'S OBVIOUS NOW.
THIS IS THE PLANET OF MY FATHERS, RULED BY MY SISTER. MY FRIENDS ARE FIGHTING TO SAVE IT. THIS IS WHERE I NEED TO BE.
YOU SAY YOU'RE MASTER OF THE DARK? THE VOID?
I'M THE MASTER OF THE SUN.
AND YOU KNOW WHAT THEY SAY.
SUN'S OUT...
...GUN'S OUT.
KZZ-AAMM

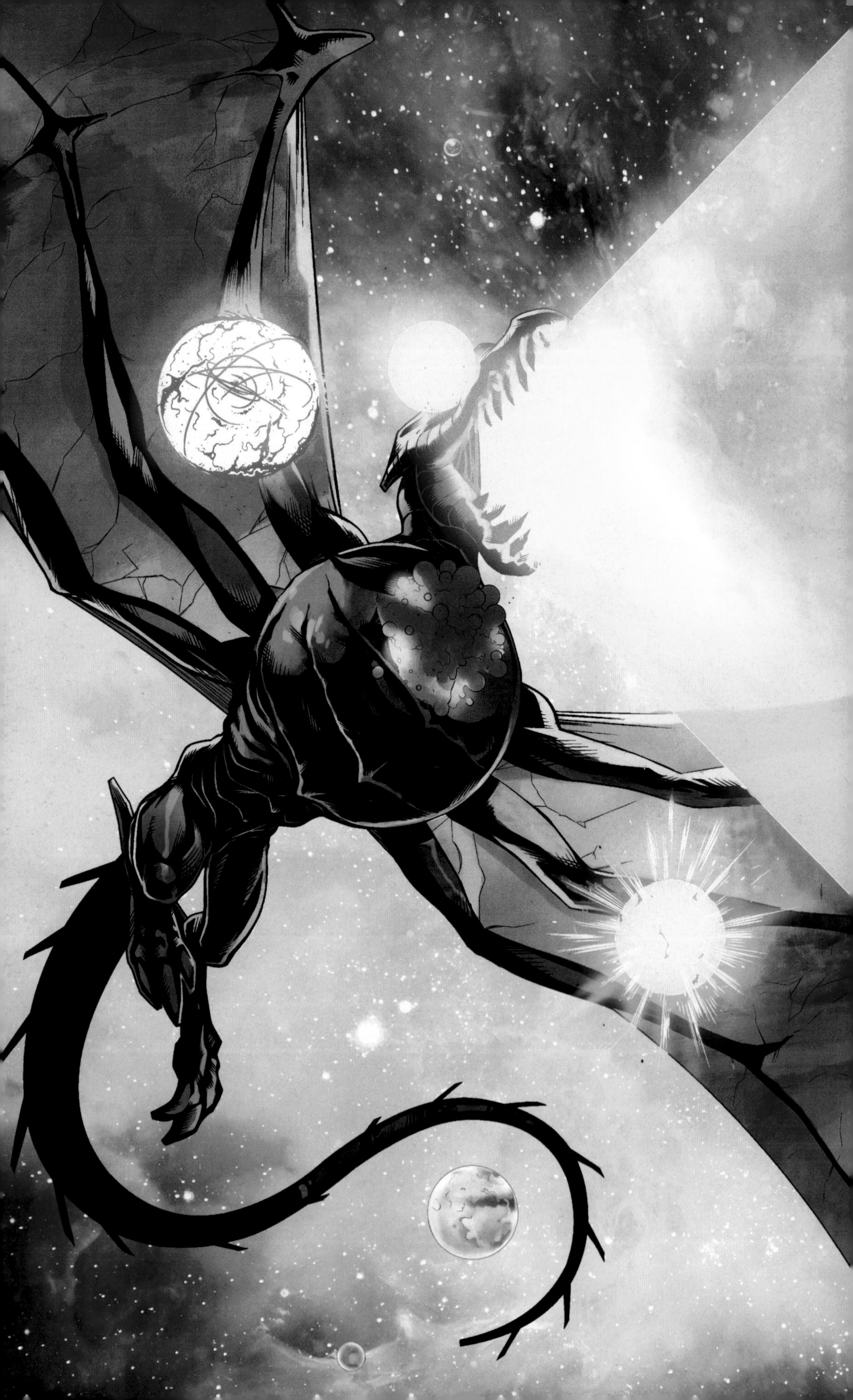

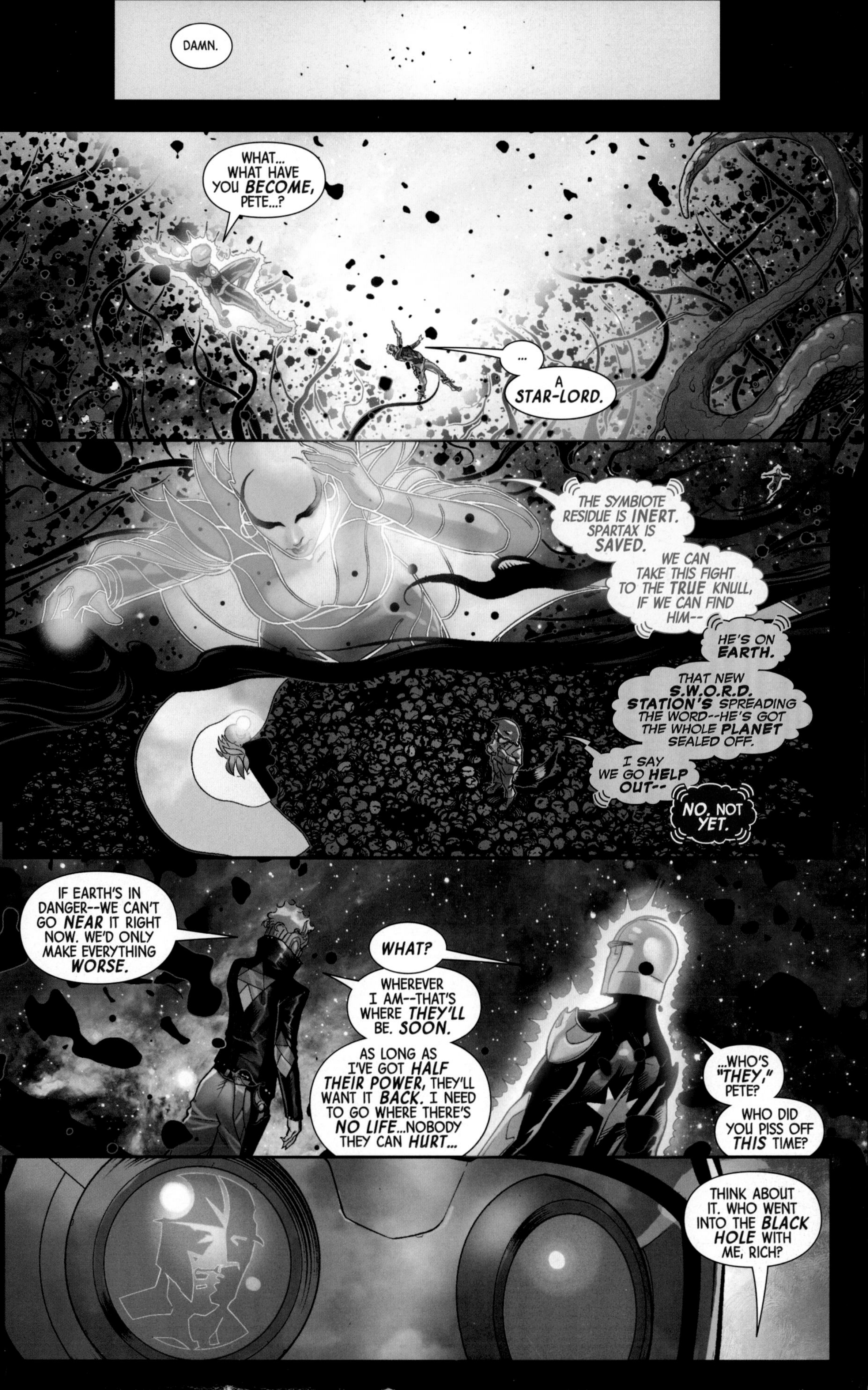
DAMN.
WHAT... WHAT HAVE YOU BECOME, PETE...?
...
A STAR-LORD.
THE SYMBIOTE RESIDUE IS INERT. SPARTAX IS SAVED.
WE CAN TAKE THIS FIGHT TO THE TRUE KNULL, IF WE CAN FIND HIM--
HE'S ON EARTH.
THAT NEW S.W.O.R.D. STATION'S SPREADING THE WORD--HE'S GOT THE WHOLE PLANET SEALED OFF.
I SAY WE GO HELP OUT--
NO. NOT YET.
IF EARTH'S IN DANGER--WE CAN'T GO NEAR IT RIGHT NOW. WE'D ONLY MAKE EVERYTHING WORSE.
WHAT?
WHEREVER I AM--THAT'S WHERE THEY'LL BE. SOON.
AS LONG AS I'VE GOT HALF THEIR POWER, THEY'LL WANT IT BACK. I NEED TO GO WHERE THERE'S NO LIFE...NOBODY THEY CAN HURT...
...WHO'S "THEY," PETE?
WHO DID YOU PISS OFF THIS TIME?
THINK ABOUT IT. WHO WENT INTO THE BLACK HOLE WITH ME, RICH?

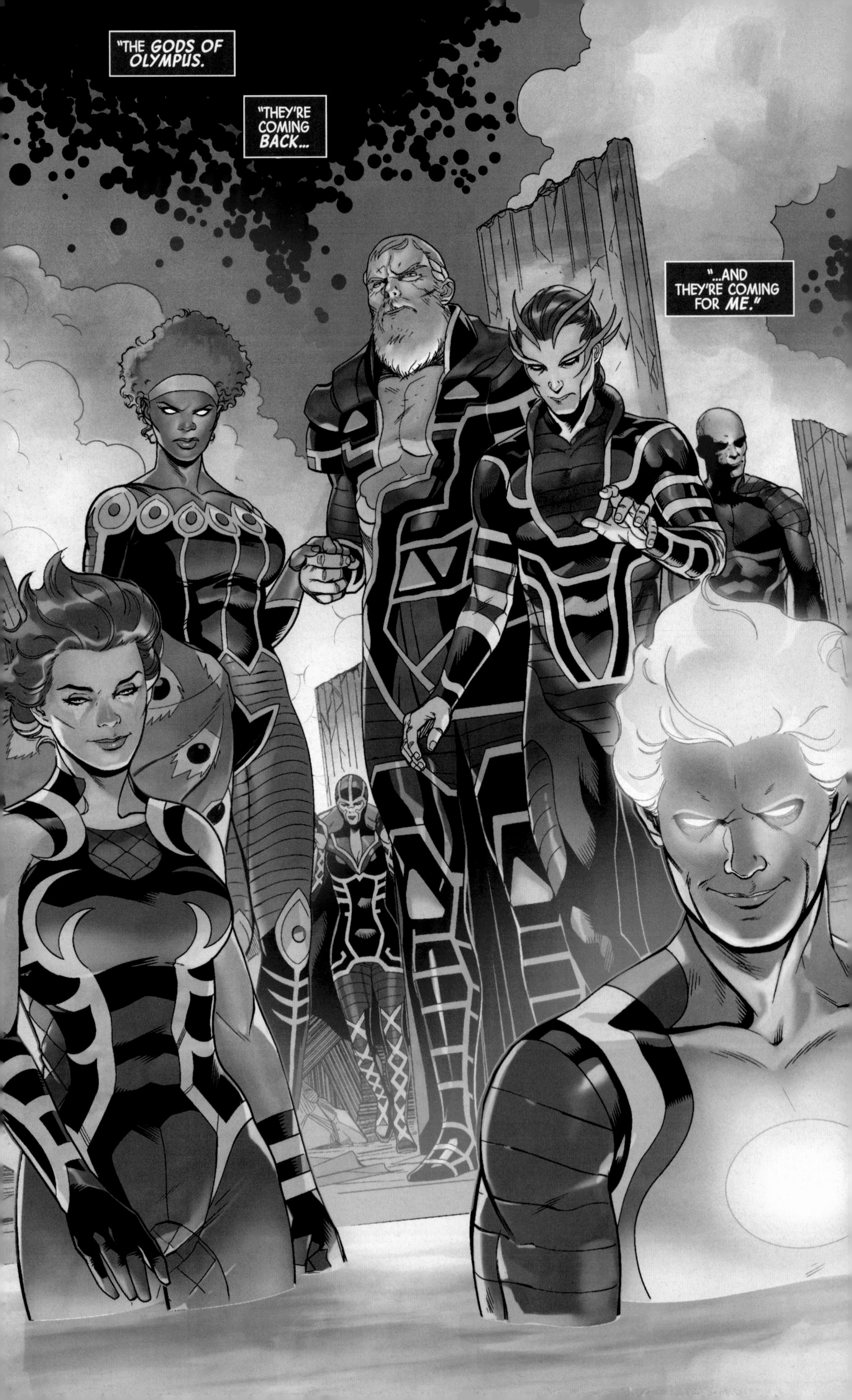
"THE GODS OF OLYMPUS.
"THEY'RE COMING BACK...
"...AND THEY'RE COMING FOR ME."

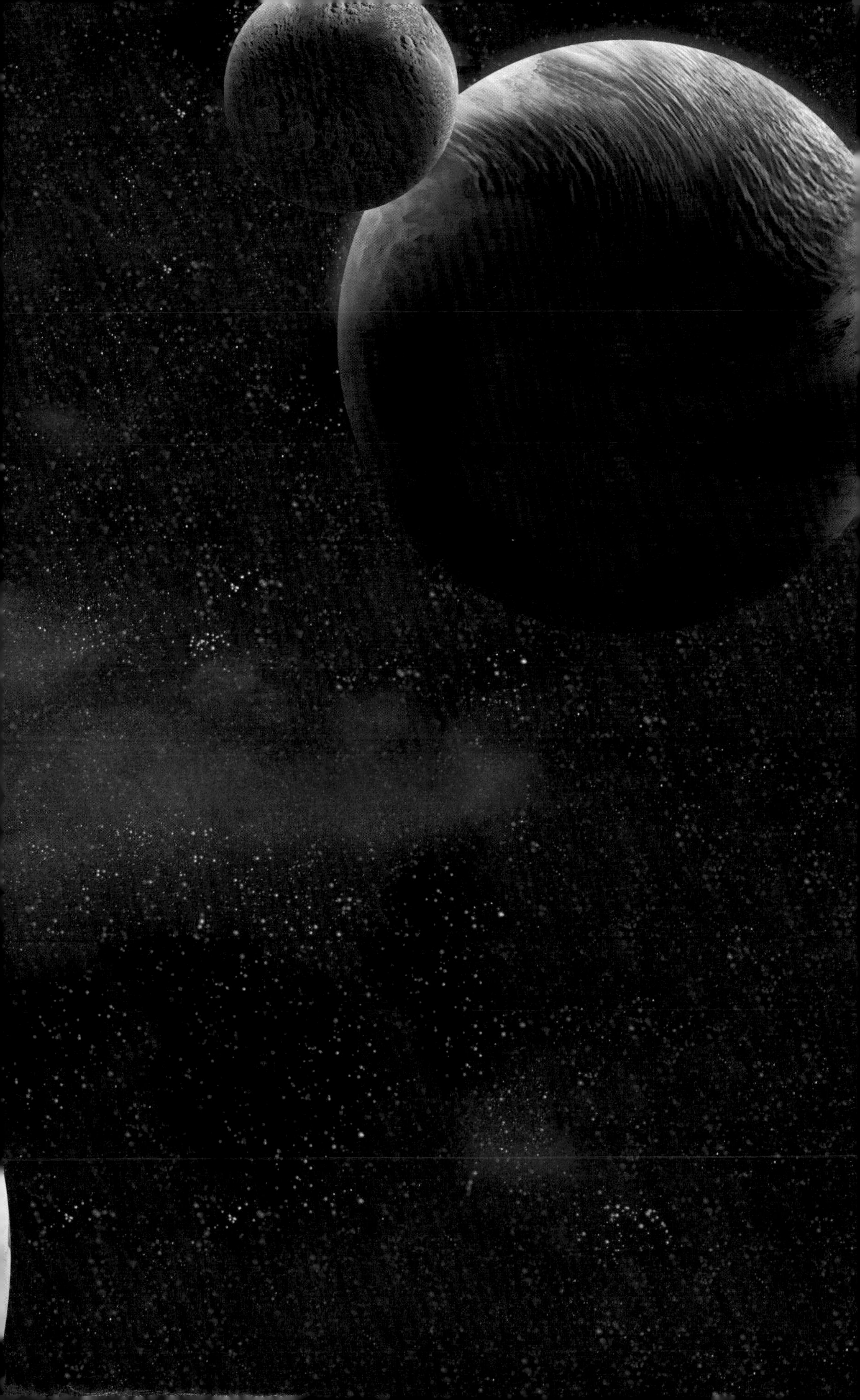

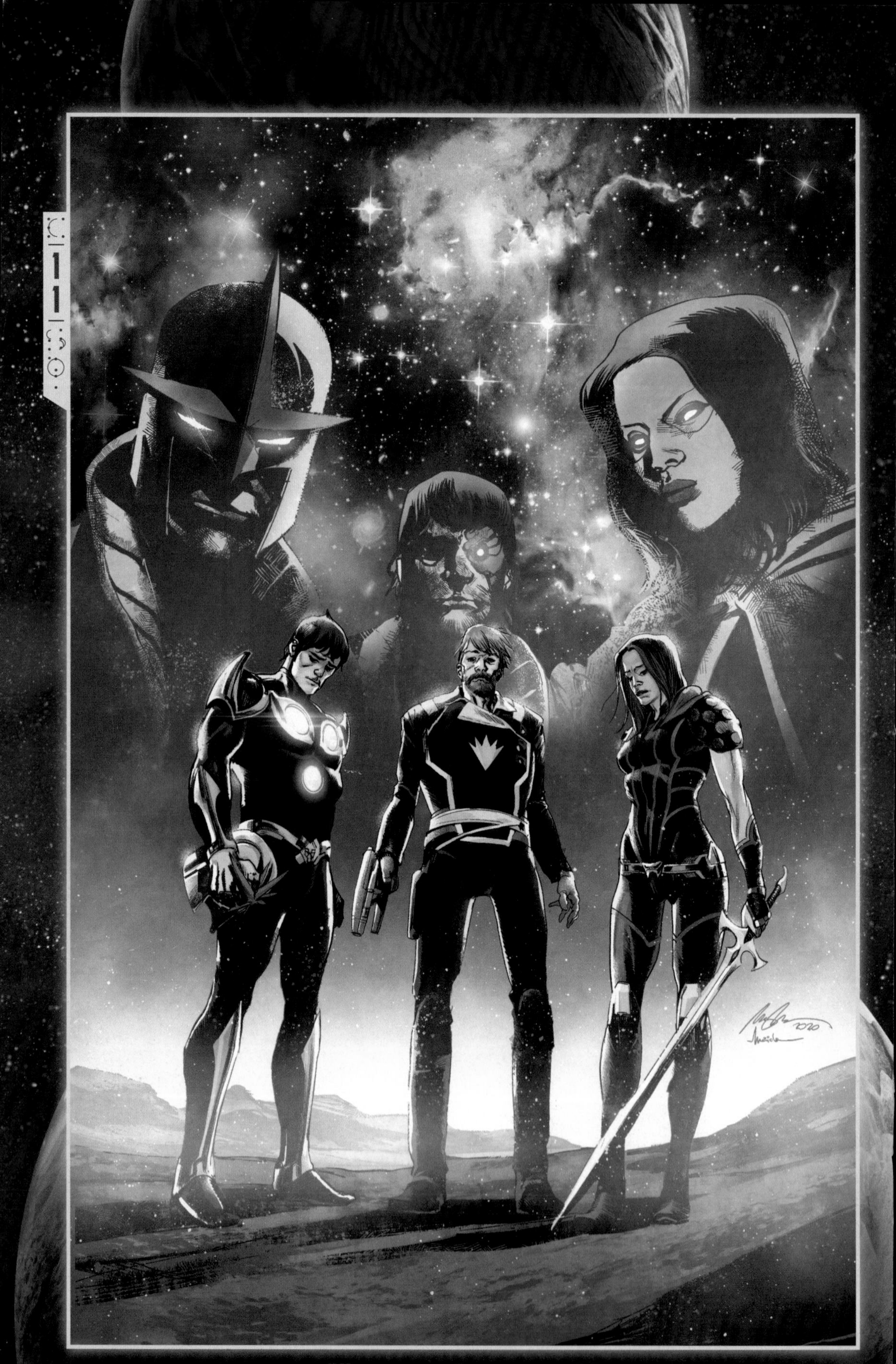

"Here we make our stand."

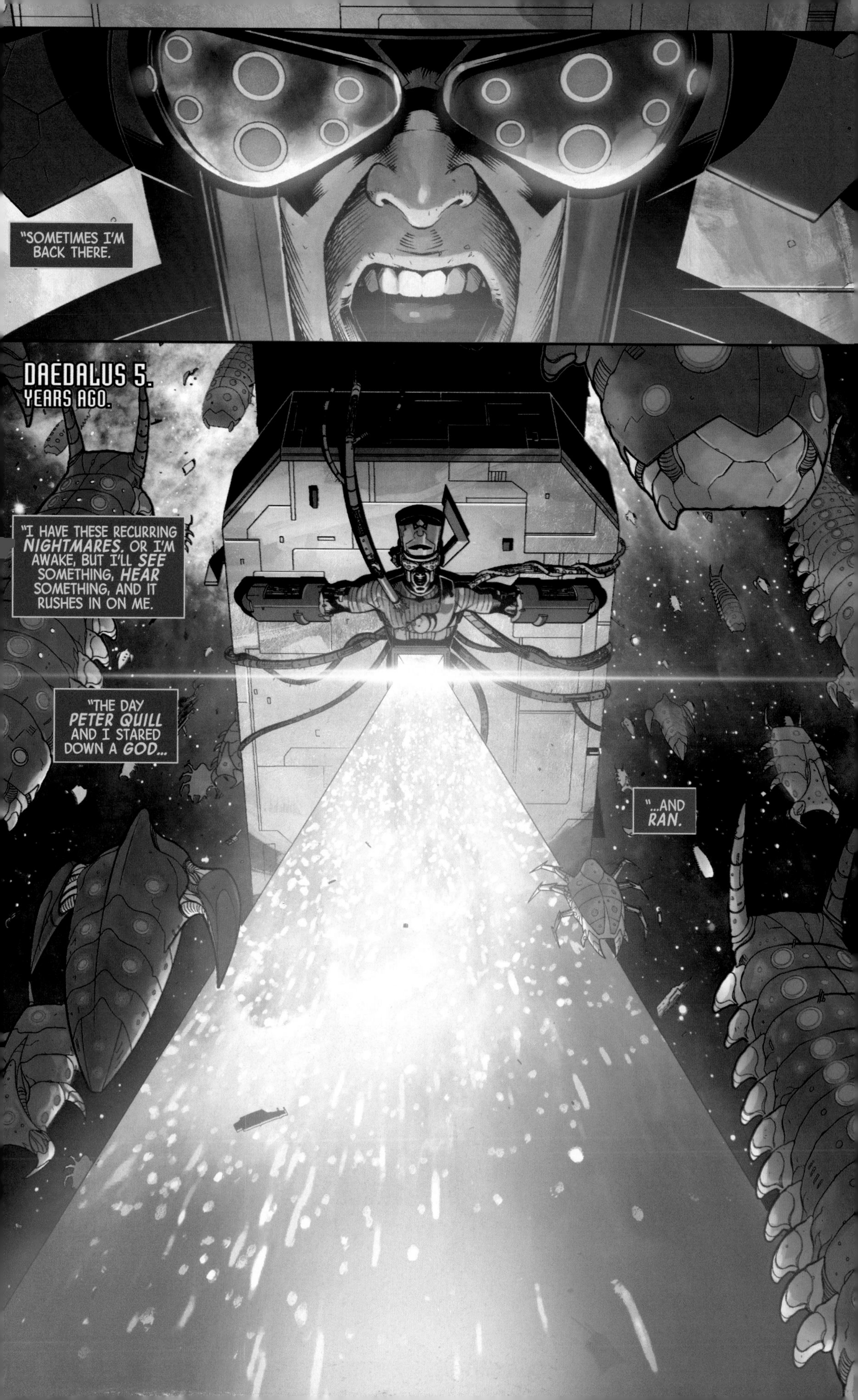
"SOMETIMES I'M BACK THERE.
DAEDALUS 5. YEARS AGO.
"I HAVE THESE RECURRING NIGHTMARES. OR I'M AWAKE, BUT I'LL SEE SOMETHING, HEAR SOMETHING, AND IT RUSHES IN ON ME.
"THE DAY PETER QUILL AND I STARED DOWN A GOD...
"...AND RAN.

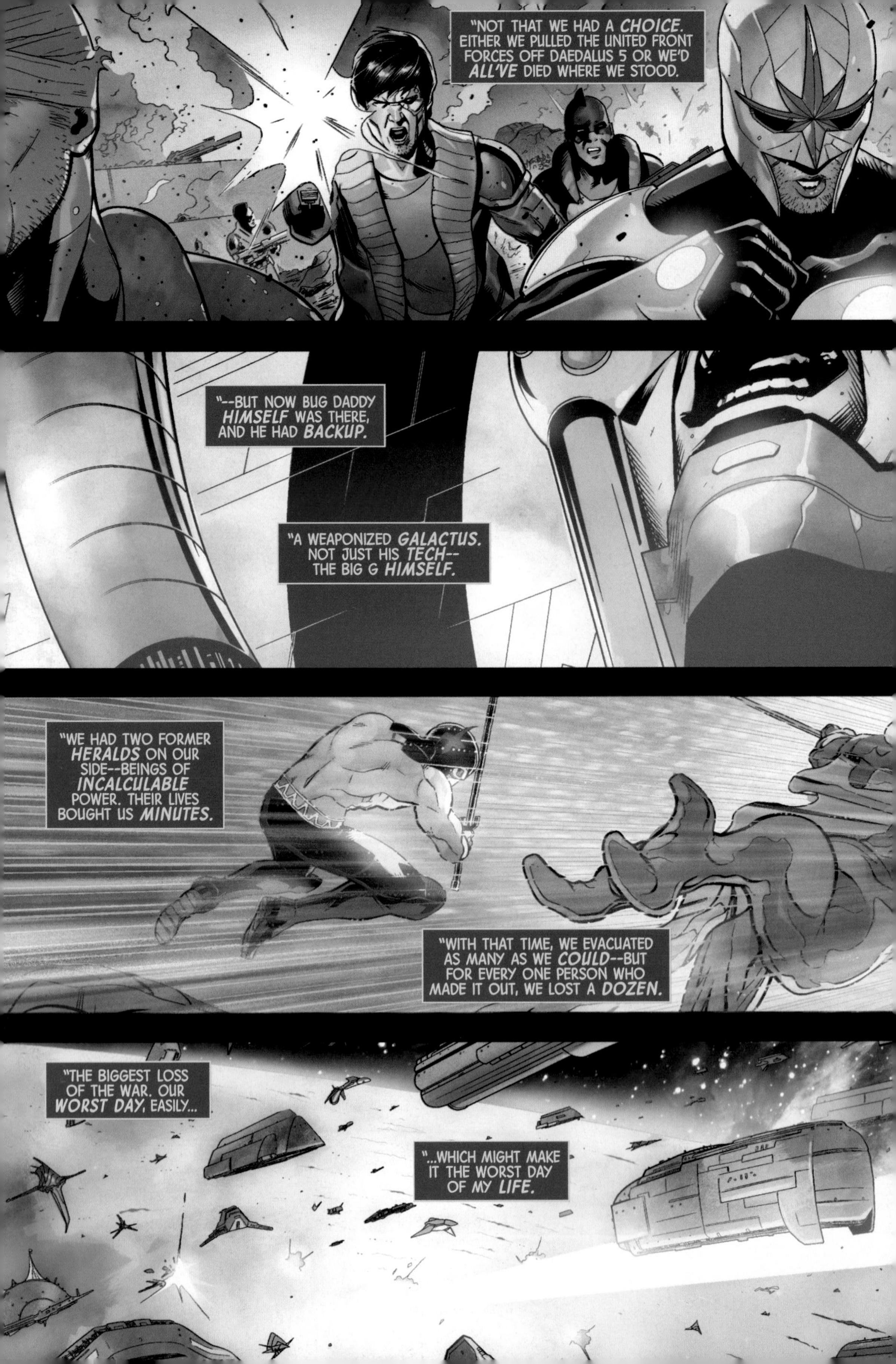
"NOT THAT WE HAD A CHOICE. EITHER WE PULLED THE UNITED FRONT FORCES OFF DAEDALUS 5 OR WE'D ALL'VE DIED WHERE WE STOOD.
"--BUT NOW BUG DADDY HIMSELF WAS THERE, AND HE HAD BACKUP.
"A WEAPONIZED GALACTUS. NOT JUST HIS TECH-- THE BIG G HIMSELF.
"WE HAD TWO FORMER HERALDS ON OUR SIDE--BEINGS OF INCALCULABLE POWER. THEIR LIVES BOUGHT US MINUTES.
"WITH THAT TIME, WE EVACUATED AS MANY AS WE COULD--BUT FOR EVERY ONE PERSON WHO MADE IT OUT, WE LOST A DOZEN.
"THE BIGGEST LOSS OF THE WAR. OUR WORST DAY, EASILY...
"...WHICH MIGHT MAKE IT THE WORST DAY OF MY LIFE.

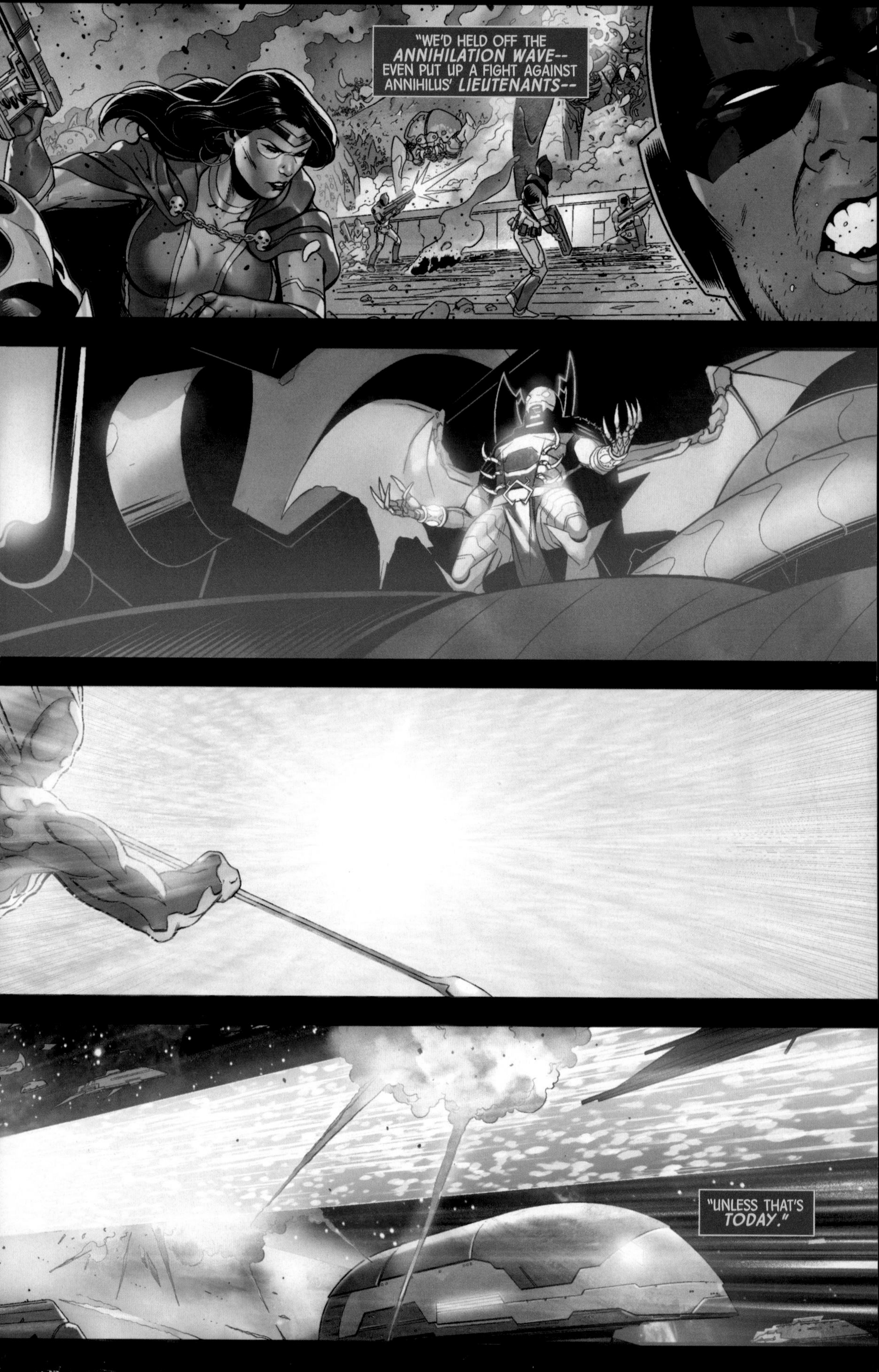
"WE'D HELD OFF THE ANNIHILATION WAVE-- EVEN PUT UP A FIGHT AGAINST ANNIHILUS' LIEUTENANTS--
"UNLESS THAT'S TODAY."

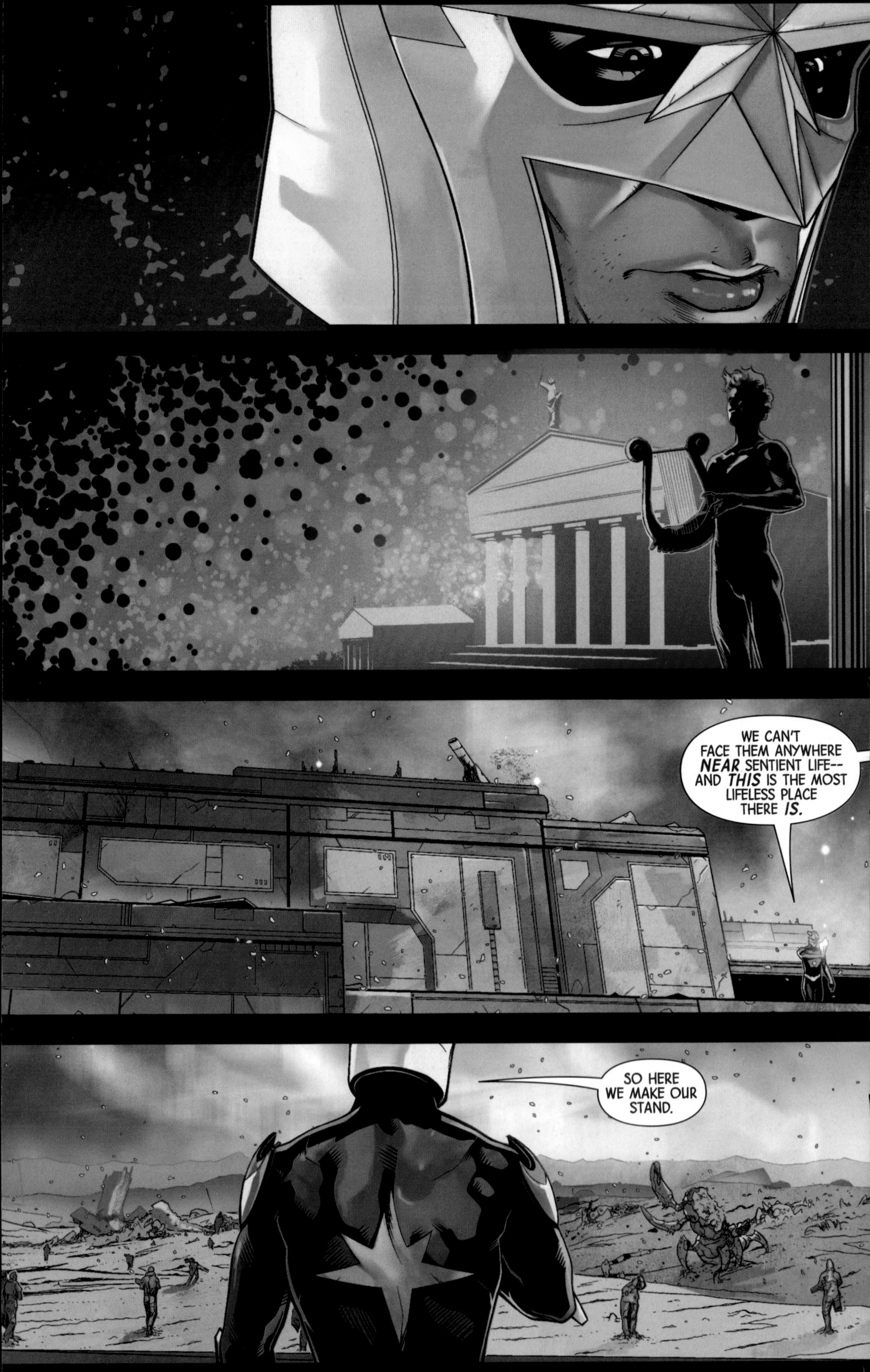
WE CAN'T FACE THEM ANYWHERE NEAR SENTIENT LIFE-- AND THIS IS THE MOST LIFELESS PLACE THERE IS.
SO HERE WE MAKE OUR STAND.

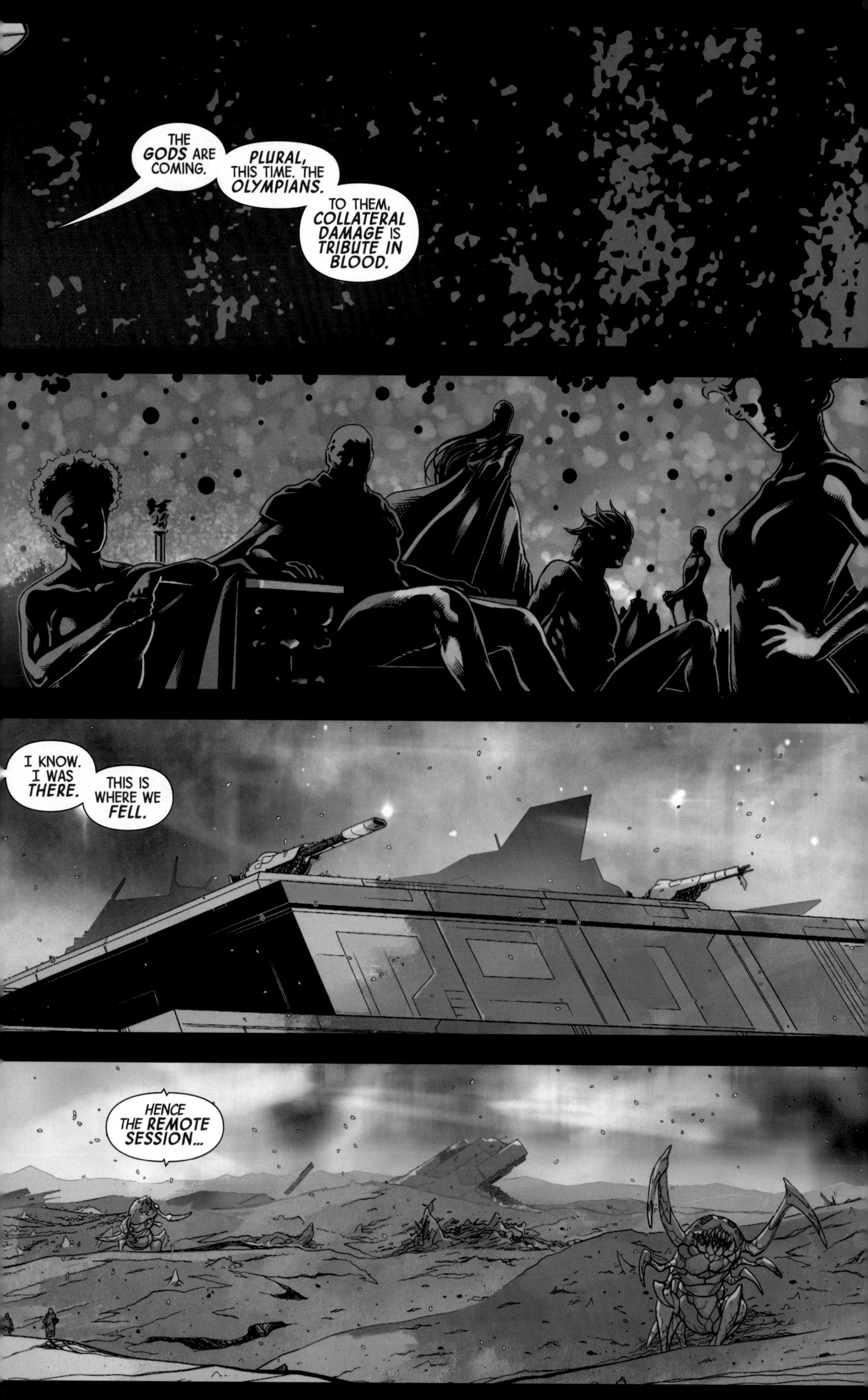
THE GODS ARE COMING.
PLURAL, THIS TIME. THE OLYMPIANS.
TO THEM, COLLATERAL DAMAGE IS TRIBUTE IN BLOOD.
I KNOW. I WAS THERE.
THIS IS WHERE WE FELL.
HENCE THE REMOTE SESSION...

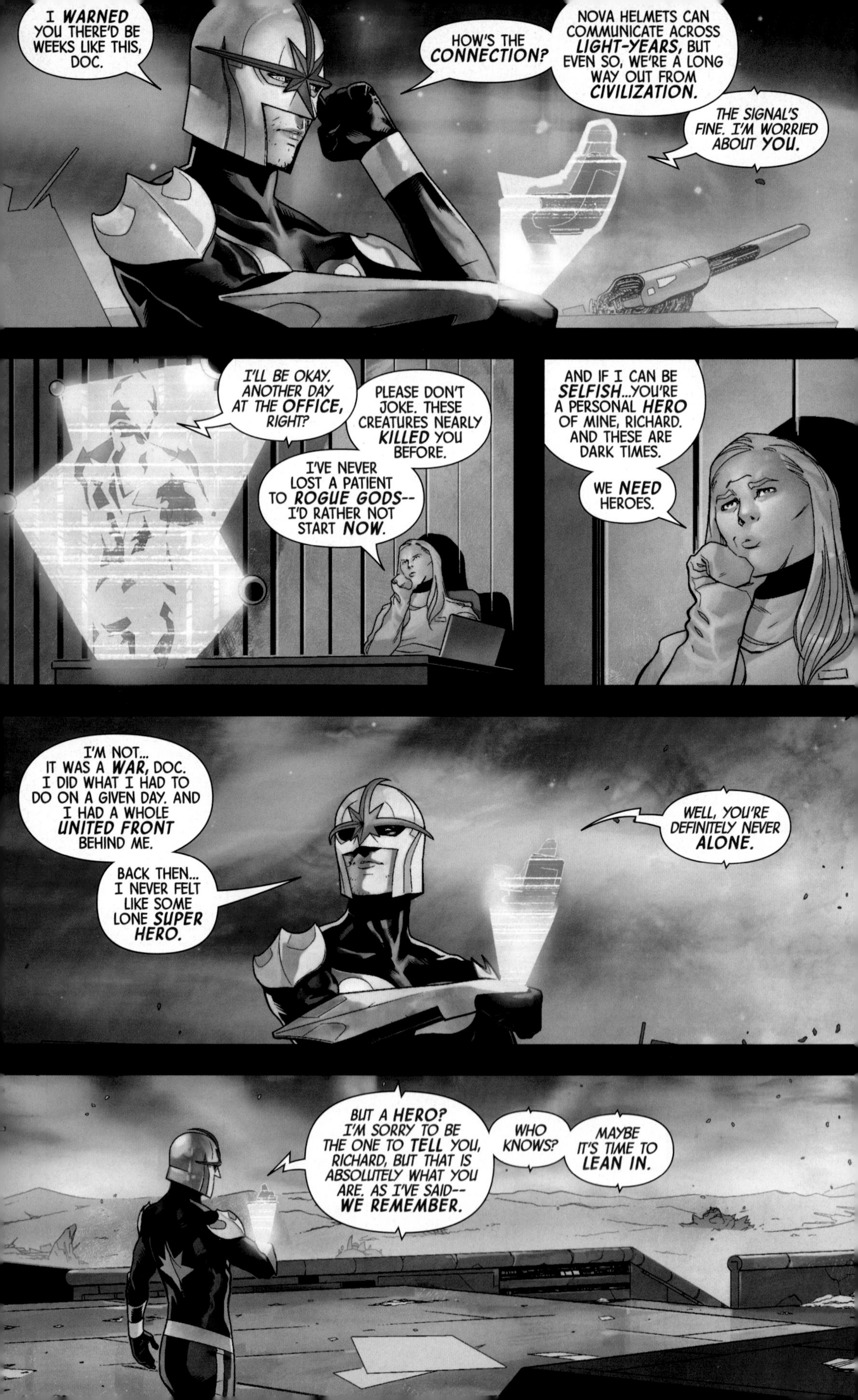
I WARNED YOU THERE'D BE WEEKS LIKE THIS, DOC.
HOW'S THE CONNECTION?
NOVA HELMETS CAN COMMUNICATE ACROSS LIGHT-YEARS, BUT EVEN SO, WE'RE A LONG WAY OUT FROM CIVILIZATION.
THE SIGNAL'S FINE. I'M WORRIED ABOUT YOU.
I'LL BE OKAY. ANOTHER DAY AT THE OFFICE, RIGHT?
PLEASE DON'T JOKE. THESE CREATURES NEARLY KILLED YOU BEFORE.
I'VE NEVER LOST A PATIENT TO ROGUE GODS-- I'D RATHER NOT START NOW.
AND IF I CAN BE SELFISH...YOU'RE A PERSONAL HERO OF MINE, RICHARD. AND THESE ARE DARK TIMES.
WE NEED HEROES.
I'M NOT... IT WAS A WAR, DOC. I DID WHAT I HAD TO DO ON A GIVEN DAY. AND I HAD A WHOLE UNITED FRONT BEHIND ME.
BACK THEN... I NEVER FELT LIKE SOME LONE SUPER HERO.
WELL, YOU'RE DEFINITELY NEVER ALONE.
BUT A HERO? I'M SORRY TO BE THE ONE TO TELL YOU, RICHARD, BUT THAT IS ABSOLUTELY WHAT YOU ARE. AS I'VE SAID-- WE REMEMBER.
WHO KNOWS?
MAYBE IT'S TIME TO LEAN IN.

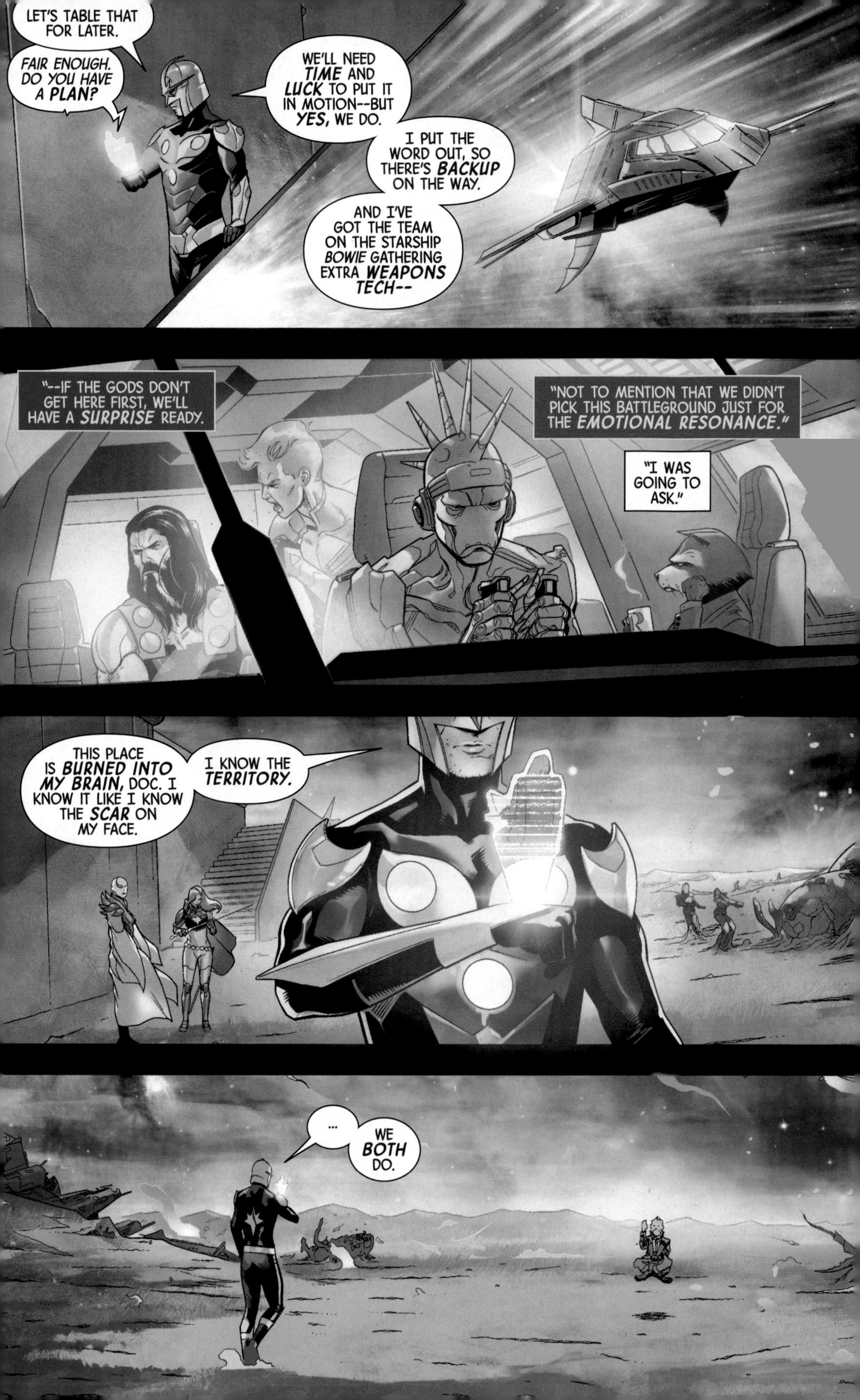
LET'S TABLE THAT FOR LATER.
FAIR ENOUGH. DO YOU HAVE A PLAN?
WE'LL NEED TIME AND LUCK TO PUT IT IN MOTION--BUT YES, WE DO.
I PUT THE WORD OUT, SO THERE'S BACKUP ON THE WAY.
AND I'VE GOT THE TEAM ON THE STARSHIP BOWIE GATHERING EXTRA WEAPONS TECH--
"--IF THE GODS DON'T GET HERE FIRST, WE'LL HAVE A SURPRISE READY.
"NOT TO MENTION THAT WE DIDN'T PICK THIS BATTLEGROUND JUST FOR THE EMOTIONAL RESONANCE."
"I WAS GOING TO ASK."
I KNOW THE TERRITORY.
THIS PLACE IS BURNED INTO MY BRAIN, DOC. I KNOW IT LIKE I KNOW THE SCAR ON MY FACE.
...
WE BOTH DO.

YES. YOU MENTIONED...

I MENTIONED. HE'S *BACK*.

PETE...HE SPENT YEARS SOMEWHERE *ELSE*. LIVED A WHOLE *LIFE*, BUT DIDN'T *AGE*...

...AND THEN HE JUST FELL OUT OF THE SKY. IN *TROUBLE*, LIKE HE ALWAYS IS.

BUT NOT *DEAD*.

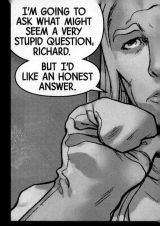

I'M GOING TO ASK WHAT MIGHT SEEM A VERY STUPID QUESTION, RICHARD.

BUT I'D LIKE AN HONEST ANSWER.

HOW DO *YOU* FEEL ABOUT THAT?

IT'S A LOT.

I MEAN, I'M--DON'T GET ME WRONG, I AM *SO* RELIEVED. IT'S A *MIRACLE*, YOU KNOW?

BUT AT THE SAME TIME... THERE'S PART OF ME THAT NEEDS TO *KNOW*--

WHAT THE HELL WERE YOU THINKING?

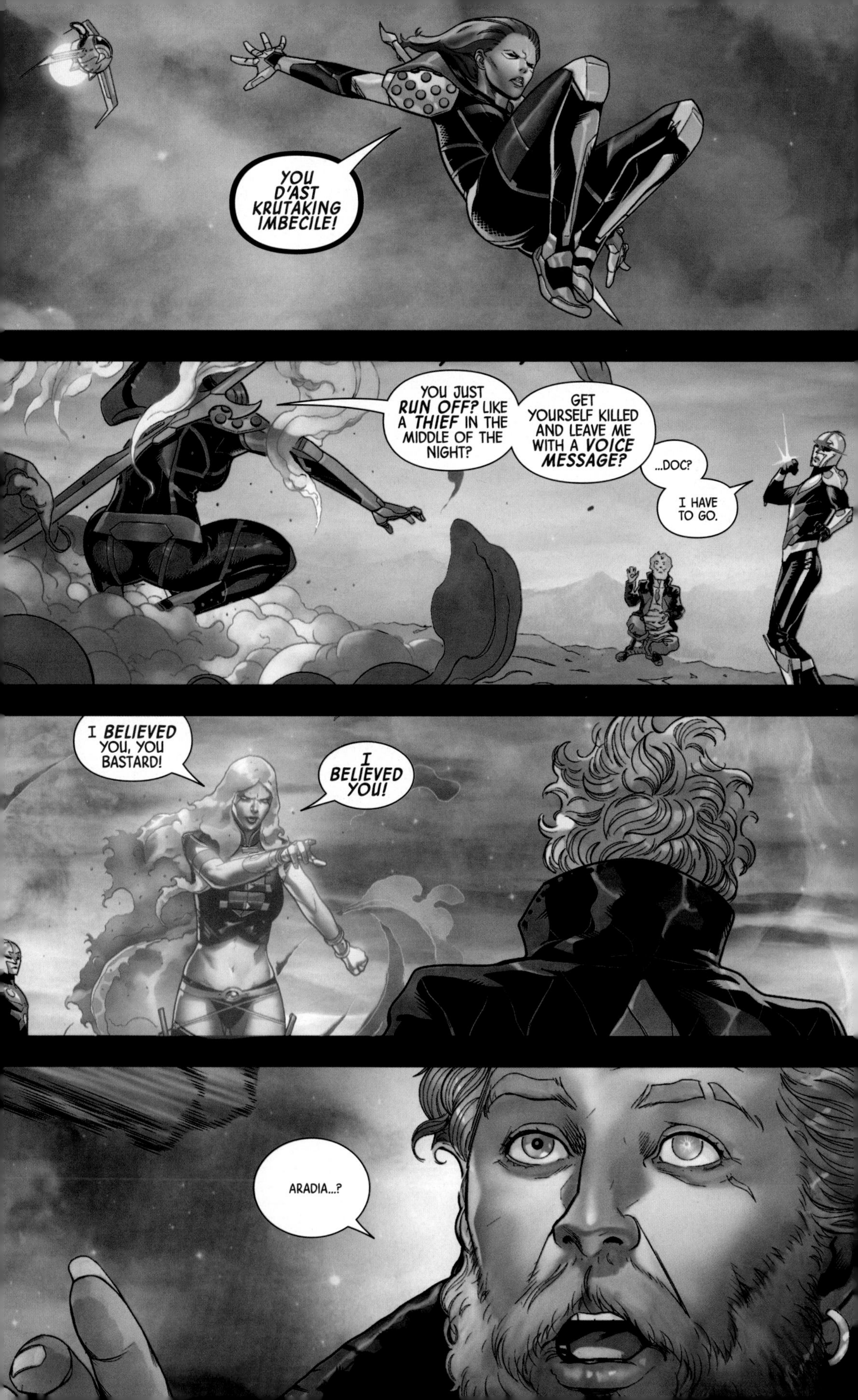
YOU D'AST KRUTAKING IMBECILE!
YOU JUST RUN OFF? LIKE A THIEF IN THE MIDDLE OF THE NIGHT?
GET YOURSELF KILLED AND LEAVE ME WITH A VOICE MESSAGE?
...DOC?
I HAVE TO GO.
I BELIEVED YOU, YOU BASTARD!
I BELIEVED YOU!
ARADIA...?

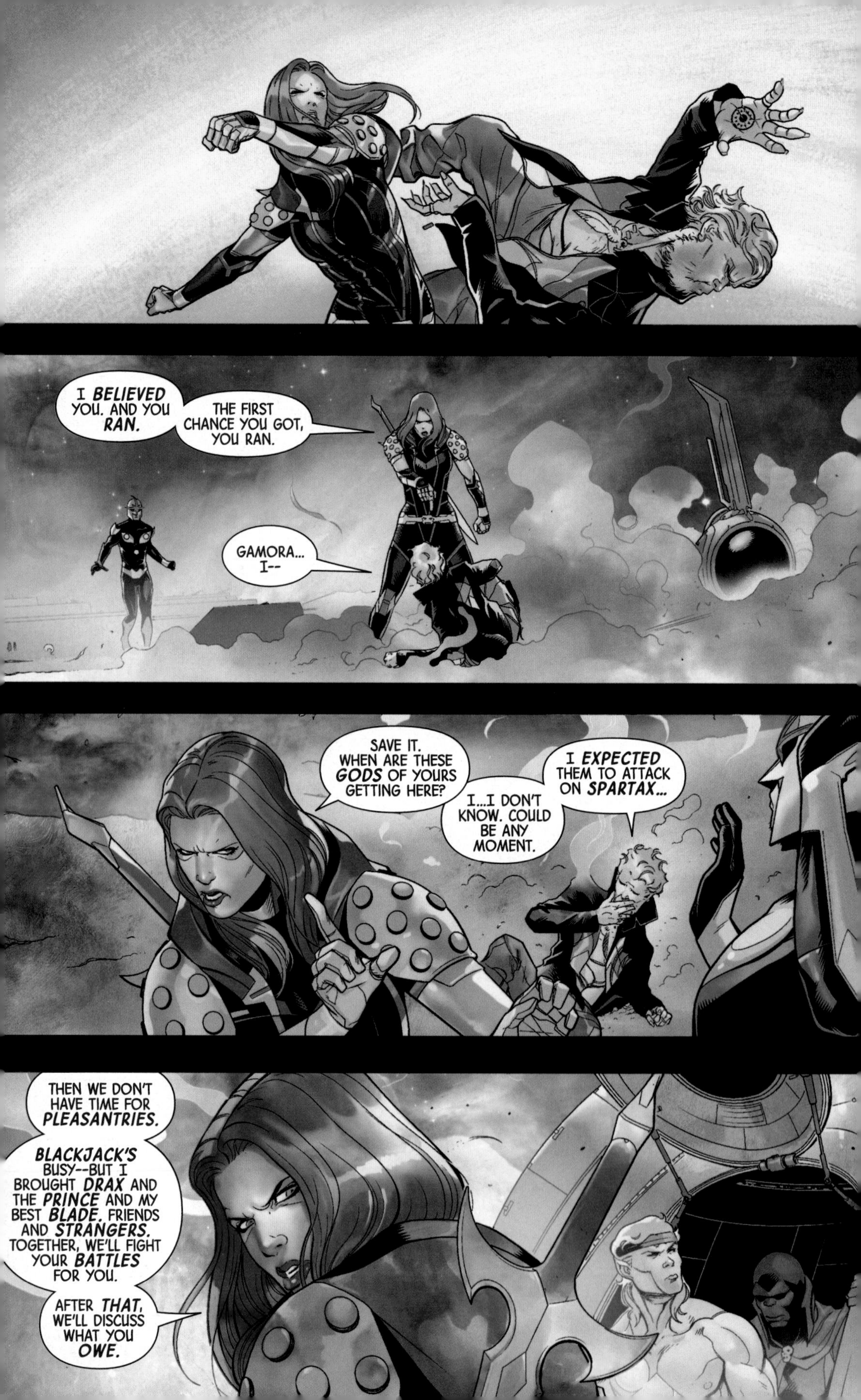
I BELIEVED YOU. AND YOU RAN.
THE FIRST CHANCE YOU GOT, YOU RAN.
GAMORA... I--
SAVE IT. WHEN ARE THESE GODS OF YOURS GETTING HERE?
I...I DON'T KNOW. COULD BE ANY MOMENT.
I EXPECTED THEM TO ATTACK ON SPARTAX...
THEN WE DON'T HAVE TIME FOR PLEASANTRIES.
BLACKJACK'S BUSY--BUT I BROUGHT DRAX AND THE PRINCE AND MY BEST BLADE. FRIENDS AND STRANGERS. TOGETHER, WE'LL FIGHT YOUR BATTLES FOR YOU.
AFTER THAT, WE'LL DISCUSS WHAT YOU OWE.

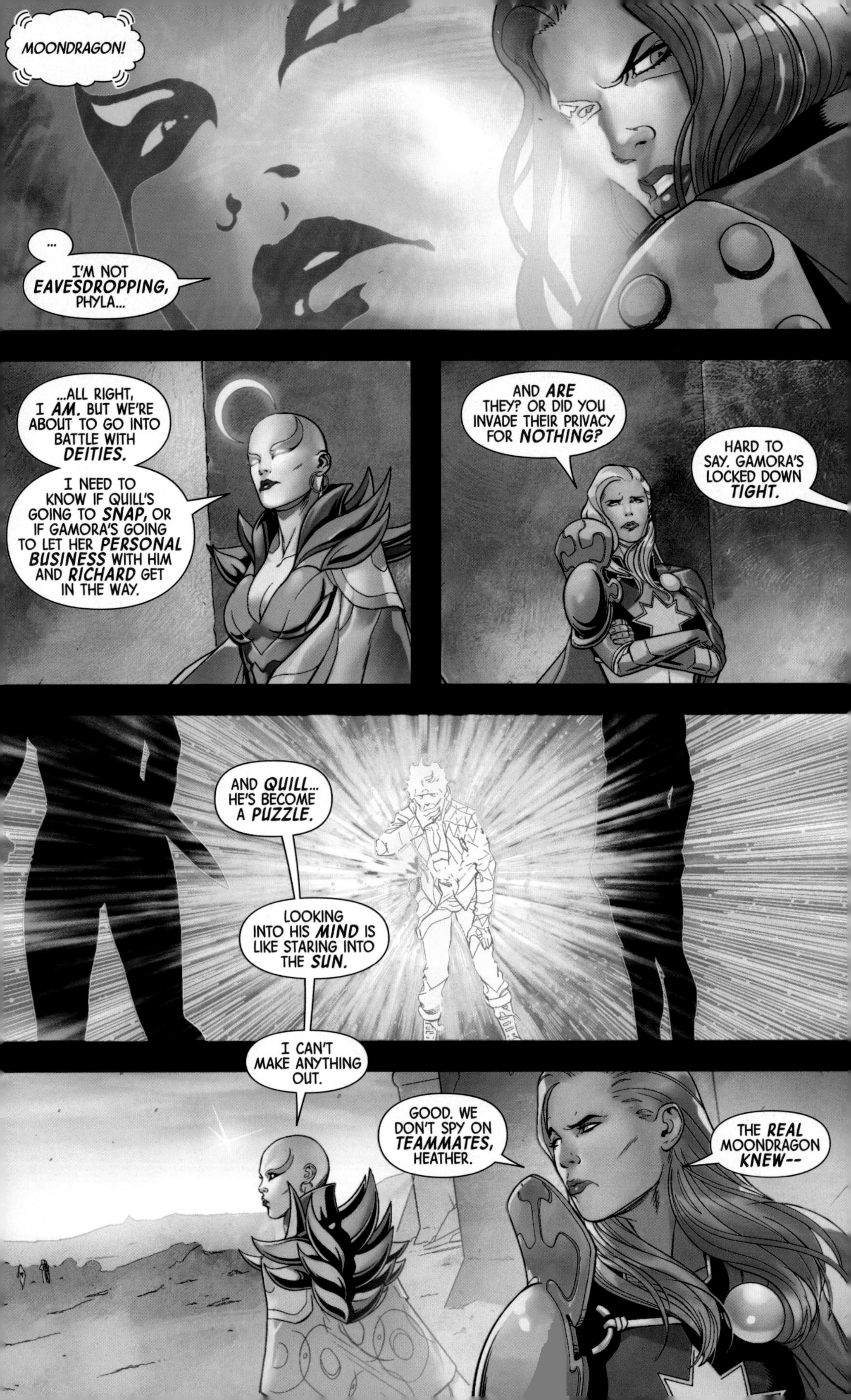
MOONDRAGON!
... I'M NOT EAVESDROPPING, PHYLA...
...ALL RIGHT, I AM. BUT WE'RE ABOUT TO GO INTO BATTLE WITH DEITIES.
I NEED TO KNOW IF QUILL'S GOING TO SNAP, OR IF GAMORA'S GOING TO LET HER PERSONAL BUSINESS WITH HIM AND RICHARD GET IN THE WAY.
AND ARE THEY? OR DID YOU INVADE THEIR PRIVACY FOR NOTHING?
HARD TO SAY. GAMORA'S LOCKED DOWN TIGHT.
AND QUILL... HE'S BECOME A PUZZLE.
LOOKING INTO HIS MIND IS LIKE STARING INTO THE SUN.
I CAN'T MAKE ANYTHING OUT.
GOOD. WE DON'T SPY ON TEAMMATES, HEATHER.
THE REAL MOONDRAGON KNEW--

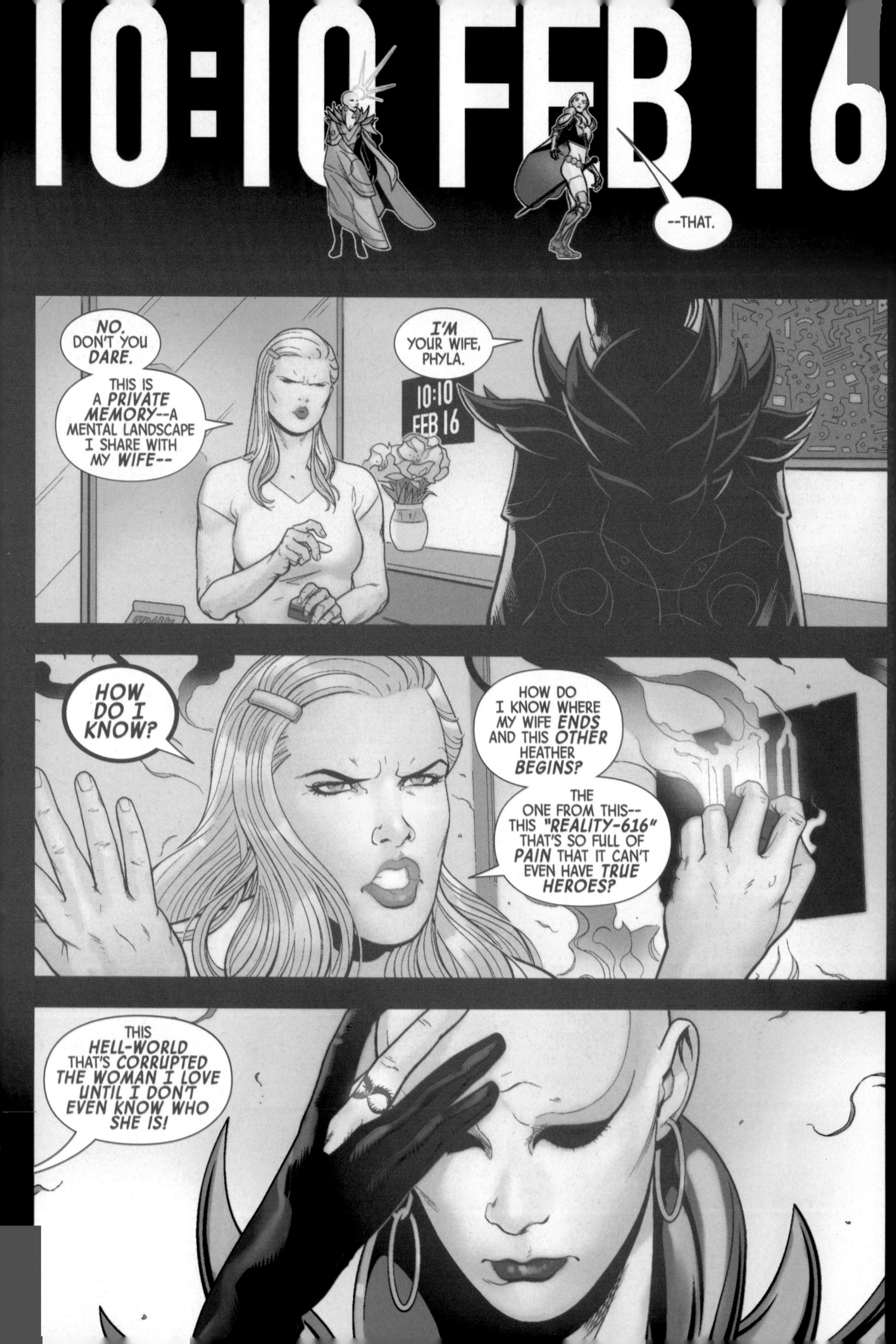
10:10 FEB 16
--THAT.
NO. DON'T YOU DARE.
THIS IS A PRIVATE MEMORY--A MENTAL LANDSCAPE I SHARE WITH MY WIFE--
I'M YOUR WIFE, PHYLA.
10:10 FEB 16
HOW DO I KNOW?
HOW DO I KNOW WHERE MY WIFE ENDS AND THIS OTHER HEATHER BEGINS?
THE ONE FROM THIS-- THIS "REALITY-616" THAT'S SO FULL OF PAIN THAT IT CAN'T EVEN HAVE TRUE HEROES?
THIS HELL-WORLD THAT'S CORRUPTED THE WOMAN I LOVE UNTIL I DON'T EVEN KNOW WHO SHE IS!

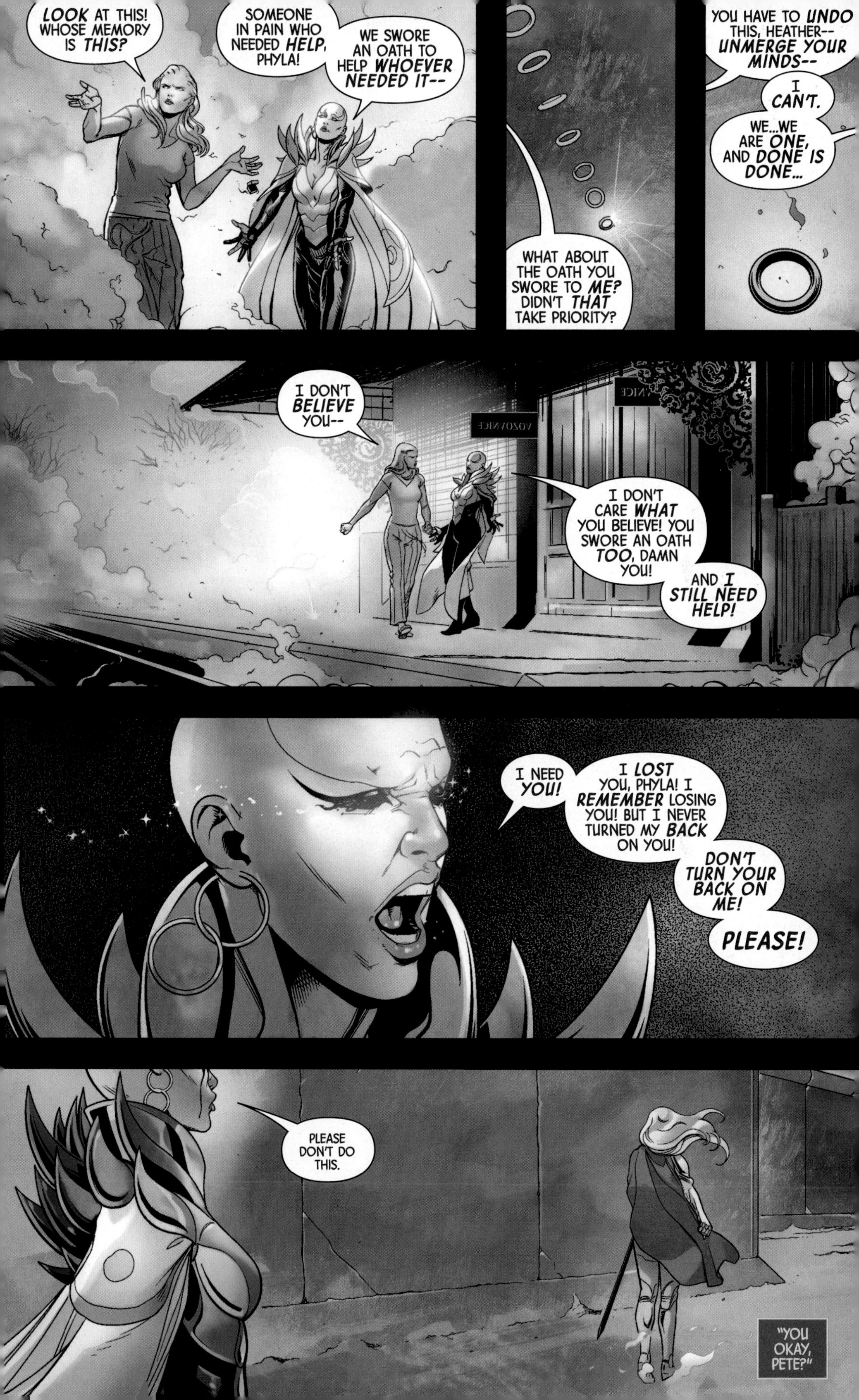
LOOK AT THIS! WHOSE MEMORY IS THIS?
SOMEONE IN PAIN WHO NEEDED HELP, PHYLA!
WE SWORE AN OATH TO HELP WHOEVER NEEDED IT--
WHAT ABOUT THE OATH YOU SWORE TO ME? DIDN'T THAT TAKE PRIORITY?
YOU HAVE TO UNDO THIS, HEATHER-- UNMERGE YOUR MINDS--
I CAN'T.
WE...WE ARE ONE, AND DONE IS DONE...
I DON'T BELIEVE YOU--
I DON'T CARE WHAT YOU BELIEVE! YOU SWORE AN OATH TOO, DAMN YOU!
AND I STILL NEED HELP!
I NEED YOU!
I LOST YOU, PHYLA! I REMEMBER LOSING YOU! BUT I NEVER TURNED MY BACK ON YOU!
DON'T TURN YOUR BACK ON ME!
PLEASE!
PLEASE DON'T DO THIS.
"YOU OKAY, PETE?"

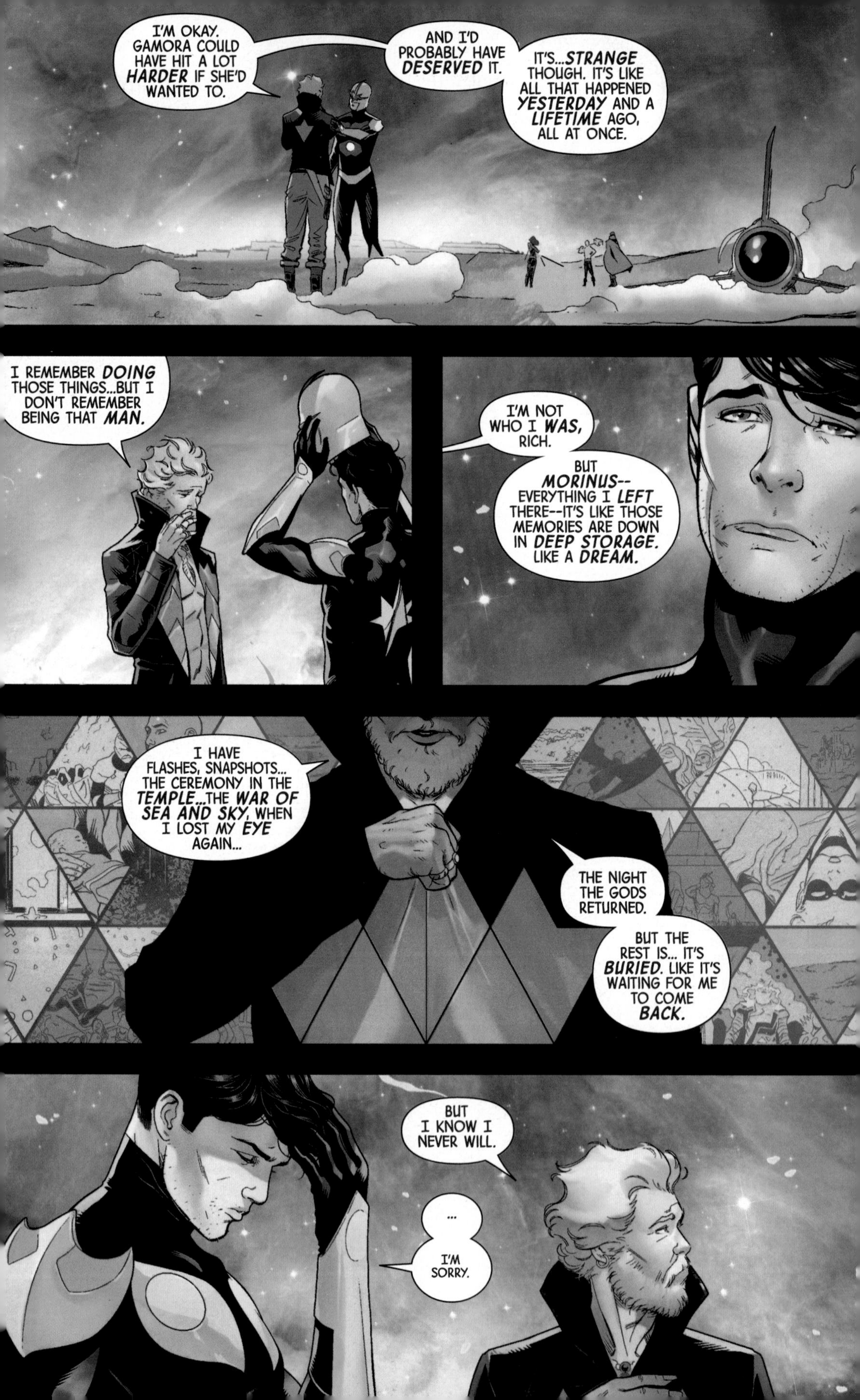

I'M OKAY. GAMORA COULD HAVE HIT A LOT HARDER IF SHE'D WANTED TO.
AND I'D PROBABLY HAVE DESERVED IT.
IT'S...STRANGE THOUGH. IT'S LIKE ALL THAT HAPPENED YESTERDAY AND A LIFETIME AGO, ALL AT ONCE.
I REMEMBER DOING THOSE THINGS...BUT I DON'T REMEMBER BEING THAT MAN.
I'M NOT WHO I WAS, RICH.
BUT MORINUS--EVERYTHING I LEFT THERE--IT'S LIKE THOSE MEMORIES ARE DOWN IN DEEP STORAGE. LIKE A DREAM.
I HAVE FLASHES, SNAPSHOTS... THE CEREMONY IN THE TEMPLE...THE WAR OF SEA AND SKY, WHEN I LOST MY EYE AGAIN...
THE NIGHT THE GODS RETURNED.
BUT THE REST IS... IT'S BURIED. LIKE IT'S WAITING FOR ME TO COME BACK.
BUT I KNOW I NEVER WILL.
...
I'M SORRY.

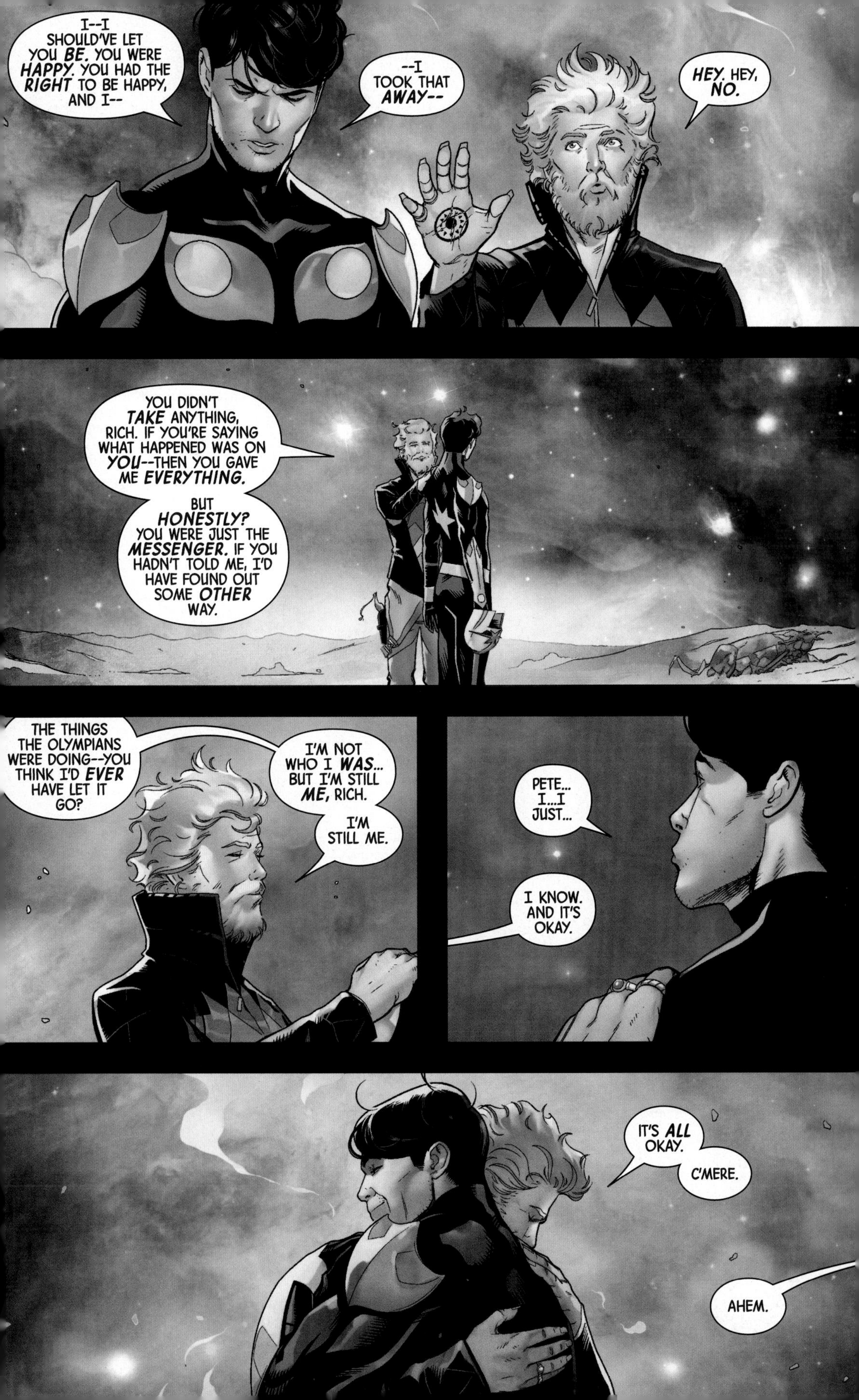

I--I SHOULD'VE LET YOU BE. YOU WERE HAPPY. YOU HAD THE RIGHT TO BE HAPPY, AND I--
--I TOOK THAT AWAY--
HEY. HEY, NO.
YOU DIDN'T TAKE ANYTHING, RICH. IF YOU'RE SAYING WHAT HAPPENED WAS ON YOU--THEN YOU GAVE ME EVERYTHING.
BUT HONESTLY? YOU WERE JUST THE MESSENGER. IF YOU HADN'T TOLD ME, I'D HAVE FOUND OUT SOME OTHER WAY.
THE THINGS THE OLYMPIANS WERE DOING--YOU THINK I'D EVER HAVE LET IT GO?
I'M NOT WHO I WAS... BUT I'M STILL ME, RICH.
I'M STILL ME.
PETE... I...I JUST...
I KNOW. AND IT'S OKAY.
IT'S ALL OKAY.
C'MERE.
AHEM.

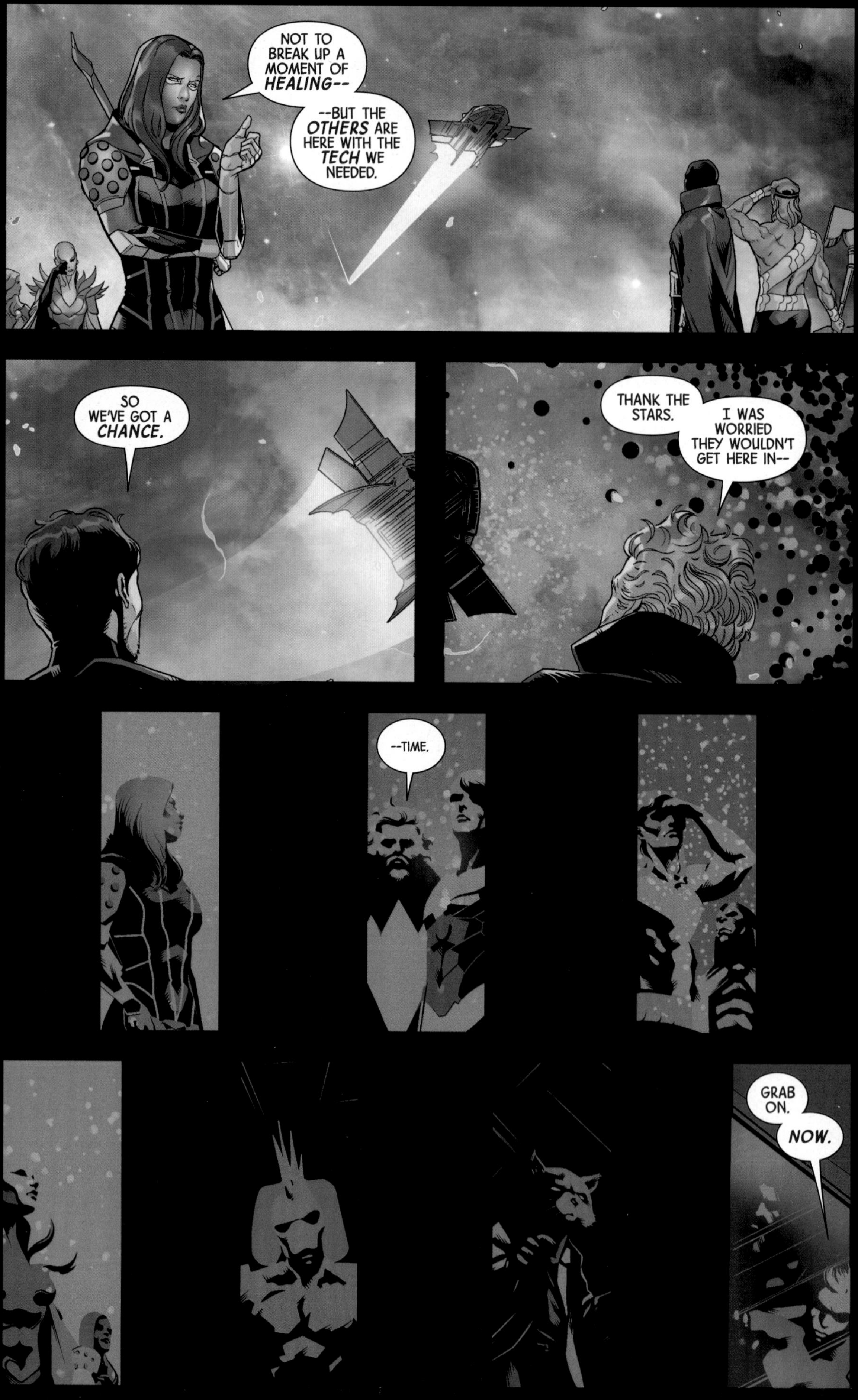
NOT TO BREAK UP A MOMENT OF HEALING--
--BUT THE OTHERS ARE HERE WITH THE TECH WE NEEDED.
SO WE'VE GOT A CHANCE.
THANK THE STARS.
I WAS WORRIED THEY WOULDN'T GET HERE IN--
--TIME.
GRAB ON.
NOW.

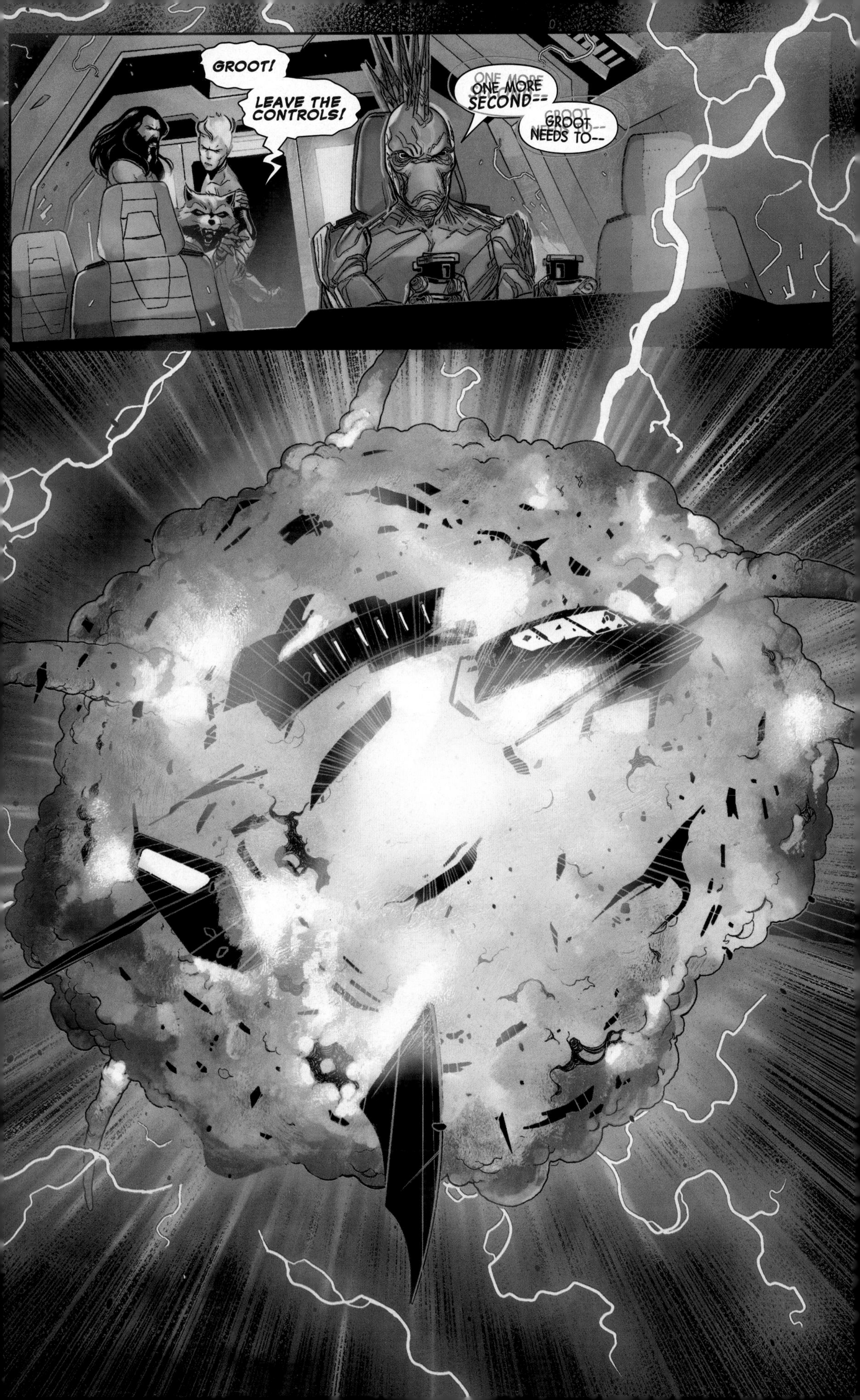
GROOT!
LEAVE THE CONTROLS!
ONE MORE SECOND--
GROOT NEEDS TO--

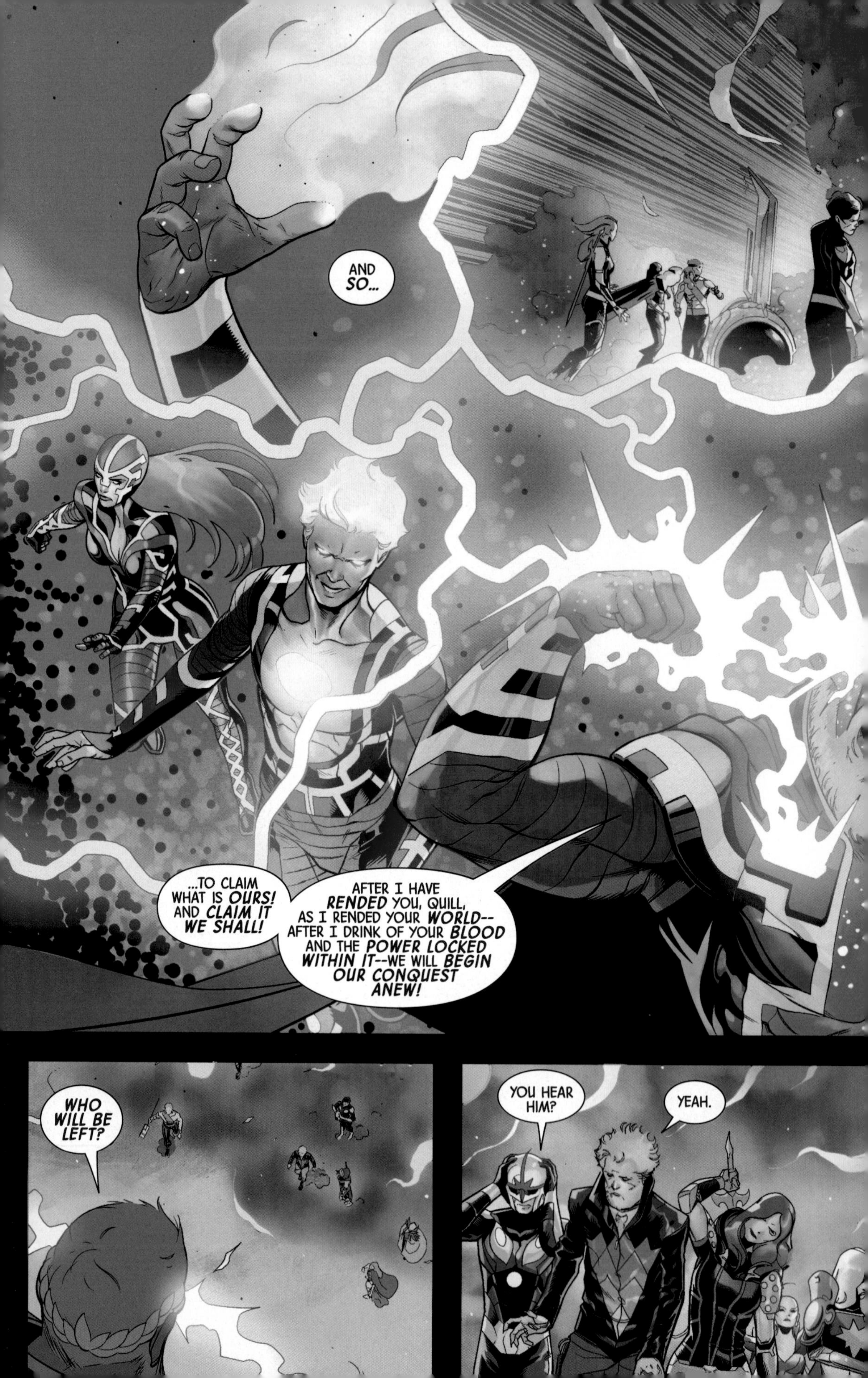
AND SO...
...TO CLAIM WHAT IS OURS! AND CLAIM IT WE SHALL!
AFTER I HAVE RENDED YOU, QUILL, AS I RENDED YOUR WORLD-- AFTER I DRINK OF YOUR BLOOD AND THE POWER LOCKED WITHIN IT--WE WILL BEGIN OUR CONQUEST ANEW!
WHO WILL BE LEFT?
YOU HEAR HIM?
YEAH.

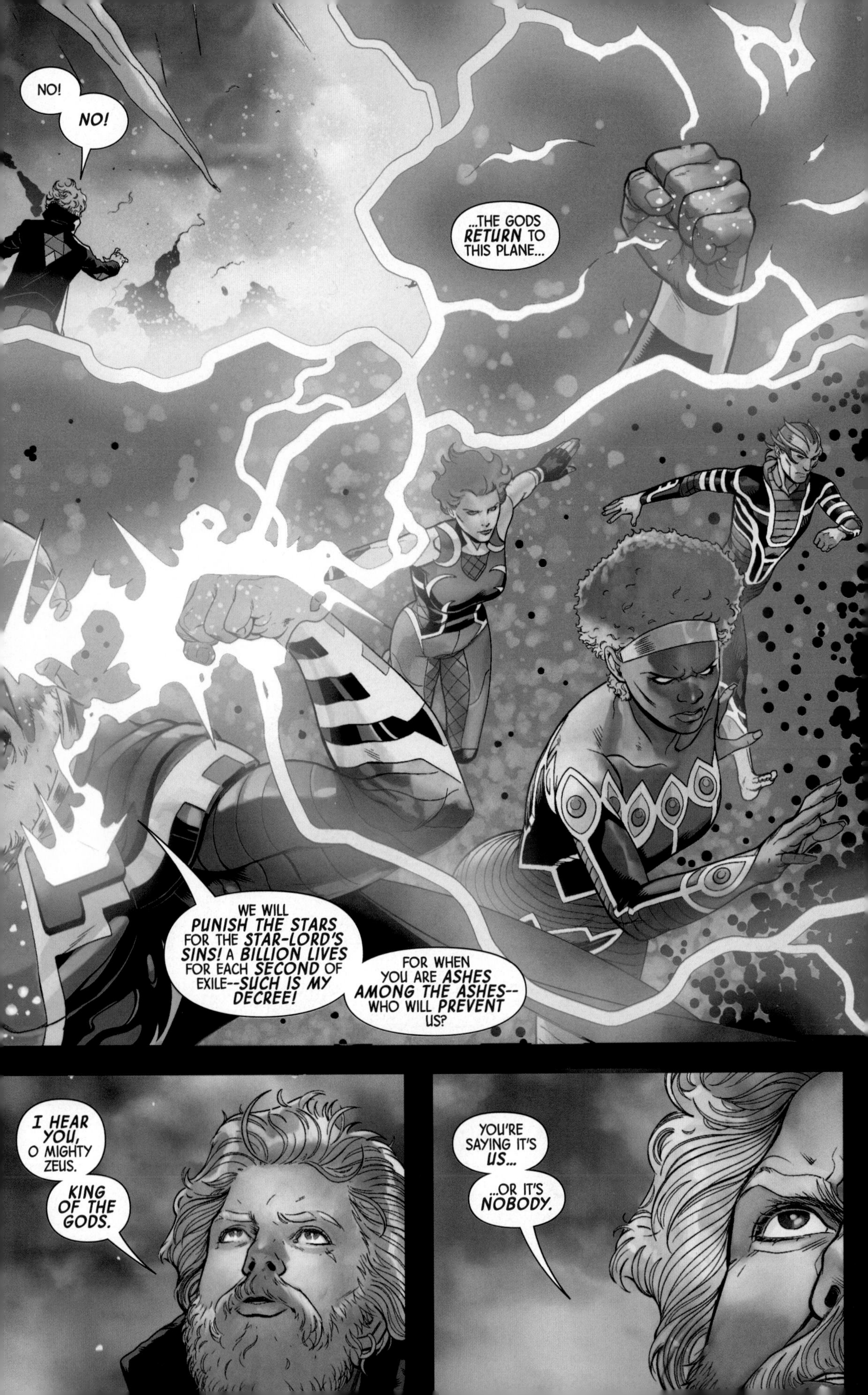
NO!
NO!
...THE GODS RETURN TO THIS PLANE...
WE WILL PUNISH THE STARS FOR THE STAR-LORD'S SINS! A BILLION LIVES FOR EACH SECOND OF EXILE--SUCH IS MY DECREE!
FOR WHEN YOU ARE ASHES AMONG THE ASHES-- WHO WILL PREVENT US?
I HEAR YOU, O MIGHTY ZEUS.
KING OF THE GODS.
YOU'RE SAYING IT'S US...
...OR IT'S NOBODY.

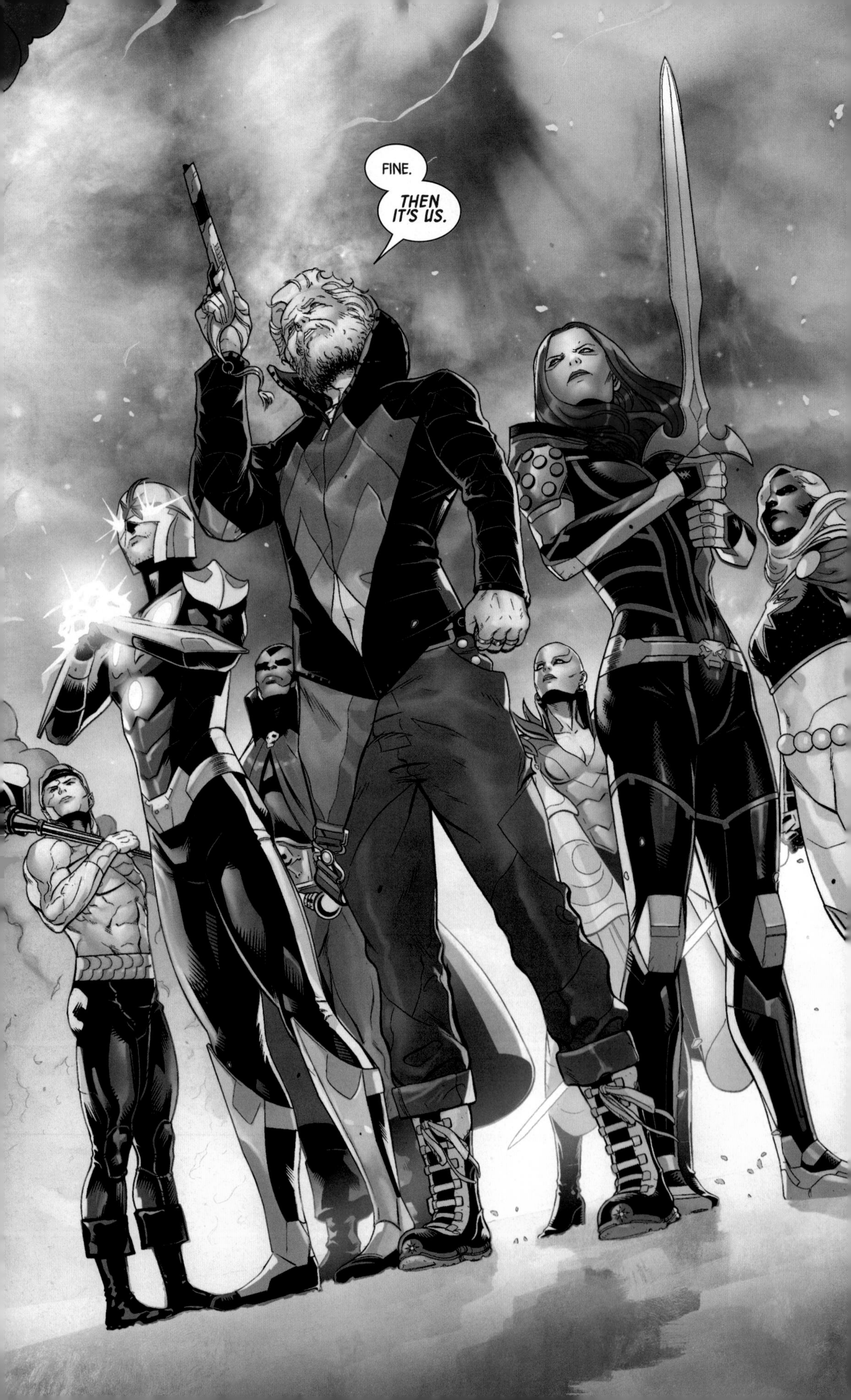
FINE.
THEN IT'S US.

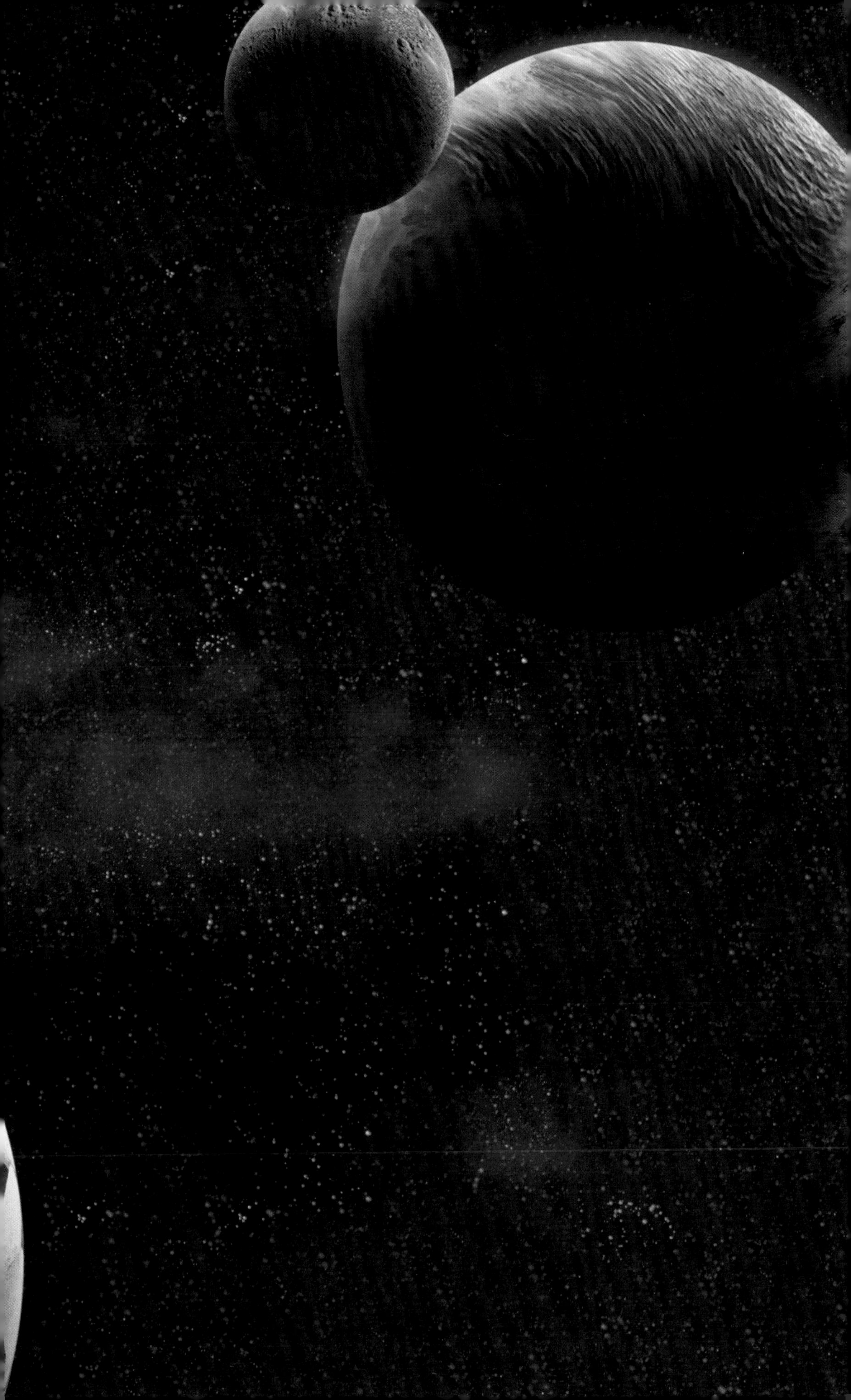

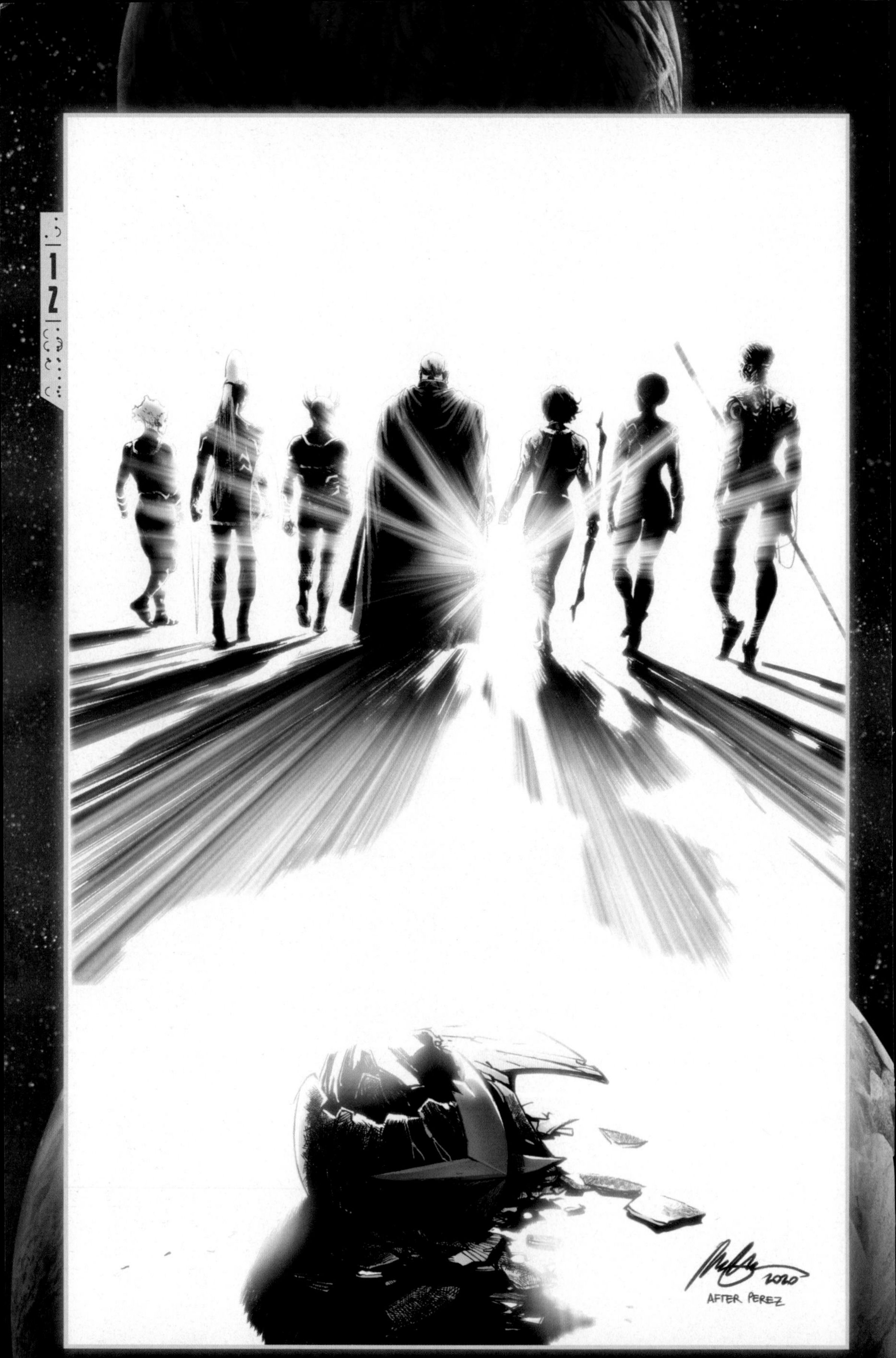
2020
AFTER PEREZ

"The time of mercy is past."

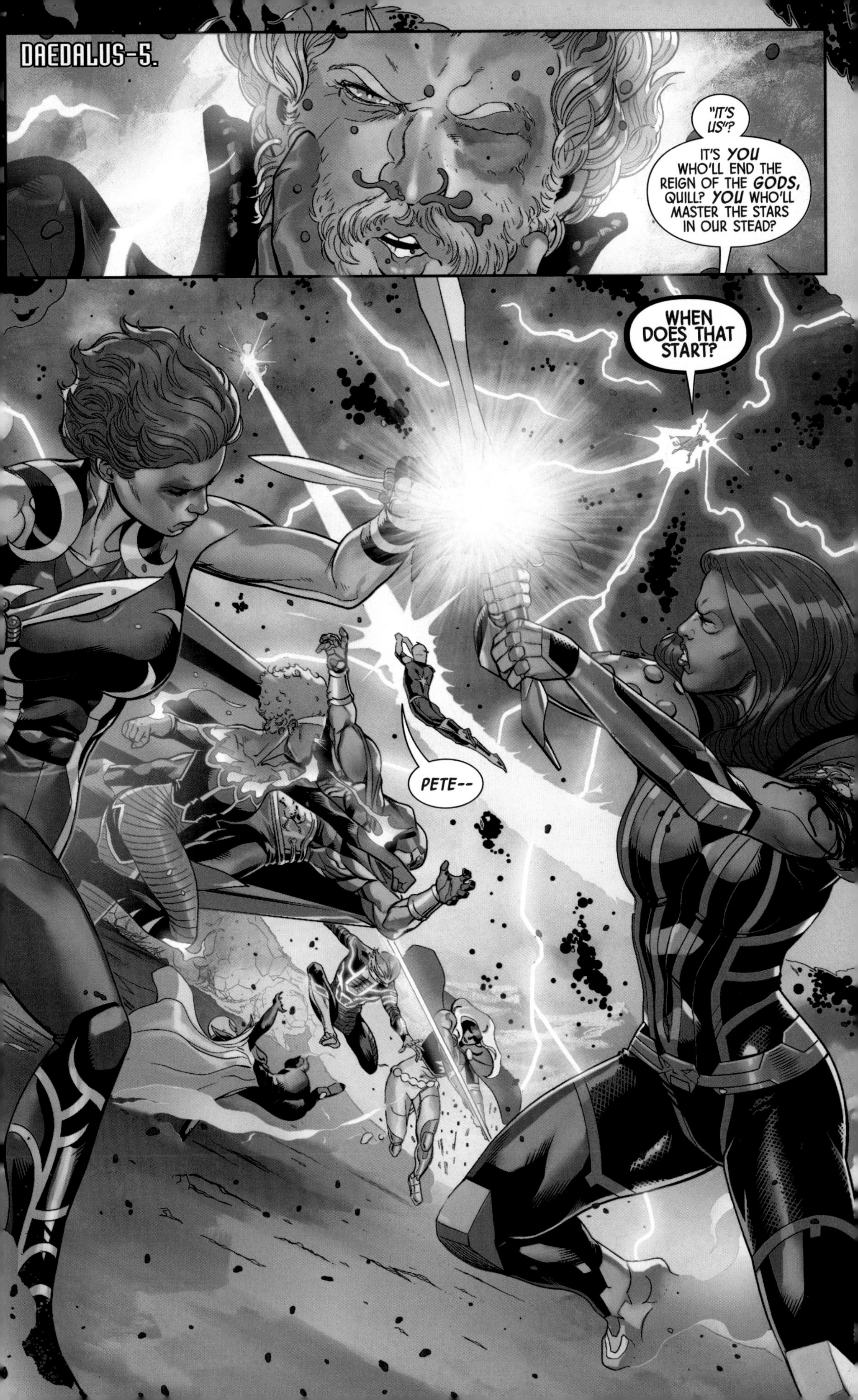
DAEDALUS-5.
"IT'S US"?
IT'S YOU WHO'LL END THE REIGN OF THE GODS, QUILL? YOU WHO'LL MASTER THE STARS IN OUR STEAD?
WHEN DOES THAT START?
PETE--

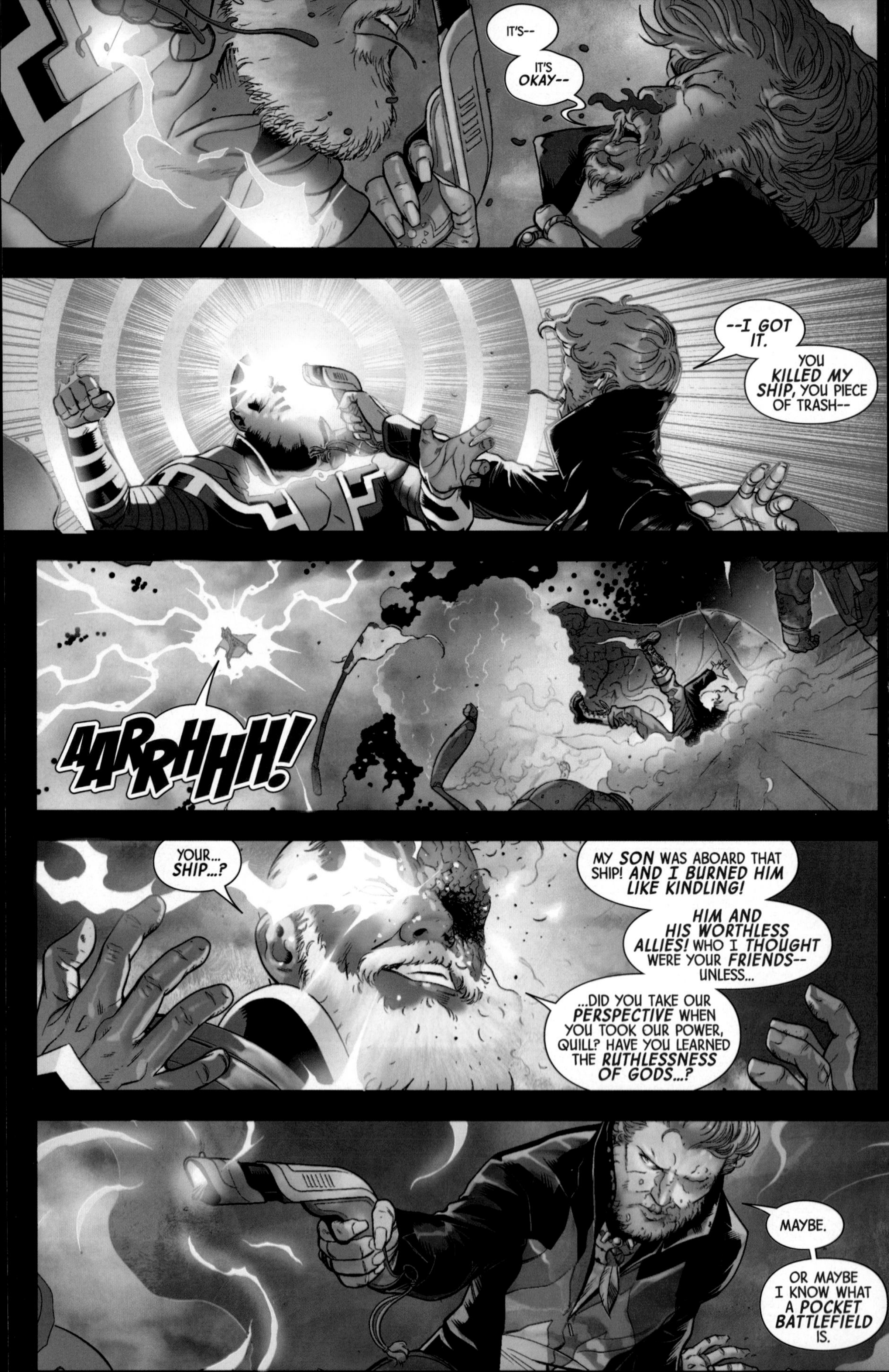
IT'S--
IT'S OKAY--
--I GOT IT.
YOU KILLED MY SHIP, YOU PIECE OF TRASH--
AARRHHH!
YOUR... SHIP...?
MY SON WAS ABOARD THAT SHIP! AND I BURNED HIM LIKE KINDLING!
HIM AND HIS WORTHLESS ALLIES! WHO I THOUGHT WERE YOUR FRIENDS-- UNLESS...
...DID YOU TAKE OUR PERSPECTIVE WHEN YOU TOOK OUR POWER, QUILL? HAVE YOU LEARNED THE RUTHLESSNESS OF GODS...?
MAYBE.
OR MAYBE I KNOW WHAT A POCKET BATTLEFIELD IS.

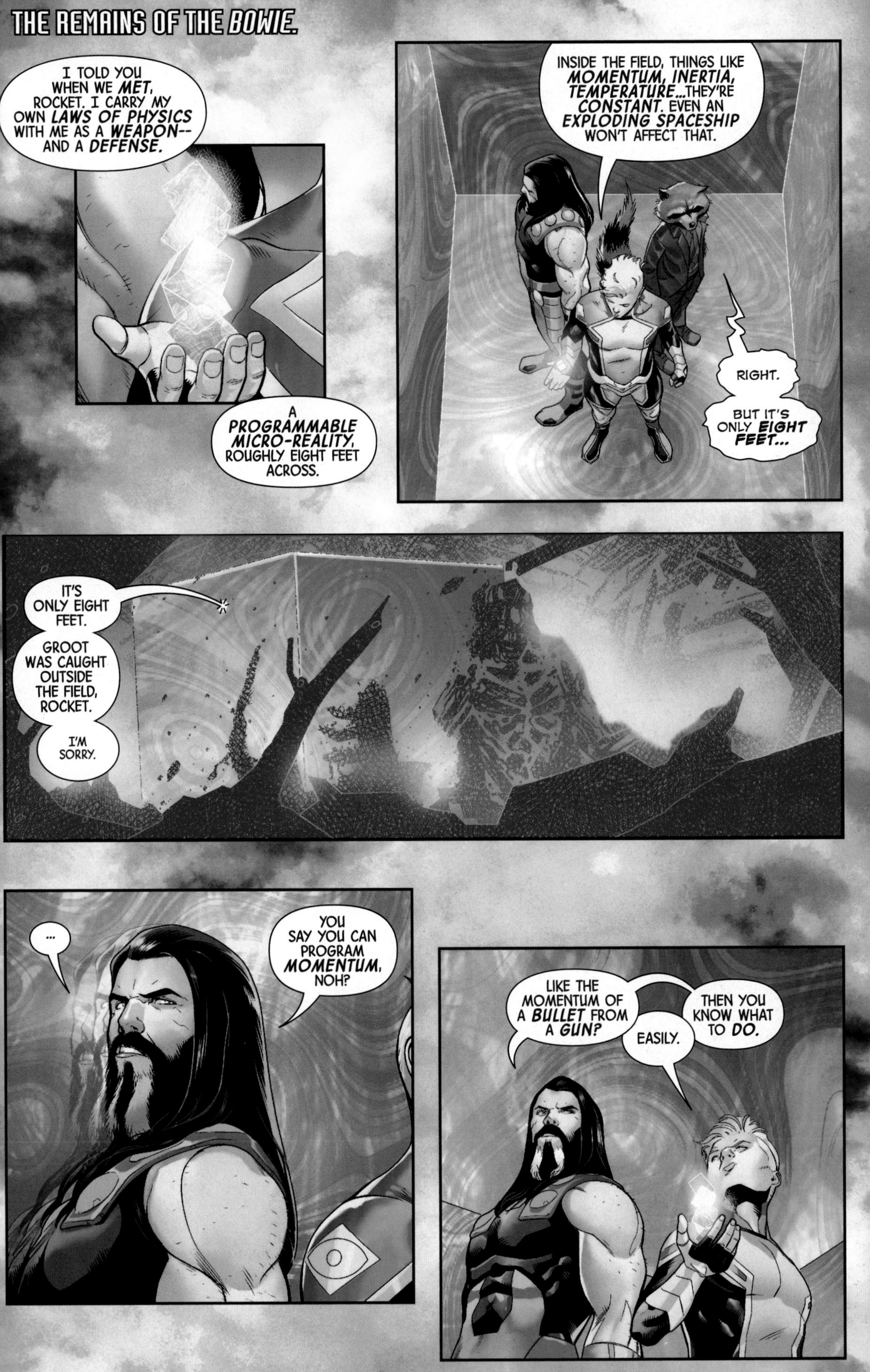
THE REMAINS OF THE BOWIE.
I TOLD YOU WHEN WE MET, ROCKET. I CARRY MY OWN LAWS OF PHYSICS WITH ME AS A WEAPON-- AND A DEFENSE.
A PROGRAMMABLE MICRO-REALITY, ROUGHLY EIGHT FEET ACROSS.
INSIDE THE FIELD, THINGS LIKE MOMENTUM, INERTIA, TEMPERATURE...THEY'RE CONSTANT. EVEN AN EXPLODING SPACESHIP WON'T AFFECT THAT.
RIGHT.
BUT IT'S ONLY EIGHT FEET...
IT'S ONLY EIGHT FEET.
GROOT WAS CAUGHT OUTSIDE THE FIELD, ROCKET.
I'M SORRY.
...
YOU SAY YOU CAN PROGRAM MOMENTUM, NOH?
LIKE THE MOMENTUM OF A BULLET FROM A GUN?
EASILY.
THEN YOU KNOW WHAT TO DO.

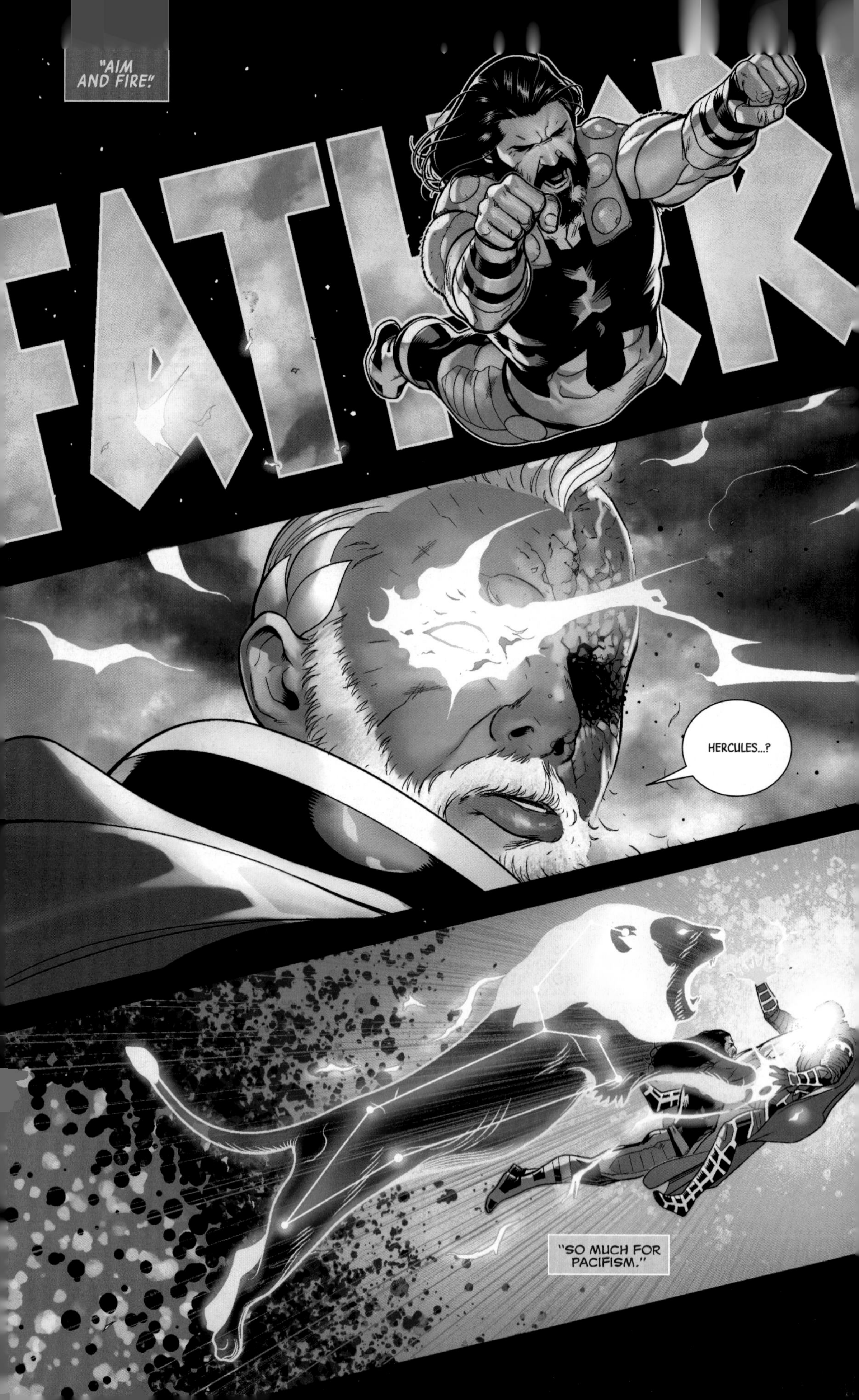
"AIM AND FIRE."
FATHER!
HERCULES...?
"SO MUCH FOR PACIFISM."

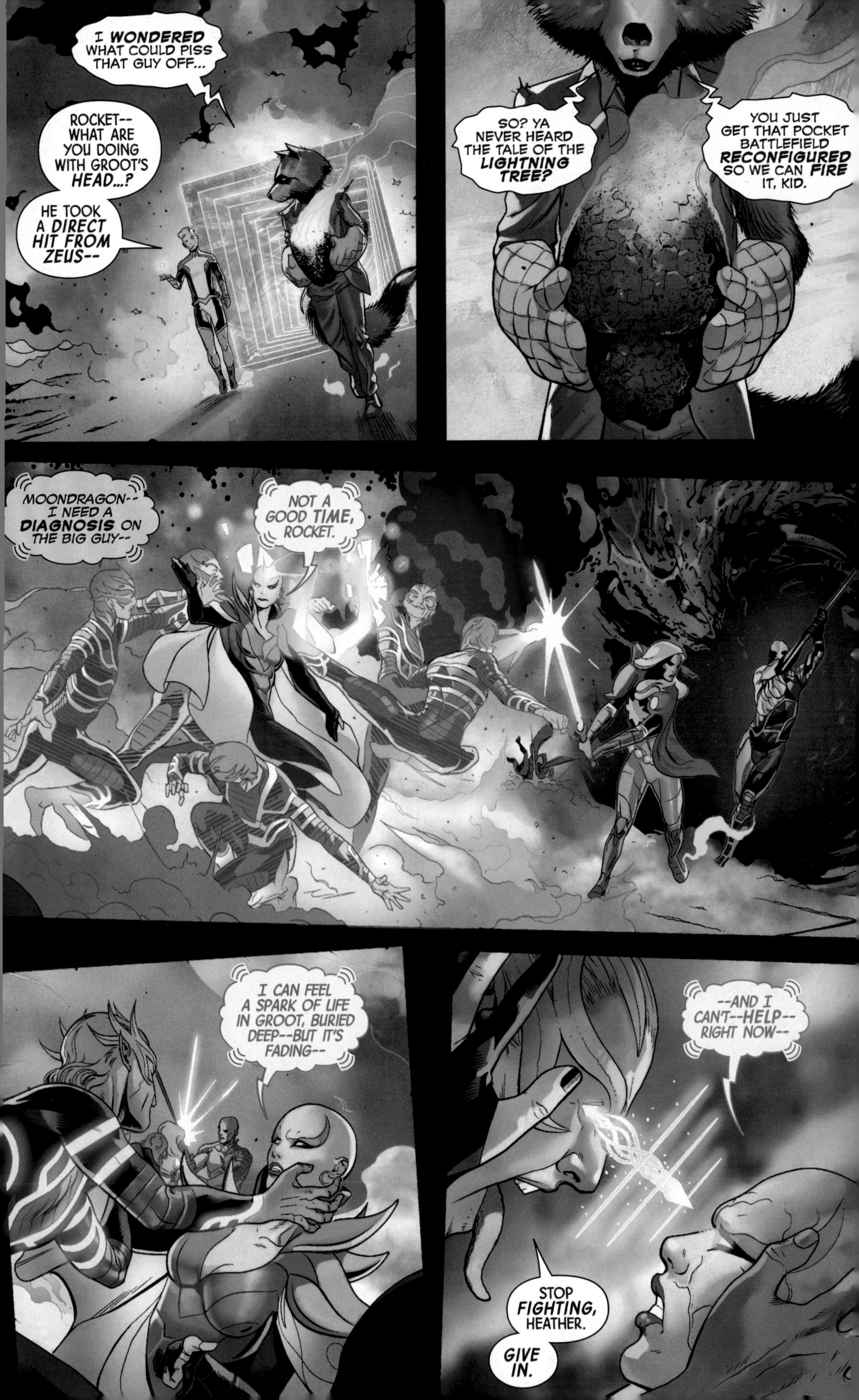
I WONDERED WHAT COULD PISS THAT GUY OFF...
ROCKET-- WHAT ARE YOU DOING WITH GROOT'S HEAD...?
HE TOOK A DIRECT HIT FROM ZEUS--
SO? YA NEVER HEARD THE TALE OF THE LIGHTNING TREE?
YOU JUST GET THAT POCKET BATTLEFIELD RECONFIGURED SO WE CAN FIRE IT, KID.
MOONDRAGON-- I NEED A DIAGNOSIS ON THE BIG GUY--
NOT A GOOD TIME, ROCKET.
I CAN FEEL A SPARK OF LIFE IN GROOT, BURIED DEEP--BUT IT'S FADING--
--AND I CAN'T--HELP-- RIGHT NOW--
STOP FIGHTING, HEATHER.
GIVE IN.

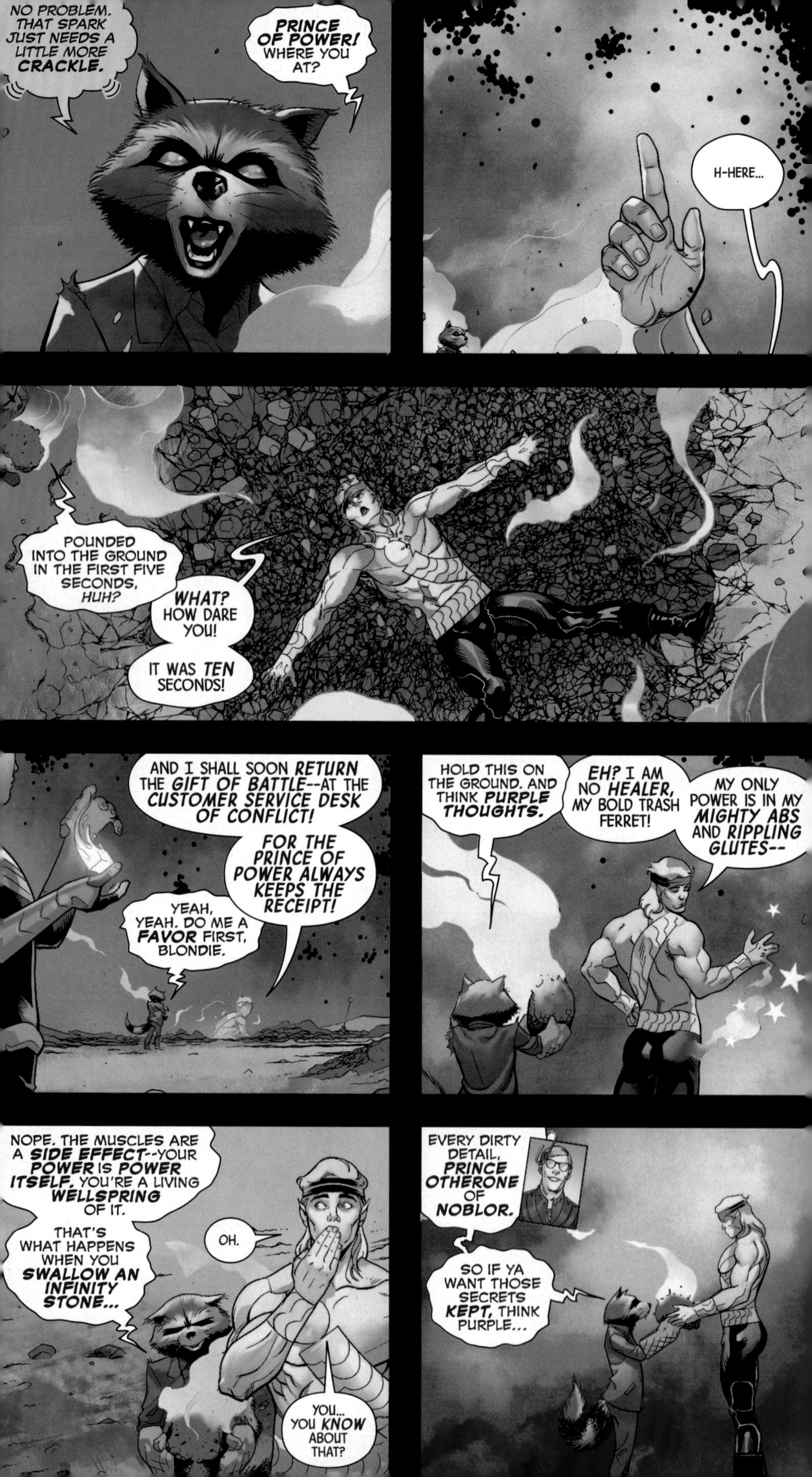
NO PROBLEM. THAT SPARK JUST NEEDS A LITTLE MORE CRACKLE.
PRINCE OF POWER! WHERE YOU AT?
H-HERE...
POUNDED INTO THE GROUND IN THE FIRST FIVE SECONDS, HUH?
WHAT? HOW DARE YOU!
IT WAS TEN SECONDS!
AND I SHALL SOON RETURN THE GIFT OF BATTLE--AT THE CUSTOMER SERVICE DESK OF CONFLICT!
FOR THE PRINCE OF POWER ALWAYS KEEPS THE RECEIPT!
YEAH, YEAH. DO ME A FAVOR FIRST, BLONDIE.
HOLD THIS ON THE GROUND. AND THINK PURPLE THOUGHTS.
EH? I AM NO HEALER, MY BOLD TRASH FERRET!
MY ONLY POWER IS IN MY MIGHTY ABS AND RIPPLING GLUTES--
NOPE. THE MUSCLES ARE A SIDE EFFECT--YOUR POWER IS POWER ITSELF. YOU'RE A LIVING WELLSPRING OF IT.
THAT'S WHAT HAPPENS WHEN YOU SWALLOW AN INFINITY STONE...
OH.
YOU... YOU KNOW ABOUT THAT?
EVERY DIRTY DETAIL, PRINCE OTHERONE OF NOBLOR.
SO IF YA WANT THOSE SECRETS KEPT, THINK PURPLE...

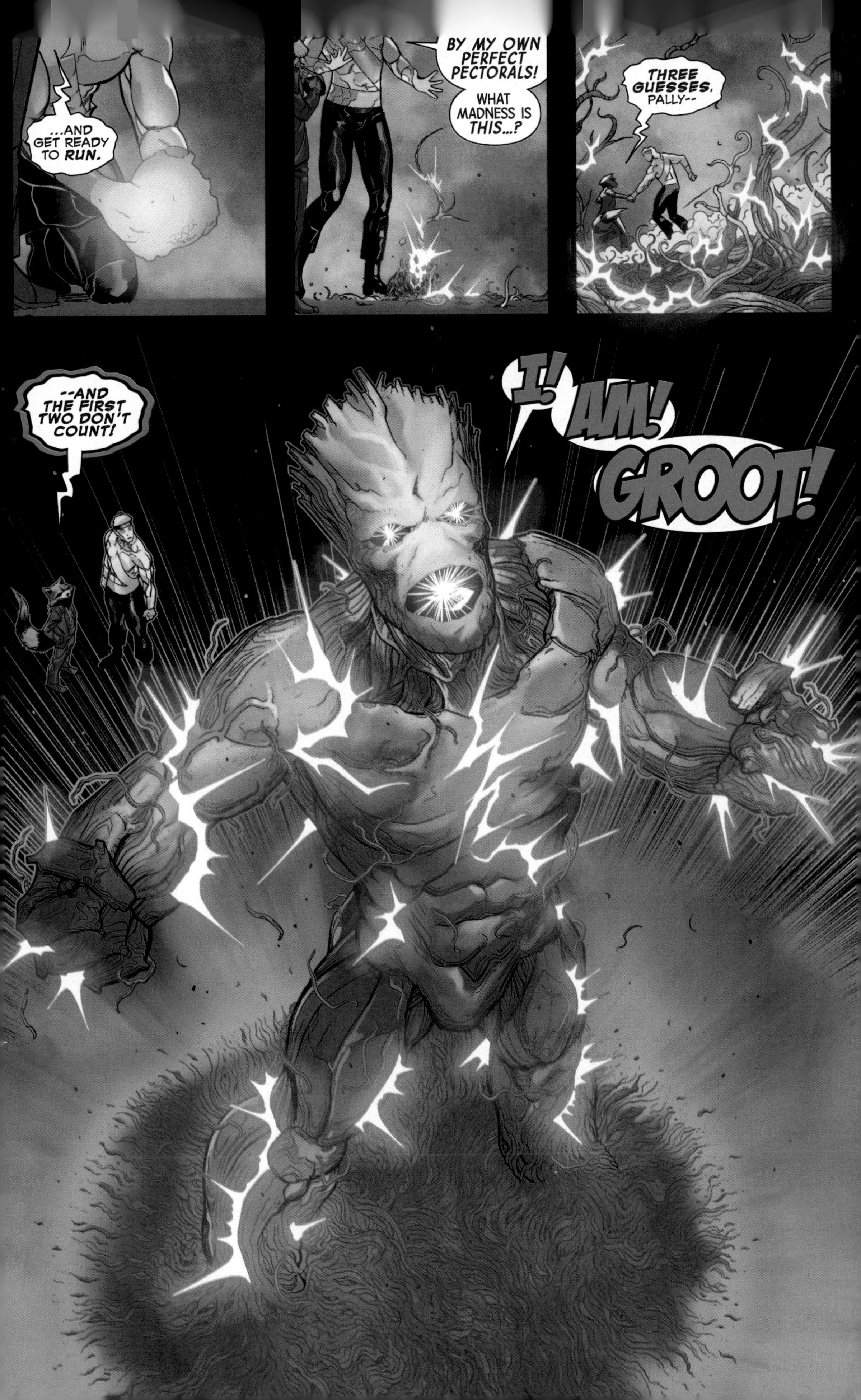
...AND GET READY TO RUN.
BY MY OWN PERFECT PECTORALS!
WHAT MADNESS IS THIS...?
THREE GUESSES, PALLY--
--AND THE FIRST TWO DON'T COUNT!
I! AM! GROOT!

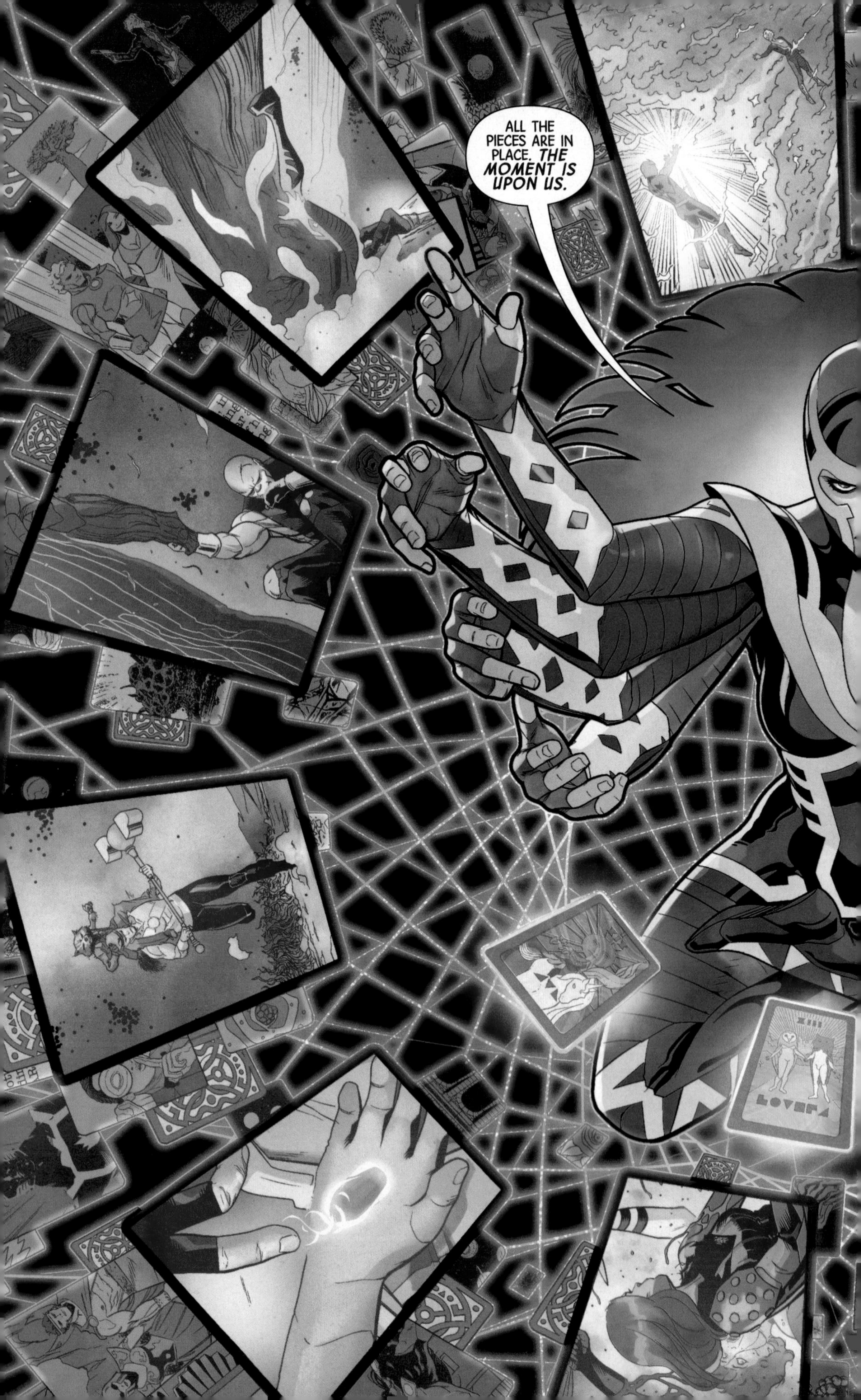
ALL THE PIECES ARE IN PLACE. *THE MOMENT IS UPON US.*
LOVERS

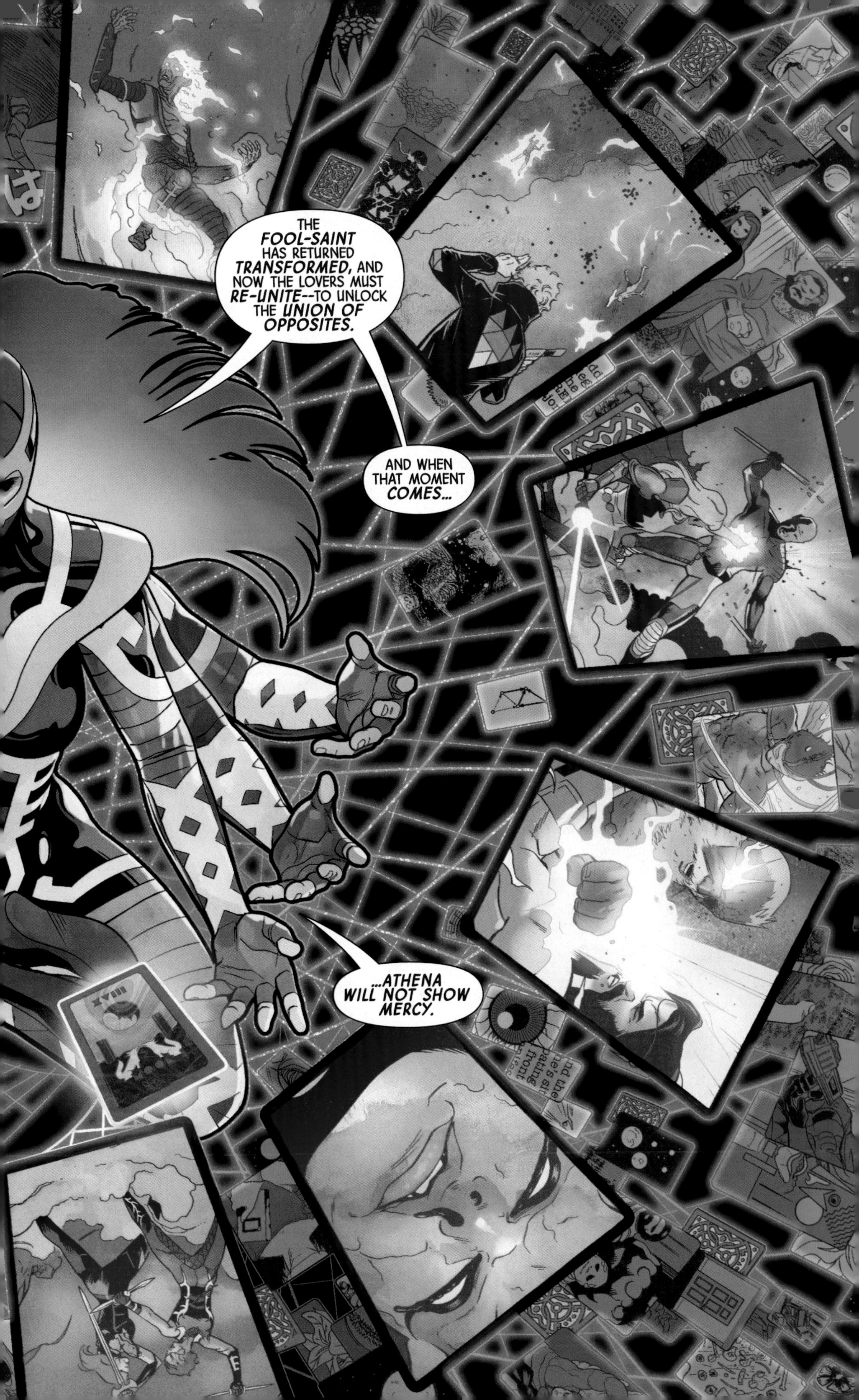
THE FOOL-SAINT HAS RETURNED TRANSFORMED, AND NOW THE LOVERS MUST RE-UNITE--TO UNLOCK THE UNION OF OPPOSITES.
AND WHEN THAT MOMENT COMES...
...ATHENA WILL NOT SHOW MERCY.

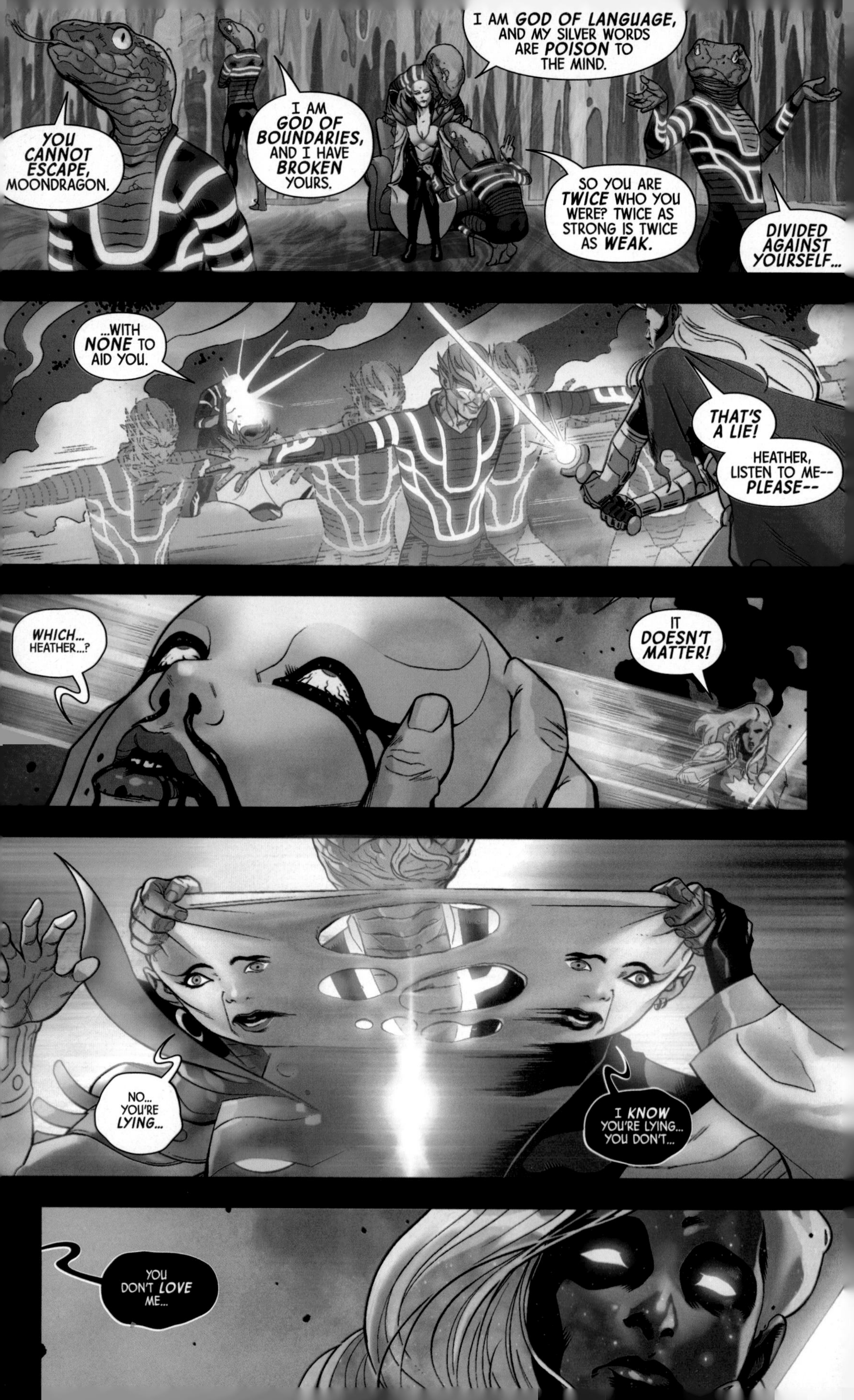
YOU CANNOT ESCAPE, MOONDRAGON.
I AM GOD OF BOUNDARIES, AND I HAVE BROKEN YOURS.
I AM GOD OF LANGUAGE, AND MY SILVER WORDS ARE POISON TO THE MIND.
SO YOU ARE TWICE WHO YOU WERE? TWICE AS STRONG IS TWICE AS WEAK.
DIVIDED AGAINST YOURSELF...
...WITH NONE TO AID YOU.
THAT'S A LIE!
HEATHER, LISTEN TO ME-- PLEASE--
WHICH... HEATHER...?
IT DOESN'T MATTER!
NO... YOU'RE LYING...
I KNOW YOU'RE LYING... YOU DON'T...
YOU DON'T LOVE ME...

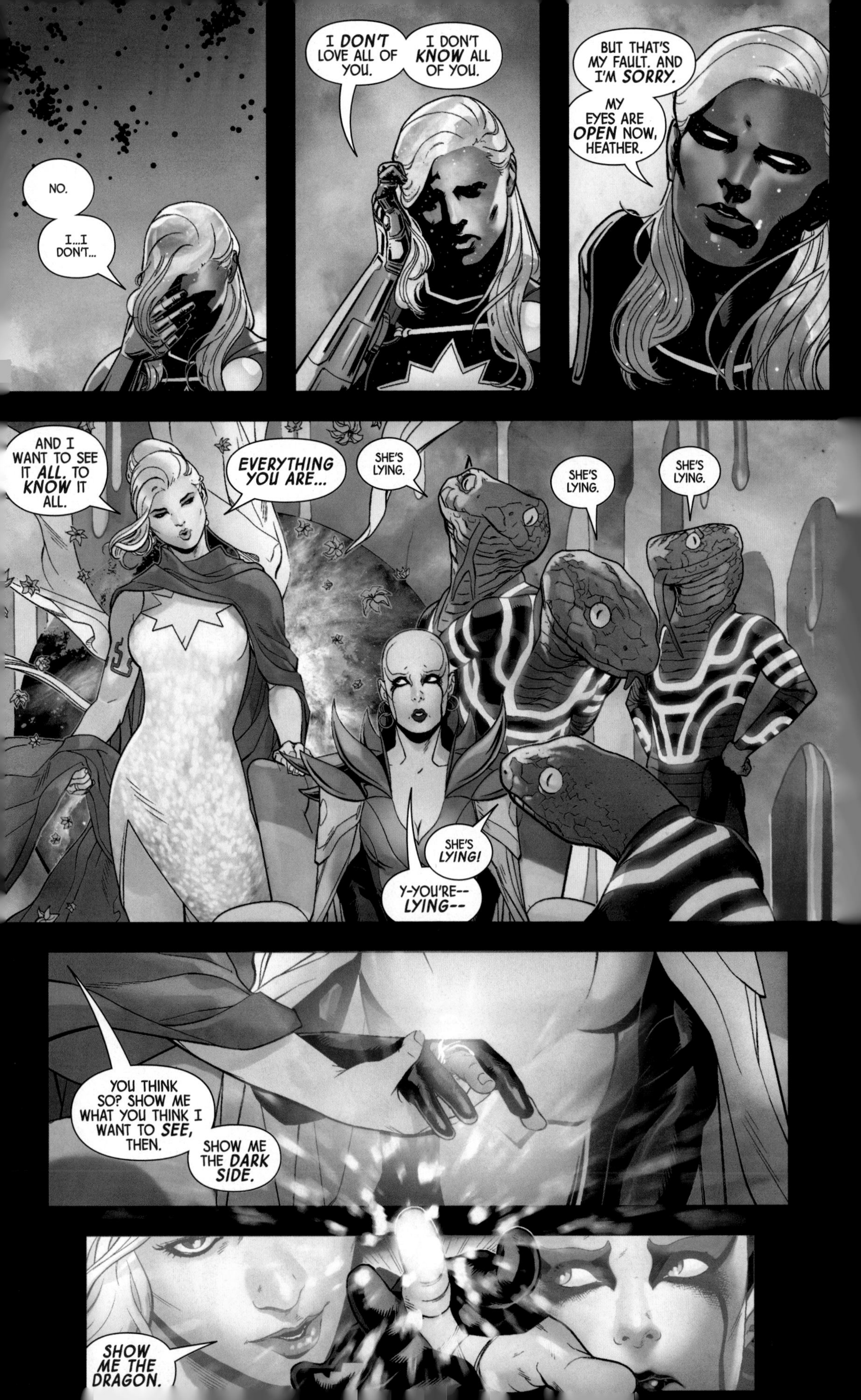
NO.
I...I DON'T...
I DON'T LOVE ALL OF YOU.
I DON'T KNOW ALL OF YOU.
BUT THAT'S MY FAULT. AND I'M SORRY.
MY EYES ARE OPEN NOW, HEATHER.
AND I WANT TO SEE IT ALL. TO KNOW IT ALL.
EVERYTHING YOU ARE...
SHE'S LYING.
SHE'S LYING.
SHE'S LYING.
SHE'S LYING!
Y-YOU'RE-- LYING--
YOU THINK SO? SHOW ME WHAT YOU THINK I WANT TO SEE, THEN.
SHOW ME THE DARK SIDE.
SHOW ME THE DRAGON.

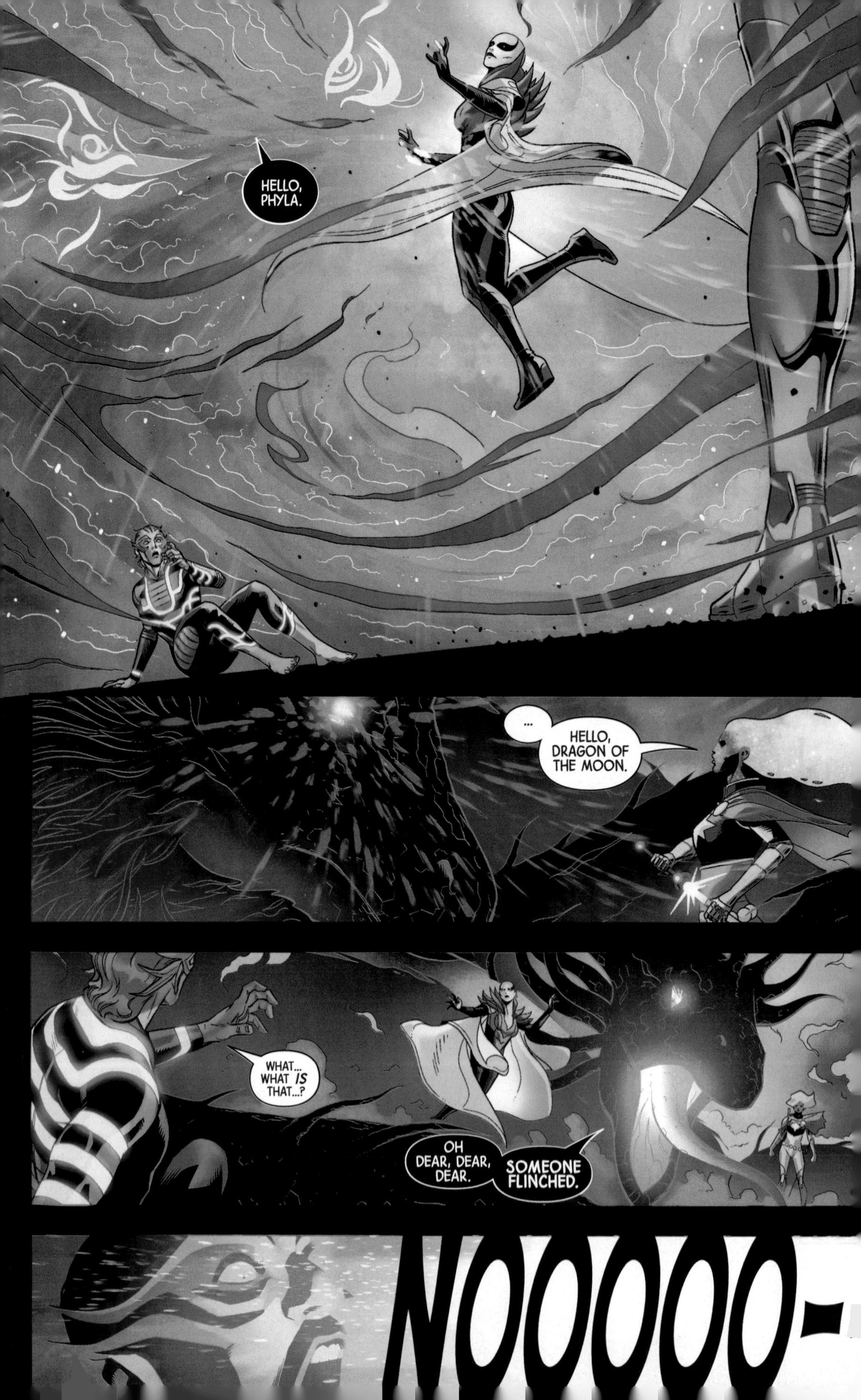
HELLO, PHYLA.
...
HELLO, DRAGON OF THE MOON.
WHAT... WHAT IS THAT...?
OH DEAR, DEAR, DEAR.
SOMEONE FLINCHED.
NOOOOO-

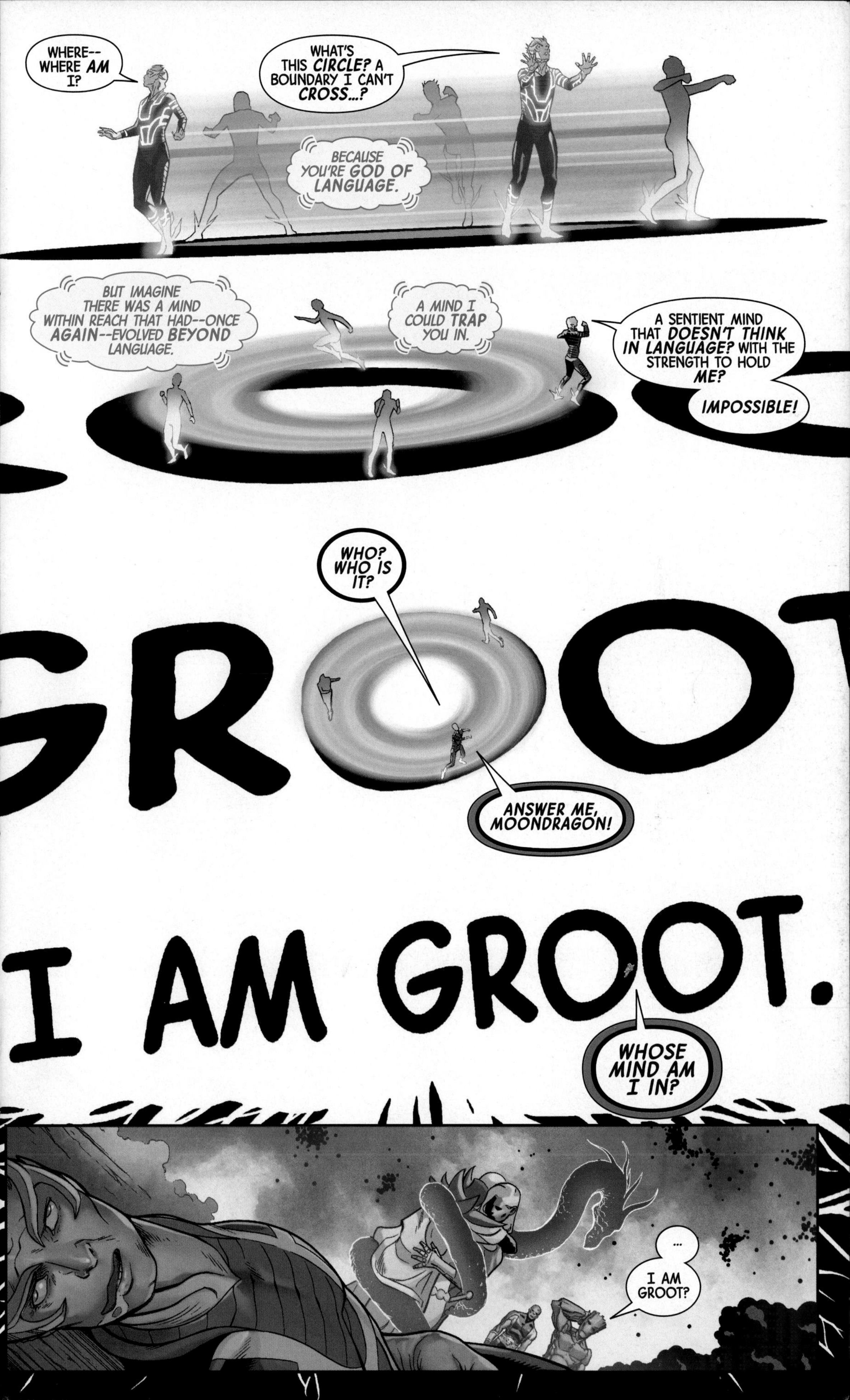
WHERE--
WHERE AM
I?
WHAT'S
THIS CIRCLE? A
BOUNDARY I CAN'T
CROSS...?
BECAUSE
YOU'RE GOD OF
LANGUAGE.
BUT IMAGINE
THERE WAS A MIND
WITHIN REACH THAT HAD--ONCE
AGAIN--EVOLVED BEYOND
LANGUAGE.
A MIND I
COULD TRAP
YOU IN.
A SENTIENT MIND
THAT DOESN'T THINK
IN LANGUAGE? WITH THE
STRENGTH TO HOLD
ME?
IMPOSSIBLE!
WHO?
WHO IS
IT?
GROOT
ANSWER ME,
MOONDRAGON!
I AM GROOT.
WHOSE
MIND AM
I IN?
...
I AM
GROOT?

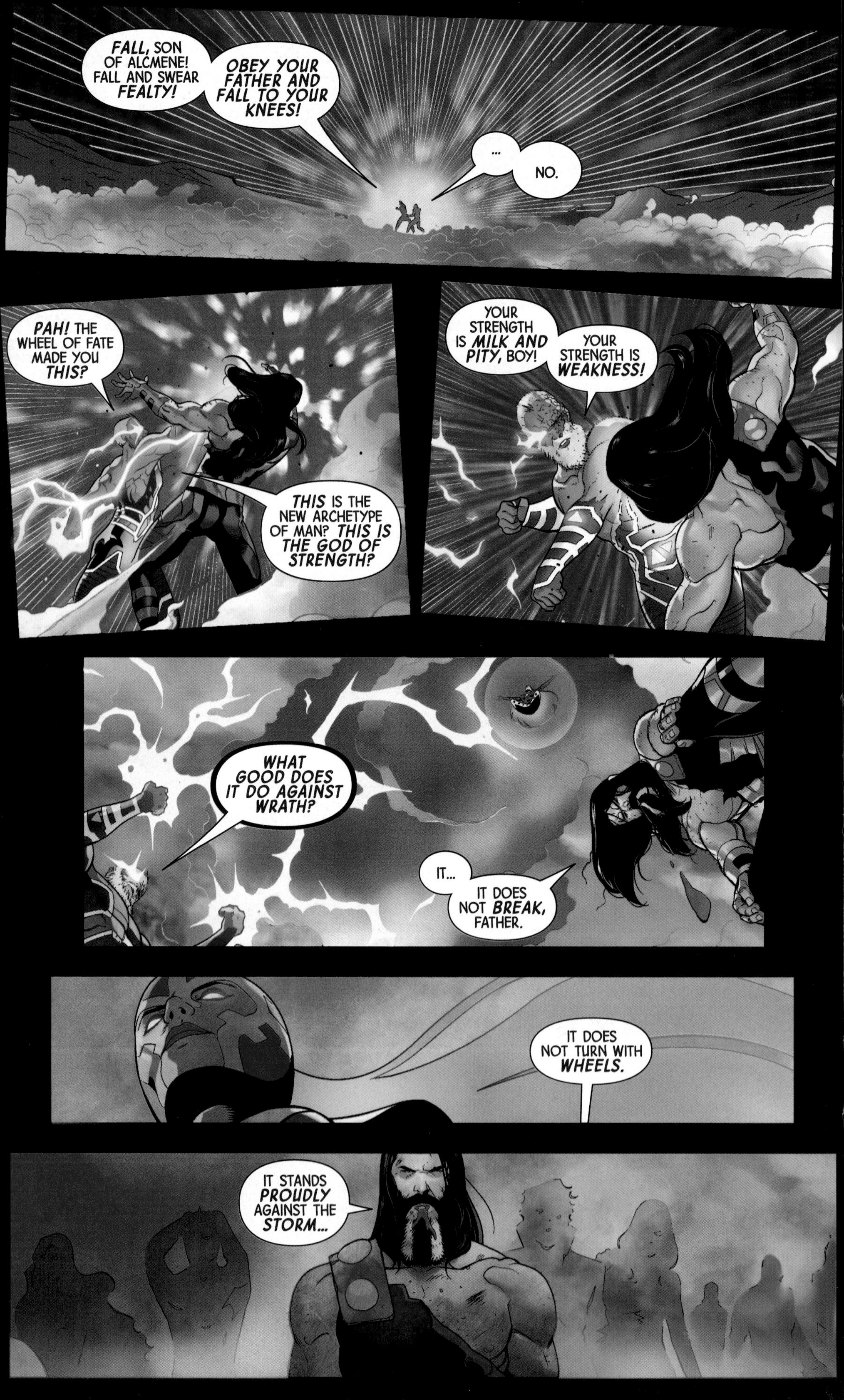
FALL, SON OF ALCMENE! FALL AND SWEAR FEALTY!
OBEY YOUR FATHER AND FALL TO YOUR KNEES!
...
NO.
PAH! THE WHEEL OF FATE MADE YOU THIS?
THIS IS THE NEW ARCHETYPE OF MAN? THIS IS THE GOD OF STRENGTH?
YOUR STRENGTH IS MILK AND PITY, BOY!
YOUR STRENGTH IS WEAKNESS!
WHAT GOOD DOES IT DO AGAINST WRATH?
IT...
IT DOES NOT BREAK, FATHER.
IT DOES NOT TURN WITH WHEELS.
IT STANDS PROUDLY AGAINST THE STORM...

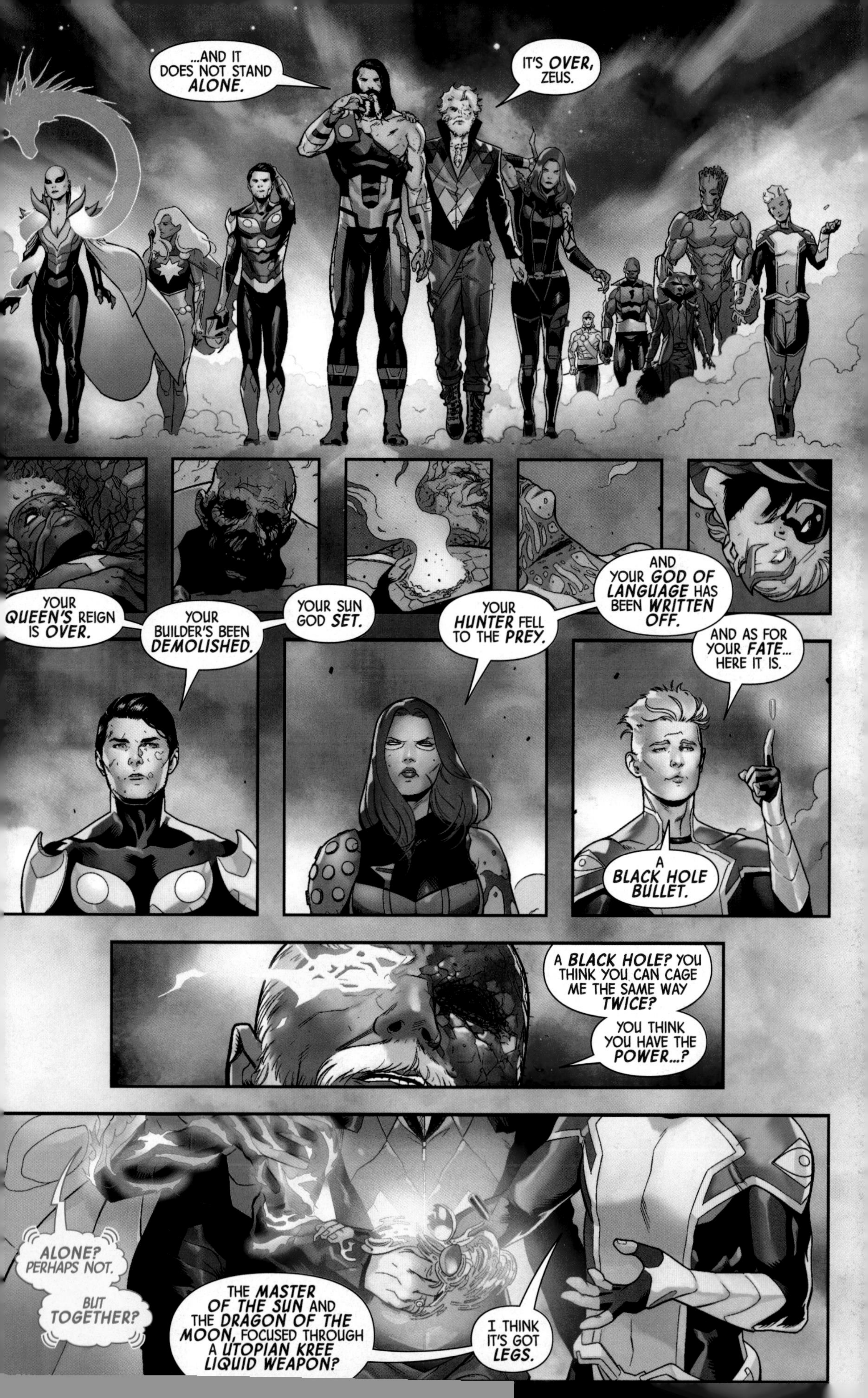
...AND IT DOES NOT STAND ALONE.
IT'S OVER, ZEUS.
YOUR QUEEN'S REIGN IS OVER.
YOUR BUILDER'S BEEN DEMOLISHED.
YOUR SUN GOD SET.
YOUR HUNTER FELL TO THE PREY.
AND YOUR GOD OF LANGUAGE HAS BEEN WRITTEN OFF.
AND AS FOR YOUR FATE... HERE IT IS.
A BLACK HOLE BULLET.
A BLACK HOLE? YOU THINK YOU CAN CAGE ME THE SAME WAY TWICE?
YOU THINK YOU HAVE THE POWER...?
ALONE? PERHAPS NOT.
BUT TOGETHER?
THE MASTER OF THE SUN AND THE DRAGON OF THE MOON, FOCUSED THROUGH A UTOPIAN KREE LIQUID WEAPON?
I THINK IT'S GOT LEGS.

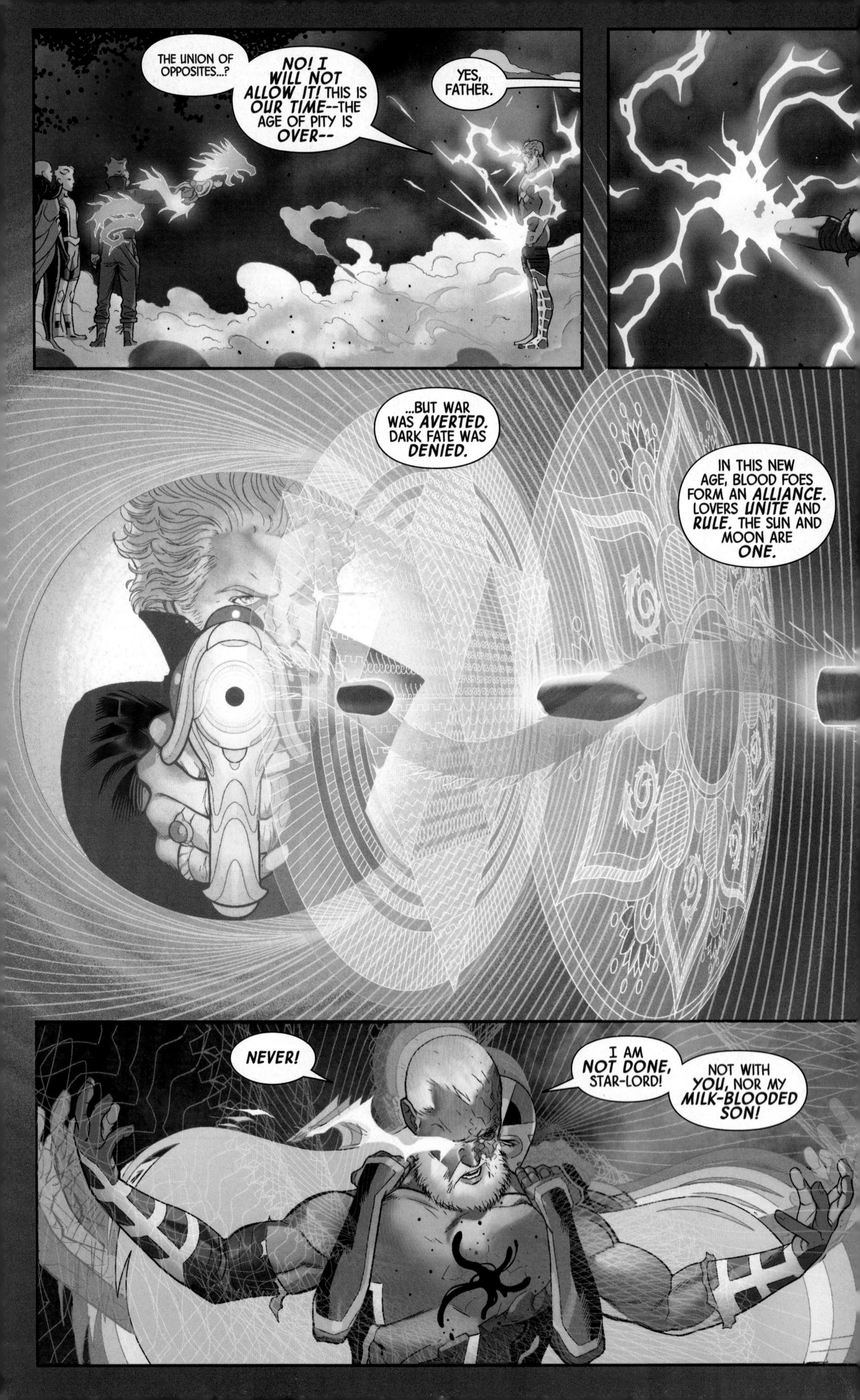
THE UNION OF OPPOSITES...?
NO! I WILL NOT ALLOW IT! THIS IS OUR TIME--THE AGE OF PITY IS OVER--
YES, FATHER.
...BUT WAR WAS AVERTED. DARK FATE WAS DENIED.
IN THIS NEW AGE, BLOOD FOES FORM AN ALLIANCE. LOVERS UNITE AND RULE. THE SUN AND MOON ARE ONE.
NEVER!
I AM NOT DONE, STAR-LORD!
NOT WITH YOU, NOR MY MILK-BLOODED SON!

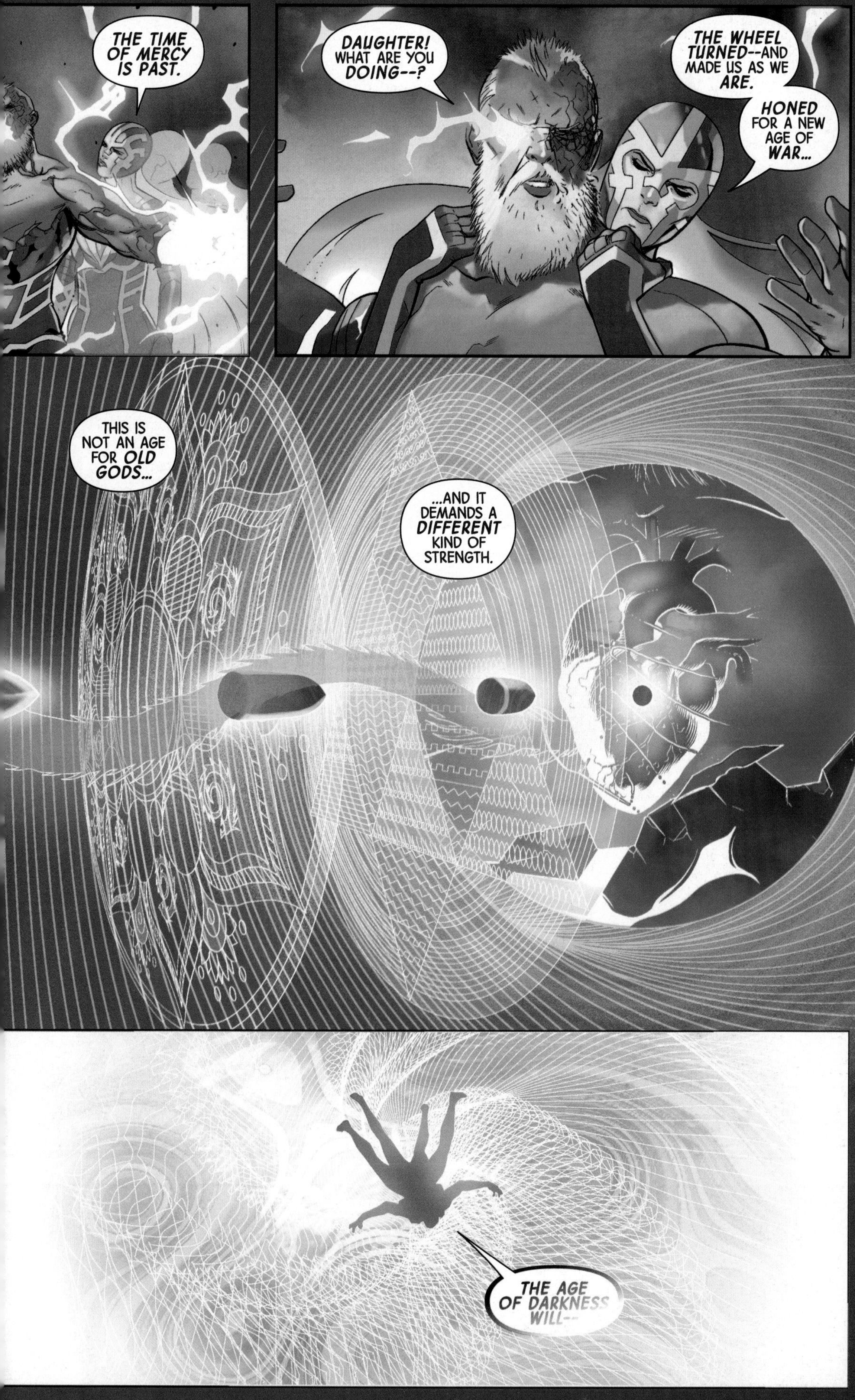
THE TIME OF MERCY IS PAST.
DAUGHTER! WHAT ARE YOU DOING--?
THE WHEEL TURNED--AND MADE US AS WE ARE.
HONED FOR A NEW AGE OF WAR...
THIS IS NOT AN AGE FOR OLD GODS...
...AND IT DEMANDS A DIFFERENT KIND OF STRENGTH.
THE AGE OF DARKNESS WILL--

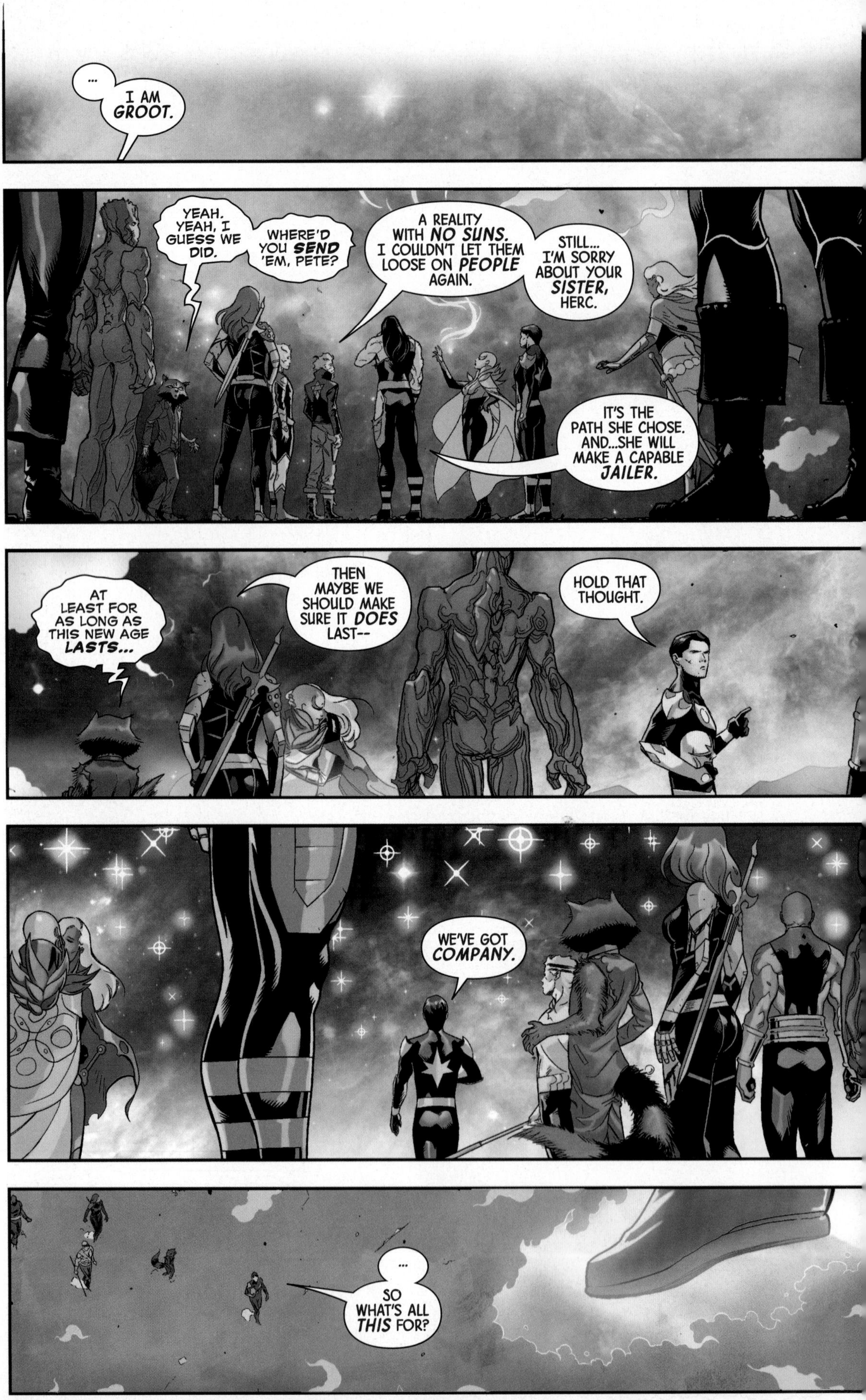
... I AM GROOT.
YEAH. YEAH, I GUESS WE DID.
WHERE'D YOU SEND 'EM, PETE?
A REALITY WITH NO SUNS. I COULDN'T LET THEM LOOSE ON PEOPLE AGAIN.
STILL... I'M SORRY ABOUT YOUR SISTER, HERC.
IT'S THE PATH SHE CHOSE. AND...SHE WILL MAKE A CAPABLE JAILER.
AT LEAST FOR AS LONG AS THIS NEW AGE LASTS...
THEN MAYBE WE SHOULD MAKE SURE IT DOES LAST--
HOLD THAT THOUGHT.
WE'VE GOT COMPANY.
...
SO WHAT'S ALL THIS FOR?

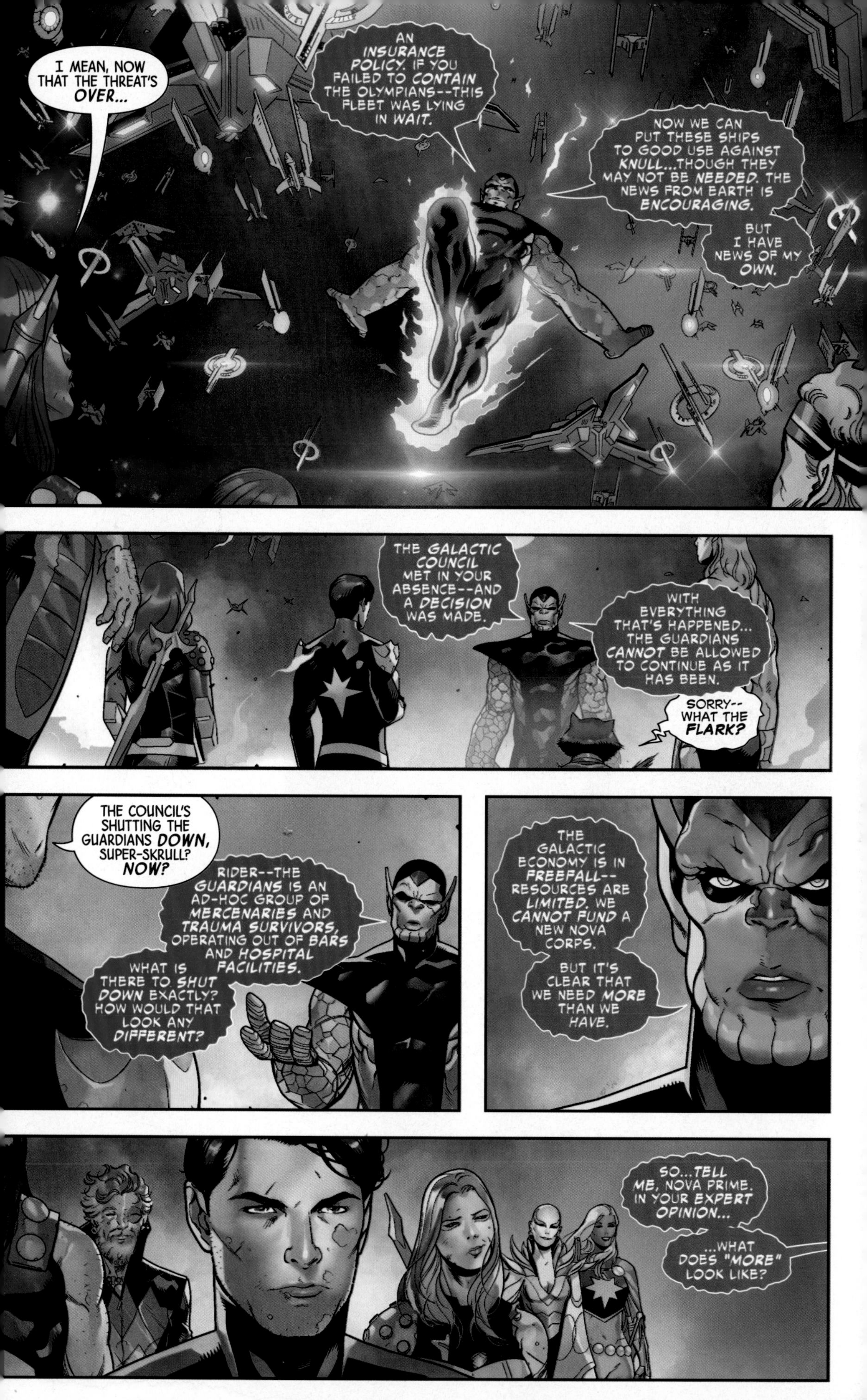
I MEAN, NOW THAT THE THREAT'S OVER...
AN INSURANCE POLICY. IF YOU FAILED TO CONTAIN THE OLYMPIANS--THIS FLEET WAS LYING IN WAIT.
NOW WE CAN PUT THESE SHIPS TO GOOD USE AGAINST KNULL...THOUGH THEY MAY NOT BE NEEDED. THE NEWS FROM EARTH IS ENCOURAGING.
BUT I HAVE NEWS OF MY OWN.
THE GALACTIC COUNCIL MET IN YOUR ABSENCE--AND A DECISION WAS MADE.
WITH EVERYTHING THAT'S HAPPENED... THE GUARDIANS CANNOT BE ALLOWED TO CONTINUE AS IT HAS BEEN.
SORRY-- WHAT THE FLARK?
THE COUNCIL'S SHUTTING THE GUARDIANS DOWN, SUPER-SKRULL? NOW?
RIDER--THE GUARDIANS IS AN AD-HOC GROUP OF MERCENARIES AND TRAUMA SURVIVORS, OPERATING OUT OF BARS AND HOSPITAL FACILITIES.
WHAT IS THERE TO SHUT DOWN EXACTLY? HOW WOULD THAT LOOK ANY DIFFERENT?
THE GALACTIC ECONOMY IS IN FREEFALL-- RESOURCES ARE LIMITED. WE CANNOT FUND A NEW NOVA CORPS.
BUT IT'S CLEAR THAT WE NEED MORE THAN WE HAVE.
SO...TELL ME, NOVA PRIME. IN YOUR EXPERT OPINION...
...WHAT DOES "MORE" LOOK LIKE?

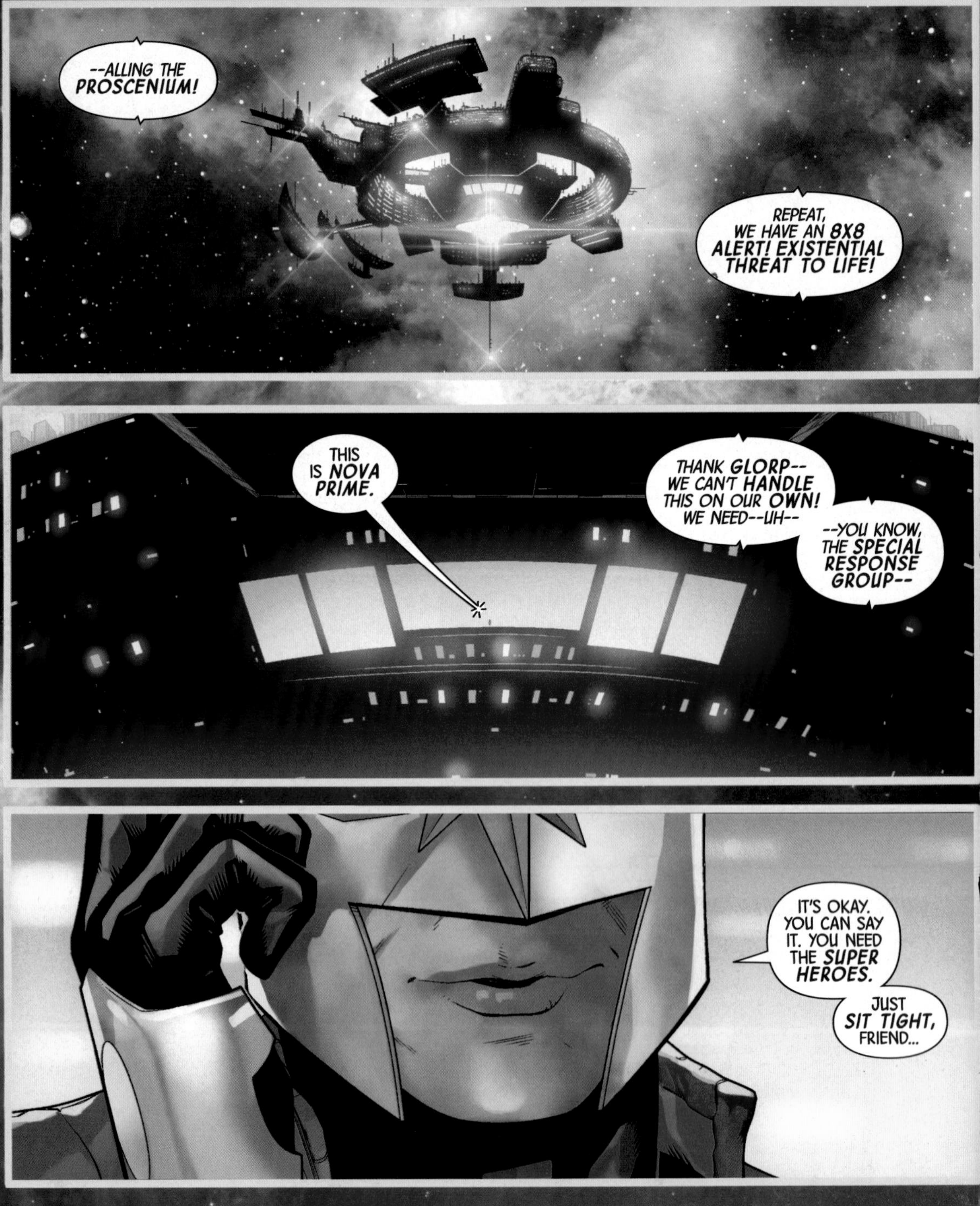
--ALLING THE PROSCENIUM!
REPEAT, WE HAVE AN 8X8 ALERT! EXISTENTIAL THREAT TO LIFE!
THIS IS NOVA PRIME.
THANK GLORP-- WE CAN'T HANDLE THIS ON OUR OWN! WE NEED--UH--
--YOU KNOW, THE SPECIAL RESPONSE GROUP--
IT'S OKAY. YOU CAN SAY IT. YOU NEED THE SUPER HEROES.
JUST SIT TIGHT, FRIEND...

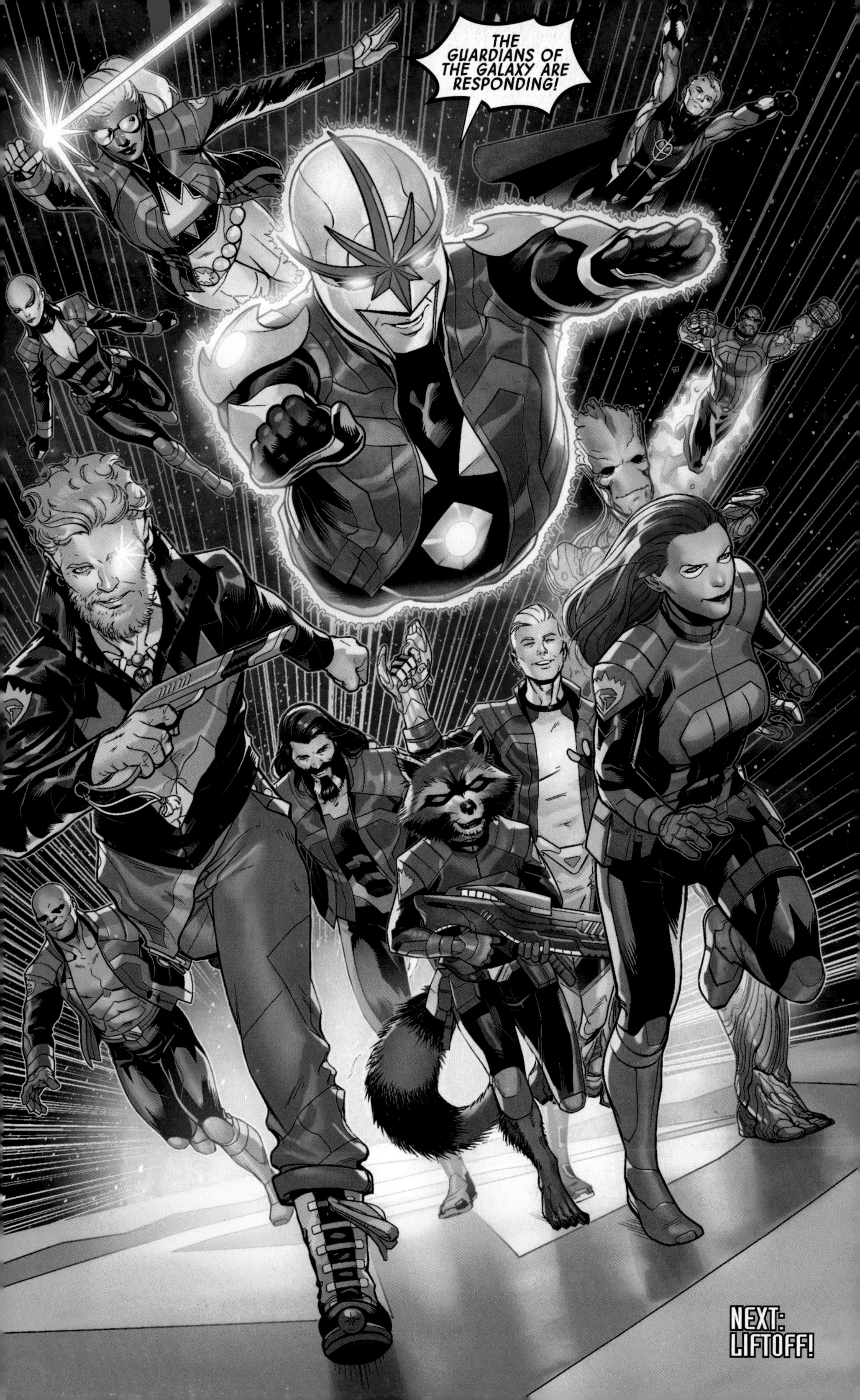
THE GUARDIANS OF THE GALAXY ARE RESPONDING!
NEXT: LIFTOFF!

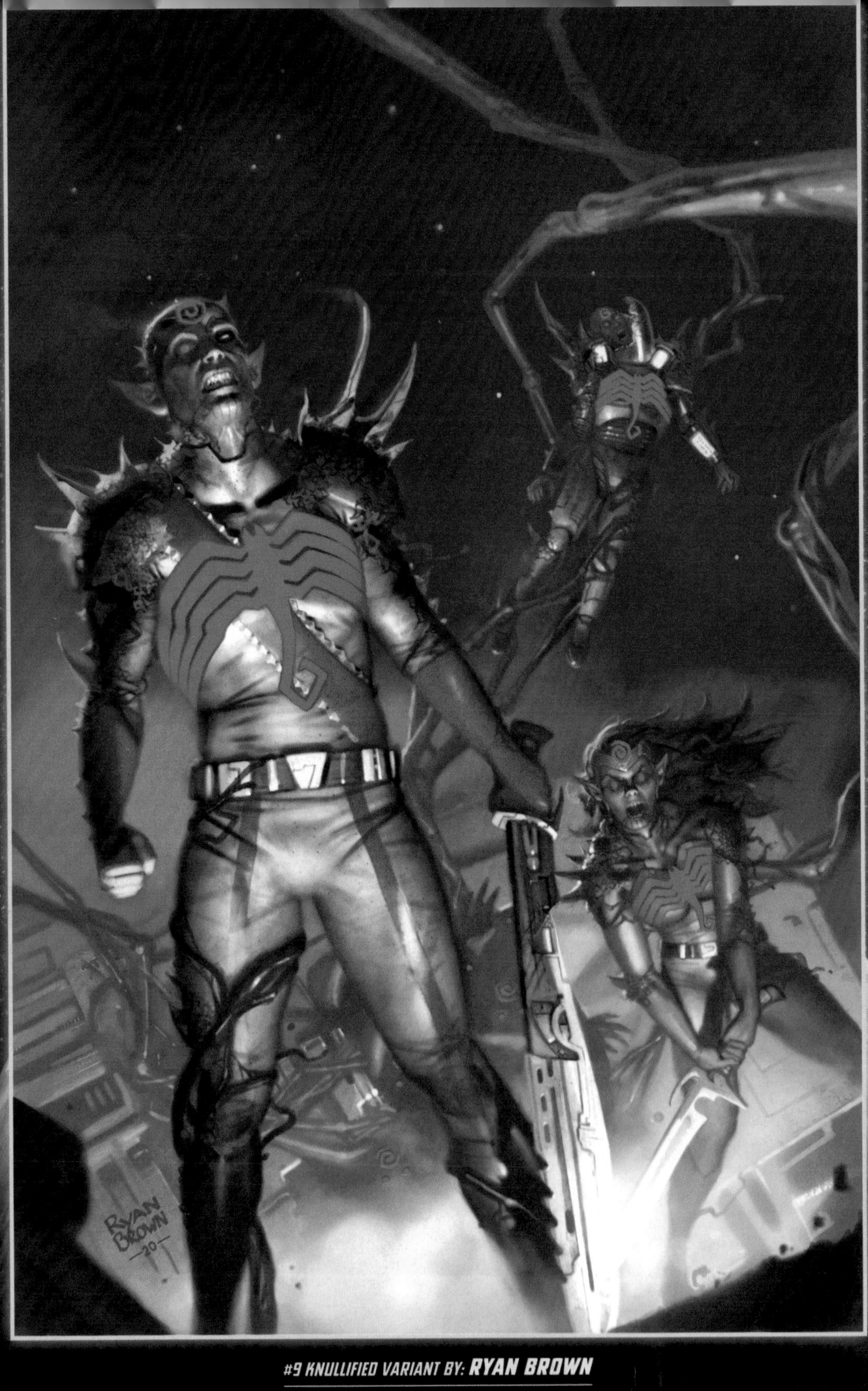
RYAN BROWN -20-

#9 KNULLIFIED VARIANT BY: **RYAN BROWN**

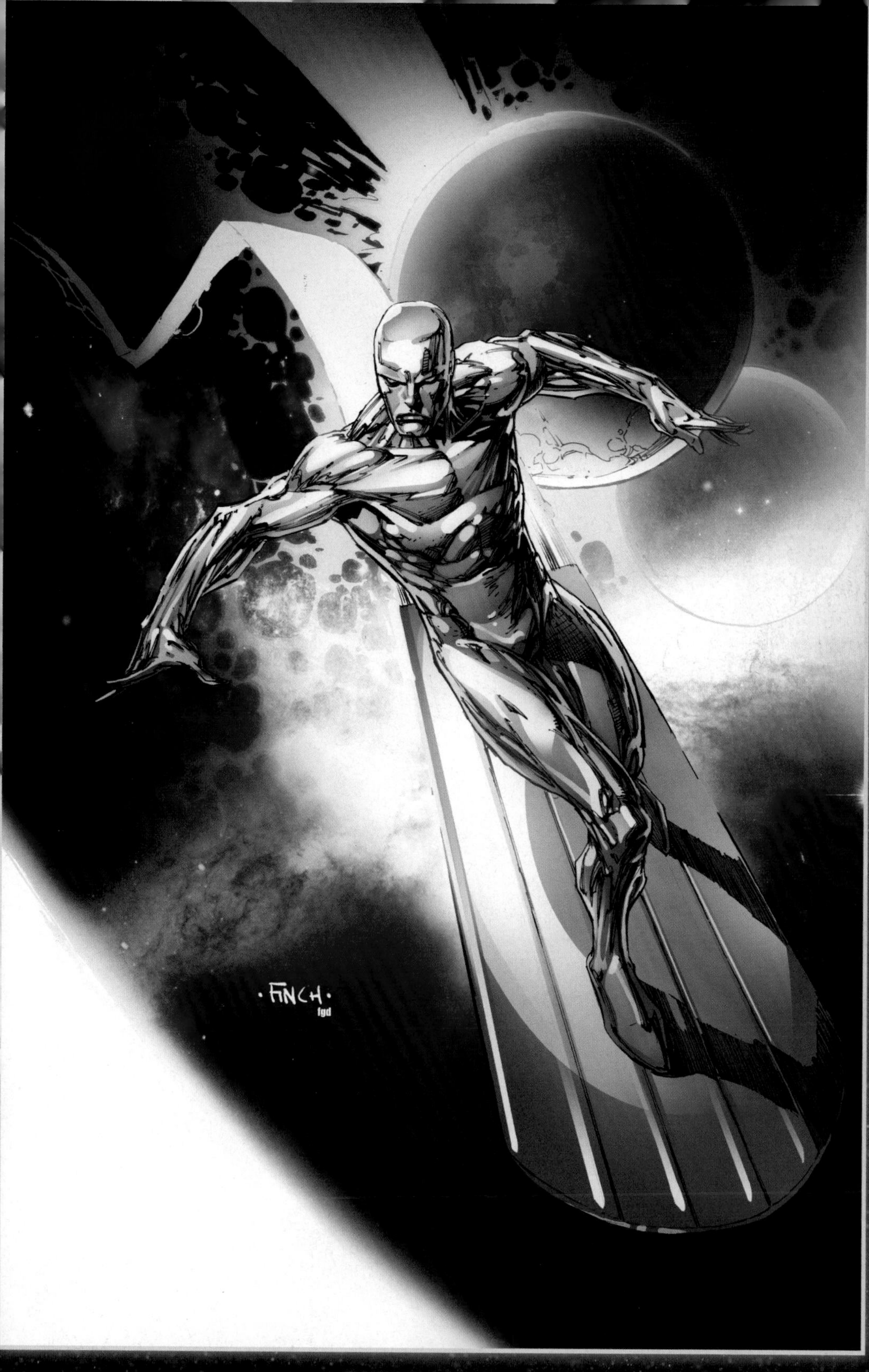
FINCH
fgd

#11 VARIANT BY: **DAVID FINCH & FRANK D'ARMATA**

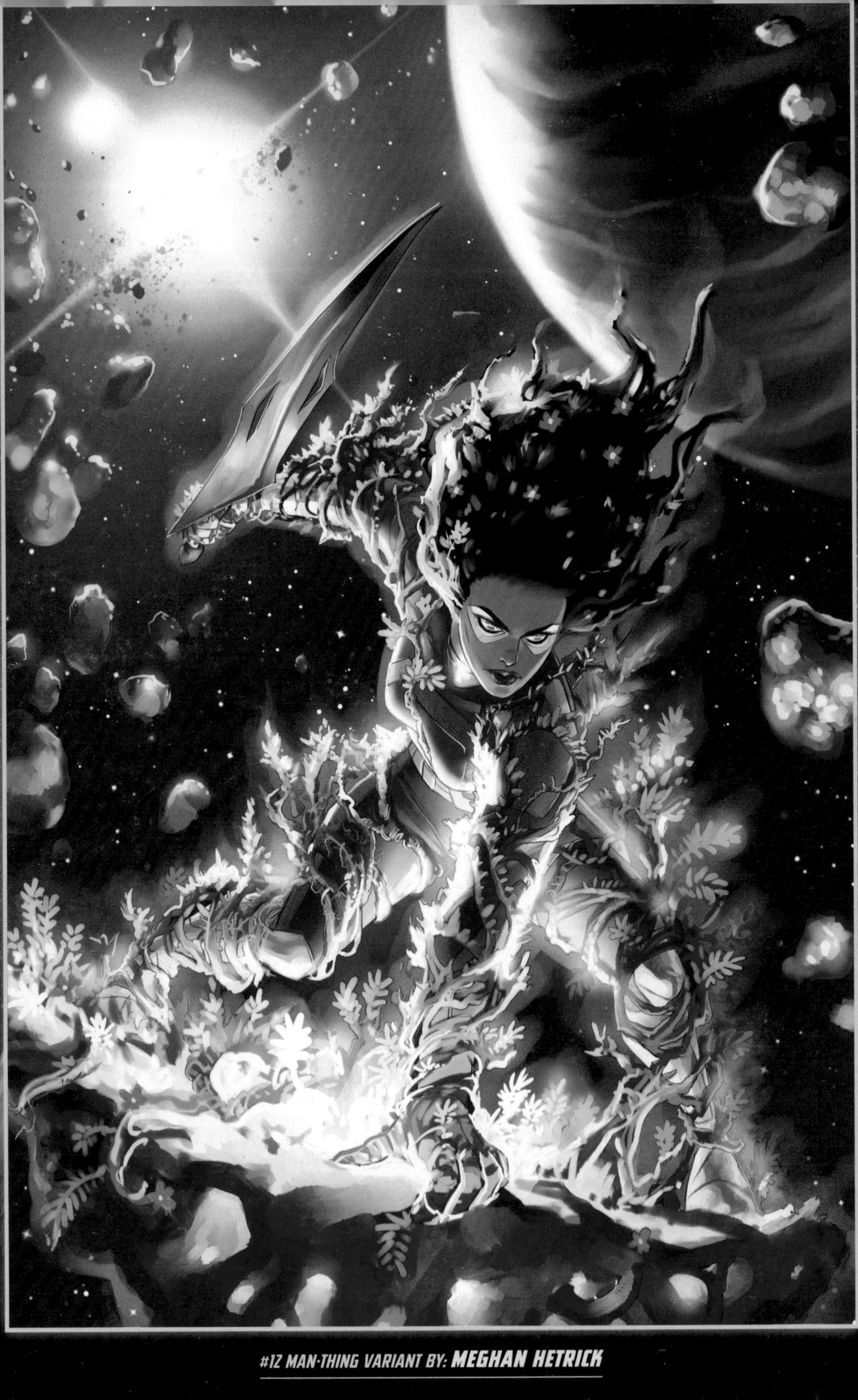

#12 MAN-THING VARIANT BY: **MEGHAN HETRICK**